W9-BDX-463

Valuation and Pricing of Technology-Based Intellectual Property

Valuation and Pricing of Technology-Based Intellectual Property

RICHARD RAZGAITIS

WILEY

John Wiley & Sons, Inc.

This book is printed on acid-free paper.

Copyright © 2003 by John Wiley & Sons, Inc., Hoboken, New Jersey. All rights reserved.
Published simultaneously in Canada.

The first edition of this book was titled *Early-Stage Technologies: Valuation and Pricing*.

No part of this publication may be reproduced, stored in a retrieval system, or transmitted in any form or by
any means, electronic, mechanical, photocopying, recording, scanning, or otherwise, except as permitted under
Section 107 or 108 of the 1976 United States Copyright Act, without either the prior written permission of
the Publisher, or authorization through payment of the appropriate per-copy fee to the Copyright Clearance
Center, Inc., 222 Rosewood Drive, Danvers, MA 01923, 978-750-8400, fax 978-750-4470, or on the web at
www.copyright.com. Requests to the Publisher for permission should be addressed to the Permissions
Department, John Wiley & Sons, Inc., 111 River Street, Hoboken, NJ 07030, 201-748-6011, fax 201-748-
6008, e-mail: permcoordinator@wiley.com.

Limit of Liability/Disclaimer of Warranty: While the publisher and author have used their best efforts in
preparing this book, they make no representations or warranties with respect to the accuracy or completeness
of the contents of this book and specifically disclaim any implied warranties of merchantability or fitness for a
particular purpose. No warranty may be created or extended by sales representatives or written sales materials.
The advice and strategies contained herein may not be suitable for your situation. You should consult with a
professional where appropriate. Neither the publisher nor author shall be liable for any loss of profit or any
other commercial damages, including but not limited to special, incidental, consequential, or other damages.

For general information on our other products and services, or technical support, please contact our Customer
Care Department within the United States at 800-762-2974, outside the United States at 317-572-3993 or fax
317-572-4002.

Wiley also publishes its books in a variety of electronic formats. Some content that appears in print may not be
available in electronic books.

For more information about Wiley products, visit our web site at www.wiley.com.

Library of Congress Cataloging-in-Publication Data:
Razgaitis, Richard.
    Valuation and pricing of technology-based intellectual property / Richard Razgaitis.—
[2002 ed.].
      p. cm.
    Rev. ed. of: Early-stage technologies. c1999.
    Includes bibliographical references and index.
    ISBN 0-471-25049-X (cloth : alk. paper)
    1. License agreements—United States.   2. Technology transfer—Law and
legislation—United States.   I. Razgaitis, Richard. Early-stage technologies.   II. Title.
KF3145 .R39   2003
346.7304'8—dc21
                                           2002193372

Printed in the United States of America.

10 9 8 7 6 5 4

About the Author

Dr. Richard Razgaitis is a Managing Director of InteCap, Inc. (formerly IPC Group). He has over 35 years of experience working with the development, commercialization, and strategic management of technology, 20 of which have been spent specializing in the commercialization of Intellectual Property. He has participated in the licensing-in and licensing-out of numerous technologies, including advanced materials, manufacturing systems, software and communications products. In addition, Dr. Razgaitis has been involved with commercialization efforts of technologies originating from federal laboratories, and he has negotiated commercialization agreements with clients in the United States, Europe, and the Far East ranging from Fortune 500 to small start-up companies.

Early in his career, he was a rocket scientist who worked at Cape Kennedy on the Apollo program from Apollo 8 through the famous Apollo 13.

Dr. Razgaitis is a Trustee and the treasurer of the Licensing Executives Society USA/Canada (LES) and of the Licensing Foundation of LES. He is also a board member of the National Inventors Hall of Fame Foundation. He speaks frequently on the commercialization of technology, specifically on valuation and pricing of technology, licensing strategy, and linking licensing and business strategies. He has taught segments of licensing courses sponsored both by LES and the Association of University Technology Managers (AUTM).

He has B.S., M.Sc., and Ph.D. degrees in engineering from the University of Illinois, Florida, and SMU, respectively, and an MBA from Ohio State University.

Dr. Razgaitis has been a registered Professional Engineer in three states and the holder of four U.S. patents.

Bill Riley,
licensing mentor at Battelle and friend.

Contents

Preface

This book is about the valuation and pricing of technology. By "technology" or "early stage technology" is meant potential new business opportunities that are at an early or mature state of Research & Development (R&D) and generally not yet to the point of having been *productized* and introduced commercially. Valuation is about determining what something is worth intrinsically. It is something that both the seller and buyer need to do for many purposes, not the least of which is to determine whether there is a basis for an agreement. Pricing is about negotiating and communicating. It is something that is done by both seller and buyer once a valuation is done. Generally speaking, valuation is something intrinsic, whereas pricing is external; valuation is an idea, pricing is an agreement.

TR R A DE™

As a framework for this book, and linking the idea of licensing value creation to the traditional meaning of *trade* as a value-creation event, we will use the acronym *TR R A DE*™. This term summarizes what this book is about: Technology Rights (TR) becoming the economic basis of a deal (Deal Economics, DE) as determined by Risk characterization (R) and the Art (A) of creating deal-making opportunities.

JUDGMENT

Technology licensing in particular exhibits an apparent paradox: the licensed subject matter to be valued is subject to highly structured and rock solid scientific laws and principles, but the deal-making, including valuation, can appear to be subject only to whimsy. The paradox is only apparent. The world of certainty is a limited one. Where life is lived is inherently where generalizations apply and a certain fuzziness is inevitable. We live in a place that constantly requires us to make estimates and predictions, knowing that ideas submerged in words like *truth* and *certainty* and even *knowledge* do not really fit. Estimates and predictions can be faithful to underlying assumptions and beliefs, so that they are valid and self-consistent, but they cannot be *true* in the sense that knowledge of a historical occurrence or a scientific fact can be. This condition is not really a limitation; it is the nature of practical everyday life.

For some, the lack of certifiable, demonstrable, knowable outcomes leads to the following question: is valuation a pointless exercise? Although it can be, in general (another generalization) it is not. There is substantial value in performing a valuation. As we shall see in this book, there exist methodologies, underlying principles, and ideas that can be of great benefit in the determination of fair value creating agreements. As no one can know whether one's future includes an automobile accident, such lack of certitude does not induce reasoned individuals to drive without learning how, or following the rules of the road, or exercising caution, or staying sober. So here in the domain of valuation, the impossibility of certainty should not lead one to assume that there is no method or tool of value, or that rules of experience cannot be of help, or that the counsel of the wise cannot guide, or that sober, reasoned judgment is not of real practical benefit.

This form of thinking, often termed "wisdom" or "reasoned judgment," is as old as the Bible and, in another domain, Aristotle. This book is about applying such reasoned judgment in the arena of technology valuation. It is an Aristotelian principle that one should not expect more precision from any subject than that subject matter is capable of providing. So in providing such reasoned judgment in matters of valuation, especially in the context of technologies, it should not be expected that comparable levels of knowledge or certainty are possible as that of the scientific underpinnings of the technology being licensed. Fortunately, comparable levels of knowledge are not needed to be of benefit to the user.

The purpose of this book is to aid the practice of technology licensing. The target reader is the licensing practitioner. In the case of the experienced practitioner, it is hoped that the experience of reviewing a codification of valuation methods and principles can be useful in integrating what such an individual may have learned through one-by-one experiences. Further, this book addresses some methods, such as Monte Carlo, that may not be familiar to even experienced licensing professionals. In the case of those new to licensing, this book may function well as a textbook suitable for one-semester self-study. For those between the stages of beginners and old timers, this book may be a useful reference and introduce some ideas and insights usable in everyday business practice. It is also hoped that this book could serve as a text for specialized classes in valuation.

DISCLAIMER

It many not be necessary, but it is probably prudent, to point out what should be obvious: this is not intended as a proof text in support of a litigation. The context of the valuation methods considered here and my associated observations and suggestions is in support of opportunity licensing, not enforcement. Further, each licensing and valuation opportunity is specific to the given fact situation; so it is unwise and can even be misleading to take a passage of static words and assume that it can be applied without consideration of the specific circumstances by the exercise of reasoned judgment.

Acknowledgments

2002 EDITION

This book is a re-titling and extension of an earlier edition entitled *Early Stage Technologies: Valuation and Pricing*, published in 1999 also by John Wiley & Sons. By titling this book *Valuation and Pricing of Technology-Based Intellectual Property* we hope to make clearer that the scope of the valuation methods and their application in pricing encompasses a broad spectrum of technology from early-stage to fully-developed. The principal distinction of this book is the focus on valuation of technology that has not matured into products and operating businesses for which other more traditional valuation methods can be employed such as price/earnings ratio analysis and discounted present value models using established earning growth rates. As will be discussed, *technology*, *early-stage technology*, and *intellectual property (IP)* valuation and pricing will, in most circumstances, be treated as synonyms.

The origins of these books can probably be traced to a conversation I had with Lou Berneman who, on behalf of the Association of University Technology Managers (AUTM), asked me to teach the valuation section of AUTM's introduction to licensing course. That invitation, and honor, has become an annual event for me for some dozen years now and lead to my writing the valuation chapter in AUTM's License Practice Manual[1]. I owe thanks to Lou, AUTM, and in particular the two thousand plus students who have participated in that experience; these many interactions have helped me solidify my own thoughts and defog some aspects.

I wish to also acknowledge the useful interactions and discussions I have had with my consulting colleagues at InteCap, Inc. (www.intecap.com). In addition to the individuals I mentioned in the earlier edition, I have benefited by discussions with Lew Koppel, David Tenenbaum, Liza Bloomer, David Haas, Jeff Snell, Jeff Brown, Dan Wald, Dan Gitlin, Kevin Arst, and particularly Brian Oliver with whom I have worked on numerous client projects. These words and the responsibility for them are solely my own; the book does not represent the views or position of InteCap or its employees. Also thanks is due Susan McDermott, acquisition editor at Wiley, for the stimulus of and faith in a new edition of this book.

Based on these writings and my consulting practice, I have also had the privilege of leading two-day workshops on valuation and pricing for clients. These highly interactive experiences have also been very helpful to me in making certain points clearer and in developing additional examples and providing summary roadmaps of key ideas. I thank these workshop participants for their astute questions and the interesting discussions.

In this book we will still consider six valuation methods, and I am tempted to say, "just six methods," akin to renowned scientist Martin Rees's interesting book and title: *Just Six Numbers*.[2] Here, I have expanded the discussion of Industry Standards (Method 1) to include a discussion of paradigm licensing where standard valuation ranges are often applied and certain distinctions between what is commonly known as the market method and how it relates to industry standards. The chapter on Rating/Ranking (Method 2) has been expanded to provide additional examples and tools that can be used for both valuation and the related purposes. The Rules of Thumb Method (Method 3) includes an expanded discussion of stacking, stage of development, and risk issues and their effect on valuation, and what I hope is a useful roadmap chart. The Discounted Cash Flow Method (Method 4) includes an expanded discussion of risk and rate-of-return available for different risks and another new roadmap chart. The Advanced Methods chapter (Method 5) has an expanded discussion of the use of real options, though a fuller treatment of this subject awaits a separate book (forthcoming in 2003) entitled *Dealmaking Using Monte Carlo and Real Options Analysis*, also published by John Wiley & Sons. The Auction Method chapter (Method 6) is relatively unchanged from before.

Other changes include a discussion of license strategy choices and their effect on valuation and royalty base issues, a discussion introduced in Chapter 3 and expanded in Chapter 11.

Throughout the book, I have made numerous changes and clarifications in the hope of making the points clearer and more useful. Arthur Schopenhauer (1788-1860) in an 1844 edition of his classic book, *The World as Will and Representation* (or *Idea*) originally published in 1818, wrote: "Now, as regards this second edition, in the first place I am glad that after twenty-five years I find nothing to retract; my fundamental convictions have been confirmed, at any rate as far as I myself am concerned."[3] From this perspective, his 1844 edition, and his final 1858 edition included his 1818 text unchanged. In contrast with that genius, I have tried to change anything and everything that I could to make the book better. I am still not done with it, but it is the best I can do at the moment. It does not represent my final views on the subject of technology valuation and pricing. I have intended it to be an educational contribution to my profession, not as a proof text on some narrowly defined dispute, but as a systematic discussion of tools, methods, and principles, that can be developed and applied to that most challenging task of estimating what a technology could be worth.

To help with future writings and errata, I would appreciate receiving suggestions and corrections at *TechVal@razgaitis.com*. I will maintain an errata list at *www.razgaitis.com*.

NOTES FROM 1ST EDITION

Much of my life has been spent in learning. Some would say I still have a long way to go (which is true, but details on that are more appropriate to a confessional). Here I want to offer heart-felt thanks to you many "teachers" of valuation and pricing.

For 14 years and 2 months, I had the privilege of working for Battelle in Columbus, Ohio. During the early years of this period I had the opportunity of working for Battelle Development Corporation (BDC), a wholly-owned subsidiary that had been responsible for commercializing Battelle and outside-inventor technology since 1935. During those years at BDC, I happened to be present during the retirement transition of an unusually talented group of individuals who took the time and had the patience to share with me over a period of years their insights from an incredible breadth of experience. Although the content of this book is mine, I would be remiss not to acknowledge the influences that this unique opportunity afforded me. Bill Riley, to whom this book is dedicated, hired me into BDC. Bill was an endless source of experience-filled marketing and deal-making histories; many of those stories deserve a string instrument composition to elevate them to more-than-Irish ballads—really more like Homeric Epics. Bill's 29 years with Battelle, long-term participation in the Licensing Executives Society (including a term as LES President), and wise memory were, for me, like attending an academy of licensing learning.

Ken Shaweker was also a 30 year veteran of licensing experience, mostly at Battelle. He was BDC's IP Counsel. As our lead attorney, he was a model of reasoned judgment combined with sagacity in developing solutions to meet worthy business objectives and taught me a lot about agreements and people. Steve Dickerson, another 30 year man and head of BDC for many years, was tireless in his enthusiasm and pursuit of opportunities. In negotiations he was both gracious and quick-thinking, a very potent combination. Dr. Charles Schwartz was, unbelievably, our 50-year man (I put this in the category of Hank Aaron's lifetime home run record—amazing and not soon to be broken). His breadth and currency of technical insight was astounding; and as to kindness and patience, I have known only one other that deserves mention in the same breath. Art Westerman ("just" a 40-year man) in addition to his business development skills was a great writer and teacher of business writing (sorry that I didn't learn better than I did).

There were many others at Battelle who were not part of the retirement transition but who were part of my licensing and valuation 'faculty': Barry Bissell, Bob Zieg, Bill Huffman, Roland Adoutte, Don Williams, Gene Eschbach, and many others. I owe a very special debt to four very talented administrative assistants whose teachings often had to be by the rescue method: Carol Cremeans, Shirley Russell, Shari Dean, and Mary Ann Dillon.

My association with the Licensing Executive Society (LES) has been a constant source of learning from many people who have also become friends. If I start mentioning names, I would never know where to stop. LES is simply an outstanding group of individuals who have universally been both gracious and wise, an uncommon combination.

I am likewise indebted to my many teachers at Bellcore, now Telcordia Technologies, part of SAIC, another very special organization. In the midst of revolutions in communications technologies, and the networking marketplace, and even in our corporate structure, there were many who took the time to help and educate.

I would also like to thank my present colleagues at IPC Group and in particular Dan McGavock, Jim Malackowski, and Mike Lasinski.

Perhaps I owe my greatest learning debt to those many individuals with whom I negotiated, or attempted to negotiate, licensing agreements. Your reasoned and articulate explanations of how you viewed the subject opportunities have swirled through my memories many times and continue to do so even many years later. It is an axiom of negotiation that deal-making is a mutual-learning experience. I don't know how mutual it has been, but for me it has been the learning laboratory and my thanks goes out to all of you.

This is not the kind of personal book that causes me to focus on the contributions of my family. But it has been their encouragement and patience and source of earthly purpose that has kept me going: so to you, Carol (my loyal wife of 35 years) and children of whom I am so proud—Rich, Rennie, Christy, Jodi, and Leslee—I say thanks. These six have all at one time or another asked "What exactly is it that you do?" This book provides a good bit of the answer (hey, guys—I know it's hard to believe anybody actually gets paid for this, but this is what I do).

NOTES

1. "Pricing the Intellectual Property Rights to Early-Stage Technologies: A Primer of Basic Tools," Vol. 2, Part VII, Chapter 4; Association of University Technology Managers (AUTM), License Practice Manual.
2. Rees, Martin, *Just Six Numbers*, Basic Books, 1999. However, his subtitle of "The Deep Forces that Shape the Universe," pales our subject here.
3. Schopenhauer, Arthur, *The World as Will and Representation*, translated from the German by E.F.J. Payne, Dover Publications, Vol. 1, 1969, p. xxi. Although his book on epistemological philosophy is generally far afield from our purpose here, Schopenhauer's core idea that we apprehend not the subject of our consciousness but only a representation of such subject is useful and applicable to our understanding of any valuation model we may use and develop. We will return to this idea in closing observations in Chapter 12.

CHAPTER 1

What Is Technology Licensing?

INTRODUCTION

This book describes how to develop a value for technology rights being offered or bought. There are many books that treat the subject of valuation in various business contexts; this one focuses on valuation of technology licenses and assignments.

DISTINGUISHING TECHNOLOGY LICENSING FROM BUSINESS AND PRODUCT LICENSING

One can think of three discrete species of licensed rights: businesses, products, and technologies. Business transactions, which are usually outright sales or assignments, are those situations where a going concern with manufacturing, sales, and marketing, established customers and channels with a revenue and profit history, and all the other elements necessary to operate as a stand-alone entity are being transferred. Products licensing relates to those license transactions that enable the buyer to duplicate the making of some device, system, or service that has already been completed and proven by the seller. In this situation, the buyer will need to provide the necessary surrounding business assets to realize a profit from the license. The term *technology agreements*, on the other hand, commonly is used to designate transactions for pre-commercial designs and data, normally without the evidence of large-scale manufacturability or possibly even a single legitimate customer. In some cases, the final or best formulation has not yet been established. Another way of thinking of technology is as a work product of research and development (R&D). Put yet another way, R&D is a business operation which has as its successful result technology. Such a R&D work product can range all the way from a raw concept, at one extreme, to the results of many years and many millions of dollars' worth of investigation with comprehensive data books, samples, test results, financial projections, and business plans, as well as outside verification by certification agents and potential customer feedback from trials.

The key ingredient missing from technology licensing that is present in both business and product licensing is a commercial track record. Without such ingredient, the customary

approaches to product and business valuations do not work because the underlying data relied on do not exist. To make this more concrete, consider an automotive example. In early
1999, Ford Motor Company made an offer to buy and ultimately bought Volvo's automotive business. In developing the valuation of this transaction Ford, as the buyer, was able to
study many years of financial and operational data as well as forecasted performance based
on such data. This is the nature of sale of business transactions. Alternatively, Ford could
have licensed from Volvo the right to make and sell Volvo cars in the United States in Ford
plants based on Volvo proprietary information and patents. Again, in such a situation, Ford
would have been able to study an extensive historical basis of the costs and revenues of
making a Volvo car, and use such information to develop projections of profitability. This
would have been a product transaction, because Ford would have had to use its business assets to make and sell the cars. An example of a technology transaction would be Ford's acquisition of the rights to an uncommercialized Volvo invention that Ford could then
develop and use in their manufacture of Ford cars, or for some other business purpose. With
such technology transaction species, there is often no product or business history because
what is being licensed is newly developed and has not yet reached the stage of a product.
Although the tools and methods discussed in this book can be of use in business and product transactions, the main objective here is in support of technology licensing.

Technology licensing is becoming an increasingly important transaction category but
does not have the abundance of tools and experience available to business and product
transactions. This book is intended to contribute to the field of technology valuation.

SELLERS AND BUYERS IN TECHNOLOGY LICENSING TRANSACTIONS (TR R A DE™)

The vehicle of technology transactions is a contract between a seller and buyer, normally a
license. Such license conveys technology rights from the licensor, or seller, to the licensee,
or buyer. For simplicity, hereafter the licensor will be referred to as the seller, and the licensee as the buyer.

The transaction between buyer and seller is a trade. Sometimes the trade is as simple as
money from the buyer in exchange for assignment of a patent by the seller. In most cases,
the trade is much more complex. But it is always a trade. Building on this fundamental idea
we have devised the acronym *TR R A DE*™ to structure our discussion. Within the scope
of the book, all transactions are founded on the *TR R A DE*™ framework: *TR* is used to
designate *Technology Rights* conveyed in the licensing transaction. *R* is the risk involved in
any transaction, *A* represents the art of deal-making, and *DE* is deal economics. Each of these
elements of a transaction will be further discussed throughout this book.

Depending on the complexity of the transaction, there can be numerous other agreements accompanying the license. For the transfer of physical assets, such as lab equipment
or technology prototypes, there may be a separate purchase agreement. For circumstances
where key employees are to leave the seller and join the buyer, normally there will be employment agreements. If the seller agrees to provide subsequent technical assistance to the

buyer, there will be a separate services or consulting agreement. If the buyer is going to provide a licensed product to the seller for the seller's use in some other product, there will be a supply agreement. Sometimes, the parties choose to create a separate non-disclosure agreement so that it stands independently of the license. In the case of equity transactions, there are numerous other agreements that are needed related to stock purchase, incorporation, and shareholder issues. The legal details of all such licenses and related agreements are outside the scope of this book. Here we will focus on valuation and pricing and refer to the bundle of contracts as a singular license agreement, or "deal."

The process of valuation and pricing determines the transaction *deal economics*, (the *DE* in our acronym). So, in shorthand form, this book is about *TR* for *DE*.

TECHNOLOGY AND INTELLECTUAL PROPERTY

Technology Rights are usually expressed in three forms of intellectual property (IP): patents, trade secrets (also known as: knowhow, or proprietary technical information), and copyrights. Such IP can be considered as the form by which the technology rights are documented, protected, and conveyed.

It will be assumed that IP protection exists when considering the valuation of technology. There is always some uncertainty about the breadth and strength of such protection, and this uncertainty factors into the value determination. If there are issued patents, there can be some uncertainty surrounding interpretation of claim language or even the validity of the patent itself. If the patents are still pending, then there will be uncertainty about what will be allowed by patent offices in various countries of the world. There can also be uncertainties about trade secrets. It may not be well understood how "secret" the trade secret really is; it could be that many other labs and companies have independently arrived at the same information or soon will do so. Also there is always some risk of inadvertent disclosure of the trade secret by the seller or buyer or by some third party that would damage the value of the underlying technology asset.

The extent and strength of IP protection are dimensions of a valuation. An extreme example of such effect is the absence of value if the inventing organization publicized all the details of its invention in such a way as to preclude obtaining a patent or any other form of IP protection. So the absence of protection can and normally does preclude value. However, the converse is not true: it is possible to have very strong patent and trade secret protection and still not have much or any value because, for example, of the absence of a market for the product made by the underlying technology. Thus, IP protection is a necessary but not a sufficient condition for value to exist.

Considerations about which forms of IP should be used in which contexts, and analysis of the strengths and weaknesses of each, are outside the scope of this book. In the valuation examples considered it will be assumed that the *TR* are protected in some way or combination of ways. When risk issues are considered, or when comparisons are made to reference agreements, then strength and extent of IP protection will be identified as a factor to be considered when performing a valuation.

SOURCES OF TECHNOLOGY LICENSING

In the opening discussion of this chapter, we recognized that technology licensing is just one of three broad categories. The natural question arises, is technology licensing important in the business world? The answer is yes, and it is becoming increasingly more important.

In the United States alone, R&D spending exceeds $1 billion each business *day*. According to Battelle (www.battelle.org) which has long surveyed R&D spending in their summary published in R&D Magazine[1], R&D expenditures in the United States in 2002 are estimated to be nearly $286 billion, representing an increase of 3.6% over 2001 and a compound growth of 4% over 2000. Of this total, the federal government spending will be $75.5 billion, about 26% of the total; approximately 25% of this total is spent by the National Institutes of Health alone, 50% by the Department of Defense, and the balance by all other agencies (NASA, DOE, NSF, EPA, etc.). Total industrial spending on R&D will be $195 billion. The balance, $15.4 billion, will be provided by universities, institutes, and various other not-for-profit organizations.

The R&D intensity of such spending can be measured in two ways: the industries into which the R&D monies go, and the relative R&D spending as a percentage of revenues. Based upon international R&D data, according to R&D Magazine, just five business sectors account for 82% of all such spending:

1. Information Technology (hardware, software, and services): 32%
2. Pharmaceuticals and Health: 18%
3. Automotive: 18%
4. Electronics and Electrical: 10%
5. Chemicals: 5%

R&D company spending as a percentage of revenues ranges widely from nearly 20%, for information technology hardware and software, to less than 1%, for petroleum refining. Again, according to the Battelle/R&D Magazine study, six R&D U.S. industry sectors spend, on average, more than 10% of revenues on R&D.

1. Computer communication equipment: 18.5%
2. Prepackaged software: 17.1%
3. Telecommunications apparatus: 13.3%
4. Pharmaceutical preparations: 12.4%
5. Radio, TV, communication equipment: 11.2%
6. Semiconductor: 10.2%

In addition, according to this same article, many other industry segments spend between three and eight percent on R&D, including: aircraft, chemicals and allied products, computer and office equipment, electrical, electronic computers, household audio and video, automobiles, phone communications, and photographic equipment. A more complex, and subtle, question is this: what is this money buying? One of the trends of the 1990s, which is continuing in this decade, is increasing pressure on R&D departments and individual scientists and engineers to justify the investment in measurable returns to shareholders and stakeholders. This appears to be reflected in more well-targeted R&D programs, and a more applied focus. Nevertheless, substantial portions of the above R&D will not, and in some cases, cannot be used by the inventing organization. In other cases, the fruits of the R&D will be used in partnership, teaming, merger and acquisitions, and other relationships that will involve some form of technology being licensed, transferred, or in some way committed to a third party. Such transfers and commitments involve in some way the assessment of the value of the subject technology.

One measure of the work product of R&D is in patent data. In the U.S., in 2001, there were 326,508 utility patent applications submitted, substantially all "technology" subject matter, and 166,039 patents granted (according to U.S. Patent and Trademark Office; www.uspto.gov). In addition, many technologies are protected solely by treating them as trade secrets or copyrighted software for which there is no comparably available statistic.

Another measure of R&D, patenting, and licensing activity is available through the Association of University Technology Managers (AUTM: www.autm.org). They obtain data on their member organizations by surveying, with the most recent data being that for 2000.[2] This data is particularly interesting because for the most part the member organizations do not develop technology for their own businesses but rather for the pursuit of educational and societal good and make available the fruits of such R&D through licensing. Highlights from their 2000 report are as follows:

- 190 reporting institutions
- Total R&D spending was $29.5 billion (a little more than 10% of the U.S. R&D spending).
- Total invention disclosures of 13,032. Because universities generally publish the results of their R&D, they primarily rely on patents (and software copyrights) to establish intellectual property rights, in lieu of trade secrets.
- Total patent applications filed of 6,375, or about 50% of the invention disclosures.
- Total patents issued of 3,765.
- 4,362 new license and option agreements entered into during the year.
- A total of $1.26 billion in adjusted gross income received during the year from 9,059 license and option agreements.

Unfortunately, no comparable data is available for license and option agreements and payments for companies. Increasingly, individual companies such as IBM are providing such information in their annual reports to shareholders. For IBM such licensing revenues exceed $1.5 billion.

The preponderance of such industry R&D funding is designed to create technologies that the company itself will commercialize. However, it is a common outcome that companies create more technology than they can exploit in the businesses they operate and the markets they serve. Even with the prevailing trend of running much more focused R&D operations, companies inevitably create technology that does not find a home in a business unit. Sometimes this is because of a change in direction since the time that a specific R&D project was launched. In other cases, it just happens that creative people in the labs come up with "Aha's!" that are outside the business scope of their company. In still other cases the technology is needed and used in a company's product, but it can also be used in other fields; licensing is a way to extract hidden, additional value from such technology. Regardless of the reason, a company finding itself with orphan technology should consider how technology licensing can be used to extract value from the asset and benefit its shareholders.

An important segment of the venture capital industry invests in technology startup situations. Although more weight is put on the management team and the associated business plan, when the startup is based on a technology, then valuing the technology should be part of the overall valuation of the startup. As patents are being increasingly used by established companies to fend off unlicensed upstarts and new entrants, assessing the value of the technological intellectual property should play an increasingly important part of venture capital valuations.

Another context for technology valuation arises when a company transfers technology from its R&D lab in one country to a business unit in another country. There are tax issues associated with making sure that an appropriate imputed payment (royalty) is made intra-company.

A final example, but by no means a final category, occurs with in process R&D and the need under new FASB regulations to perform purchase price allocation for the acquisition of businesses. Although beyond the scope of this book, this situation arises when two companies are merging. At the time of the merger the companies may seek to write off some of that intangible value in an acquired company that would otherwise have to appear as goodwill and would thereby be amortized, adversely affecting company-reported earnings. The accounting environment relating to such matters is rapidly changing.

ISSUES IN TECHNOLOGY LICENSING

Valuation in business is about forecasting the future value of operating profits and cash flows. The buyer is paying to enjoy a stream of future positive cash inflows that it could not otherwise experience. When there is a history of sales, costs, and profitability there is generally a stronger belief that the future can be predicted. This is based on an innate belief that the past is a harbinger of the future. Due diligence in such cases focuses on two issues: confirming the historic data, and testing various hypotheses as to why the future should be worse, the same, or better than the past.

With technology licensing there is no past in the above commercial sense—or as is sometimes expressed tongue-in-cheek, "your track record is all in front of you." So, the issue of forecasting is the same, but all the data needs to be developed from scratch. It should be recognized that when a new technology is to be deployed in making an existing product there are "data" on which to develop a history. Although this is certainly not an optimal situation, it does have advantages. With product and business licensing, it is easy to become so anchored in the past and its extrapolation that one can miss flaws in the data and hazards, or opportunities, in the future. In a sense, when developing a forecast for technology licensing, it is easier to consider everything because one starts from a blank or near-blank piece of financial paper. Absence of data also helps prevent the rigid mindset that the future can be determined by the past. In general, there exists an inertia effect that keeps business circumstances from changing overnight, which supports the notion of relying on historic data. However, in the past decade we have seen such numerous revolutions in business models—ubiquitous and mobile connectivity to information, electronic commerce, and genetically-targetted therapies, for example—that one should be ready to scrutinize any forecasts regardless of the extensiveness of a historical record.

Overall, the uncertainty in technology licensing is higher than product or business licensing. This difference can be narrowed by skillful due diligence and analysis, but the fact remains that converting the results of R&D in a manufactured and sold product involves additional hurdles and possible opportunities for failure.

A TAXONOMY OF TECHNOLOGY LICENSING

There are various ways of categorizing the circumstances under which licensing valuation, pricing, negotiation, and deal-making occur. Although a discussion of the "how-to's" of licensing in each of these categories is beyond the scope of this book, it is useful to have a common reference of licensing situations.

Technology licensing can be understood to take place under six situations, as discussed below:

1. *Enforcement Licensing.* The seller (licensor) believes it has the right and opportunity to enforce patent claims, and/or perhaps misappropriated trade secrets, against a buyer (licensee/believed-infringer) whose licensing need is a freedom to practice. In many cases the buyer is already using the technology in commerce and may already be aware of the seller's patent(s). This is sometimes called *stick* (or "the taxman cometh") licensing. Valuation can occur in pre-litigation contexts, or expert opinion in litigation, or settlement discussions.

2. *Opportunity Licensing.* The seller has a technology IP and possibly other assets that it believes will be of value to a buyer who is seeking new or expanded new revenue opportunities. Such licensing would normally include knowhow of some kind. This is sometimes called *carrot* (or "have I got a deal for you") licensing. Valuation normally occurs in anticipation and in the midst of a negotiation.

3. *Opportunistic (as distinct from Opportunity) Licensing.* The buyer seeks out a technology owner for the purpose of securing rights to a technology and perhaps other licensable assets. Prior to such contact, the seller may not have realized that it

possessed licensable value, or it may not have been previously willing to license its technology. Valuation typically occurs first by the buyer in anticipation of making the seller an offer, and by the seller and by both parties in the negotiation.

4. *Divestiture Licensing.* The seller is exiting a business area that includes technology and, typically, other assets such as physical plant, property, equipment, people, and trademarks. Traditional M&A (merger and acquisition) activities would encompass this form of licensing, though M&A transactions are normally of operating businesses. So in our context, divestiture licensing would more likely be related to technology assets and rights that were unused or underused by the seller and for some reason has become part of the M&A transaction. Divestiture licensing can resemble opportunity or enforcement licensing depending on the circumstances. Valuation typically includes non-technology elements, such as the value of equipment, buildings, and so forth. Often the value is expressed as a lump sum payable in cash or cash and securities, though there can also be earnout and other future payments.

5. *Partnering Licensing.* The seller is seeking a business partner who will provide certain resources (such as complementary technology, key people, market access, and money) to a joint effort in further R&D, product development, manufacturing, and/or sales. The technology license is normally just an element of a panoply of supply, joint invention, facility access, marketing, and other agreements. Valuation occurs in anticipation of and during the back and forth of partner negotiations and can be expressed in royalty payment or splitting terms, or in revenue apportionment in accordance with some form of a capital contribution calculation, which would include a value for the technology contributed to the partnership.

6. *Startup Licensing.* The seller is licensing to a new business (a NEWCO) being formed expressly for the purpose of commercializing the technology by making and selling products and services. Buyers, who may be traditional venture capitalists, private investors, or strategic investors, normally seek many things from the seller, not least of which are the employment of the key people. The closing documents associated with licensing are mountainous and include incorporation papers, corporate bylaws, employment agreements, stock purchase agreements, and the technology license itself. Valuation occurs in the preparation of term sheets in anticipation and midst of negotiation of the formation of the NEWCO and for subsequent rounds of investment. Equity is normally the principal valuation consideration.

In the first three categories, the agreement structure and valuation issues tend to be substantially simpler than in the last three categories. To keep our considerations manageable, we will not attempt to include a discussion of all six categories of technology licensing as we go through each of the six valuation methods. In Chapter 10 we will cover the special situation of taking equity as a principal form of compensation, which normally occurs with Startup Licensing, but can occur in other circumstances. For convenience, most of the illustrations used in this book will use Opportunity Licensing as an assumed context.

PRICING VERSUS VALUATION

Valuation and pricing are two terms used for closely related ideas. As used in this book, the term "valuation" means the direct output of the valuation tools and methods developed in Chapters 4 through 10 without consideration for how such value should be presented or packaged to make it attractive or acceptable to the other party.

"Pricing" is about using the valuation findings to reach an agreement. Pricing is the internal and external communication of perceived value. Pricing is also the concrete answer to valuation, the specification in monetary or equivalent terms of what is offered for sale. Valuation, as we shall see, tends to produce a range of numbers, either as a result of different methods used or as an expression of uncertainty in value; pricing is the proposed number. Yet another way of expressing the difference is this: Valuation is an opinion; pricing is an offer which is designed to lead to a negotiation and, ultimately, an agreement and commitment.

Pricing is the customary way in which parties say "yes" or "no" to a deal; in most cases, once a potential buyer has passed through an initial screening process for strategic fit, there is a price at which the buyer will buy and a price above it for which the buyer will walk away.

Pricing also relates to transaction time. Although technology licensing is not normally amenable to "blue light specials" (à la K-Mart), a seller may establish a lower price for a quicker deal and this would be a legitimate strategy. If the time period is so short as to preclude a reasonable period for due diligence, then the buyer will only consider a "fire sale" offer—a price so low that, within a very wide range of conceivable outcomes, the buyer is confident that the deal is worth doing. If the due diligence time period is reasonable but short, and the seller is offering a price that can be derived by a reasonable valuation, then this approach can create a higher priority due diligence effort by one or more buyers. Conversely, a seller may adopt a high price strategy and be willing to conduct a more expensive and lengthy marketing campaign. Because technology tends to age more like apples than fine wine, one runs the risk of being passed by by playing too hard to get.

Pricing issues, then, relate to negotiation tactics and, in some cases, company strategy. Valuation is focused on the underlying asset's intrinsic worth. Both issues will be addressed, although the focus will be on the latter.

A highly recommended book is one of the less-famous Arthur Miller plays, (appropriately titled) *The Price*. Like other great works, this play has multiple levels of interpretation. The presented level is the price of some used furniture.[3] The seller, one of two brothers in the play, has invited a used furniture dealer, an 89-year-old Russian, to bid on the family furniture of his father's estate. There is wonderful interplay between the brother and the savvy buyer. The brother keeps wanting to hear "the price." The buyer keeps providing him insights about the furniture, business, and life in general because, in broken English, "the price of used furniture is nothing but a viewpoint and if you wouldn't understand the viewpoint is impossible to understand the price (sic)."[4] This apt comment about a viewpoint determining the price summarizes much of what will be later developed in this book.

CONCLUSION: OVERVIEW OF THE REST OF THIS BOOK

In Chapter 2, we will consider possible components involved in a licensing transaction, rights and other things conveyed by the seller and money and other things paid by the buyer, and risks embodied in the future projections. *Risk* is so important a factor that it is used to represent the second *R* in *TR R A DE*™.

Chapter 3 provides an introduction to the six valuation methods presented in Chapters 4 through 9 (one method per chapter). Risk is dealt with in quantitative terms in Chapter 7 through the use of a Risk Adjusted Hurdle Rate, RAHR (represented by the symbol "k").

Chapter 10 deals with some special issues when equity is a component of the transaction, especially with startup situations.

Finally in Chapters 11 and 12 we consider how the value of license agreements can be structured and negotiation principles. Such structuring and negotiation are what make technology rights deal-making an *Art*, the letter *A* in our acronym *TR R A DE*™.

To recap, this book will deal with *Technology Rights (TR), Risk (R), Art (A)*, and *Deal Economics (DE)*.

> Troilus: What's aught but as 'tis valu'd?
>
> Hector: But value dwells not in particular will. It holds his estimate and dignity
> As well wherein 'tis precious of itself As in the prizer.
>
> Troilus and Cressida II[5]

NOTES

1. "2002 R&D/Battelle Research Funding Forecast," article authored by Dr. Jules J. Duga and Tim Studt, in *R&D Magazine*, January 2002.
2. *AUTM Licensing Survey: FY 2000, Survey Summary*, 10th Anniversary Edition, AUTM.
3. The hidden levels have to do with the price of life paid by two brothers, their wives, and the brothers' parents. The play focuses on the price of the furniture, but the other "prices" keep reappearing. It is a wonderful story.
4. Arthur Miller, *The Price* (Penguin Books, 1968), Act I, p. 38.
5. *The Yale Shakespeare, The Complete Works*, Barnes and Noble, 1993, p. 336, line 54ff. Thanks to Edward J. Bander who identified this excerpt in the context of valuation in *The Breath of an Unfee'd Lawyer: Shakespeare on Lawyers and the Law*, Catbird Press, 1996.

CHAPTER 2

The *TR R A DE* Substance, and Its Risks and Psychology

INTRODUCTION

This chapter deals with three issues that underlie the rest of this book: the determination and specification of the transaction exchange itself, the perceptions and characterizations of commercial risks, and the psychology of valuation (and pricing) in the context of making projections with a high degree of uncertainty.

Licensing is really about trade, hence the acronym *TR R A DE*™ introduced in Chapter 1. Trade means an exchange in which two parties transfer to one another different things, but *both* perceive they received more in value returned or a more useful form of value than what was given up. If both parties did not view the trade in this way, it simply would not take place. Further, both parties necessarily prefer to possess that which was acquired in lieu of that which was given up. Thus, trade is a value-creating event for both parties.

In common forms of trade the exchange is easy to value and rapid to execute, whether it is trading $1 for two bananas, or one party providing piano lessons in exchange for the other party mowing the piano teacher's lawn. With technology licensing, there is a wide range of elements that can be offered by the seller and by the buyer. The specification and valuation of these elements is the subject of this book. In this chapter we will consider further the "*TR*," or *Technology Rights* issue introduced in Chapter 1, and the "*R*," or *Risk*, the second R in *TR R A DE*™.

IDENTIFICATION OF TECHNOLOGY RIGHTS TRANSFERRED

Both the buyer and seller have beliefs as to what should be on the list of rights transferred. It is not uncommon to find that even well into a negotiation one or both parties are surprised to learn that something they had assumed was part of the deal is not in fact being offered. This discovery leads to setbacks in the negotiation process and, in some cases, a complete breakdown in the relationship. In all cases such a misunderstanding will lead to an error in valuation because valuing a technology needs to be done in the context of all the assets, which includes a specification of the rights being transferred. Consider three kinds of licenses: (1) outright sale, (2) non-assert, and (3) limited license.

Outright Sale Agreements

In the case of an outright sale, what is being offered is the ownership of the patents and related IP rights, such as trade secrets (know how). This would appear to be simple: "Here it is, you buy it." However, the buyer and seller can have different perspectives on what "here" and "it" means. The buyer may expect and reasonably need some hands-on learning, often termed "tech transfer" assistance in order to be able to make use of the technology; this could involve months of access to the seller's experts. In special cases, the buyer may even require that certain key employees of the seller become employees of the buyer, because the need for such expertise is perceived to be ongoing and critical to the commercial success of the project. The buyer may also expect to receive ownership of equipment and fixtures that were used in the R&D process. The buyer may also want representations and warranties concerning the seller's rights to the patents and other forms of intellectual property, guarantees that the patents are valid, assurances that the use of the technology as described by the seller does not infringe a third party's patents, and so on. The buyer may also want a representation that it will not require the use of any other patent owned or controlled by the seller even if such patent is not directly related to the technology.[1] Likewise, even with this simple agreement, the seller may expect more from the buyer than just money. For example, the seller may want the retained right to practice the patents or at least to be free from the threat of being sued by the buyer for infringement of the transferred patents' and improvement claims (a so-called "non-assert" provision). If the valuation includes royalty or other forms of future conditional payments, the seller may insist on minimums, guarantees, and reversion rights, depending upon future outcomes.

Non-Assert Agreements

In a "non-assert" license, the buyer is essentially acquiring freedom from a future lawsuit by the seller; it represents the opposite extreme from the initial example of outright ownership. On the surface, this also appears to be a simple agreement—basically, the buyer is paying for something *not* to happen. (In reality, the buyer does "get" something:

assurance that it has the freedom to practice within the scope of the seller's patents included in the agreement.) Yet despite the apparent simplicity of this type of license, there are numerous elements of the deal requiring clarification as being included or excluded. For example, what about future patents that the seller may invent or obtain? Are such unspecified and even presently unknowable patents included within the scope of the non-assert? Will the non-assert right apply to all countries in which corresponding patents have been obtained? Does the seller have to represent that it will require any competitor of the buyer to pay the seller at least as much to acquire such a non-assert (the so-called "most favored nations" clause)? In turn, the seller may want some form of reciprocal non-assert for the same, related, or completely unrelated technology.

License Agreements

With a limited license or simply a "license," the grant to the buyer is more extensive than the non-assert but less than an outright sale and considers many dimensions of business practice. Will the buyer be able to make anything it wants under the license or only certain products or categories of products? Will it be able to make, use, and sell, or just one or two of these rights? In which countries will such rights be enabled? How long will the license last? Will the buyer have the right to license third parties (the so-called "sublicensing" right)? Will the buyer be able to sell its right to a third party (assignability)? What will the seller be obligated to provide? Commercial data? Customer lists? Equipment and facilities? Tech transfer support? Improvement inventions? Defense of the patents? Who pays to maintain the patents in all their various jurisdictions? What happens if the patents are later found to be invalid? Can either party terminate the license without cause and cost? If not, under what conditions could termination be effected? Will agreements to supply raw materials or buy or provide finished products be part of the trade? Obviously all these questions require interaction amongst the technical, business, and legal people on each side and should be factored into making a valuation.

The answer to each one of these and many other questions affects the value of the transaction, some more so than others. Accordingly, the specification of the "*TR*," the *Technology Rights* which is used here to encompass all such terms, is essential to performing a valuation.

It should also be said that this is not a legal textbook. Therefore the reader is encouraged to refer to many such texts on legal issues to obtain a fuller and authoritative treatment of such agreements.[2]

SELL-SIDE SOURCES OF VALUE: THE BOX

The critical starting point of any valuation is defining exactly what is being offered for licensing.[3] Yet, it is not uncommon that long into a marketing campaign, or deep into a negotiation, it becomes frustratingly obvious that the parties have not had a common or even similar idea of what is being licensed. Here we wish to consider what a seller may offer and a buyer may seek in a license agreement. In the next section we will reverse the view and consider what a seller may expect and a buyer may offer in consideration for such agreement.

It is useful to develop a shorthand for this discussion: we will use a metaphorical Box and its contents to designate the subject matter of a license being valued. What might such a Box contain? Clearly, we begin with the right to practice the technology being licensed. But even this simple idea contains two very important terms that must be defined: technology and right.

1. *Technology.* What exactly is the *technology* being licensed? How does it relate to the issued patents that might be in the Box? For instance, does technology mean that the buyer can use the claims of the licensed patents, however it is able to do so, and only that? Or, is the scope of the technology only incompletely encompassed by the issued patents? What about pending patent applications whose ultimate claims are not known at the time of the negotiation? What about improvement inventions that might arise at the seller's R & D labs or that the seller may acquire rights to in the future? What does improvement really mean in relation to the technology?

2. *Right.* This is another term capable of a rich range of meanings. What is the uniqueness of licensed right? Is it exclusive? If so, what are the terms? Does it apply to all potential applications (fields of use)? All territories? For all time? Does exclusivity preclude the seller's right to practice? Is the right to sublicense included in such an exclusive right? What about the right to assign?

It is common that sellers are willing to consider alternative Boxes with respect to the technology and right issues. There are two things that are important about changing Boxes: How does it affect value? How does it affect deal doability?[4]

1. *Valuation.* Any change in the contents of the Box should, in general, cause a change in the value of a license to the Box's contents. Accordingly, without locking on a definition of the content of the Box, it is not possible for valuation to take place by either the seller or buyer. One is tempted to conceive of creating an à la carte menu by which each element in the Box is individually priced, such that any buyer can self-price the deal by the selections it makes, something like this: nonexclusive royalty is 2%; with exclusivity there is a 3% adder (5% total); the sublicensing right is 1%; two years of improvements cost an additional 2% but five years of improvements are on special today for only 3%; and so forth (or the equivalent in present-value, lump-sum payments).

2. *Doability.* In licensing situations, the number of possible elements is so large, and their value can so interact with the presence (or absence) of other elements, that to create such a valuation model would require an overwhelming level of analysis. Although such an approach works for restaurants and custom-built homes, the idea of a single Box with à la carte pricing incorporating all the possible deal variations is simply impractical for technology licensing. Fortunately there are practical solutions.

The obvious solution is for the seller to prescribe only one Box and value it accordingly—as Henry Ford said, you could have any color of a Model-T automobile, as long as it was black. Such a one-size-fits-all approach is likely to be rejected by potential buyers as including more than they want to pay for or less than they need. In many cases, a potential buyer will have very particular interests and values, and will seek a licensing Box unique to its business situation.

If an à la carte Box cannot reasonably be valued, and a one-size-fits-all Box has low or no deal doability, what is to be done? As a starting point for marketing and negotiations, the seller creates a baseline Box of what it conceives is an appropriate configuration of its interests and its target buyers, but with an analysis of one or two alternatives to establish a range of values and an estimate of value sensitivity. Regardless of these choices and complications, the Box must be defined before the valuation process can begin if its result is to have a rational basis.

So far, we have considered technology and rights as two elements of the Box. What else is there? Well, the list is long indeed. The following list provides brief descriptions of additional possible elements that could be appropriate to and included in such a licensing Box.

- *Patents and other intellectual property.* This could include pending patent applications, formalized trade secrets, copyrighted content and software, and even trademarks.

- *Proprietary technical information (PTI).* Although this can be grouped under IP trade secrets, it is useful to consider the wealth of technical information that is typically created by a seller as being broader than the more restrictive, legal term of trade secrets. Included in such PTI could be laboratory notebooks, unpublished white papers, project plans, management presentations, a selected compendium of published articles whose results are pertinent and valuable to the licensed technology, assessments of competing technologies, market assessments including customer surveys or focus panel results, and the like.

- *People.* There could be individuals employed by the seller who would be interested in joining the buyer and so continuing to stay involved with the technology. The seller can agree to permit the buyer to recruit selected individuals and even provide inducements to key employees to go with the technology. As part of such transfer, the seller can provide the buyer, and the people transferring employment, the right to use all their "head IP" as it relates to the subject technology. Such seller commitments are subject, always, to the willingness of such people to become transferring employees of the buyer's company, but incentives can be committed to by either the seller or buyer or both.

- *Hardware.* The technology can be expressed in a wide range of physical forms from special raw materials, to models, R & D prototypes, development breadboards, test samples, and so forth, all the way to saleable inventory.

- *Facilities.* This can range from the offerings of a complete operable production plant embodying the licensed technology or a factory that manufactures the licensed technology as a product, down to specialized facilities/infrastructure that can be removed, shipped, and reinstalled at the buyer. Alternatively, a lease arrangement could be used whereby the buyer would use the seller's facilities on a short-term or long-term basis.

- *Software.* The seller could have software programs that model the performance of the technology and are useful in R & D and/or production design and/or production control.

- *Customers.* Commercial accounts could be transferrable to a buyer. In other cases, there could be trials with potential customers, or expressions of intent to buy that could be available.

- *Suppliers.* The seller could have identified and even qualified certain vendors who can supply needed materials or services, with the attendant specifications. The seller itself could agree to be a supplier of a needed component (an element that could be a source of high deal value to the seller).

- *External contracts.* There could be sources of funding, including R & D funding by third parties, such as a government agency, which the buyer might acquire as part of the agreement. Likewise, commercial services that are currently provided by the seller could be transferred to the buyer.

- *External licenses.* The seller may have operating permits, government approvals, or other licenses to the subject technology collecting revenues that can be transferred. Alternatively, licensed rights to third-party patents could be included here, or under "other IP," and could be an important source of deal value if the seller has the right to sublicense or assign.

- *Patent prosecution and maintenance.* If the patents are assigned (sold), then their prosecution and maintenance normally becomes the responsibility of the buyer. If the patents are only licensed, then the buyer or the seller could undertake the financial obligation, or it could be shared.

- *Infringement enforcement.* A common concern is, what happens after the deal is done if a third party infringes or appears to infringe on licensed claims? A seller-licensor could agree to enforce the licensed patents to ensure the buyer's exclusivity. If nonexclusive, the seller may accept the responsibility to take action against unlicensed third parties who compete with the buyer. In either case there may be some threshold of infringement before the seller would be obligated to take action.

- *Infringement defense.* A different infringement concern by the buyer has to do with the risk associated with its freedom to practice what it licensed from the seller. The seller could indemnify the buyer against claims by the third party against the buyer for a specific product.

- *R & D/consulting services.* The seller could provide R & D services (commonly termed *tech-transfer assistance*) for a transition period, or an indefinite period. A prescribed level of such services could be included in the license, and/or the commitment to provide such services under specified terms.

- *Regulatory support services.* There could be circumstances whereby the use of the technology will require some form of regulatory approval and the seller could be of assistance to the buyer in seeking or transferring such approval.

- *General representations and warranties.* It is, of course, common for the seller to warrant that it has the right to sell or license what it is offering to the buyer, but the seller could offer additional representations and warranties.

Although few agreements have all these elements, it is useful to both the seller and buyer to consider what can, should, and should not be included to maximize the relative value of the opportunity to both parties, particularly for technologies with significant commercial potential. It is especially useful for the seller to create a summary of what is in the Box—or Boxes, in the case of multiple scenarios. This practice allows all the affected individuals within the seller's organization to possess a common understanding of the dimensions of a potential deal. In any case, such a specification is necessary to create a baseline on which a valuation can take place. Further, it is also useful in communicating with potential buyers so that an early understanding can be reached, or the Box appropriately adjusted, to accommodate the deal being envisioned.

These possible elements are not equally important, nor are they unrelated to each other. The IP is, for example, closely tied to both the *technology* and *rights*; it would not be uncommon that a license deal would have only these core elements in the Box.

BUY-SIDE EXPRESSIONS OF VALUE: THE WHEELBARROW

In the previous section, the focus was on the value provided by the seller to the buyer, using the metaphor of the Box, as the contents for the technology, the rights to use, and the related value-affecting aspects of a license. Here, we wish to consider how the buyer may provide value to the seller. As before, a metaphor will be useful.

One frequent measure of value of a license is the royalty rate, as in "this deal is for a 5 percent license." Actually, a royalty rate by itself is an incomplete description of value. The seller is rightfully concerned about the size of the check that it expects to receive, not the royalty rate used in calculating the amount owed under the license, regardless of the rate, and regardless of whether it is usage-based, time-based, or event-based. To effectively capture the concern of the seller (and buyer), the slang term *Wheelbarrow* has been utilized in reference to the buyer hauling cash to the seller in a wheelbarrow. Accordingly, while a royalty rate is a common negotiation point, both parties are ultimately concerned with the size of the Wheelbarrow. Here, the Wheelbarrow is used to reflect all of the various forms of value provided by the seller to the buyer. The seller provides a Box of technology, rights, and other deal elements, whereas the buyer provides, in the form of one or many Wheelbarrows, value payments to the seller.

There are two common forms of value contained in such Wheelbarrows: a single payment, such as "the buyer paid $10 million for the license," and a royalty rate.

1. *Lump-sum license.* A single-payment license, commonly termed a *lump-sum* or *paid-up* license, is the simplest valuation structure.[5] It represents a check, or more commonly a wire transfer, usually made simultaneously with executing the license. It represents the only payment that the buyer will make. However, even in this simplest of arrangements there may be other important forms of value provided by the buyer, such as granting the seller access to certain patents belonging to the buyer (*cross licensing*), a supply agreement whereby the buyer agrees to provide products made by the licensed technology, or even some other technology, under more favorable terms than are commercially available. Thus, even for such simple, single-payment licenses, the Wheelbarrow may contain something notable beyond the closing payment.

2. *Royalty license.* A pure royalty-based license, also known as a *running royalty license*, is the inverse of the single-payment license: the single-payment license is a fixed sum paid upfront for unlimited (or in accordance with the terms of the license), subsequently free use, whereas the pure royalty license has only payments due on use (make, use, or sell) and only on such use. However, a critical factor in determining value is the royalty base against which such royalty rate is applied. A common negotiation involves a determination of the appropriate base. Consider the situation of a quick disconnect that is being licensed for use on the terminals of an automobile battery. The seller may argue that the appropriate royalty base is the selling price of the automobile because such terminals are, say, used only on batteries in automobiles. If the buyer is a battery maker, such an approach will be unacceptable regardless of how low the royalty rate is because the battery maker has no control, or even knowledge, of the selling price of the automobile with the battery in it. Further, the battery maker is likely to argue that the connector royalty should not be based on the selling price of the battery itself because the connector is only a small part of the battery and in fact does not contribute to the basic function of the battery. The buyer is likely to propose a royalty base on the selling (or fair market) price of the connector component itself. The negotiated royalty rate will be done in conjunction with the negotiation on the appropriate royalty base: a 1 percent royalty based on the selling price of the battery, for example, could alternatively be a 25 percent royalty based on the connector's cost or fair market value, and yield the same cash amount in the Wheelbarrow.

In addition to these two common elements, there are many other possible elements that can be used in any combination in the Wheelbarrow to provide value to the seller:

1. *Upfront payment(s).* A common value element is the use of one or multiple *upfront* or *license fee* cash payments. Upfront payments are unconditional and precede the anticipated commercial use by the buyer. One such payment is made on closing or

within a specified number of days of closing (e.g., 30 days). Additional "upfront" payments could be made at specified dates, such as on the first and second anniversary of the license. In this case, the term *upfront* is used to specify payments that are committed at deal execution but may be deferred to specific dates after closing. As used here, such form of value is unconditional and additional. It is unconditional in the sense that regardless of the buyer's later decision not to use the licensed technology or even termination of the license, such payments are still due. It is additional in that other subsequent forms of value payments, such as royalties, are a separate contributor to the Wheelbarrow of payment. One important negotiation issue is the ability of the buyer to credit such payments against future royalties owed; not surprisingly, sellers gravitate to no and buyers to yes. The reasonable answer lies in the calculation of the royalty: If the full value of the license has been ascribed to the royalties, and some of the running royalties have been moved to be fixed, upfront payments, then the answer should be yes because they are in fact prepayments; on the other hand, if the royalties were calculated to represent the license value remaining after the upfront payments, then the answer should be no.

2. *Annual payments.* Another form of fixed cash payments is the use of annual payments payable on each anniversary of the license for as long as the license is in effect. Sometimes this form of payment is referred to as *license maintenance fees* or *minimum royalties* (or simply *minimums*). Normally the use of *minimums* is restricted to those periods when earned royalties can reasonably be expected and the magnitude of the minimums is scaled on some proportion of the magnitude of expected royalty payments, and such payments are commonly credited against earned royalties during that period (and such credits may or may not be applicable, i.e., carried forward, to subsequent periods).

3. *Milestone payments.* Such payments are specified amounts that become due upon the crossing of some milestone event. In the area of pharmaceuticals, such milestones could be the entry into each phase of clinical testing, or any regulatory approval. Other kinds of milestones could be key R & D achievements, and/or the commitment to building a commercial plant of specified minimum size, and/or the first commercial sale. A special type of milestone payment would be a payment due upon termination of the license.

4. *Option payments.* One form of option payment is an initial payment made by the buyer to allow it to conduct additional R & D, or market assessment or other feasibility activities, to enable it to make an informed licensing decision. Such a payment has the effect of compensating a seller for withholding the licensing opportunity from the market during the option period. Other types of option payments are possible. One example is the option to maintain exclusivity of the license beyond a certain date. Another example would be to acquire an additional field of use or territorial right. Yet other examples would be to acquire a companion technology, to

buy out the license (a one-time payment to end all future royalties), and to make other payments to buy down the royalty rate (a payment that lowers the effective royalty for all subsequent sales).

5. *Royalty adjustments.* Many creative adjustments have been used with a baseline royalty rate. A *wedding cake* royalty is one that decreases in rate with increasing sales, such as 5 percent on the first $5 million, 3 percent on the next $10 million, and 1 percent for all additional sales. Such sales could be annual—that is, with each anniversary the royalty again begins at 5 percent in this example—or cumulative (i.e., total sales since the onset of the license).

    Alternatively, an escalating royalty could be used where the royalty rate actually increases with increasing sales, under the reasoning that higher sales would correspond to higher licensee profitability. This might also be used to restrict or control the output of the buyer's licensed goods. A *multimarket royalty* is another approach, where different, specified royalties are used for individual products (fields of use) and/or territories.

    Yet another strategy calls for certain sales to be *royalty free* (possibly to aid market introduction or some other purpose). Sellers might seek to include in the same or an alternative royalty calculation something called *convoyed sales*, additional products or services that the licensee might anticipate selling as a result of selling the goods embodying the licensed technology.

    Similar to a milestone payment, a *kicker* is a royalty premium paid upon the occurrence of some milestone. For example, the baseline royalty rate might be set at 5 percent, but if the performance of the technology exceeds some specified level, there is a 2 point kicker, making the royalty paid actually 7 percent. Of course, the opposite could be negotiated by the buyer, such that there is a 3 point "deflator," making the royalty paid 2 percent if the technology meets only some lower standard. Other adjustments in royalty rate could be based on market share, payments made to third parties for the right to practice patents needed to practice the licensed technology, step-downs in rate if the licensee elects to convert its license from exclusive to nonexclusive or if certain (but not all) patents expire, the making public of licensed trade secrets, the passage of a specified period of time, or even the profitability of the relevant product line or company (though such a provision can be perilous to the seller because of accounting complexities). Another complex royalty adjustment can exist with respect to the royalty base itself. In some licensing situations, the sales made by a certain buyer of a technology might be primarily as a result of one or more patents in the Box.

    Alternatively, such patents could be relatively minor contributors to a later sale by that same buyer. The parties could deal with this situation by adjusting the royalty base and possibly the rate itself to deal with each of these possible future situations. A final example is that of sublicensing royalties. The royalty amounts paid to the seller under the buyer's sublicenses could be different from that which would have been paid by the buyer for its own making/using/selling. This could be done by apportioning the gross amount of such sublicensing revenues between the buyer and seller.

6. *IP rights.* A grant-back is one type of IP right in which the buyer can provide rights to its own improvements to the subject technology to the seller, either for the seller's own internal use or to enable the seller to offer additional technology to its other technology licensees. Another example of IP rights provided by the buyer would be rights to patents or other forms of IP owned by the buyer but unrelated to the subject technology; such an arrangement is commonly termed a cross license. Another form of this type of value would be an agreement to provide the seller with a product that it, in turn, could sell based on the subject technology, or even some unrelated technology. Publicity by the buyer of the seller's role as a technology provider could create value to the seller in the form of goodwill and market recognition.

7. *Commitment to purchase goods/services.* The buyer could agree to purchase goods made by the seller at terms that are commercially favorable to the seller in a so-called supply agreement. Another example would be the buyer's commitment to purchase professional services, such as R & D in the area of the licensed technology or some other area; such an arrangement is common when the seller is a university and the buyer is a large company. Depending on the terms of these types of commitments, it could be value neutral to the parties, a value provided by the buyer, or even a value provided by the seller.

8. *Equity.* The provision of a share of ownership in the buyer can create a source of considerable value, or even the total value in lieu of any cash payments, royalty, or any other form of value in consideration for a license. Another variation is that the seller has an option to purchase a specified number of shares at a prescribed price per share by a prescribed date, and/or similarly the right to convert fixed or royalty payments into equity. Another form of equity value could be provided by the buyer by its infusing capital into the seller in exchange for shares in the seller's company. Such a cash infusion could provide the seller with a strategic advantage with respect to other fund-raising activities. Based on the circumstances, such a transaction could be value neutral, or value favoring the seller, or value favoring the buyer.

Although these eight elements do not exhaust the possibilities, they do reflect the commonly used means of creating a Wheelbarrow of value to the seller. As with the Box, it is unlikely that there are many agreements that include all possible elements, but the flexibility afforded by the inclusion of an element and its specific implementation can be important in reaching an agreement. Agreements with only unconditional payments, such as paid-up licenses, or licenses with only fixed periodic or event-driven payments, may have higher valuation risks because of their lack of certitude. Generally, though, these agreements result in a simpler document, both in construction and in implementation.

Conversely, agreements whose value is primarily dependent upon conditional elements (e.g., royalties) may have less valuation risk but higher complexity in document construction and ultimate implementation. An illustration of such possible elements of the Box and the Wheelbarrow is shown in Exhibit 2.1.

In general, for less important and less valuable technologies, the parties tend to gravitate to simpler Wheelbarrows (and Boxes). However, as current trends continue into the twenty-first century, technology owners will increasingly recognize their fiduciary responsibility to maximize their return on assets, and as time to market urgency increases, sellers will be more inclined to license out even their crown jewels for appropriately large Wheelbarrows. Likewise, we can expect all buyers to consider quite literally the world of technology in-licensing of boxes based on externally created technologies for the prospect that they can become strategic new businesses and, thereby, warrant highly crafted license-in arrangements. The twenty-first century is expected to become a new economy of licensing by the increasing use of highly tailored Boxes and value-optimizing Wheelbarrows for opportunities of high importance to both seller and buyer.

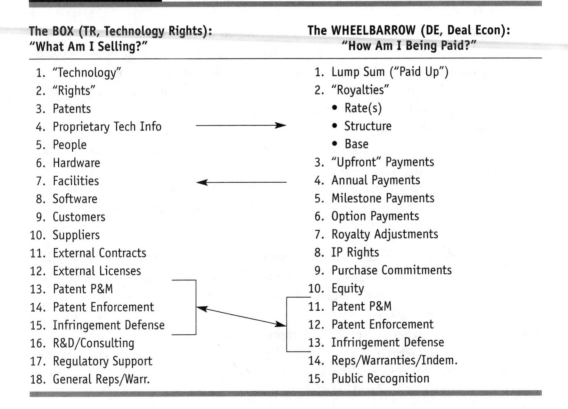

EXHIBIT 2.1   **THE FOUNDATION OF A VALUATION: THE BOX AND THE WHEELBARROW**

The BOX (TR, Technology Rights): "What Am I Selling?"	The WHEELBARROW (DE, Deal Econ): "How Am I Being Paid?"
1. "Technology"	1. Lump Sum ("Paid Up")
2. "Rights"	2. "Royalties"
3. Patents	• Rate(s)
4. Proprietary Tech Info	• Structure
5. People	• Base
6. Hardware	3. "Upfront" Payments
7. Facilities	4. Annual Payments
8. Software	5. Milestone Payments
9. Customers	6. Option Payments
10. Suppliers	7. Royalty Adjustments
11. External Contracts	8. IP Rights
12. External Licenses	9. Purchase Commitments
13. Patent P&M	10. Equity
14. Patent Enforcement	11. Patent P&M
15. Infringement Defense	12. Patent Enforcement
16. R&D/Consulting	13. Infringement Defense
17. Regulatory Support	14. Reps/Warranties/Indem.
18. General Reps/Warr.	15. Public Recognition

Special Circumstances with "Cashless" Buyers

In some transaction situations the buyer is unwilling or unable to pay in cash, either on closing or in the near future. Startup companies are one notable category; even successfully backed startups are notorious for creativity in the avoidance of writing checks. Another category of cashless buyer is an economically distressed buyer who may have a very solid plan for profitability but is in a cash-poor position at closing. A third example is third world and even second world companies; once one leaves North America, Western Europe, and Japan, it is common to encounter negotiating situations where the buyer is unable or unwilling to pay in hard currency, especially upfront.[6]

In the case of startup companies, we will consider special issues of equity in exchange for *TR* in Chapter 10. For distressed companies, there are usually two avenues available to make the deal economics (DE) work. One way is by delaying or reducing payments otherwise due until the commercialized technology is anticipated to yield positive net cash flow and compensated by increased later payments because the seller in fact has become a risk capital lender as well as a technology provider. A second way is by creative investigation into non-cash ways that the buyer can remunerate the seller, such as supply agreements under highly favorable terms either of the licensed technology or some other product made by the buyer.

In the case of third world companies, in addition to the two ways used with cash-poor companies there has arisen a third and ancient way: barter. The way barter works in a licensing context is generally as follows. The buyer agrees to pay a third party in the buyer country using the buyer's country's currency for a determined quantity of an exportable commodity with a quantifiable value. The third party then ships pre-paid the exportable commodity to a fourth party in a first world country. The fourth party then pays for the shipment by paying the technology seller in a bankable currency. There are numerous variants possible. For example, there could be multiple intermediaries buying and re-selling the exportable commodity until it becomes a bankable currency to the technology seller. Another variant is that the third world company "pays" some third party not in the third world currency but with some other commodity that it makes or resells. Clearly the use of bartering is much more complex, not to mention risky, than being paid in a first world currency. However there may be licensing opportunities where a third world company is the best route to the marketplace. In such a situation entering into a barter transaction may be warranted.[7]

Special Circumstances with "R&D" Sellers

There are numerous examples of technology sellers who perform R&D as their core "business." Included in this category would be universities, government labs, and private R&D entities such as SAIC, Battelle, AD Little, and SRI.

One element of value to such R&D sellers is to have funding to sustain active programs within the field of the licensed subject matter or in other fields. This can lead to circumstances where the license fee(s) can be committed in a way that benefits both the seller and the buyer. For example, a portion (or all) of the upfront license fee could be committed by the seller to further a not yet investigated area related to the licensed technology and which, if successful, could become the basis for a second generation product line. By earmarking such expenditure, with terms and conditions regarding rights to new inventions, the buyer can get more for its payment than just the subject license and, thereby, justify paying more than sought by the seller just for the offered *TR*. From the perspective of the R&D seller, valuation in these situations brings in other factors and rules of thumb, such as the "man year rule" or the "invention factory rule"[8] which are outside the scope of this book.

Defining the Technology Rights (*TR*) of the *TR R A DE*™

Ordinarily one expects the seller to be primarily responsible for defining and pricing the opportunity being offered. However this generalization has limitations. In many cases the licensing opportunity derives from need discussions originated by the buyer. In other cases the opportunity is created by both parties by mutual recognition of the possibility that a licensing deal can create value for both parties.

Regardless of the context, it is important that early in the discussions both parties agree on what is in and out of a possible deal. Ultimately such detail becomes an essential component of the executed agreements, often in the form of attachments of formal specifications. At the negotiation stage, the contents of the offer can be expressed as informally as bulleted points on a vugraph or transparency all the way to an offering book for more complex situations, although one should always obtain legal advice on such matters. Such summaries are included in documents known as "heads of agreement" or a "term sheet;" normally these documents have laid out, in addition to the *TR* specification, other key business terms including some of the key financial terms (*DE*).

If the negotiations are to be in the context of an auction, (covered as Method 6 in Chapter 9), then the deal definition comes from the seller and is formal and fixed. More frequently, the deal definition (*TR*) is itself a subject of negotiation between the parties. It is said that no two deals can ever look alike because the buyers and sellers are unique and want and value different things.

Another virtue of early definition of the *TR* is that deal-breaking issues can be identified. Examples of buyers' expectations that might become deal-breakers include the following:

- Representations and warranties that the patents offered are valid, or that the technology "works." Essentially, asking the seller to take the risk without the responsibility or control of getting the technology from the R&D stage to successful operation at a commercial scale.

- Commitment to enforce the patents against any and all infringers irrespective of the economic significance of such infringement.

- Inclusion of other patents or technologies which may not directly relate to the scope of the license.

Such issues can arise for many reasons. In some cases buyers are mistaking a technology license for a product or business license: by definition, a technology license requires a buyer to take responsibility for getting it from "here" (R&D work product) to "there" (commercial fruition). In other cases, buyers have low tolerance for risk, either because they see the overall risk of the project as being extraordinarily high, or they just have low tolerance for risk. In still other cases, buyers will keep asking for more *TR* until they hear a firm "no" simply as a negotiating strategy: How do we know we got all we can until they are ready to throw us out? (This is sometimes known as the "Brooklyn Negotiating Strategy.") Regardless of the circumstances, it serves both parties well to reach this understanding early, and record such understanding in writing even if in the form of a summary table. Such record keeping can be particularly useful when other parties within the buyer's organization join the negotiations at a later stage and presume or feign to presume certain things are included in the deal that have been excluded. Also, at the stage of documenting the *TR* table it is essential that the parties representing the seller gain organizational unanimity of the scope of what is being offered to avoid creating "take away" situations late in negotiations; such situations are always harmful to the negotiation process and can lead to the breakdown of a pending agreement.

Just as there are deal-breaking requests made by buyers there can be seller *TR* offers or structures that can be deal-breaking to a buyer. Examples include:

- Guaranteed commercial outcomes which, if not met cause the buyer to face substantial punitive consequences

- Requiring the buyer to grant back its improvements so that the seller can then license or disclose such improvements to third parties to compete with the buyer

- Requiring broad cross-license rights from the buyer's extensive patent portfolio in areas unrelated to the subject matter of the license.

Again, to avoid facing a broken deal after substantial effort, it is in the interest of both parties to work out the deal content issues early in the due diligence process. Another crucial reason for such *TR* definition is its necessity in order to assess *Risk* (*R*) and determine the appropriate *Deal Economics* (*DE*).

What about the feasibility of creating a pricing table for each possible (non deal-breaking) element of a transaction that can be used with any potential buyer or what is known as "á la carte pricing?" Unfortunately, such pricing works in restaurants and even when buying automobiles but it generally isn't feasible in technology licensing. In general, there are too many elements that can be negotiated that simply cannot be quantified on a one-by-one basis in a pricing book. Some exceptions exist. One such exception occurs when the technology can be used to make two different products (say, A and B) and in three different territories (say, 1, 2, and 3); in such cases it is possible that a limited pricing table can be created along the following lines:

- The *TR* for "A" and "B" are priced separately for use in all territories (1, 2, and 3) making a two-element pricing structure, or
- The *TR* for all products (A and B and any other) are priced separately for each of three territories (1, 2, or 3) making a three-element pricing structure.

The former situation makes sense when the buyer is a large international company that is likely to want to pursue worldwide exploitation of one, but not both, products. The latter situation makes more sense when the buyer is a smaller company whose marketing interests are focused in one territory but wants to put the underlying technology to as many uses as possible.

In this example, it is possible (in theory) to conceive of creating a matrix of rights: two products in two rows and three territories in three columns and pricing each of the six resulting cells. It has been reported that term sheets have been offered that have nine products matrixed against nine territories creating 81 cells all for one underlying technology. Such an approach may be workable for special situations such as licensing soft drink franchises in various countries, and it is conceivable for special technology licensing situations such as nonexclusive rights to a medical diagnostic tool protected by worldwide patents. In general, however, segmenting license prices into more than two or three components is rare. And rarer still (in fact, unheard of) would be a *TR* term sheet that shows the added cost of each of a dozen elements possible in an agreement.

PRINCIPLES OF VALUE

Before turning our attention to valuation methods and tools, let us consider certain underlying principles of value and valuation.

Specificity

One valuation method is the use of industry standards, which is based on the concept of identifying a comparable license agreement from public literature. However, for many situations, the contents of the box and the structure of the wheelbarrow will result in a valuation highly specific to the parties and parameters of the deal. This means that it is difficult if not impossible to find an exact or even near-exact comparable agreement on which to base a valuation. Also, this situation should make all of us cautious in characterizing any deal in terms of one or a few simple metrics, or in presuming that whatever the wheelbarrow looked like in our most recent deal is what it should look like in our next deal. There are simple licenses—for example, the non-exclusive licensing of a single patent in exchange for a single lump-sum payment—where the deal is clearly nonspecific, but this is a less common situation.

Risk

A dictionary definition of "risk" when used as a noun conveys an idea of possible loss or injury. When used in a license valuation context, "risk" means that the seller and buyer understand that things could turn out adversely in the context of the projected "most likely" situation assumed when performing a valuation. Risk can be thought of as the likelihood and impact of an outcome less favorable than the "most-likely" one.

In this sense risk is tied to the optimism (or pessimism) used to create the valuation. By itself, risk does not have meaning. Like the old vaudeville joke—"How are you doing?" ("*Compared to what?*")—risk needs a point of comparison. For example, if a buyer were knowingly to make very optimistic projections of how soon the technology could be brought to market, and of the top line growth in sales and the bottom line profit margins, then there would be a very high likelihood that such a project will not meet such projections. Put another way, this would be a high-risk deal for the buyer.

However, if the buyer were instead to make very pessimistic assumptions on time to market entry, sales, and margins, then the risk becomes lower, though it is never zero, because there is always the risk that the entire project could fail prior to the first sale.

Does this variability of risk mean that no rational basis exists for creating valuations and assessing risk? The answer must be "no," or this would be a very short book. There is another dimension to risk not considered in the previous examples, namely, the "upside" potential. Generally sellers and buyers are equally interested in upsides as well as downsides. In the optimistic projections the "downside" (i.e., risk) is large and likely, and the "upside" small and unlikely. In the pessimistic projection, the situation is reversed. Generally both the seller and buyer are interested in grasping and characterizing such upside potential in their projections and valuations; examples of this will be presented in the Monte Carlo Method in Chapter 8.

Consider a simple example. Suppose the seller offers a buyer the right to flip a coin and to be paid by some third party based on the number of successive "heads" that turn up. Specifically, the deal for the buyer is this: if the first flip is "heads," the buyer gets $1 million, if the second flip is also "heads," the buyer gets $10 million (total), and if the third flip is also "heads," the buyer receives a total of $100 million; however, at the first "tails" the game is over. There are the following four pay-off possibilities for the buyer who acquires this seller's "technology" (where H stands for heads, and T for tails):

H-H-H = $100 million
H-H-T = $10 million
H-T = $1 million
T = $0

How would a rational buyer characterize the risk and value such an opportunity? The mega-optimist[9] would say this is a $100 million opportunity with high risk while the mega-pessimist would say there is a 50:50 chance it is worth nothing. The statistical value of the coin flip possibilities is shown on the next page using a decision tree format. The value of each mode is simply the average of the two subsequent outcomes as each possiblity is equally probable.

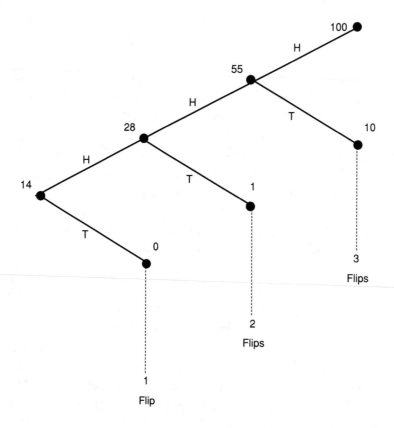

So, statistically the value of this opportunity is $14 million.

This means that statistically, if a buyer could acquire many such technologies, say 20 or more, it would very likely experience an *average* benefit of $14 million over the 20 or more "licenses" even though no one license yielded or even could have yielded exactly $14 million because the only possibilities are $0, $1, $10, and $100 million. From this long-term/many-deal perspective, the buyer should be willing to pay a seller of such rights almost up to $14 million to secure the right to "play" (assuming it does not have to make any other investments or deploy other buyer assets).

Say the parties agree that the buyer will pay $11 million for this opportunity. The most *frequent* outcome would be that the buyer would lose money on the deal, because half the time the buyer would get zero (tails first), and of the other half of the time the outcome would be evenly divided between $1 million and either $10 million or $100 million. Yet, if the buyer can play enough times, then the $100 million prize will occur with sufficient regularity that even paying the seller $11 million would be profitable to the buyer. For the 20-deal example, the buyer would average a profit of $3 million per "license" and, could thereby expect a total profit of $60 million.

Practically speaking, technology licenses require many years before great successes can be realized (failures can come early). Buyers and sellers recognize that in their business lifetimes they will generally not have a statistically significant number of deals that they can be so confident in such statistical methods, though for large corporations doing many deals such analysis is reasonable and appropriate.[10] Accordingly, it appears that buyers generally discount very high but rare upsides in their valuation analysis. Sellers, of course, normally take pains to point out to prospective buyers the existence of the upside potential.

Venture capitalists in particular receive offers that sound like the coin toss payoff example. Here is an actual letter:

> What we are asking for is Forty Million Dollars ($40,000,000), which will provide the capital needed....As planned, at the end of the two-year period we will have ramped up to 100 percent with an expected pre-tax profit of $211,832,258.[11]

Although one appreciates the precision of the projected returns, any reasonable buyer recognizes that what is being pitched here is a very high risk opportunity, or worse. It is useful to consider the kinds of risks that a buying opportunity may entail.

Business planning for future events involves risk. The decision to maintain status quo in a business situation, say by refusing to license, involves risk. *Risk* is business shorthand for saying that the future may turn out more adversely than our most careful planning and forecasting leads us to believe today. In technology licensing, risk has many potential sources:

- *Technology itself.* Depending on its stage of development, there could be risks associated with R & D activities, product development, and design for manufacture. Unexpected environmental difficulties, rising costs of raw material, or special manufacturing requirements could hamper technological success.

- *The market.* Forecasting market need, acceptance, timing, willingness to pay, and the attendant competitive response can be very challenging, depending on the nature of the technology and the time horizon. Such forecasts naturally tend to underaccount for emerging, unknown technologies that might compete, or might assist, the commercial value of the subject opportunity.

- *IP issues.* The IP protection of the seller's patentable technology might be incomplete at the time of the transaction, leading to risks associated with ultimately allowed claims. IP of third parties may be required, or useful, to the practice of the subject technology, which may add licensing-patent-avoidance costs to commercial estimates. Trade secret protection could be lost by human error or misappropriation.

- *Government and society.* Government policy, or societal values, can make it difficult or impossible to realize commercial value (take the nuclear power industry as a 30-year example).

In fact, any reasonably comprehensive enumeration of risks can be so disheartening as to be disabling, as an ancient (ca. 1000 B.C.) text says:

> Whoever watches the wind will not plant;
>   whoever looks at the clouds will not reap.[12]

Risk is unavoidable, but not all risks are equal. It is possible to characterize the risk of a specific opportunity by specific analysis of the business issues and uncertainties. Such a characterization can be used with various valuation approaches, as will be discussed in the next section, to account for the risk. A particularly useful way to deal with risk is through the framework of the wheelbarrow by using, for example, value heavily weighted by royalties, equity, or conditional fixed payments, where it makes business sense to do so.

What other kinds of risks exist? Fully enumerated, there are at least 36, as Dilbert contends in Exhibit 2.2. However, for our purposes the risks can be grouped into five categories.

R&D Risks

Although there is no bright line of demarcation at the end of R&D and the beginning of design for manufacturing, usually what is meant by "R&D" is the demonstration of a practical means of doing something. In this context, "practical," means that the quality control, the speed, and the cost of making the product appear to be sufficient and the product can be made and sold at a profit.

The nature of R&D is to attempt to anticipate the principal unknowns that require resolution prior to design for manufacturing. The problem is that one can never anticipate the things one does not think of and one can never be sure that everything that should have been considered was considered. There are many famous catastrophes,[13] and lesser ones, that show the danger of R&D hubris.

In some technology licenses the seller purports to provide *TR* that is complete with respect to its R&D. In other cases, the seller notes known unfinished R&D. In all cases, the buyer in its due diligence needs to consider not only the investment in time and money to complete all the R&D, seller's perceptions excepted, but also to characterize the risk associated with successful completion.

EXHIBIT 2.2

DILBERT reprinted by permission of United Feature Syndicate, Inc.

The real risk of failure at the R&D stage is not normally that the technology cannot be made to work but that it is too difficult and costly to be made to work. With rare exceptions, to be commercial it is necessary that the technology is extensively used and, so costs are important.

Manufacturability Risks

Manufacturability risks refer to all the perils that one faces in creating a production environment that will repeatably and cost-effectively produce the product designed by the R&D process. These risks are associated with converting a technology that has been demonstrated in a limited number of examples at lab scale into something that can be replicated many times at a commercial scale. Also involved in such conversion is the idea that less skilled people will be deployed in the manufacturing process in order to keep costs low.

There are many ways technology can fail at this stage. In chemical processes, R&D is frequently done in a batch mode whereas in many commercial high-volume operations, it needs to be done in a continuous mode to be profitable. This can be a difficult transition.

In commercial operations one needs to be concerned with waste product disposal issues. In the R&D process, certain internal recycling operations may have been assumed that in a commercial context turn out to be difficult to accomplish.

In the case of semiconductors, the ratio of good parts to total parts made, or the yield, is the critical factor in the process economics. Although there may be extensive data at the R&D scale on yield, it is possible that when a large-scale production facility operates, the yields will not be as high as needed, or that significant additional development will be required to achieve necessary yields.

Marketing Risks

Even with a product that performs as designed and can be sold at low cost because of efficient manufacture, it is not certain that a sufficient number of customers will purchase the product to warrant its existence.

It is surprisingly difficult to predict what customers will do with respect to a specific offer-for-sale opportunity. This is compounded in technology licensing because at the time of the license the exact nature of the product features and cost may be unknown. Also, the "market" changes its opinion with time. If you asked people in 1990, if they wanted an "internet," what would they have said? If you asked people in 1985, if they wanted a "fax machine," what would they have said? A "PC" in 1980? A "microwave" in 1970?

It is important to recall such examples as the PC Junior (IBM), Corfam (DuPont), supersonic airlines (Boeing), Betamax (Sony), Video On Demand (Time Warner), buying furniture and pet food online, and many others to realize that even very good companies with smart people spending large sums on market research have been humbled, regularly.

Competitive Risks

When considering the risks associated with a *TR* buyer making products and selling to its customers, it is easy to lose sight of the fact that this is more than a two-party process. When a technology and its derived products are being evaluated at the licensing stage, assumptions are made about what competitive products will exist when the subject one is introduced and how competitors will respond. All companies are searching to meet customer needs. While a technology buyer thinks it can disadvantage such competitors in the competition for customers, there are known competitors and unknown who are thinking and planning the same thing. This unending stream of suitors for customers is a wonderful situation for the marketplace, but it creates a risky environment for companies making new product plans.

If a technology is going to yield products that will displace currently sold products, one can be sure that the competitors making such products will not stand by and say, "sure, you go ahead and take my customers because I'll just do something else" (such as go out of business). Competitors have shareholders who expect profits and management who is accountable for same, and salespeople with quotas, and product managers who are hired and fired based on their ability to create and maintain a competitive edge. All these people and companies are not going to give up without a fight.

Even if a technology is intended to create new products and services for new markets, the competitive response is still there. All companies are looking for opportunities for new revenues and higher margins. If a new product is introduced in a new market, it will spawn a competitive response provided the business looks attractive. When a football coach is watching his first string team beat up his third string team on a Wednesday, he should not assume that Saturday's game is in the bag; his opponent's first string is also beating up its third string that same day.

Legal Risks

One simple example of a legal risk is Prohibition. Early in the twentieth century the government outlawed the making and selling of alcoholic beverages. More recently, the government has put such hurdles in the use of nuclear power as to effectively extinguish that industry in terms of new plants. Designers of new encryption techniques face serious scrutiny for use and export. The cost and therefore, utility, of many chemical products is significantly affected by environmental regulations. In recent years there have been cost penalties and outright prohibitions associated with the use of certain chemicals in packaging (polystyrene cups for example).

Another form of legal risk is contained with the very nature of patents. In the United States, approximately 3,000 patents are issued every Tuesday that, for approximately 17 years (20 years from the date of filing), bar the making, using, and selling of a defined and claimed process or product.[14] Because U.S. patent applications are secret until they are issued,[15] and there are literally several hundred thousand such pending applications, it is conceivable that one of those pending applications could mature into a valid, enforceable patent that would prevent one's practice of a licensed technology.[16]

With software technology such patent-blocking risks have increased significantly. Although software patentability has been established for some years now, it has not been a significant business issue. It appears that with the increasing proliferation of software tools and processes coupled with the enormous market value of software companies (Microsoft is presently more valuable than GM), in the future the blocking effect of software patents will increase the risk of deploying new technologies.

Overall Characterization of Risk

There is no formula that can be used to derive the risk of a technology licensing project. There has been significant study in two related aspects: success rates for new product development and for pharmaceuticals in particular. A recent study published in *Research Technology Management* summarizes 16 prior studies on the commercial success rates of new product launches; these studies claimed success rates from a low of 40 percent to a high of 67 percent.[17] Further, this study examines data looking at seven stages in the new product development process, starting with "raw ideas" and ending with "economically profitable." The study concludes that the ratio from Stage 1 (raw idea) to Stage 7 (economically profitable) is 3000 to 1: that is, it takes 3,000 starting raw ideas to make one profitable success. Most of the mortality, according to the study, occurs in the R&D process (although that is conditional upon certain definitional issues) Depending on one's interpretation of "completion of R&D," the data suggests that from 4 to 100 projects are required for one commercial success. This leads to the conclusion that both of the following statements are true: (1) 60 percent of new product projects succeed (from Stage 6 to Launch/Stage 7) *and* (2) 99.7 percent of ideas submitted fail (from Stage 2 to Stage 7).[18]

An interesting question and relevant issue to technology licensing is this: do technology licenses have a higher success rate? The argument can be made that the answer is yes for two reasons: (1) there exists a willing buyer who, at arms length and without compulsion, elects to pursue the subject opportunity, and (2) by separating the inventing/R&D performing organization from the manufacturing/selling organization, it is possible that a better result will occur, despite "hand off" (tech transfer) issues, because each could be the best at what they do.

Another area in which considerable study has occurred is the development of pharmaceuticals. One widely cited figure is that it takes 10,000 active molecules identified to create (on average) one pharmaceutical sold in the marketplace; this would suggest that the mortality, if that's the right word, in the pharmaceutical development business is approximately three times the 3,000:1 findings for typical industrial products. A study attributed to Shearson Lehman Hutton suggested the following ratios at various stages: 20:1 at IND (the filing of Investigation of New Drug), 10:1 at Phase I Clinicals, 4:1 at Phase II, 1.8:1 at Phase III, and 1.2:1 at New Drug Application (NDA).[19] Another study concludes 1 out of 5 INDs received NDAs.[20]

As will be discussed in detail in Chapter 7, the overall commercial risk is normally characterized by one numeric factor designated by the symbol "k." Such "k" is known by a variety of terms: risk factor, hurdle rate, Risk-Adjusted Hurdle Rate (RAHR), and return-on-investment required (or expected); we will generally use RAHR. It is the one value by which all the previously mentioned risks are expressed, and it is used to assess the present value of a prospective future benefit.

Chapter 8 will deal with the Monte Carlo Method, a powerful and more recently developed tool for characterizing risk. With this approach we will see risk expressed as a probability distribution of financial outcomes somewhat like the heads and tails example used earlier.

Just as with the "price of used furniture,"[21] risk is a *perspective*. Inventors tend to see risk as primarily embodied in the creation of the original concept; from their perspective, the risk post-invention is, in comparison, small. R&D managers, having a broader perspective, see the successful R&D project as having wrung out most of the risk. Design-for-manufacturing people see the primary risk in creating the cost efficient, reliable "factory" that actually makes things. Marketing people see the identification of customer segments and the cost-benefit equation and competitive response as being the real risk. Salespeople see the risk as being what it takes to get a customer to lift his or her pen and sign a purchase order. Lawyers see risk everywhere; it's their calling. And, shareholders don't want to hear about risk; they just want to see 20+ percent growth in share price (or else).

Uncertainty

Risk just considered can be thought of as an expression of uncertainty. That is, if we somehow had a time machine that could transport the parties to a time 20 years hence with access to all the business effects, favorable and not, of having entered the license and having not entered the license—a kind of *Wonderful Life* James Stewart movie experience—then the risk would be erased by our privileged future knowledge. Unfortunately for business and valuation purposes (but certainly a blessing in other ways), the future is unknowable to us.

Our purpose here is to consider *uncertainty* apart from its obvious connection to *risk*. When performing most accounting business functions, we expect reasonable exactitude and certitude. If one wonders what the cash balance in liquid accounts is at any moment, one does not accept the answer from the treasurer that such a figure cannot be known, or can only vaguely be known. Likewise with raw material inventories: It is either in our control, and therefore on our books, or it is not. If we have it in our control, somebody had better be ready to give a complete and accurate accounting.[22] Selling is perhaps a little more ambiguous, but each business defines (in accordance with generally accepted accounting standards) a criterion for what constitutes a sale, and thus the sales revenue and backlog at any time is similarly knowable. This belief system forms the basis for having an accounting firm audit a company's books and issue a report that represents fairly the financial position of the company and the results of its operations in the past year on a basis consistent with that of the preceding year (recent headlines not withstanding).

This perspective changes when pro forma (projected) business models are created. The need for internal consistency and mathematical accuracy remains (the columns must sum properly, and the assumptions and related calculations must be self-consistent), but the need for certitude is further relaxed. However, there is a general understanding that pro forma values will be achieved or exceeded or there will be some form of accountability. This causes the responsible parties to be quite conservative, although their managers are known to boost such projections, as has been the source of much of the humor in Dilbert cartoons. In licensing contexts, it is common that the nature of such projections lacks the business history of typical pro forma projections. Further, if only a conservative, can't-miss approach is taken, then it is likely that many worthy licenses will be forgone. Although there are valuation tools that specifically deal with this issue, there is an underlying perspective that licensing technology is a risk-bearing process, and one can rarely afford the luxury of having a high degree of certitude regarding high-value opportunities.

Pricing

Pricing is the specific values that are associated with the wheelbarrow and communicated, frequently by the seller to the buyer. A useful vehicle for such pricing communication is a *term sheet*. A typical term sheet is a two- to three-page document of summary, bullet-like points that characterize the box and the specific values associated with each of the relevant wheelbarrow elements. It can be initiated by either the seller (the most common situation) or the buyer. It provides sufficient summary financial aspirations (or determined expectations) that specify the results of the valuation model and associated trade-offs.

Pricing intertwines with negotiation, much as it would in selling and buying homes. One can price high and expect to wait a long time for just the ideal buyer for whom such price is acceptable, or price low to attract competitive interest to achieve a rapid sale. One can price a little above the expected final value to leave room for counteroffers and the give and take of negotiation, or one can price firm and inform prospective buyers that no offers less than the stated price will be considered (at least at this time). Pricing strategies are outside the scope of this chapter.

PSYCHOLOGY OF NEGOTIATIONS AND BUYING

The personalities and processes of the seller and buyer significantly affect the perceived value and associated risk of a deal, and the speed (or lack of it) of reaching an agreement. Generally in license negotiations, sellers play the official role of optimists, providing reasoning that leads to higher estimates of future successes, while buyers are the pessimists dedicated to thinking of things that can go wrong. Clearly the respective motivations drive such perspectives: the seller wants to receive a high price, whereas the buyer not only wants to acheive the highest profit possible, but also wants to avoid a situation where the company has paid more than can ever be realized by its commercial efforts.

If both parties conform to their natural inclinations, deals would be rare events—they would occur only in those cases where a pessimist perceives the opportunity more valuable than an optimist! This is similar to the joke about the optimist being one who believes we live in the best of all possible worlds and the pessimist fearing that this just might be true. So, in order for deals to occur, sellers will need to gain a comprehension of the downside that any buyer faces in converting a technology to a business, and buyers will need to grasp that really good things can happen and maybe the overall risks are not as great as they may seem.

From this perspective, negotiation is a teaching process whereby buyers persuade sellers to think less of their technology and sellers persuade buyers to think more of the opportunity.

Buyer Perception and How It Can Affect Value

There are many factors that can affect this mutual teaching and persuasion process. For starters, seller professionalism and credibility is important. There is no practical way that a buyer can completely replicate every assertion of a seller without redoing the entire R&D program. If the buyer perceives the seller to be the "Joe Isuzu" of technology licensing it will either lose interest in the negotiation or so low-ball its offers that a deal becomes unlikely.[23]

Exhibit 2.3 shows the results from a study run with two groups, a test group, and a control group.[24] The results for the control group are shown in the first column under "Setting A." A statistically significant number of individuals were asked, one at a time, to review a notebook describing the seven items shown at the left. Based on such descriptions each individual was asked to say how much they would pay for the item with the understanding that no transaction was to take place. The entire process was repeated for "Setting B," with the results showing that in every case the mean value of willingness to

EXHIBIT 2.3	SUBJECTIVE FACTORS AFFECTING BUYERS		
"Consumer Products Book"	**Mean in Setting A**	**Mean in Setting B**	**(B-A/A)**
Dress 1	$27.77	$41.50	49%
Dress 2	$21.09	$33.91	61%
Tent	$69.95	$77.73	11%
Men's Sweater	$13.91	$20.64	48%
Lamp	$28.36	$40.41	42%
Electric Typewriter	$131.45	$165.36	26%
Chess Set	$35.29	$43.15	22%

Source: Feinberg, R. A., APA Proceedings, Division of Consumer Psychology, 1982, p.28

pay was higher than Setting A ranging from a low of 11 percent higher to more than 60 percent higher.

What was different in Setting B? The experimenters placed a "Masthercharge" logo (the experiment was conducted prior to the name change to Mastercard®) on a desk near the notebook. Even though it was clear that no actual purchase was to take place, the interpretation was that the mere presence of a credit card as a means of payment unconsciously influenced the evaluation of the willingness to pay. It is this belief that makes retail stores go to great lengths to display every credit imaginable on their entrance doors and at their counters; they know, or believe, that people will pay more if they can pay with plastic.

How does all this relate to technology licensing? Consider the following two examples. In the first case the seller is an unknown university located well off the beaten path, requiring a planes/trains/and automobiles experience to get there. The principal investigator on the project believes that duct tape and alligator clips are the primary tools of good R&D labs. Moving aside some coffee-stained old newspapers, the buyer examines some of the data recorded in pencil on looseleaf paper. For lunch, the prospective buyer is treated to fast food. As the buyer leaves, the principal investigator commends the prospective buyer for having been the first person to have ever bothered to look at the project.

Suppose the exact same technology was instead found in the following setting: Harvard University. The buyer has difficulty arranging a visit because, apparently, many other prospects have been previously scheduled. When greeted at the lab, the principal investigator looks as the lab does, impeccable. The latest in data acquisition tools are everywhere. There is a hum of efficiency and excitement among the technicians and grad students. The data is available in electronic form as well as copious and artistic notes in a shelf of lab notebooks. Lunch is at the Harvard Faculty Club and Henry Kissinger stops by to congratulate the principal investigator on receipt of his or her second Nobel Prize and asks how the new breakthrough invention (being discussed) is going.

Would a prospective buyer come away from the second experience thinking more highly of the opportunity than from the first? Would it make a difference in perception if at the buyer's organization it becomes known that a license is being considered from a prestigious university and a "name" professor?

The lesson here is that sellers should do all they can to present themselves and the opportunity in the best light possible. This is not to say that one should become Joe Isuzu, because not only would it be ethically inappropriate, it would also be counter-productive. Rather, the seller should make every effort to present as thorough and well-considered a presentation as possible. Optimism can be expressed by using scenario-projections such as "conservative," "most likely," and "optimistic."

The same lesson also applies to the buyer. Typical licenses provide conditional payments to sellers in the form of royalties or equity based upon the ultimate outcome once the technology is in the hands of the buyer. Sellers want to have their technology in the best, most-professional (and enthusiastic) hands. So, buyers need to temper their skepticism lest they appear so negative that the seller wonder's why they are even interested. However, the same caution against becoming a Joe Isuzu buyer applies.[25]

CONCLUSION: TWO FINAL POINTS ON
BUYING AND SELLING

Returning to the Arthur Miller play, *The Price*, we are reminded that valuation is a function of perspective and, is therefore individual. Two different prospective buyers each following legitimate valuation approaches can come to two significantly different valuations because of widely differing perspectives on what is "most likely" as an outcome and the attendant "risk." For the seller, the challenge is to find that prospective buyer who, because of some combination of experience, general optimism about the future, relevant assets, and especially with significant needs for new products, will grasp some of the seller's upside enthusiasm. "Hungry" buyers tend to see more opportunity.

> He who is full loathes honey,
> but to the hungry even what is bitter tastes sweet.

> Proverbs 27:7

And, finally, pricing is the leverage point of all negotiations. No buyer will ever say to a seller, "This is a great deal, are you sure we would be paying you enough?" That is about as likely as a hockey player apologizing for causing a collision. So, regardless of the price, the seller will hear (even right up to the moment of contract signing) that the price and risk are too high.

> "It's no good, it's no good!" says the buyer;
> then off he goes and boasts about his purchase.

> Proverbs 20:14

NOTES

1. Such represenatation are generally not appropriate to technology licensing as by definition, the seller is not likely to know or be able to control how the technology is ultimately put into practice by the buyer.
2. John W. Schlicher, *Licensing Intellectual Property*, Wiley Intellectual Property Series, 1996; Harry R. Mayers and Brian G. Brunsvold, *Drafting Patent License Agreements*, Second Edition, Bureau of National Affairs, 1987.
3. Much of the following material is taken from Chapter 2 (Richard Razgaitis) of *The LESI Guide to Licensing Best Practices* (Goldscheider (ed.), New York: John Wiley & Sons, Inc., 2002).
4. Deal doability is a grammatically incorrect but useful slang expression that expresses the expected ease with which a particular licensing opportunity will be successfully marketed by a seller. One common example of increased deal doability is the seller's ability and willingness to provide post-licensing technical support to decrease the risk of the buyer's successful and speedy adoption of the technology.
5. Strictly speaking, such form of payment is a royalty—a prepaid, or paid up royalty and, so, should be called a lump-sum royalty. However, as the term royalty is normally used as a short hand for "running royalty," that is, a buyer payment that is made in proportion to the buyer's use of the technology, we here will refer to such fixed cash payments without the designation "royalty" affixed.
6. These comments are not intended to apply to large multinational companies that may be headquartered in a country outside the geography of North America, Western Europe, and Japan. Such companies are capable of writing large checks in any currency.
7. "Bartering as a Means of Technology Transfer," presentation by Steven R. Maimon of the Hunter Group, Inc., given at the Licensing Executive Society Summer Meeting at Williamsburg, VA.
8. "Valuing/Dealing with Non-Cash Consideration," presentation given by Richard Razgaitis at the Licensing Executives Society Advanced Licensing Course, Charleston SC, March 13, 1997.
9. Defined as that person who believes he could douse hell with one bucket—while the pessimist fears that the optimist could be right.

10. A more practical measure is the number of deals in the career horizon of the buyer. Given the increased pressure on near-term returns, individuals may be far less prepared to consider statistical returns.

11. Michael S. Malone, *Upside*, September 1992.

12. From the Old Testament book of Ecclesiastes, Chapter 11. The entire paragraph that deals with risk management, and other matters, is as follows: 1 *Cast your bread upon the waters, for after many days you will find it again.* 2 *Give portions to seven, yes to eight, for you do not know what disaster may come upon the land.* 3 *If clouds are full of water, they pour rain upon the earth. Whether a tree falls to the south or to the north, in the place where it falls, there will it lie.* 4 *Whoever watches the wind will not plant; whoever looks at the clouds will not reap.* 5 *As you do not know the path of the wind, or how the body is formed in a mother's womb, so you cannot understand the work of God, the Maker of all things.* 6 *Sow your seed in the morning, and at evening let not your hands be idle, for you do not know which will succeed, whether this or that, or whether both will do equally well* (New International Version).

13. Two examples come to mind. The first one is home movies of the gyrations and collapse of the Tacoma Narrows bridge that failed less than a week after being opened; there was an era where this was required viewing for every engineering freshman. The second example is of the numerous early aviators with their now-bizarre looking "aircraft" failing with sometimes comic and sometimes tragic outcomes.

14. The life of a U.S. patent is 20 years from filing. Assuming it takes three years to get from filing to issuance, the useful life on issuance would be 17 years.

15. There are exceptions associated with securing foreign patent rights when the application can publish prior to issuance.

16. Although it is possible that the holder of such blocking patent would be amenable to providing a license, there is no assurance that this is the case and the economics of such a second license could significantly harm the overall economics of the original transaction.

17. Greg A. Stevens and James Burley, "3,000 Raw Ideas = 1 Commercial Success!" *Research Technology Management*, published by IRI, May–June 1997, p. 16-27.

18. Ibid.

19. "Commercializing Biomedical Technology," in *Licensing Economics Review*, June 1991, p. 9, cited an Immulogic Pharmaceutical Corporation presentation at an international conference on Commercializing Biomedical Technologies, held at Harvard School of Public Health, April 1991.

20. Analysis of INDs filed during 1976–1978, published in *Scientific American* (April 2000): 74ff.

21. *The Price.* Miller, Arthur, Penguin Books, 1968, Act I, p. 38.

22. Of course even in such circumstances, there are practical limits to knowledge because of the cost of knowing compared to the value of such knowing. In the raw materials example, one could include the number of pencils in all the company storerooms and desk drawers as a business asset. In principle, such assets could all be counted and known to whatever degree of certainty one was willing to pay to obtain. In practice, a principle of reasonableness is applied that pursues such analysis and measurement only insofar as it is really important to the management of the business or the shareholders. There are other examples, such as the ownership of the right to extract oil, where the magnitude of such reserves are not only subject to the market value of oil and extraction technology, but are also in a real sense unknowable.

23. In the late 1980s, the Isuzu automobile company ran a series of television advertisements that made fun of the car salesperson's character by having one Joe Isuzu say the most outrageously puff statements ever heard coupled with small on-screen footnotes providing the corrections.

24. Feinberg, R.A., APA Proceedings, Division of Consumer Psychology, 1982, p. 28.

25. Dear Isuzu Lawyers: I actually like Isuzu cars; I have owned four of them. So, the use of "Joe Isuzu" is not intended as an adverse reflection of the product of the Isuzu company or its employees, dealers, or shareholders.

CHAPTER 3

Overview of Valuation Methods

In this chapter we will anticipate the six methods to be studied in Chapters 4 through 9. We will also consider how the use of royalties and equity greatly aid in dealing with high-uncertainty valuations. Finally, we will consider the appropriateness of using seller's cost as a valuation method or basis. This is an important issue because it so commonly, and generally inappropriately, arises in technology licensing discussions.

KNOWLEDGE VERSUS CERTAINTY: THE VALUE OF METHOD-BASED JUDGMENT

Beginning in Chapter 4, we will consider the first of six valuation methods. The purpose of this chapter is to provide an overview of these methods and the context of their intended use. Also, we will address the issue of seller's incurred cost as a measure of value.

There are two polar perspectives that could be applied to the subject of technology valuation: (1) that there exists a rigid, certain method that yields one and only one answer independently of the evaluator, or, at the other extreme, (2) there cannot exist any real method for dealing with high-uncertainty situations such as technology licensing, so any proposed method is simply disguised guesswork. The first perspective directs one to slavishly follow the result while the second perspective says not to bother creating a result in the first place.

The six valuation methods embodied in Chapters 4 through 9 reject both of these polar views. There exist tools and approaches that *are* worth applying because they provide practical guidance and rescue one from pure guesswork. On the other hand, the very nature of the problem being addressed does not admit to the kind of certainty that a purely analytical perspective would expect.

This position of extolling a position of intermediacy between certainty and ignorance has a long history. Aristotle argued that it is a sign of an educated mind *not* to expect more certainty from a subject than it can possibly provide. If we deal with geometry or algebra, we anticipate and require certainty; it just cannot be possible that adding a column of numbers can produce a result that depends upon the opinion of the adder, or the circumstances of the moment, or that the Pythagorean Theorem is just one man's opinion. However, when we deal with artistic interpretation, we understand that the observer is a participant in the art in the sense of its interpretation; so it is that art can mean different things.

In ancient Greek thought there was an important word for this position of intermediacy: phronēsis, (FRO-knee-sis), usually translated as "judgment." The use of the valuation methods discussed in Chapters 4 though 9 is an example of that kind of judgment. Because we are dealing with unique technologies and specific profiles of sellers and buyers, and particularly with the issue of forecasting future events, it cannot be that a certain, unarguable result can be produced. Yet there are tools that can, with skill, experience, and judgment, provide very valuable guidance to an important business question: How much is this deal worth?

Drawing on another parallel, in the early days of computers a term was coined to explain bad outputs—GIGO, or garbage in…garbage out. The computer cannot improve bad or false data or improperly crafted algorithms (at least not yet). Similarly, the methods discussed in Chapters 4 through 9 rely on information and application that is as close to mirroring reality as is possible; otherwise, it can be GIGO here too.

AN OVERVIEW OF THE SIX METHODS

The first method considered, in Chapter 4, is the use of Industry Standards. This is based on the idea of working to find as many relevant agreements as possible that bear some resemblance to the technology and deal in question. For reasons that will be discussed, it is rare that a "right on" comparable agreement is found that can be directly used to infer a value. Rather, an interpretive process works on families of agreements to characterize the nature of the terms agreed to in other agreements so as to give guidance to the subject valuation.

In Chapter 5 we consider the Rating/Ranking Method. This method provides a more formal way of characterizing how one technology and/or one agreement differs from another. It requires a reference agreement or standard in order to base a valuation. For this reason it is normally used in conjunction with the Industry Standards Method.

The use of Rules of Thumb is considered in Chapter 6 as the third method. Such rules, guidelines really, are generalizations derived from observing how parties reached previous agreements. The most common form is the so-called 25 Percent Rule. It establishes a principle for apportioning a percentage of the revenues received by the buyer based on the anticipated profitability.

Chapter 7 presents the Discounted Cash Flow Method. This method introduces the Risk Adjusted Hurdle Rate (RAHR, often designated by "k") as a means for characterizing the overall commercial risk. Using such a risk factor, the magnitude and timing of future cash flow benefits can be analyzed and apportioned between the seller and buyer.

Advanced methods are considered in Chapter 8, principally the Monte Carlo Method. This method is similar to the Discounted Cash Flow Method except that it relies on probability analysis of estimated ranges to produce a statistical prediction of the expected value. In addition, we will consider in this chapter some other non-traditional perspectives on valuation that deal with high-uncertainty and/or long-term payoff situations.

Finally, the Auction Method is presented in Chapter 9. In a sense, Chapter 9 brings us full circle back to a market-based approach that is the basis of Chapter 4. However in the case of auctions, the seller creates a market for the specific opportunity being offered for license.

In Chapter 10 some special valuation issues relating to the seller taking an equity position in the buyer (usually as a startup) are reviewed. In general, these issues rely upon the six basic methods developed throughout the book.

Finally, in Chapter 11 we consider how valuations determined can be expressed in various forms of payment. And in the closing chapter, Chapter 12, some principles of negotiation are discussed.

THE POWER OF SCALED PAYMENTS: ROYALTIES AND EQUITY

The most difficult situation in high-uncertainty valuations, such as technology licensing, occurs when the result has to be a single number payable at closing. Here all the future uncertainty has to be shrunk to the most certain of all entities, that of a single, fixed number now. Although the methods to be presented in this book, working in concert with good judgment, are capable of performing such a feat, there is no escaping the fact that when dealing with high-uncertainty futures there is an acute tension in creating an absolutely certain present.

The establishment of royalties, however it originated in the antiquarian past, is a powerfully enabling tool for dealing with uncertainty. Because the amount of payment is tied to a rate multiplied by a to-be-determined number, usually sales, there is a built-in way of causing large payments for large outcomes (at least in terms of sales), and vice versa. Accordingly, using royalties makes the valuation task easier because all the future uncertainty has to be reduced to a single *rate*, not a single number (dollar amount). This is by no means easy, because there is a wide variation in what an appropriate rate should be. However, it is important to note and credit the great utility of royalties as a tool that can be used in conjunction with all six valuation methods.

Likewise, equity is a powerful way to make a valuation correspond to outcomes. Equity, even more than royalty, is more closely tied to value because of its connection to profitability which, over time, determines the market value of a company, recent internet company valuations excepted. As we shall see in Chapter 10, there are some limitations on the use of equity. Nonetheless, when equity can be used it is a tool, like royalties, applicable to all six valuation methods.

ROYALTY RATES, BASES, AND STRUCTURES

It is useful at this point to define what we mean by royalty and discuss how royalty structure issues can affect valuation

First, let's define a royalty rate: it is a *rate*, typically expressed as a percentage, which is multiplied against a *base*, typically expressed in dollars (or other currency), which yields a currency payment from the buyer to the seller for the use of the technology typically for some period, such as a calendar quarter.[1] The royalty rate is only meaningful in the context of a specified royalty base.

Determination of, and Adjustments to, the (Royalty) Base

The normal starting point for the determination of the base is the revenue received by the licensee for sales of product or services incorporating the licensed subject matter. Often, such revenue is reduced by certain specified deductions such as shipping, insurance, returns, and allowances. Clearly buyers like to have this list of allowed deductions long, and sellers want it short.

Beyond these deductions, buyers may argue for further reductions in the base because, the argument often goes, the licensed subject matter contributes to or affects only a part of the overall product that is being sold by the licensee. In such a case, the licensee might reason that the device incorporating the licensed subject matter has four key functions, say each equally significant to its customers and equal in cost to make and so equal in profit margin to the licensee, and the licensed subject matter only enables one of such four functions, then the royalty base should be, according to this line of reasoning, reduced by 75%. So, if a royalty was determined to be 5%, and the device sold by the license would net $100 after deduction of, say, shipping and returns/allowances, then the licensee would by the above reasoning be proposing to pay 5% of just $25, or $1.25 per device sold. The idea of reducing the royalty amount by factoring the base is discussed further in Chapter 11.

Considering the interesting example of licensing in music industry, there are several illustrations of how buyers (music companies) use royalty base creative adjustments. Say the royalty agreed to for an artist/composer was 10% and the expected wholesale price of the CD was $10; it would look like the royalty would be $1 per CD sold. But, not so fast, Ms. Mariah Carey wanna-be. There is a long-established practice of allowing deductions of 10% of units shipped for breakage. This originates with vinyl records (LPs), which only those born in the first half of the preceding century are likely to remember; this format did break relatively easily. Rather than account for each individual broken record, the practice was widely established that allowed the 10% deduction, though from the perspective of the artist/composer this seems high. So, now it appears that the 10% is applied against $9 yielding 90 cents. Not so. When the CD format was introduced in the mid 1980s, record companies argued that the cost of converting to this new format was significant and, accordingly, a reduction for the high cost of packaging compared to then standard techniques was appropriate. Somehow it became common to deduct 25% for such special costs associated with CD packaging. So, now, according to the music company's perspective, the 10% would be applied against a further reduced base of $6.75 yielding just 67.5 cents. But, you know, making the artwork and printing of the CD "liner" (the folded insert) is very expensive and we, the record company think it is only fair to deduct this as well. This base-shrinking exercise is a kind of "Where's Waldo?" game[2]. The artist/composer/licensor keeps trying to find his or her base, and the licensee is saying "no it's not there," "no it's not here either," and so forth.

In the case of technology licensing, there are situations where the buyer may propose deducting the cost of goods sold (COGS) to reach the base, or even, in addition, the deduction of certain overhead costs. For reasons discussed in Chapter 11, this is not a recommended approach, nor is it common practice, although from a buyer's perspective the attraction is obvious.

Sellers can (and sometimes do) make the argument that the base, in certain circumstances, be greater than just the revenues associated with licensed subject matter. Consider the following example. The buyer is a company with a non-competitive ink jet printer technology but with excellent inks. Its printer market share is close to zero and, accordingly, it sells minor amounts of high margin inks. The seller is prepared to license excellent ink jet printer technology that will enable the seller to obtain significant printer market share though the margins on the printer itself are low because of the competitive environment and because the margins on the follow-on ink sales which (in this hypothetical example) are high because customers tend to buy ink from the same manufacturer as the printer. In this situation the seller might propose a low royalty rate on the revenues from the sales of printers by the licensee and, in addition, another royalty on follow-on replacement ink sales under the principle that but for the enabling licensed ink jet technology there would have been negligible or no replacement ink jet sales.

This discussion is intended to make clear that a royalty rate only is meaningful when it is defined with respect to a base, and that sellers logically reason for no deduction and even an expansion of the base to non-licensed subject matter sales while buyers push for multiple deductions and may go catatonic at the suggestion of expanding the base to include other products.

Licensing in a Value Chain and the Effect on the Rate and Base

From a seller's perspective, it would be appealing to collect a royalty on the manufacturer of, say, a chip that incorporates the licensed technology, and also on the device that incorporates the chip, and also on the system that operates by the interconnection of the components, and (while we're at it) on each unit of use of the system. This generally is not possible because of a legal doctrine known as exhaustion of rights, a subject that is beyond the scope of this text. The practical situation, however, in most cases, is that the seller can license at just one point on the value chain, though it may be possible for the seller to choose to the point of the chain. So how to choose (when choice is both necessary and practically possible)?

Licensees, for obvious reasons, generally resist paying royalties and seek to push that burden on some other party in the value chain. So, in the above example, if the seller calls on the system integrator and attempts to enter negotiations on a royalty based on the selling price of the system, it is likely to hear that such discussions should take place with the makers of the components who sell to the system integrator. If the seller takes that counsel, it is likely to hear the further suggestion by the component manufacturer that actually the proper party is the chipmaker who supplies the component manufacturer, and so on; this is yet another version of the "Where's Waldo?" game. In many cases, sellers find themselves directed to the smallest, cheapest possible 'thing-maker.' With increasingly complex technology being embedded deeper and deeper into chips and firmware and software this is not an uncommon situation. From the seller's perspective, negotiating a royalty payment with a chipmaker selling chips at, say $500 each, automatically shrinks the base compared to a device based on such chips that may sell for tens of thousands of dollars, and a system of devices that sells for tens of millions.

It would be possible that the royalty payment to the licensor could be calculated in such a way to yield the same dollar value to the seller. For instance, there could be a 50% royalty on the $500 chip, yielding $250 a chip; if four such chips are used in each device, this would have the effective royalty of $1,000 a device, though it would be paid by the chipmaker. Alternatively, at least in principle, the licensor could have negotiated a royalty rate with the device manufacturer of 10% on a revenue of $10,000 per device and receive the same $1,000 royalty amount. Thus, if ten such components were required by an integrator to create a system for a network operator, then the licensor would receive $10,000 for each system sold. Thus, in the alternative, the licensor could have licensed the system operator at a royalty rate of 1% on, say, a $1 million network system and receive that same $10,000. All such payments are one-time royalties, namely: the royalty is paid one time triggered by the selling event of the respective product on which the base is established. All subsequent use of the equipment by the licensee's customer is then not subject to a royalty.

As one might imagine, sellers might find attractive the prospect of being paid on the use of the above network incorporating the technology rather than on the one-time sale of the chips, the components, or the system. This approach would have the appealing-to-the-seller feature of providing a royalty stream on the ongoing use of the network. This is similar to the above example of the ink jet manufacturer making most of its profit on the recurring sales of ink rather than the one-time sale of the printer, and like the appeal of giving away razors to secure the recurring revenues and profits of the razor blades.

Industry practice, and the nature and significance of the technology and the scope of its IP protection, will affect which of the above licensing options will be practicable. But, the royalty rate must be connected to both the base and the structure to be meaningful.

Exclusivity and Size of Licensed Market

Another important factor affecting royalty rate, and potentially the royalty amount, is the issue of exclusivity and how this may affect the size of the licensed market.

Every licensor wishes for the situation of a high royalty rate and a 100% penetration of the potential licensed market, and wants to avoid the converse situation of a low royalty rate combined with a low market penetration. However, the choices facing licensors in most cases are between two intermediate alternatives: (1) do I license exclusively at a high royalty rate to one licensee who in turn will have a modest market penetration, or (2) do I license non-exclusively at a low royalty rate to multiple licensees who in aggregate may reach essentially 100% of the license addressable market?

As a general rule, the royalty rate for exclusive licenses is higher than non-exclusive licenses. The customary rationale is that such exclusivity creates higher margin sales for the licensee that enables it to apportion an increased portion of the profits to the licensor. We will consider this effect later in this chapter and in Chapter 6 on the Rules of Thumb Method. Correspondingly, each non-exclusive licensee faces a competitive environment with respect to the same technology because of the market presence of other licensees that has the effect of depressing prices and margins and the capacity to pay royalties and still make a fair return on investment.

There are two current and recent examples of significant licensing revenues achieved by non-exclusive licensing. Stanford University, on behalf of itself and the University of California at San Francisco, licensed its Cohen-Boyer gene splicing patent to nearly 500 companies and received over the lifetime of this patent more than $250 million in royalties for U.S. practice only.[3] The other example is quite controversial but nonetheless illustrative of the principle that non-exclusive licensing can lead to a lot of money. The late Jerome Lemelson, and his estate, has received in the 1990s more than $1 billion in royalties from non-exclusive licensing from some 800 companies for a method of reading bar codes in managing manufacturing inventory covered by a patent which issued 38 years after its original submission in 1954. In both these examples, the royalty rates were and are low, and correspondingly the payments are low from any one licensee. However in aggregate there are many licensees and products and the total magnitude of royalties is very significant. What is also notable about these two examples is that in the one instance, Cohen-Boyer, all the licenses and royalties occurred as a result of opportunity licensing, whereas in the Lemelson situation all or substantially all of the licenses and royalties are as a result of enforcement licensing (patent litigation or the threat of litigation).

The Effect of Significant Lump Sum Payments

Earlier we discussed how the buyer may seek creative ways of diminishing the royalty base so as to reduce the royalty payment. In a somewhat analogous way, the seller may seek significant fixed payments to minimize their downside risk in case commercialization proves unsuccessful, or of limited success, while retaining upside rights through their royalty interest.

Returning to the music industry let us consider an interesting, recent example. Mariah Carey has been a very popular artist. In the 1990s, she had nine record albums that sold on average 8 million copies each, a very large number, including one that sold

23 million copies. At least since 1991, she is the highest selling female artist according to SoundScan, Inc.[4] In 2001, she entered into a contract with EMI Records to create five new albums. She is reported to have received an $80 million guarantee[5] (which works out to $16 million per album, or more than $1 million per song) of which $21 million was paid upfront at contract signing in April 2001. In September 2001, the first album, *Glitter*, was released; through January 2002 the album had sold just 500,000 copies and had less than glittering reviews. In January 2002, it was reported that EMI would make an additional payment of $28 million to terminate the contract, meaning they paid $49 million for one album (for which production and promotion costs were also significant) that sold 500,000 copies.[6] If we assume that the royalty base on the copies sold was $10, then Ms. Carey received in fixed payments an effective royalty rate of 980% ($49 million in payments on $5 million in royalty base), which cannot be what EMI had in mind when they signed the contract. Had her five albums sold her previous average of 8 million copies each, the royalty base would have been $400 million (again assuming a base of $10 per album), which would have meant that her upfront payment of $21 million was just 5.25%, and her total $80 million guarantee was 20%, of such projected revenues. So, with these assumptions, EMI was guaranteeing Ms. Carey the equivalent of a 20% royalty on the sales of five albums at her previous average album sales numbers. However, the guarantee provision, and the termination outcome, resulted in a much higher effective royalty rate, illustrating the risk that a buyer takes when it commits to guaranteed payments.[7]

VALUATION METHODS/TOOLS
USED IN COMBINATION

There are two senses in which the valuation methods are used in combination. One way is that a technology is commonly valued using two (or more) different methods so as to compare the results. When different methods lead to similar ranges, it increases one's confidence in the utility of the result. When the methods do not lead to similar results, then it is time to reexamine the assumptions and retry the methods.

Another sense in which methods are used in combination is that each of the methods can be thought of as a tool to support other methods. For instance, the Discounted Cash Flow Method helps create equivalencies in cash value for different times and conditions that can be used to help better identify and interpret a comparable license (Method 1 in Chapter 4). Rating/Ranking (Method 2 in Chapter 5) is often used with Industry Standards and with Rules of Thumb. Monte Carlo (Method 5 in Chapter 8) is built upon Discounted Cash Flow (Method 4 in Chapter 7). Auctions (Method 6 in Chapter 9) are normally evaluated using other methods such as Industry Standards and Rules of Thumb. Rules of Thumb are frequently used with Discounted Cash Flow to apportion profitability between seller and buyer.

Accordingly, it would be a mistake to latch on to one method as the one and only way of conducting valuations. It would be like choosing to have only one tool in your tool box.

WHAT ABOUT COST AS A METHOD?

You may note from the previous outline that the seller's cost is not considered as a valuation method. Some might consider this as missing the most obvious method. However, with few exceptions (as we shall presently discuss), seller's costs are irrelevant. As the following illustration shows, the seller's cost could be a benchmark as to the buyer's costs to design around the offered license.

Seller's Cost Perceptions and How They Can Affect the Deal-Making Process

One common issue affecting a seller's perception of value and price of an opportunity is its costs incurred. There is a logic to this perception because, after all, the cost is what the seller paid for the technology, so why shouldn't the buyer be willing to pay at least the same amount? However, the logic is false in the following sense. What the seller bought was an option to a business opportunity that would result from an R&D success. If the R&D project is a success, then the seller would be foolish to consider its costs as the value. If the R&D project fails or underperforms, then the seller needs to be reminded that it bought an option, and options can go up and go down; in this case, it went down, perhaps even to zero.

Although it is an extreme example, consider buying a ticket in a lottery. If one pays $1 for the ticket, one has bought an option on, say $1 million, if all the little numbers on the ticket line up with all the little balls in the scrambling machine. If they do, the option price of $1 is irrelevant to the ticket's value because it is (in such case) exercisable for $1 million. If the balls do not replicate the ticket holder's string of little numbers, then the option price of $1 is also irrelevant to the ticket's value because it is an option on nothing. So regardless of what happens, the purchaser of a lottery ticket can be certain that his or her ticket will *never* again be worth $1, because costs are irrelevant. Consider a real-life technology example (one of many). Kendall Square was once a high flying computer company. In August 1993, the company was valued at $360 million and shares were selling for $25 apiece. In October 1994, Kendall Square was selling for less than 5 cents (cents!) a share. In between those dates, one poor soul had invested $65 million in real money.[8] In the more recent internet and telecomm sections other stock (equity) meltdown examples have demonstrated this point.

In the case of technology that turns out to be a disappointment, sellers sometimes still believe that its cost should invoke a combination of perceived significance and pity on a buyer. Here's another example. In 1990, the investors of Optical Data, Inc. threw in the towel on their $10 million investment made over a nine-year period. A business journal article summarized the decision as follows: "Though it was touted as breakthrough technology, the company was never able to create a market for its products."[9] The resulting patents were being offered at $1 million. Although the linkage between the stated value ($1 million) and the historic costs ($10 million) is not overtly stated, the implication is made that there is a bargain in the offing as the IP can be had for "only" 10 cents on the dollar.[10]

An Example Negotiation Driven by the Seller's Perception of Its Costs Determining Value

For projects that a seller believes will be successful, it tends to view value in a return-on-investment way. Although this is closer to being value-based thinking, this idea is flawed as well, as Exhibit 3.1 will illustrate. This example shows how sellers and buyers can misapprehend each other. In one case they miss a deal and in another they reach a deal but through a false rationale.

Shown in the left column is the seller's R&D cost with an added "justifiable" margin that the seller believes it should be entitled to based on its costs. Such a perspective is really based on a manufacturing model of R&D: that selling prices can be determined by some form of "cost plus" pricing, even though such an approach is increasingly rare even for commercial operations.

In the three columns to the right of the dotted line in Exhibit 3.1, the buyer's perceptions of value are shown. For "Case A" we see three components to such perceived value: (1) the cost if the buyer had to repeat the R&D, plus (2) the incremental cost to avoid the intellectual property barriers surrounding the seller's technology (i.e., patent claims), plus (3) the value of having the head start of picking up the seller's project without attempting to independently recreate the results. In Case A, the buyer's perceived total value is shown as being just below the seller's costs. And here is an illustration of a cost-based valuation which

EXHIBIT 3.1   SELLER AND BUYER PERSPECTIVES ON COST AND VALUE

is valid. Therefore, the seller's initial reaction will be negative to a buyer's offer of such an amount because it would have the effect of acquiring the technology for less than the seller's own costs. Sellers naturally resist the idea that successful projects can be worth less than they cost. Unless the seller can be persuaded that the buyer's value is in fact an accurate representation of value, then no deal will be done.

In Case B, the same components of value have resulted in a buyer's valuation to be greater than the seller's perception. In this case a deal should be readily possible but only because it so happens that the seller's perception of "justifiable margin" matches the buyer's perceptions of the three components of value that it considered. So the deal is, in a real sense, an accident.

Shown to the far right in Exhibit 3.1 is yet another dimension of buyer valuation. Every investment that a buyer considers making should be compared to other uses of the investment resources. The decision to acquire the seller's technology should be made only if that decision happens to be the very best use of the incrementally available investment resources. This column shows that there is an alternative that can be acquired for much less than the seller is offering for the subject opportunity. Because no two opportunities are ever exactly alike, the buyer has to add or subtract an "apples to apples" comparison between the third party alternative and the seller's proposal. In this example, the buyer has concluded that the seller's technology does have an incremental value above the third party's alternative, but not enough to reach the seller's perceived value. If the seller perceives that the third party alternative is something that will affect only this one prospective buyer, then even a demonstration of the basis of such lower valuation will be unpersuasive to the seller. However, if the seller can be convinced that all potential buyers will have third party alternatives like or approximately like this one, then a seller might be convinced that its perception of "justifiable margin" is wrong. This suggestion sets the stage for the first valuation method, the use of industry standards, in Chapter 4.

Summarizing

There are numerous problems with these lines of cost-as-value reasoning.

- Sellers rarely, if ever, know their *true* costs. In many technology development projects, the cost accounting of the work leading to the licensable technology is only part of a continuum of investment.

- When the costs are determined for a seller's technology, the value of the starting or infused IP is almost never assessed.

- The seller's development costs often do not correspond to the costs that the buyer might incur in attempting to recreate the technology, because of the differences in capabilities, insights, and approaches.

- The IP rights of the seller generally may make it difficult, and possibly impractical, for the buyer—in terms of investments required, other resources, time delay, and overall project risk—to recreate the seller's technology in a way that the buyer is free to use commercially. So, the replication of the seller's cost is likely to be illusory.

- On the other hand, the seller could have made excessive investments in the development of the technology because of poor choices of approach or other reasons and might thus have a cost basis for the technology in excess of what a reasonable seller should pay, even given the above considerations.

- The risk associated with the commercialization technology is, normally, reduced by the seller's development. Such risk would need to be undertaken by the buyer in an independent development. Even some developments that appear easy turn out to be far more difficult than imagined.

- In some cases there could be an important value of what is sometimes called *negative know-how*: knowledge of processes or approaches that do not work well or at all. It is possible that the seller's technology incorporates an approach that is the only practical way the technology can be made to work, although independent technical experts who have not participated in the development or the technology might believe, wrongly, that another or many other approaches can be made to work commercially.

- There is the seller's value of *now*. In most instances, a reasonable buyer is willing to pay a premium to accelerate its time to market.

- Finally, the cost of creating IP is often simply unrelated to its value. As one far-afield example, Chuck Close is a famous, contemporary artist who paints huge portraitures. Early in his career (1967–1970) he used very highly diluted paints applied by an airbrush technique; he is reported to have painted eight of these amazing paintings with one 60-cent tube of Mars black paint. Technology is not the same as paintings, but the principle is that it is possible to create a valuable technology and not have incurred a commensurate cost.

Yet, if a buyer really believes that its costs to recreate and be free to practice the subject technology are in fact $1 million, including the factors just addressed, which includes the cost to avoid the IP rights of the seller, then this benchmark is likely to be a relevant benchmark.

What Do Sellers Sell?

What do sellers sell? Value. "Price is never the *cause* of value."[11] Price, or valuation, is the quantification of value. Buyers buy value, never the seller's costs.

There can be negotiation utility in knowing the seller's costs, although such knowledge and use can be confusing. Let us imagine a technology created by the seller at a cost of $1 million that has, by some combination of valuation methods, a present value of $10 million, the inverse of the previous Optical Data Company example. The parties agree that they will divide up the $10 million payment into an upfront component and a royalty component. There might be good reason why the seller would like as a downpayment an amount equal to the costs incurred, namely $1 million if it is warranted by the value. This creates a comfortable logic that the seller got back its costs upfront and will achieve its return on investment from future royalties. In this case, it is likely that the buyer will find this acceptable. However, the logic and comfort of such math only works because the value determined independently of cost turned out to be 10 times the cost. If it is equal to the cost, or worse, then the concept does not work.

Finally a suitable use of cost is for the seller to measure the value-generation performance of its R&D function. If over time the seller finds that the cumulative payment received (value) is less than a suitable return on investment (i.e., costs) then the seller should conclude that R&D is not a good business to be in, at least as it has been constituted.

CONCLUSION

The need to make assumptions and create models and scenarios to obtain a valuation can be troubling. What if the assumptions are wrong? What if the models are incomplete? What if the scenarios were too optimistic or too pessimistic?

The problem is that all these issues are present every day. When buying the stock of a publicly-traded company, one is forecasting the future in terms of the company's revenues and profits, the attitude of its customers and competitors, the skill and staying power of its management, and even the enthusiasm for other investors in bidding up or selling down the stock.

Valuation of business and product licensing transactions is similarly linked to assumptions, models, and scenarios. One huge assumption made in such circumstances is that the past is a predictor of the future. Unfortunately, there are many circumstances in which that has not proven true, and important deals involving the sales of businesses or licensing of products have created adverse outcomes for one party or the other. The purchase of the Snapple business by Quaker Oats and NCR by AT&T, both of which were later sold off, cost shareholders more than $1 billion. In each case the future was not accurately predicted by extrapolating the past. Similar though less spectacular examples exist for product licensing. Alas, we know less about the future than we often think we do.

Also, many key factors in a valuation are not really knowable. Management goes bad. Competition gets good. Customers change their minds. New technology emerges. Government interferes with commerce. Such things happen all the time. In the case of technology licensing, these uncertainties and risks are compounded with others. The solution is not despair but good judgment. Develop the best model possible, use appropriate methods, exercise judgment (FRO-knee-sis). The result is much better than guesswork, and in many cases provides a surprisingly good answer for both the seller and the buyer.

NOTES

1. Other variations include a royalty expressed in dollars for each unit sold (the base).
2. "Where's Waldo?" is a children's game with the point of trying to find a character, Waldo, hidden in various scenes. It's not as easy as it sounds.
3. Thanks to Kathy Ku of Stanford for this information. Licensing took place for U.S. use only because prior publication precluded the securing of foreign patent rights. Stanley Cohen and Steven Boyer were inducted into the National Inventors Hall of Fame (Akron, Ohio) in 2001 in recognition for their invention.
4. Statistic cited in *Wall Street Journal* article, "Latest Twist in Mariah Carey Saga; New Multialbum Deal," May 9, 2002, p. B1.

5. According to a *Wall Street Journal* article, "Latest Twist in Mariah Carey Saga; New Multialbum Deal," May 9, 2002, p. B1, the total deal value was $100 million.

6. This example is based on an article by Alex Kucynski and Laura M. Holson: "Record Company Cancels Mariah Carey's Contract," *New York Times*, January 24, 2002.

7. The next chapter in Mariah Carey's career has been inaugurated by a new contract in 2002 with Vivendi-Universal, as reported by the *Wall Street Journal*, "Latest Twist in Mariah Carey Saga; New Multialbum Deal," May 9, 2002, p. B1. Ms. Carey's deal appears to be approximately $20 million to produce three albums over the next five years with between $5 and 8 million in the first year for his first album; although there are limited details it appears that these figures are a combination of license fees and funding of production and promotion costs, so it is not clear what she will receive solely for the license. It appears likely that she will receive her primary compensation in earned royalties on album sales.

8. Budkely, William M. "Missing the Boat: Yachtsman Bill Koch Lost His Golden Touch with Kendall Square." *Wall Street Joural*, October 27, 1994, p. 110.

9. "Everything Must Go," *The Business Journal,* Portland, Oregon, January 27, 1992.

10. The irony, of course, is that the patents could be worth much more than the $10 million investment if, for example, the claims covered significant commercial practice by third parties even in products unrelated to the original venture. However, if the patents only protect a product and process that has no commercial value the patents by themselves will have no value, regardless of the cost incurred.

11. Mack Hanan and Peter Karp, *Competing on Value*, AM Acom, 1991.

CHAPTER 4

Method One: Use of Industry Standards to Determine Valuation

In this chapter we begin our study of the six valuation methods with the use of industry standards to determine valuation. We will first consider what is meant by industry standards and how they can be helpful in valuation efforts. We will also examine their important limitations. Then we will review different possible sources of industry standards data. Finally we will characterize the limitations of this method and introduce the complementary method presented in Chapter 5, the Rating/Ranking Method.

THE CONCEPT AND LIMITATIONS OF "INDUSTRY STANDARDS"

The term *industry standards* is used here to designate the existence of a database of previous deals in a sufficient number and specificity that buyers and sellers can, by reference to such data, agree upon a fair transaction price. The concept conveys the idea of norms or standards that can serve as a guide, somewhat like a complex price book. In some circumstances the concept references an accepted, exact value somewhat analogous to an IEEE or ANSI standard. In most usages, however, the term industry standards is used to designate a value of value range that can be taken as normative of certain kinds of transactions but for which exceptions can and do occur.

Such norms do exist in many contexts: used cars, corporate bonds, office floor space, peaches, and collector baseball cards. Before considering the utility and limitations of such norms for licensing valuation purposes, it is helpful to understand the circumstances where industry standard norms are usefully applied.

In general, industry standards work well when the item being sold or rented can be characterized by two simple factors—the category and the quality—and when a sufficient number of publicly available, similar transactions that comprise a market history can be determined.

As an example, in the case of used cars, *category* could mean 1993 Ford Taurus with the *quality* represented by: four-door, leather interior, all power, 240,000 miles, runs well. In the space of one sentence, it is possible for the prospective buyer to have a reasonably accurate understanding of what is for sale: probably something that looks pretty bad, but with the possibility of some high-maintenance miles left in its life. With a brief telephone call or email exchange, a prospective buyer can rapidly and accurately decide whether this is indeed a purchase of potential interest subject to subsequent due diligence (test drive, mechanic's inspection, etc.) to confirm what is already believed to be true.

The second key aspect of the utility of industry standards is that there also exist a sufficient number of similar transactions and that such information is generally available to buyers and sellers. Continuing with the Ford Taurus example, it is unlikely that any car fitting this exact description has been sold. However, there have been so many Ford Taurus's sold that the database is sufficiently large enough to enable characterization of the effect on value of 240,000 miles even though no one car sold in the database exactly matches this specification. Further, a small industry has emerged which tracks such information and publishes it in various colored "books" and on the internet. So, both seller and prospective buyer can have a reasonable understanding of what the specific car is worth based upon the agreements reached by many thousands of previous sellers and buyers.

Another example is office space. For the metropolitan New York area there is one firm (Newmark, *www.newmarkre.com*) that publishes quarterly what amounts to a pricing book for all kinds of office space designated by Manhattan neighborhood. How about "Grand Central?" The weighted average asking rental rate is $33.56 per square foot per year in the fourth quarter 1991, up from $29.82 a year earlier—you can look it up. Are you more a "Sixth/Rock" (New York for Rockefeller Center area) company? Then it's $41.01, up from $39.13. Do you want to rent on "Park Avenue?" You're talking $45.68.[1]

Another example of a valuation blue book is actually bright red with an intriguing title: *What's It Worth?*[2] It is a compilation of more than a thousand summaries of recent decisions and settlements from personal injuries and wrongful death. The alphabetized injury categories range from *abdominal* to *wrist*, and cover, in a stream of sad summaries, just about every body part in between *a* and *w* (no *x, y, z*). A herniated disk at LS-51 was worth $1.8 million, but one at C6-7 was $700,000.[3] In the case of the LS-51 disk, an expert panel, a jury, deemed the injury deserving of an award of $2.15 million which led to the settlement paid by a hotel of $1.8 million. In the case of the C6-7 disk, a utility agreed to pay the $700,000 prior to a judgment. This is an unfortunate context, but a valuable resource in assisting injured and responsible parties in determining appropriate financial remuneration. The book contains the judgment of judges, juries, and plaintiffs-defendants on the economic value of something very difficult to quantify. The large number of such cases, and the availability of published information, in such matters makes it possible to use Industry Standards to make comparisons and thereby estimates of the value of a specific injury or life.

An example closer to the subject of this book is the selling and buying of corporate bonds, a debt instrument. For simplicity, consider one class of bonds known as *zero coupon* bonds or *zeros*. A zero is simply the obligation of the issuing company to pay the owner of such a bond the face value at the face due date, say $100,000 on January 1, 2010. If the current owner of the bond wants cash now, the owner becomes a seller looking for a buyer. Like the Taurus example, the category here is, simple: a $100,000 zero due January 1, 2010. And, just like the used car example, there exist groups whose business it is to publish market information on what previous sellers and buyers agreed upon for like purchases, depending upon the quality of the bond. An added feature in this example is that there are also groups who provide objective quality measures, called rating agencies, in accordance with established criteria, such as "AAA" or "B" by which the buyer can assess the risk of default. Again, the key elements are present: published market information, large number of deals, and standards by which quality can be assessed.

This is all very nice for bonds and square feet and used cars. The level of specificity enables an efficient market to exist where bonds can be traded with little due diligence. Unfortunately, no such simple "book" or "AAA" rating system exists for the selling and buying of technology. Why not? With certain exceptions, technology transactions cannot be managed like used cars and bonds. One problem is simply that technology almost by definition is unique or at most has few pre-existing examples. (There are exceptions to this limitation: A new catalyst material used in a conventional chemical process can be unique of itself but it still belongs to a readily describable category). Another problem is that of describing the quality of the technology in simple, economically-relevant terms; the dimensions of technology performance tend to be so numerous and detailed that there is no parallel to "runs good" or "AAA." (Again, a new catalyst material can serve as a counter-example). Finally, the number of published similar or "like" transactions is almost always very limited and without such a database of information no "book" can exist.

For business or product licensing, there may be sufficient performance data in which there exists some possible classification and valuation standards such as those expressed in multiples of revenues (such as 1X revenues) and/or multiples of after tax earnings (such as 20X, also known as the P/E, price/earnings, ratio) and/or multiples of the free cash flow (such as 10X). However, even in such cases and with such metrics, the tumultuous and unpredictable world of business still requires substantial specific due diligence and judgment to create a specific valuation. Even on the public stock market, there are huge variations in the P/E multiple based on the market perceptions of future value.

For technology licensing, there is by definition no "standards" for multiples of free cash flow (there may be cash flow, free or otherwise), of profits (probably none), or of revenues (perhaps not yet, but maybe one happy test customer).

Therefore, one should not expect this chapter to present a notebook of numbers that can be used in every technology valuation. No such all-inclusive notebook exists here or elsewhere. Yet, there is important value in obtaining and understanding market-based data on technology transactions. In almost all technology licensing situations there exists some discoverable previous transactions which can provide useful insight into value, based on what such previous buyers and sellers agreed to. In almost all cases some significant interpretive work will be needed to apply the data to the present circumstance. This will be the focus of the next chapter and Method two, the Rating/Ranking Method.

The Unique-Universal Paradox

There is a paradox that exists with the use of the industry standards method. How can *any* previous agreement be "like" the opportunity in question? As discussed in Chapter 2 regarding The Box and The Wheelbarrow, there are so many dimensions to a technology agreement, how can any historic deal be useful in valuing my specific opportunity? Put in yet another way, our dilemma is this: we are seeking not simply to know how other people priced their agreements (however interesting that may be); we want to know, we need to know, how to value and price *our* opportunity.

Before considering three possible answers to this question, let us directly address the paradox: how can different things be comparable? Let me use the example of foreign films (from a U.S. perspective). In watching many of these films, you find yourself immersed in characters, and plot, that is really different from your own life. The film-evident cultural norms can have features that are very different from our everyday experiences. It is easy to feel that "these people" are "so very different." But, by the end of most such movies, one really concludes that in important ways they are just the same as people I know, and me. At a deep level, they have similar fears and aspirations, disappointments and hopes, sadnesses and joys. At the end of a well-done immersion experience you can easily identify with the characters and their respective dilemmas even though their everyday worlds at an outward level are nothing like your own.[4] Great plays by great playwrights, say *Death of a Salesman* or *The Price* by Arthur Miller, or *Hamlet* or anything by Shakespeare, survive time and venue differences to connect with us in our circumstances. It has been said that "we read to know that we are not alone." Unless we are reading our own biography, which for most of us is not likely to be literally possible, what we read is never directly about us; but there can be something in the midst of all the differences between a book's characters and the people around us that connects deeply with us. This is the *unique-universal* paradox, where we encounter unique, distinct experiences so different in their particulars but underneath and inside there is something universal that makes it personal and immediate.[5]

In a licensing context, looking at historical agreements can be something like this. In them, we are looking at final terms agreed to by traders, one selling and one buying, who were expressing a common business language in seeking their self-interest, all-things-considered. Here, the unique-universal paradox means that though no two deals are ever exactly alike[6], behind the differences are certain business universals such as projected sales and profit, required resources investments, and overall perceived risks and uncertainties that guided the parties in reaching the terms of their agreement. It is this unique-universal feature that we will discuss in this first method of valuation.

Segmentation of the "Industry Standards Method"

The Industry Standards Method, can be thought to comprise three different sub-methods: (1) the market or comparables approach, (2) paradigm licensing, and (3) rating/ranking.

(See Exhibit 4.1.) We shall now consider broadly how each of these three could be applied in technology licensing.

Market (or Comparables) Approach   One of the traditional approaches to the valuation for anything is commonly known as the *market* (or, sometimes, the *comparables*) method. The simple underlying idea is that there exists a historical transaction that was valued by other parties that can be used as a direct prediction of the value of the present opportunity. Referring to the above discussion of real property, we can generally determine by public records filed with the appropriate property tax agency the price that was paid for a property together with the legal description of what was sold. If we can find a property that was sold recently that is comparable in size, quality, features, accessories, and so forth, it is likely to be a good indication of the value of our property's value. In residential real property such comparables are generally widely available because many homes can be considered as belonging to similar, widely relevant categories such as: four bedrooms, two and one-half baths, two-car attached garage, on a quarter-acre lot, in good condition. In commercial real estate, the situation can be more challenging. Recently, the Empire State Build-

| EXHIBIT 4.1 | METHOD I: USE OF "INDUSTRY STANDARDS" TO DETERMINE ROYALTIES |

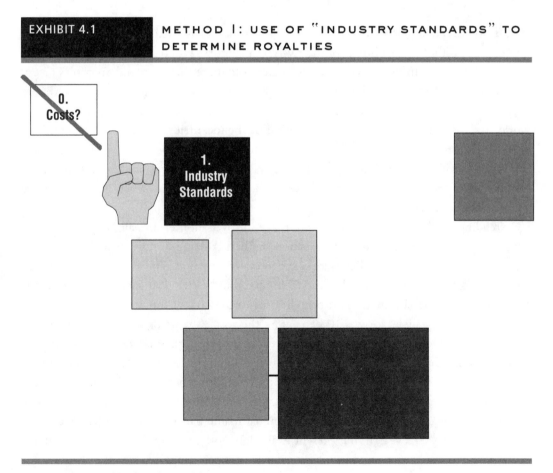

Source: © 2003 Razgaitis, richard@razgaitis.com.

ing in New York City was sold; by definition, there is an inherent uniqueness to this property and the terms of the sale. Taking another New York example, the Mets baseball team, which has a strong component of intellectual property value associated with its trademark and tradename, was recently valued in anticipation of a sale that created significant controversy because the sellers had been expecting a much larger figure.[7]

Applying such examples to technology licensing, the market valuation approach is the use of the terms of one or more comparable license agreements to estimate the value of the subject technology licensing opportunity. In some instances one is able to find one or more agreements that appear to be very closely related to the subject opportunity and deal structure. However, even in this fortuitous case one needs to ask whether the price (and terms) of the found agreement(s) reflects present market value. It is possible that the seller in that historic case sold too cheaply, for whatever reason; or, in the alternative, that the buyer paid dearly, perhaps because of something akin to dot-com fever.

In many cases, applying the market valuation approach leads to numerous, say a dozen or more, agreements in the same broad technology category but no one of which, for different reasons, is exactly or near exactly comparable. In this circumstance, one may yet be able to estimate a royalty range from this family of agreements.

Paradigm Licensing Rates   *Paradigm* has become a widely used buzz word as a result of one of the most influential books of the twentieth century: Thomas Kuhn's *The Structure of Scientific Revolutions*. In that scholarly book, which sold more than one million copies (every author's dream), Kuhn applied a term used by linguists to describe how irregular verbs are declined ("I *am*," "You *are*," "He *is*," etc.) to how scientists adopt and cling to models of world (e.g., Ptolemaic geocentric vs. Copernican heliocentric structure, or quantum vs. classical mechanics). Such scientific models, according to Kuhn, become paradigms, meaning they are widely adopted as explaining the way the world works and are not subject to scrutiny any more than we wonder why we say "I am" but "you *are*" when in both cases we are conveying the idea of being.

Extending the proliferation of paradigm usage into yet another domain, we can consider a segment of the Industry Standards valuation method as being the use of widely accepted standard rates and terms. Paradigm rates exist in many domains. When one eats in a restaurant, there is the understanding that the table server and other wait staff will be compensated for such service by an amount proportional to the cost of the meal, somewhat like a royalty. Historically, such rate was 10 percent; in the past 20 years or so it has been 15 percent; now one frequently hears 15 to 20 percent as an appropriate range for a tip. Another example of paradigm rates is the maintenance cost of enterprise software. If a company licenses a software product for, say, a payment of $1 million, there is in addition an annual payment (which typically begins after the first year) for maintenance that is based on a percentage of the license fee. Historically such annual maintenance fee was 15 percent of the license fee ($150,000 a year, in our present example); more recently, like table service, it appears to be increasing into the 15 to 20 percent (or greater) range.

Closer to our subject is the area of trademark licensing. There is a general understanding that many such transactions will be valued within widely-accepted ranges. One example of this is shown in Exhibit 4.2, taken from a book on trademark licensing rates by Battersby and Grimes.[8] Exhibit 4.2 taken from the first page of their book, shows three products for which trademark licensing of different types could occur: adhesive bandages, afghans (the blankets, not the nation), and aftershave lotion. For each product type there are seven columns that correspond to the various types of sources of trademark value: art, celebrity (such as George Foreman), character (such as Waldo), collegiate, corporate, designer (Ralph Lauren), event (Olympics), and sports (Yankees). Then for each product row, Battersby and Grimes show the range of royalty rates, as determined by a combination of surveying and expert panel, that appear to be widely accepted in the industry. However, notice these values have fairly wide ranges such as 3 to 10 percent or even 1 to 10 percent, so it makes an important economic difference where you end up in that range. Further, Battersby and Grimes point out, as one would expect, there may be certain "hot properties" where rates above the range can occur and in other cases "tight margins" (and, presumably,"not so hot" properties) where the opposite occurs. Two very different recent examples of hot properties are Jennifer Lopez and George Foreman. Signatures Network Inc. has entered into a licensing agreement with Ms. Lopez for the use of her intellectual property (photographs of her) in T-shirts, posters, calendars, back-to-school items, and other to-be-announced products

EXHIBIT 4.2

INDUSTRY STANDARDS CAN WORK WELL IN 'STANDARD INDUSTRIES' SUCH AS TRADEMARK & "CONTENT" LICENSING

Licensed Product	Class	Art	Celebrity	Character/ Entertainment	Collegiate	Corporate	Designer	Event	Sports
Adhesive Bandages	5		3-10%	5-10%		8-10%		10-15%	8-11%
Afghans	24	5-8%	3-10%	8-12%	6.5-10%	5-9%	3-8%	10-15%	8-11%
After Shave Lotions	3		3-10%			3-7%	3-8%		1-10%

However
- Hot properties
- Tight margins
- Stacking
- "The Base"
- Still wide ranges
- etc.

Source: © 2001 Aspen Law & Business, www.aspenpublishers.com.

with sales estimated to reach $20 to 40 million in just six months.[9] Although the royalty terms of this license were not disclosed, it would not be surprising if the royalty rate exceeds the range suggested by the Battersby and Grimes tables because of the current fervor and fame of J-Lo.[10] (Separately, Ms. Lopez, following a classic field-of-use licensing model, has licensed her IP for a new fragrance, *Glow*, various restaurants, and probably thousands of other uses.) Although a very different kind of IP, George Foreman achieved his own licensing notoriety in 1999 by licensing his name and image to the makers of George Foreman Grills for a paid-up amount of $137.5 million and stock, a gargantuan sum which is probably outside common trademark licensing guidelines.

So, when considering even published standard terms, one must recognize that values beyond such guidelines can occur. Consider for a moment the possible celebrity endorsement of another boxer, Mike Tyson, relating to the three items shown in Exhibit 4.2. On an adhesive bandage, I would think rights to Mr. Tyson's IP could command a high-end royalty given his close association with such items; on the other hand, I would think the use of his name endorsing, say, an aftershave lotion would seem to have less economic value to a licensee. So, even with these comparatively simple licensing deal structures for the use of a person's image and likeness on a well-established product category, there remains substantial room for uncertainty. If we were to consider an even narrower classification, say the use of Notre Dame or Ohio State University on sweatshirts or hats, we could expect to find that the uncertainty shrinks dramatically to fairly standard terms that are widely accepted.

Another example of paradigmatic licensing often occurs with content licensing, such as book, music, and other multimedia publishing. Author royalty rates typically range from 5 to 15 percent, although, like the trademarks discussion, exceptions can occur with hot authors and topics (such as with the forthcoming, separate books by former President Bill Clinton and present Senator Hillary Clinton). Music publishing has similar rates though there is the complication of potential separate royalties for the author of the lyric, the composer of the tune, the performing artist, and the producer. For the lyric, the tune, and the artist, typical royalty rates are also in the 5 to 15 percent range; for a deal which includes the producer, a so-called "all in deal," the royalty range is likely to be 10 to 20 percent, but again exceptions occur. Recall that a royalty rate is only meaningful in the context of a royalty base (as discussed in the preceding chapter).

A clear example of paradigm licensing is the royalty for licensing music for recordings. This rate is determined by U.S. statute and is currently capped at eight cents per song per album; in the industry this is known as the *stat* rate. So when you see an infomercial offering 40 tracks of "one-hit wonders," the promoter paid no more than $3.20 in licensing rights for the copyrighted content per CD, and often they pay even less.

As discussed later, an industry leader can, by their licensing terms, create a licensing paradigm. For a time, IBM offered non-exclusive bare patent licenses to essentially any one of its patents for use in personal computers (PCs) for a 1 percent royalty, any two for 2 percent, and so forth up to a maximum of 5 percent. Although IBM appears not to follow this practice at this time, its actions could be taken as establishing 1 percent a patent as paradigm rate for licensers with comparable portfolios.

Another occasion where standard licensing terms are often proposed is when the implementation of the technology follows some prescribed standard such as promulgated by IEEE. This can arise because there is a consortium licensing on behalf of its members or because a single company wants to establish a standard set of terms and values for what it believes will be many licensees. An example of the latter type is given in Exhibit 4.3, based upon information obtained from the cited web site (www.bell-labs.com/news/1997/april/29/schedule.html) for licenses to Lucent patents relating to the shown "G" standards, which relate to various compression standards.

In all these disparate examples, the paradigm emerges because there are a large number of transactions involved and they relate to a relatively well defined business model. So the promotion and selling of goods by the use of trademarks, or the creation and selling of music or book content, or the licensing of tens of thousands of IBM patents to the many PC manufacturers, all had to find some way of practically dealing with large numbers of transactions with licensees who were using their acquired rights for comparatively uniform business purposes and benefit. This situation of large transaction numbers in common business situations is what makes paradigm licensing tend to emerge as an industry practice.

Example Agreements Used with the Rating/Ranking Method   A third type of the Industry Standards method is the use of one or more historic agreements from which one can make systematic comparisons to the subject opportunity even though such agreements may not be directly in the same technology or market application areas. Such systematic comparison constitutes the second method of valuation, the Rating/Ranking method, which we will take up in Chapter 5. As we shall see, Rating/Ranking is a systematic method of making comparisons of the subject valuation opportunity to something else. To the extent that such "something else" is very close to our subject opportunity, the Rating/Ranking method reduces to the market approach discussed above, namely, that we merely point to the "something else" and assert that our opportunity should be valued as that comparable was. Normally, in technology licensing, because of the range of subject matter, and the distinctiveness of the individual box and wheelbarrow of each agreement, we find ourselves in a situation where we have identified multiple historic agreements that provide useful insights but no one of them is sufficiently close in subject matter or deal terms that we can merely point to its value and reliably use it as our own. In such circumstances, we can use our found agreements with the Rating/Ranking method to develop a reasoned estimate of value.

SOURCES OF INDUSTRY STANDARD DATA AND INFORMATION

There are many different sources of technology licensing industry data. There are individuals, organizations, and even countries that have surveyed license transactions and published the results. Some companies have published what amounts to standard pricing terms for certain of their technology licenses. Court cases can be another source as some license

EXHIBIT 4.3	FEE AND ROYALTY SCHEDULE FOR LICENSING LUCENT PATENTS FOR G.721, G.723, G.726, G.727, G.728, AND G.729*

Effective April 2, 1997 (Revised)

CLIENT (SINGLE PARTY SUPPORT) **	G.723.1 or G.729A	G.729	G.728	Multi-Function—All Four Stds. Bundled	ADPCM G.721, G726, & G727
Option 1					
Unit Royalty Per Channel	Per Channel	Per Channel	Per Channel	Per Channel	Per Channel
<100 Thousand	$0.42	$0.60	$2.00	$2.58	$2.00
100 Thousand - 500 Thousand	$0.35	$0.51	$1.70	$2.18	$1.70
500 Thousand - 1 Million	$0.27	$0.39	$1.30	$1.67	$1.30
	$0.21	$0.30	$1.00	$1.29	$1.00
Fees:					
License Initiation Fee	$50,000	$50,000	$50,000	$50,000	$50,000
Minimum Annual Royalty (Equivalent to 10K Channels/Annually)	$4,200	$6,000	$20,000	$25,800	$20,000
Option 2					
Unit Royalty Per Channel					
<100 Thousand	$0.51	$0.75	$2.50	$3.20	$2.50
100 Thousand - 500Thousand	$0.42	$0.65	$2.15	$2.73	$2.15
500 Thousand - 1 Million	$0.33	$0.57	$1.90	$2.35	$1.90
>1 Million	$0.26	$0.38	$1.25	$1.61	$1.25
Fees:					
License Initiation Fee	$10,000	$10,000	$25,000	$25,000	$25,000
Minimum Annual Royalty (Equivalent to 10K Channells/Annually)	$5,100	$7,500	$25,000	$32,025	$25,000

Option 3

Fully Paid-Up License - License restricted to Single Party Support (Client-Based) software application for Promotional Distribution, either separately or as a part of a free software bundle up to a maximum of 10 Million Channels.

| EXHIBIT 4.3 | *(Continued)* |

CLIENT (SINGLE PARTY SUPPORT) **	G.723.1 or G.729A	G.729	G.728	Multi-Function—All Four Stds. Bundled	ADPCM G.721, G726, & G727
Option 3a	One time Payment of $65,000				
Option 3b	Initial Payment of $35,000.00, Followed by a second payment of $25,000.00, 12 months later, an third payment of $20,000 twenty four month after the first payment.				
Fees:					
License Initiation Fee	$10,000.00				
SERVER (Multi-party support)					
Unit Royalty Per Channel	$3.00	$4.20	$14.00	$18.15	$14.00
Fees:					
License Initiation Fee	$50,000	$50,000	$50,000	$50,000	$50,000
Minimum Annual Royalty (Equivalent to 5K Channels/Annually)	$15,000	$21,000	$70,000	$90,750	$70,000

*Lucent Technologies will license the related patents on a personal, nonexclusive and nontransferable license agreement bases. All Fees and Royalty Rates are subject to change without prior notice, and Lucent reserves the right to withdraw this royalty and fee schedule in total or in part at any time.
**Quantity Discounts Are Cumulative

agreements are actually made public. Additionally, there are firms that have developed databases which can be accessed under various arrangements. Finally, there is the opportunity for one to develop one's own industry data book over time.

We will now consider sources of such industry standard data and information organized in the following eight categories:

1. Surveys

2. Proposed or established norms

3. Shopped term sheets, price lists

4. News, publications, and the licensing society/practitioner network

5. Journals, proprietary databases, reports, and consultants

6. Published agreements

7. Court cases

8. Lifetime and organizational learning

In each of the subsequent sections we will consider these various sources and show examples of data that are available. It should be emphasized that these samples are not intended to create a data book on previous licensing deals; this would be a massive undertaking well outside the scope of this book, and when complete it would still not replicate what is available for corporate bonds, office space, or used cars. Rather, the point of the cited examples is to show illustrations of how such information can be found and used for the specific valuation sought.

SURVEY RESULTS AS A SOURCE OF INDUSTRY STANDARDS DATA AND INFORMATION

There exist numerous surveys of technology license agreements. Some of these have been government sponsored, some gathered by associations, some by companies, and some by individuals. Like all surveys, such data have numerous inherent limitations relating to the nature of the respondents (biased? statistically significant?), the raw data (survey data accurately acquired? relevant to a valuation? sufficient detail?), and the summarized presentation (bias in summarization and statistical analysis? useful information?).

As discussed in Chapter 2, there is a rich mosaic to most licensing transactions involving many different kinds of elements of what is provided by the seller and paid by the buyer. However, most licensing surveys have focused on a single financial parameter: the royalty rate. There are many dangers in thinking of royalty rate as being the determinant of value. As will be discussed in Chapter 11, there are many variables in structuring licensing payments. The parties may agree to a substantial upfront (or other period) payment and, in compensation, will arrive at a lower royalty. There can be cross licenses back from the buyer to the seller that offset an initial royalty valuation so the reported number is very low or even zero. There can be other aspects of the transaction, such as a supply agreement, that have significant enough value to the seller as to warrant low or no royalties.

Further the royalty *rate* by itself has a dangerously ambiguous meaning. Sellers and buyers care not about the rate but the payment *amount*. The conversion is simple: royalty amount = rate × base. The key element is the "base" against which the royalty rate is applied. Take, for example, a computer chip that embodies a commercially significant and patented functionality. If a large manufacturer makes both the chip and the board on which the chip sits and the box into which the chip breathes life and the system that operates only because said chip functionality exists, what is the royalty base? The buyer will suggest the chip itself, which may be a few dollars[11]; in which case the buyer might gladly accept even a 20 percent royalty on even a $100 chip.[12] But the seller could argue that the board and the box have no functionality but for the patented technology on the chip. Compared to the fair market value of the chip alone, the box can be much more valuable: 10 times as much, even 100 times as much or more. Even system solutions based on the patented technology could be subject to an argument that such sales be part of a royalty base. So, what would a 2 percent or 20 percent royalty mean without sorting through such critical matters? It is important to keep in mind that even when royalty rate information can be usefully extracted from published sources, there is more work to be done to complete a valuation.

License Survey Data from Japan

For many years the Japanese government gathered and published license royalty information. These data were obtained because for a period of time, the approval of the Japanese government was needed for any license entered into between a Japanese company and a non-Japanese company. An example of such data is shown in Exhibit 4.4.

As with any survey, (at least) three questions should be asked: Does the survey contain source bias? . . . data coherence? . . . utility? Clearly this survey has significant bias just by its scope: the data are solely for licenses with Japanese companies. It is also limited in time; these surveys ended many years ago so it does not reflect current market conditions. Another aspect of bias is not distinguishing between business, product, and technology licensing. All other factors being comparable, product licensing generally would be expected to be more valuable than technology licensing because the subsequent investment required is less, the time to profits is less, and the risk is reduced. Grouping such agreements with technology licenses is like performing statistical averages on a combined population of men and women; clearly it is possible to do this in some aspects, but leads to misleading results when extended to averaging of height and weight or other matters. Although technology is not as subject to trends as, say, clothing fashions, one should be careful when comparing valuations across significant time spans. It is widely accepted that patents are more highly valued in the 1990s than they were in the 1970s, due in large part to a trend toward higher probability of enforcement. There can be other factors. In the case of licenses to Japanese companies in the 1970s, it is likely that the technology being transferred was, on average, less advanced and thereby less valuable than technology being licensed today.

On the issue of data coherence, it appears that no attempt was made to characterize the subject matter licensed in terms of business importance (or potential), patent protection (strength, extent, life), or the existence of other forms of consideration (supply agreements, cross-licenses, grant-backs). The information that is available does not quantify the magnitude of the initial or minimum payments, only their existence.

Finally on the issue of utility, how might such information be used to perform a valuation? As an example, consider Exhibit 4.4 as a tool to prepare a valuation of a technology for making a new laser. One immediate limitation is that these data do not contain a laser category. The closest one can get would be to examine the data for electrical licenses which could include electric power generation and distribution, radios and TVs, and who knows what else; the category may not even include a single laser license. However, assuming our way past these questions, let us examine the "electrical" column of data. Provided is a histogram of data for royalty rates: namely, 32 out of 240 total agreements provided a royalty of less than 2 percent, 55 between 2 and 5 percent, 24 between 5 and 8 percent, 11 over 8 percent, 54 with "other" royalty rate, and 62 with no royalty. Which was the most-common rate? Zero royalty!

EXHIBIT 4.4 KEY FINANCIAL TERMS OF ALL LICENSE AGREEMENTS FILED WITH THE JAPANESE GOVERNMENT IN 1975

Terms of Payment	Classification of Technology	Chemical	Metal	Machinery	Electrical	Others
Initial Payment	Required	100	54	223	119	231
	Not required	65	37	187	119	220
Running Royalty	Less than 2%	5	6	16	32	28
	Over 2% and less than 5%	42	24	119	55	126
	Over 5% and less than 8%	12	8	112	24	119
	Over 8%	7	4	24	11	17
	Others	48	28	80	54	69
	None	51	21	59	62	92
Minimum Payment	Required	38	19	116	35	186
	Not required	127	72	294	203	265
Sub-total		165	91	410	238	451
No Fee, Royalty		16	4	11	2	15
Total		181	95	421	240	466

Source: Science & Technology Agency, Japan. Class A Technological Assistance Agreement for the year 1975.

68

If one considers upfront payments, Exhibit 4.4 discloses that there were 119 electrical agreements which had such payments and 119 which did not; when one considers that two agreements (the next to last row) had no fee or royalty, one would conclude that actually 121 had no upfronts.

So, by this analysis, the most common upfront payment was zero, and the most common royalty was zero! This is not a comforting outcome for a prospective seller trying to use such industry data to price a laser technology license.

Further studying the reported data, what does one conclude? In Exhibit 4.4 under "electrical," the next most common royalty rate was 2 to 5 percent, essentially tied with "other." That is not a particularly helpful statistic. Finally, when one considers all the data, one finds that there were agreement examples for each of the royalty segments from zero to more than 8 percent, including "other." Such a broad spectrum with a gross collection of agreements has so smeared out the original, potentially-valuable data that using such a table with our laser example is fruitless.

The root of the immediate difficulty is that there does not exist a small enough category of agreements that can be used to compare with the specifics of the laser.

Even if one considers another category, such as machinery, which does show a majority of agreements with upfront payments and a royalty (in this case between 2 and 5 percent), what does one do with such information in terms of preparing for technology valuation? How would one know whether the subject "machinery" technology warranted more, the same as, or less than the most common 2 to 5 percent royalty range? Furthermore, even within such range there is a significant variation: a royalty rate of 5 percent is two and half times as valuable as one at 2 percent.

For such data to have the utility of a used car, office space rental, or corporate bonds book it would have to have a much more structured and detailed presentation of information. Gathering and publishing such data would not only require a massive effort, it would jeopardize the proprietary status of such agreements.

Voluntary Surveys

Two more recent surveys are examples of voluntary surveys: McGavock, Haas, and Patin[13] and Degnan and Horton[14]. Both involved mailing out survey instruments to several thousand licensing professionals and tabulating and summarizing the findings. Although the number of respondents was modest (118 in the McGavock survey, and 428 in the Degnan survey), both of these papers provide useful insights into various aspects of licensing practices.

Although the goal of the McGavock survey was to assess the factors that affect value in license agreements, a subject dealt with in Chapter 5, the survey did report certain royalty data. Exhibit 4.5 shows a summary of the licensed-out royalty rates by industry from the McGavock survey.

By examining the category of general manufacturing, it can be seen that every column of royalty rate category contains a numerical value (based upon 21 respondents). Any at-

EXHIBIT 4.5 LICENSED-OUT ROYALTY RATES AS DETERMINED BY A VOLUNTARY SURVEY

	Royalty Rate Category						
	0–2%	2–5%	5–10%	10–15%	15–20%	20–25%	OVER 25%
Primary Industry							
Aerospace		40.0%	55.0%	5.0%			
Automotive	35.0%	45.0%	20.0%				
Chemical	18.0%	57.4%	23.9%	0.5%			0.1%
Computer	42.5%	57.5%					
Electronics		50.0%	45.0%	5.0%			
Energy	12.5%	50.0%	15.0%	10.0%		25.0%	
Food/Consumer	12.5%	62.5%	25.0%				
General Mfg.	**21.3%**	**51.5%**	**20.3%**	**2.6%**	**0.8%**	**0.8%**	**2.6%**
Gov't/University	7.9%	38.9%	36.4%	16.2%	0.4%	0.6%	
Health Care Equip.	10.0%	10.0%	80.0%				
Pharmaceuticals	1.3%	20.7%	67.0%	8.7%	1.3%	0.7%	0.3%
Telecommunications				100.0%			
Other	**11.2%**	**41.2%**	**28.7%**	**16.2%**	**0.9%**	**0.9%**	**0.9%**

Source: McGavock, et. al., "Factors Affecting Royalty Rates," *les Nouvelles*, June 1992, p. 107. Reprinted with permission from Daniel M. McGavock, Managing Director, InteCap, Inc.

tempt to use such data to value a specific opportunity within this category (which itself is a broad term) is limited because there is reason to believe that the market value could be as low as 0 percent and, at the other extreme, over 25 percent. In order to understand how the market might value a subject technology it would be necessary to go through a population of these surveyed agreements and perform an agreement-by-agreement analysis to extract specific guidance. It should be noted that the reported data for telecommunications, namely 100 percent between 10 and 15 percent royalty, is a consequence of only one respondent. It should be noted that there is a great deal of useful information in this survey, which will be referenced in Chapter 5; it is just not reasonable to expect surveys by themselves to provide the kind of information that one can use directly in support of a valuation.

The Degnan survey likewise provides useful information that will be referenced in Chapter 5. However, one example cited here is this survey's efforts to link royalty rates to an innovativeness scale. The authors designed the following three-level Innovativeness Scale:

1. *Revolutionary.* Satisfies a long-felt need or creates a whole new industry

2. *Major Improvement.* Significantly enhances product superiority in an existing product, process, or service

3. *Minor Improvement.* Creates an incremental improvement in an existing product or service

The authors then used these distinctions to survey and report royalty ranges. Their findings are summarized in Exhibits 4.6. and 4.7 for licensing-out and in, respectively.

It appears that the licensing "out" rates are higher overall than the "in" rates; this suggests that the licensing "in" data more closely correspond to technology, or at least earlier-stage

EXHIBIT 4.6   **LICENSING-OUT ROYALTY RANGE**

Royalty Rate Range (Low to High, in each category)

| EXHIBIT 4.7 | LICENSING-IN ROYALTY RANGE |

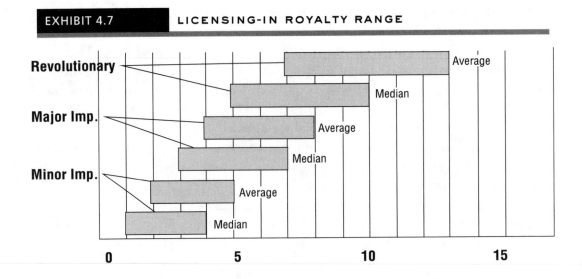

Royalty Rate Range (Low to High, in each category)

technology. The high end of the "average" values exceed that of the "median"; this is a result of one or a few very large values acting almost as outliers pulling up the average royalty rate. The key distinction based upon the "Innovativeness Scale" shows what would be expected: revolutionary > major > minor. However, the overlap in ranges is notable.

The Degnan survey also contrasted the median royalty rates for pharmaceutical licensing versus non-pharmaceutical licensing. They found that pharmaceutical licensing showed royalty rates approximately double that of non-pharmaceuticals. The reader is referred to the paper for the details.

Considering again our hypothetical valuation situation for a new laser device, the lack of a specific category of laser licenses or closely-related subject matter, the lack of information on all the other important business dimensions, and the wide range of reported royalties all reveal inherent limitation in the use of such survey data, by itself, in determining a valuation. If one uses the licensing "in" table and reasons that the technology is somewhere between "minor" and "major" and focuses only on the median data, these data suggest a royalty range of perhaps 2 to 5 percent. However, recognize that there is no connection between such data and the specific licensing opportunity.

Summary of Survey Data Limitations for Aiding Valuation

As discussed, such surveys do provide various forms of useful information. However, their capacity to provide guidance in determining a valuation is limited. The primary reasons this is so are as follows:

- These data frequently cite a wide range of possible royalties within each technology category.

- There may be limited characterization available that connects the royalty rate data to the extent and value of the IP: that is, patents only, many patents, new patents, strong patents, patent suitable to make high margin product for a large market, for a large market, and so on.

- The royalty base in some cases may not be clear. Without understanding the base it may be impossible to determine the significance of a royalty rate (royalties based upon the entire selling price of a large assembly, say an automobile, or upon a small component).

- The upfront and other fixed payments may not be defined or correlated to the specific royalty rates.

- Overall there may be lacking a characterization of the many other important terms of a license such as exclusivity, term of the agreement, right to sublicense, improvement rights, etc.

- There may be inherent vagueness in product categories: "electrical" would presumably cover an integrated circuit and a curling iron. "Mechanical" could cover everything from a complete automobile engine to a staple remover.

- There is usually an inadequate number of segments of data (because of the scarcity of data). For instance, there are multiple important areas within telecommunications, entertainment/media, pharmaceuticals and medical products, software, and e-commerce. Generally these are omitted entirely or subsumed within very different types of technology licensing.

- Surveys by their nature contain dated information, which may not be relevant to the present time. Also it is not usually clear how far back in time the data reported by respondents was gathered.

- Surveys tend to be biased by the nature of the survey segment, membership in a particular society, trans-national licensing to a specific country, and so on.

- Many of these agreements likely had other commercially significant provisions that affected the numbers. One of the common elements of licenses between companies is a supply agreement provision; often this takes the form of the licensee agreeing to supply the product to the licensor for use or resale. The pricing of such a supply agreement can be such that it influences the valuation of the license; one extreme would be a licensor's willingness to provide a license for no upfront money or royalty in exchange for favorable pricing under a supply agreement. Without a specification of such terms, it is impossible to interpret the meaning of a table of negotiated royalties. Another example would be the existence of cross licenses.

- There is no characterization of the stage of development of the technology licensed. In some cases the licenses were surely for fully-developed products with an already proven market; in other cases, the licenses may have been for unproven inventions still at an early R&D stage.

The observations are not intended to be critical of such surveys. Valuation of technologies is a challenging and important assignment, so every scrap of information is appreciated. However, it is important to understand that such broad surveys have, by themselves, limited usefulness in preparing a valuation.

PROPOSED OR ESTABLISHED NORMS

We have previously considered paradigm licensing as one example of established norms. A related source of industry standard data and information is judgment of experts which may be expressed as capturing prevailing values and practices or may be in advocacy of what they believe should be such values and practices. Most licensing practitioners tend to focus on certain technology areas and compile data according to their own experience, by networking with colleagues; and by absorbing published information, develop a formal or informal database of what something might be worth. From time to time various experts are willing to publish their opinions at meetings and in journals. These valuation opinions are generally unscientific (that is, unstatistical) but insightful. They exhibit many of the same limitations discussed in the previous section, but they have the advantage that there is a natural segmentation because of the experience and judgment of the expert.

In this section, four examples of such expert judgments are provided. These examples by no means exhaust those available nor are they to be taken as firm and fixed opinions. One of the dangers of publishing anything is that one's opinion may change, but the publication remains throughout the ages. In general be cautious because expert opinions may be dated and may no longer be held by the expert. They are highly contextual (they are judgments based upon the expert's experience however broad or narrow that might have been), and they are subject to interpretation (what an expert meant by a categorization or characterization may not be easily interpreted and applied by others to other contexts). However, obtaining such expert opinion is a useful addition to a database of industry standard information.

Multimedia Licensing Expert Example

Another content licensing example has to do with multimedia royalties in the context of developers licensing context of producers. It is included here because in at least some cases it has the unproven, higher risk nature of technology licensing.

Patricia Martone made a presentation at a Licensing Executives Society meeting that summarized royalty rates in the industry for four kinds of multimedia: text, still images, motion pictures, and music.[15] A summary of her presentation is given in Appendix 4A, and following are some example values:

- *Text Royalties.* 5–20 percent for books; $500–$1500 for small segments
- *Still Images.* generic photos $50–$75, unique photos $200–$650

- *Motion Pictures.* $3,000–$10,000 per minute
- *Music.* 5–13 cents per song.[16]

Again, remember that this judgment was expressed in 1995, and in the context of the expert's experience. Thus, these values should be cautiously considered.

What was particularly useful about Ms. Martone's paper is that she provided background in the industry dynamics including risks, costs, and profitability. Such context provides additional insight into the situation "behind the numbers" and greatly assists valuations because one can compare contexts.

Drug and Diagnostic Expert Examples

Because drug and medical diagnostic licensing has been such an important and active area for universities, there have been numerous publications of licensing experiences including valuation. Exhibit 4.8 gives an expert opinion by Tom Kiley who proposed normative royalties in certain pharmaceutical applications (rDNA designates recombinant DNA, and MAb monoclonal antibody).[17]

Again this is presented not for the purpose of providing authoritative values, but as an example of the availability of published expert opinion. In particular, it should be noted that the 1990 publication date of Mr. Kiley's paper dates the information and, in the rapid pace of this industry, may no longer be reflective of his present thinking.

Another example of expert judgment in this technology area is shown in Exhibit 4.9 based upon a publication by George Korey and E. Kahn.[18] The context for this table was early stage licensing from universities to industry. This example illustrates how such expert opinion can also include other important dimensions of an agreement such as upfront payments and minimum payments.

A useful adjunct to Exhibit 4.9 is the specification of the underlying assumptions; these are specified by Korey and Kahn and provided in Exhibit 4.10.[19]

In Chapter 9, an example will be given of the licensing of an early-stage drug com-

EXHIBIT 4.8	ANOTHER PROPOSED TABLE OF INDUSTRY STANDARDS	
Proposed "Standard" Royalties	**Exclusive (%)**	**Non-Exclusive (%)**
Developmental rDNA drug	7–10	3–4
Approvable rDNA drug	12–15	5–8
Therapeutic MAb	5–7	3–4
Diagnostic MAb	3–4	1–2
Drug delivery component	2–3	0.5–2

Source: © 1990 by Thomas D. Kiley. IPH Newsbrief. Reprinted with permission.

EXHIBIT 4.9	MORE TABLES OF ROYALTY RATES (FOR THE MEDICAL INDUSTRY)

Technology/Industry	Earned Royalty	Up-Front Payments	Minimum Payments
Reagents/Process	1–3%	Patent Costs	$2–10K
Reagents/Kits	2–10	Patent Costs	2–10
Diagnostics In Vitro	2–6	$5–20K	2–60
Diagnostics In Vivo	3–8	5–20	2–60
Therapeutics	4–12	20–150	20–150
Medical Instrumentation	4–10	5–150	5–20 (Yr 1)
			10–25

EXHIBIT 4.10	UNDERLYING ASSUMPTIONS FOR TABLE NO. I [EXHIBIT 4.9]

1. Up-front payments may be combined and such terms are deal dependent.
2. The high end of up-front payments is usually associated with a "hot" technology in a developing field.
3. Exclusive world wide licenses; anything else diminishes the royalty rates.
4. Licensee holds no equity in licensor. If equity is held or is part of the transaction, then the rates are reduced.
5. There is no claim of infringement by the licensor against the licensee. If a claim exists then the up-front payments can be significantly increased to recapture presumed royalty payments that may have been owed.
6. Terms regarding crediting of any up-front payments toward running royalties are negotiated on a deal-by-deal basis.
7. No significant sponsored research agreements are involved, otherwise the royalties are usually reduced.
8. Overseas licensing rates sometimes command a slightly lower set of rates.
9. Up-front payments are based on 1989–90 dollars.
10. The technology which is licensed may or may not have been issued a patent, but the patent has been applied for and a reasonable opinion exists that the technology is patentable under the laws of the United States and at least one other country.

Source: Reprinted with permission from Genetic Engineering News, July–August 1991, p. 4; published by Mary Ann Liebert, Inc., Larchmont, NY.

pound for an upfront payment of $20 million. One needs to be reminded that expert opinions deal with normative, common situations—events that have occurred with sufficient frequency and regularity that it is possible to make generalizations. However, by definition, generalizations do not cover all examples.

Major University Expert Example

As a final example of expert judgment, Lita Nelsen of MIT presented her approximate characterization of what buyers were willing to pay sellers such as MIT in a paper presented to AUTM in 1989 and summarized in Exhibit 4.11. In this case, the royalty rates all correspond to early-stage inventions, protectable by patents (because of the need for universities to retain the right to publish).

Repeating aforementioned caveats, these figures are more than 10 years old. Further, they were based upon experience and expert judgment but were in the context of MIT and the level of technology that was being licensed under the licensing perspectives then in place. Put in succinct terms: your results (and experience) may differ.

What is special about expert opinion is its subjectivity. Experts, like everyone else, are captive to their experience and perspectives. However in such captivity experts see patterns and can extract generalizations that can be very valuable, particularly for fields such as technology licensing which cannot be easily characterized by statistical means.

EXHIBIT 4.11	EXAMPLE TABLE OF ROYALTIES DEVELOPED BY EXPERIENCE BY A UNIVERSITY LICENSING OFFICE

Product	Royalty	Comments
Materials		0.1–1% for commodities; 0.2–2%
processes	1–4%	for processes
Medical Equipment/Devices	3–5%	
Software	5–15%	
Semi-conductors	1–2%	Chip design
Pharmaceutical	8–10%	Composition of Materials
	12–20%	With clinical testing
Diagnostics	4–5%	New Entity
	2–4%	New Method/Old Entity
Biotechnology	0.25–1.5%	Process**/non-exclusive
	1–2%	Process**/exclusive

**Expression systems, cell lines, growth media/conditions.
Source: This table was first presented at the Association of University Technology Managers (AUTM) 1989 annual meeting, and is reproduced here with the permission of AUTM and the author. Copyright 1989, Lita Nelsen (MIT).

SHOPPED TERM SHEETS AND PRICE LISTS

As will be discussed in Chapter 11, *term sheets* refer to generally short documents of a page or two that summarize the key financial terms of a proposed licensing transaction. They can originate with either the seller or the buyer, depending on which party is initiating the negotiations. Although a particular term sheet is not normally published, it may become informally available, depending on the approach of the initiator and any associated confidentiality provisions. It is normal business courtesy, apart from any confidentiality provision, not to distribute term sheets one may receive. However, over time an active licensing practitioner can be the recipient of or become exposed to numerous term sheets.

Term sheets, although they are succinct by nature, can be very useful in understanding at least an aspirant's perception of value associated with a particular box and wheelbarrow. Because they are brief documents they are often incomplete with respect to all the important deal issues. It may not be knowable whether anyone accepted such terms as are offered. Because they are often the basis of starting a negotiation, it would not be surprising to have even a successful negotiation result with very different terms than contained in such term sheet either because the nature of the box or wheelbarrow changed, or there was a change in the perception of value.

Licensing price lists can also be a source of industry standard terms and data. Price lists may be distinguished from term sheets in that there is some presumption that agreements already exist relating to the subject technology and financial terms. Another distinctive element is that price lists are generally publicly available information.

Such price lists, or more-accurately pricing tables or pricing categories, become necessary when a seller is in the fortunate position of having to deal with many different buyers and users. Rather than attempt to negotiate individual agreements, the seller in such circumstances prepares a form agreement with financial terms. Although buyers can still seek "exceptions," the seller normally takes the position that it is bound to keep the same terms for all buyers and cannot thereby enter into reduced payment arrangements without having to rebate or renegotiate with all previous licensees.

One use of price lists occurs when a university has developed a technology that it expects to be widely used on a non-exclusive basis. This could occur, for example, as a result of an invention of a fundamental and widely needed diagnostic tool. Another example would be a software technology, such as a speech recognition algorithm. Although such pricing begins to look like right-to-use licenses commonly employed for selling products, in the context of the approaches described here are for *technologies*—and lack some combination of packaging, documentation, commercial data, technical and product support, warranties, etc. The buyers in such technology licensing understand that what they are obtaining will require further development and adaptation to be usable.

Another context where price lists arise is under the threat of patent enforcement. Such licensing involves numerous other issues which are outside the scope of this book.

In both opportunity and enforcement licensing situations, one should be cautious with the use of pricing data because the seller may have had many other considerations in mind when deciding on a value (such as pricing at a very low level to create momentum to develop the approach as a de facto standard). Nonetheless, the existence of price list values can create an expectation in the mind of buyers that such are industry standards.

One very detailed example is from an actual licensing program for two related patents, one for a digital display and one for LCDs. A price list was widely produced that specified the royalty rates in each of seven categories of products with a different rate for each patent for each category. Example categories included: (1) vehicles, (2) VCRs, CD players, microwave ovens, (3) meters and gauges, and (4) wrist watches, clocks, timers. The royalty rates quoted per patent ranged from a low of 0.125 percent to a high of 7 percent, depending on the product category (this was in the late 1980 time frame). It appears that the distinction in rates was partly a result of the royalty base, and partly the seller's perception of the relative value of the technology rights to the buyer's product.

Another example was IBM's practice in the early 1990s of licensing essentially all its portfolio on a nonexclusive basis for 1% per patent up to a maximum of 5 percent for all the patents in its portfolio in the field of information handling systems (which did not include manufacturing apparatus).[20] Further such licenses provided an initial payment of $25,000 unless only a single patent was licensed, in which case the payment was $5,000. Although an approach of 1 percent per patent, regardless of patent or particular application, can appear to neglect opportunities to value specific licenses more highly, IBM at that time had a portfolio of approximately 10,000 living U.S. patents, and this apparently was a cost-effective way of dealing with such numbers and complexity. When a large and important industry player such as IBM creates such pricing, regardless of the rationale or intent, it can broadly influence prospective licenses in other negotiations within the same field, and licensees can, thereby, develop an expectation of paying not more than 1 percent per patent and 5 percent in aggregate for a nonexclusive license.

Another example of price list information arises with licensing under various standards. In formulating standards, such as may be developed formally or informally by organizations such as the IEEE, there can arise the situation where patent holders will make rights available to any practitioners of such standard under terms that are widely publicized, in some cases even on the World Wide Web. (See Exhibit 4.3.)

NEWS SOURCES OF LICENSE AGREEMENT INFORMATION

Useful license agreement information can sometimes be found in various news publications such as the *Wall Street Journal, Business Week* and other business magazines, press releases, business sections of newspapers such as the *New York Times*, proprietary searchable databases such as LEXIS-NEXIS, industry-specific journals and publications, and, increasingly, numerous internet sources of information.

Some recent examples of this source of agreement information include:

- Court proceedings disclosed that Duracell had agreed to pay Kodak a royalty of 0.225 cents per battery cell for licensed power-tester/indicator technology.[21]

- LXR Biotechnology, Inc., sold their 19 patents and two dozen pending applications in four technology packages (Cardiosol, Eilrex, Lexirin, & Apoptosis) for $968,829 in a sealed-bid auction.[22]

- Rambus, the owner of certain, SDRAM (synchronous dynamic random access memory, a type of random access memory semi-conductor) patents is reported to offer royalties under a "default contract" (presumably as a list price) at 1-2 percent (on a chip basis) and 3-5 percent (for memory controllers). After obtaining numerous licensees, Rambus was found to be to guilty of fraud in obtaining its SDRAM patents in a lawsuit with Infineon Technologies[23]; however, this judgment has been recently overturned.

- "Gateway paid about $13 million for 47 Amiga patents. . . . It was a treasure chest."[24]

- Intel settled a patent infringement suit and entered into a cross license with Intergraph by Intel's payment of $300 million.[25]

- Microsoft paid $175 million in 1998 to Citrix for a license to its technology that expired in 2002 for a special kind of "groupware."[26]

- Microsoft paid $100 million to use patents owned by Inprise Corp. (formerly Borland International, Inc.) and, in addition, buy Inprise stock valued at $25 million (about 10 percent of Inprise). Inprise holds some 100 patents relevant to a variety of PC software applications including spreadsheet technology. It was rumored that this substantial payment was affected by a fear that arch rival Sun Microsystems, Inc. might acquire such rights and enforce them against Microsoft.[27]

- Visx, Inc. receives a $250 royalty from doctors every time they use its pulsating lasers (which they sell for $500,000) for vision-correcting laser surgery.[28]

- Artists and record labels (collectively) receive a 3% royalty on *blank* CDs, and 2% on audio CD burners.[29]

- "Celera also announced, as expected, that it would transfer the marketing and distribution of its database of gene information to its sister company, Applied Biosystems, which makes equipment for studying genes and proteins. . . . The announcements are the latest in a series of strategic shifts and reversals for Celera, which, like Applied Biosystems, is a unit of the Applera Corporation. . . . Celera, based in Rockville, Md., was created by Applied Biosystems in 1998 to sequence the human genome and make a business of selling access to that information to drug companies and academic research labs. Celera was made a separate company because that business was so different from Applied Biosystems' equipment business. . . . But yesterday executives said that the information business ought to be a part of Applied Biosystems after all. Scientists designing complex experiments involving multiple genes will now be able to use the Celera database and then place online orders with Applied Biosystems for test kits for those genes. . . . Tony L. White, chief executive of Applera, told analysts yesterday that the information business would be more valuable as part of Applied Biosystems because 'there is evidence that pure data businesses are not viable in this industry.' That is partly because the public Human

Genome Project is providing similar data free of charge, he said. . . . Applera has concluded that Celera's information business will probably earn $62.5 million from existing customers over the next four years before interest, taxes, depreciation and amortization. If it does not, Applied Biosystems will make up the difference. . . . Applied Biosystems will also pay royalties to Celera based on sales of data and of some test kits it sells. The companies said the royalties would amount to about $200 million to $300 million over 10 years.[30]

- Microsoft has announced its intention to change its licensing structure to a "subscription" model. As a result of initial discussions with their major clients certain pricing information is emerging. In a *Wall Street Journal* article it is reported that Microsoft's "Office Suite Plan" is seeking annual royalty (subscription) rates in the range of 25 to 29 percent.[31] One large pharmaceutical company said that under Microsoft's new sales plan its costs would have been "$21 million for software licenses over three years."[32]

- Sony Corp. agreed to pay InterTrust Technologies, Inc. a $28.5 million upfront license fee, in addition to undisclosed royalties, to license all 23 of its U.S. patents (and presumably any foreign counterparts), many relating to digital rights management (DRM).[33] (InterTrust sued Microsoft in 2001 under these DRM patents relating to Microsoft's Windows CP and Microsoft.NET products.)

- A jury awarded a research medical center licensor, the City of Hope National Medical Center, $300 million in what it determined was unpaid royalties by Genentech. Genentech had agreed in 1976 to pay royalties of 2 percent on any product manufactured using a City of Hope patent that enabled inserting human genes into bacteria to produce useful proteins.[34] In a follow-on decision, the jury also determined a punitive award of $200 million, making the total finding against Genentech for these licensing rights $500 million.[35]

- In addition to royalty and lump sum information, it is also possible to learn of other forms of payments for rights to IP and IP-based companies. For example, a recent *Red Herring* article on companies building fully integrated biopharmaceutical systems and sources and magnitudes of investments included the following information (all $ are in millions): Exelixis has received $35 from VCs (venture capital), $125 from public equity, $65 in equity from a strategic partner, and $89 in research funding from a strategic partner for a total of $314; Tularik (from the same sources) received $138, $176, $13, and $160, totaling $488; Human Genome Sciences received $10, $1154, $55, $270, totaling $1489; and Millennium Pharmaceuticals received $9, $1260, $300, $600, totaling $2,169.[36]

- The recorded music industry is introducing new subscription and single payment online listening and recording services in response to the competitive threat of pirated song sources. Although this is a rapidly changing area, FullAudio Corp. had announced their intention to permit CD copying for 99 cents a song, which is effectively a paid-up royalty (presumably for non-commercial use).[37]

- Martek Biosciences, as reported in an article by Christopher Byron in *Red Herring*, appears to be forecasting potential revenues from licensing baby formula additives (DHA and ARA) assuming a royalty rate of 5 percent on the retail selling price of baby formula is attainable from companies such as Mead Johnson (a division of Bristol-Myers Squibb) and Ross Products, a rate that the author of the article says "seems too high . . . No well-managed company with an established retail brand is likely to surrender 5 percent of its revenues to a third party unless there is some overwhelming reason to do so."[38]

- Industry information can be useful and relevant in illustrating deal structure as well as licensing terms and values. Microsoft with Samsung Electronics Co. is developing a software OS (operating system), code name Stinger, for mobile telephones that will enable them to perform many PC functions and to interface with other devices. Nokia, in partnership with Ericsson, Psion, and Motorola have joined forces to develop a competing next generation mobile phone OS known as Symbian. On top of the Symbian OS, Nokia has developed its own proprietary system it calls Series 60, which is has decided to license to other phone makers for nominal fees including the source code to encourage its becoming a widespread standard. According to a *Wall Street Journal* story, Nokia is charging "just a few dollars a phone on top of the $5 Symbian charges for its operating system."[39] Microsoft has responded that Nokia and Symbian is "underselling" their value, suggesting that Microsoft is seeking higher license fees.

- One can receive daily email briefs from www.vcbuzz.com on VC funding generally in and near internet-related startups. For just one day, June 25, 2002, they reported on Vernier Networks (received $24.2 million in Series C round funding bringing their total to date to $34.5 million), Confluent Surgical ($20 million, Series C), Ironport systems ($16.5 million), Paracor Surgical ($16.3 million, second round), Chip Express ($16 million), Qsent ($12 million, Series B), think3, Inc. ($10 million), Princeton eCom ($10 million), Expresiv Technologies, Inc. ($9.8 million), Iridigm Display Corporation ($8 million), Alteer ($4.5 million), Bartech Systems ($3.5 million), Critical Technologies ($1 million), and Vivisimo ($300,000). If you were on distribution for the year 2002 you would have received paragraphs on $12 billion worth of such funding. Like most equity investments, the subject investments are to more than just IP, but these data can be useful in conducting such an analysis as well as being used in performing equity valuations (a subject we will examine in Chapter 10).

- Older examples that were cited in the earlier edition of this book are:

  - Rodime was reported as having established a royalty rate of 7 percent on disk drives covered by its patent, and IBM took out a license but under unknown terms.[40]

  - Microsoft was reported as collecting a royalty of $33 a copy for Windows 3.1, $43 for Windows 95, and between $80 and $90 a copy of Windows NT Workstation.[41]

- Texas Instruments was reported seeking royalties of as high as 10 percent on the price of semiconductor chips ("triple the usual level"), and for licenses applicable to PC royalties in the range of 2 to 3 percent of the PC selling price.[42]

Because such information sources are not generally providing the source material of the subject agreement, but their understanding or what they have been told of what such source material establishes, there is always the question of the reliability of the information. In addition, such stories can omit financially significant factors of the deal box or wheelbarrow. Further, because such information arises episodically, it is not readily collected or easily accessible. With increasingly powerful internet search tools and publishers making available searching of their databases of stories it is getting easier to find news citations of agreements. Also, over time one can collect a significant clip file of such information. Even when the news source is limited in the information provided, it can provide the basis of a search and perhaps the discovery of a source document or more extensive information.

Additionally, such news information can give important insights into market trends, emerging licensing structures, and other potential noteworthy events that could affect valuation. Four examples of such possible noteworthy trends are software licensing, downloadable content licensing, network operating licensing, and so-called "reach through" licensing associated with drug discovery tools.

Software value and its licensing has been and continues to be a very significant economic activity, from IBM's mainframe software, to Microsoft's PC software, from multipurpose databases such as Oracle to specifically tailored enterprise applications such as PeopleSoft, from PDAs (personal digital assistants such as Palm's OS) to wireless telephones (or, better, communicators). It has been the source of the great wealth of many "new economy" companies and (despite recent market tumult and declines) 401K portfolios. Discussed above was the example of Nokia's interests in very low cost licensing of its *source* code for next generation mobile communicators driven in part (apparently) by the desire to prevent Microsoft or some other company from establishing a de facto control point and cost. More recently, Nokia and IBM have announced two ventures to distribute music and other media to mobile communicators and integrating Nokia's software with IBM's digital media software, basing such software on Java, a Sun Microsystems programming language.[43] Nokia and IBM are also strong supporters of the "Open Mobile Alliance" that was announced in June 2002 which appears to have as one of its objectives to prevent Windows or son-of-Windows becoming a dominating force. Part of the motivation for the alliance between Nokia and IBM is to develop digital rights management for content, such as music, initially for "light content" (ring tones, logos, and pictures) and later for "rich content" (music, movies, digital newspapers). Matsushita and Nokia have also announced Matsushita's agreement to license Nokia's mobile-phone software; terms were not disclosed but were generally noted as being low to encourage widespread adoption.[44] These forces will affect not only software licensing terms and values, but also that of content, light or rich.

Another example relating directly to content is the online delivery of music for listening and/or burning onto one's own CD. The recent legal controversies regarding Napster,

MP3.com, and others, reflect the enormous concern caused by the ubiquity of the internet and the ability to transfer faithfully digital information to literally millions of users around the world, without payment to the copyright owners. It is probably not a coincidence that sales of pre-recorded music CDs have declined year over year in both 2001 and so far in 2002 (through the first six months of 2002, overall unit sales is down 12.6 percent[45]) while the sales of blank CDs exceeded (in number) sales of pre-recorded music CDs for the first time in 2001. Music publishers are now actively seeking ways of providing reasonably priced access to their copyrighted music to an audience that has become recently accustomed to terms known as *free*. It now appears that such access will be priced in the range of $1 for the right to listen and burn a single track for one's own, non-commercial collection. Pricing and structure of content appears to be on the cusp of significant changes driven by both technology enablement and market demand.

A third example is network operation licensing. If one has a patent on way of encoding and transmitting data, the historical and dominant practice has been to license the manufacturer of the "box" that commercially embodies the invention. In this approach, the box maker is paid once for each such box it sells, and a portion of each sale (under a running royalty structure) is likewise paid once to the patent holder. It has occurred to box makers that it might be advantageous instead of simply selling their box and getting a single payment to instead give the box away and get paid on some time or usage basis. For instance during the dawn of xerography, the copiers were so expensive and usage uncertain, that Xerox® established a way of being paid for their copiers on a per copy basis. In a different domain, but by a similar idea, auto leasing is a way I pay the automobile manufacturer a per month and per mile fee in lieu of owning the (what in this example is a quite big) box. In theory, any box maker could seek to do the same thing, subject to the market's interest in paying-as-you go. A technology licensor could under similar circumstance seek to be paid a royalty not by the box maker but the network operator of the box. There are several examples of licensors aspiring and in certain select cases apparently achieving network usage as a royalty basis. Ronald Katz, who is the inventor and owner of multiple patents in the area of telephone interactivity, claims to have obtained license fees and royalties from companies such as American Express, Home Shopping Network, TCI, and MCI.[46] The ability of a prospective licensor to secure usage-based royalties will depend upon the nature of the patent claims or other IP being made available and upon industry practice.

The fourth and final example is of "reach through" licensing. In the new biology that is emerging, proprietary software and hardware tools and databases (content) are being developed that can have important significance in creating new drug discoveries. Suppose, for example, there was a version of a spreadsheet which had proprietary, embedded functions and templates such that when used with published financial information of public companies could reliably predict stocks which were undervalued and, accordingly, if purchased would outperform the market. Setting aside the question of the wisdom of licensing the tool to anyone, such an IP owner could logically expect to have its license fee pegged in some way to the benefit experienced by the licensee in its use. So rather than selling "Excel on steroids" for, say, $1000, the licensor could conceivably seek some way to receive a share of the profits of the stocks selected by licensee using the software. This would be a "reach through" royalty. Suppose that instead of a stock selector, there was a hardware/software tool, perhaps together with genomic information, that enabled a licensee to have the equivalent benefit of a stock selector by enabling it to select or design molecules that can cure specific diseases. Although it should be possible to create an upfront and annual fee licensing valuation and structure that could attempt to fairly compensate the inventor/seller, another more direct approach would be to base the royalty on the sales of new drugs discovered or developed by the use of such tools and data. It is likely that prospective licensees will resist such drug-based (reach through) royalties, preferring more conventional payment schema. However, for this fact situation, it is possible that parties could agree to just such an arrangement. One of the uses of the industry standard method is to seek out whether such deal structures have been agreed to and the particular circumstances that led the parties to find such an approach acceptable, in addition to any insights as to specific financial values. Shown in Exhibit 4.12 are 15 relatively recent license agreements in the bioinformatics area (tools and content for assisting in drug discovery and development); as shown, the shaded examples do appear to be reach through–structured royalties. This table was developed based upon information obtained from public sources.

The examples and associated discussion are not intended to endorse or forecast these as trends. They have been included to expand our understanding of the scope of application of industry standards methodology to structure and not just rates.

As with other sources of industry standard data, some precautions should be noted:

- Price lists may not reflect final negotiated values (i.e., the licensor may have been willing to take less than the published list).
- Other business issues may drive price lists. For example, in the IBM case, such practice may have been influenced by IBM's interest in trying to find a cost-effective way of licensing such a numerous portfolio.
- Stories citing rates may simply be uninformed or speculative, and may not reflect actual values. (Companies cited in such stories often decline to confirm or deny the values.)
- As previously stressed, the rate depends on the basis, and the overall deal economics depend on many factors besides just the royalties themselves.

Nonetheless, gathering such information can provide useful additional insight into market-based pricing.

JOURNALS, PROPRIETARY DATABASES, REPORTS, AND CONSULTANTS

There are several publications that regularly contain articles citing technology licensing financial terms, for example: *les Nouvelles* (published by the Licensing Executives Society), and the *Journal of the Association of University Technology Managers* (AUTM).

EXHIBIT 4.12 LICENSE AGREEMENTS (BIOINFORMATICS AREA)

	Licensor	Licensee	Technology	Relevant Date	Upfront Payment	Research Funding	Milestone Payments	Recommendation for Development	Royalty Payments on Products	License Type
1.	Martin Karplus & Harvard University	Polygen Corporation	Right to exploit and commercialize a certain computer program and software	12/10/85					Yes	C
2.	Columbia University	Molecular Simulations, Inc.	Software programs for calculating and analyzing the electrostatic interactions of protein molecules	07/01/96					Yes, with minimum pmts.	C
3.	Genome Therapeutics Corporation	Merck & Co., Inc.	Certain GTC yeast gene patents	7/10/96	Yes				Yes	A
4.	Progenitor, Inc.	Amgen, Inc.	Leptin receptor technology	1/16/97	$500K		Up to $22MM		Yes	A
5.	SmithKline Beecham p.l.c.	SmithKline Beecham Corporation	Sequencing of expressed genes and development of practical applications	08/14/97					Yes	C
6.	Genome Therapeutics Corporation	Schering Corporation	PathoGenome Database containing certain genomic sequence information	09/22/97	Yes	Yes	Yes		Yes	B
7.	Gene Logic, Inc.	N.V. Organon	Technology related to high throughput analysis of gene expression and gene regulation	03/31/98	Annual payments	Yes	Yes		Yes	A
8.	Synaptic Pharmaceutical Corporation	Kissei Pharmaceutical Co. Ltd.	Novel receptor identifier	01/25/00	Yes	Yes	Yes		Yes	A

No.				Date						Type
9.	CuraGen Corporation	Genetech, Inc.	Discovery of genes that represents potential drugs, drug targets, and clinical markers	04/13/00		Yes	Yes		Yes	A
10.	Cadus Pharmaceutical Corporation	OSI Pharmaceuticals, Inc.	Yeast technology license agreement	05/15/00	$100K, $100K maintenance fee					C
11.	MorphoSys AG	Eos Biotechnology, Inc.	Human Combinational Antibody Library technology or antibody generation	06/14/00		Yes	Yes		Yes	B
12.	Biosource Technologies, Inc.	The Dow Chemical Corporation	Technology related to the identification and characterization of genetic materials	08/04/00	$10MM	$12MM per year	up to $20MM		Yes, based on sales & added value	A/B
13.	Rigel Pharmaceutical, Inc.	Pfizer, Inc.	Technology related to the discovery of novel and selective elements of the IL-4 signaling pathway involved in the modulation of IgE synthesis inhibitor	09/15/00	$2MM	$4.7MM in first 2 years	Payments on discovery schedule.	$500K for human, $250K for animal	2%-4% on human, 1%-3% on animals	A
14.	Genomica Corporation	Applied Biosystems	Object model technology license	09/22/00					Yes	C
15.	Incyte Pharmaceuticals	diaDexus, LLC.	Computer software for use in the processing and analysis of microarray expression data	11/20/00	$75K annually					C
16.	Cambridge Antibody Technology Ltd.	Human Genome Sciences, Inc.	Antibody library & patents	06/05/01	$12MM	Yes	Yes		Yes	A

Notes:

(1) License type "A" appears to be a "license option" where the licensee helps develop licensor's technology for future product rights.

(2) License type "B" appears to be a license for an existing body of knowledge and the rights to develop future products resulting from the knowledge.

(3) License type "C" appears to be a license of existing technology to be used for a specific purpose.

There is a publication that is dedicated to licensing economics: *Licensing Economics Review*, published by AUS Consultants.

There are various consulting firms that specialize in the valuation of intellectual property that maintain proprietary databases on published or available agreements and track and collect information for such purposes. Recombinant Capital (Mark Edwards) has presented papers regularly on its study of published agreements, mostly in the biotech area. InteCap (such as the McGavock survey) also publishes regularly and maintains a proprietary database of license agreement valuations. There are numerous other firms offering such consulting and data gathering services.

Papers are presented regularly at conferences of LES and AUTM and other tech transfer (e.g., FLC) and IP conferences (AIPLA) and at various professional society and industry meetings (BIO). Increasingly, such presentations are made available in whole or part on society or personal websites, such as my own, *www.razgaitis.com*. The challenge with these sources, including my own, is finding something new, coherent, and not purely self-promotional. But here and there, there is that one insight or nugget that adds to one's storehouse, toolkit, or weaponry. And in almost all cases, you get to meet some very nice people whom you can network with informally about valuation experiences.

PUBLISHED LICENSE AGREEMENTS AS A SOURCE OF INDUSTRY STANDARDS

There are a variety of circumstances whereby a license agreement becomes publicly available. In some states, it is mandated that license agreements become published under "sunshine" laws. The author was able to obtain a summary of one such agreement covering DuPont's license from the University of Houston for a certain type of superconductor material. This agreement provided that DuPont would pay as much as $5.5 million plus royalties for the patent rights to Professor Chu's invention.[47] Because it may be useful to the reader in other respects, these license terms are summarized in Appendix 4B.

Just as in the circumstance of the legal judgments, published license agreements can be extremely valuable because they provide the complete agreement which conveys a detailed enumeration of all the elements offered by the seller and paid by the buyer.

On the other hand, this superconductivity agreement shows some of the limitations of this approach as well. The inventor was, at the time of the agreement, one of the premier superconductivity researchers and the subject matter of the license was believed to be among the most promising superconductor opportunities. The licensee was highly motivated to branch into what was believed to be an extremely exciting new market. Without comprehending the context of the negotiation, one could easily be misled into thinking that such terms were and are commonplace. Nonetheless, this is a concrete example of the result of a willing buyer and a willing seller reaching an arm's length agreement.

Another circumstance whereby license agreements become public is when the licensee is a publicly traded company. The Securities and Exchange Commission (SEC) of the U.S. Government is a repository of filings of public companies and companies intending to become public. Under SEC rules, such companies are required to disclose transactions that can have a "material" effect on the value of the company as protection for its shareholders. Because of the concern for shareholder suits, some companies interpret "material" quite broadly and so are more likely to publish license agreements. The smaller the company, for any given size license, the more likely the company will be to deem it as "material." There are SEC depositories where such agreements are filed and available to the public (see also, *www.sec.gov*). Frequently there is redaction present in such agreements, but even in these cases there can be some important business terms inferred. With the explosion of small startup companies in biotech and internet/e-commerce, there is a surprisingly large population of license agreements available.

Here we will consider two example agreements that have been published with the SEC. (In Chapter 10 on Equity Considerations, we will consider another agreement demonstrating the particular issues associated with a startup.) These are presented because they show by example one pure royalty license (apparently, no fixed payments), and one nonroyalty license (with fixed and conditional payments), and they illustrate the kind of detail one can discover by searching for published agreements.

IBM-Intuitive, Nonroyalty License Agreement

The first agreement we will consider here is a 1997 license between IBM (licensor) and the licensee Intuitive Surgical, Inc. (Intuitive) relating to the use of an endoscope (an optical imaging device used to access a body's interior through a small opening) in the practice of animal and human medicine. A full copy of this agreement is available at *www.razgaitis.com/Consulting/Valuation_and_Pricing_of_Technology_Book--Resources/*. It was obtained from Intuitive Surgical's filing (as Exhibit 10.9) with the SEC of its quarterly financial report (known as a 10-Q) on 3/22/00.[48] This agreement is interesting for several reasons. It illustrates without any redacting the full terms used at least in this agreement by a very sophisticated licensing organization (IBM), which may be currently the U.S. company reporting the largest annual royalties, more than $1.5 billion. The agreement is also an excellent illustration of what might comprise a Box and Wheelbarrow. Following is a summary of some of the agreement's provisions with respect to each[49]:

- *Box*
  - License is for the rights to practice two groups of defined patents, "LARS" and "ROBODOCS" [Art. 1.8, 9]. The LARS patent portfolio is identified in Exhibit 1 of the license as including nine issued U.S. patents, five pending U.S. patents, and numerous corresponding patents and applications in other countries. The

ROBODOCS patents consist of three issued U.S. patents and one Japanese patent.

- "Patents" are defined to include "all patents which are continuations, continuations-in-part, divisions, reissues, renewals, extensions or additions thereof (or which otherwise claim priority from the foregoing) and their corresponding patents." [1.9 and Exhibit 1]

- Technical information and other drawings, models, etc. are provided related to LARS patents [as "ASSOCIATED MATERIALS" in Art. 1.1, 2.9]

- Defined field of use excludes specified medical fields (neurology, etc.) [Art. 1.5]

- Worldwide and exclusive only within the defined field of use [2.1, 5]

- Worldwide and nonexclusive for all other fields [2.2, 6]

- For the life of the respective patents [9.1]

- IBM retains a right to practice [2.3, 7]

- License is subject to rights previously granted to third parties [2.4, 8]

- A limited sublicensing right is included [Art. 5]

- A limited warranty [Art. 7; note the important *non*-warranty language in this Article]

- *Wheelbarrow*

  - The payment upon the effective date (closing) of $1 million distinguished as $916,670 and $83,330 for the LARS and ROBODOCS IP, respectively.

  - A subsequent, "trigger" payment of $5 million distinguished as $4,583,330 and $416,670 for the LARS and ROBODOCS IP, respectively, with the trigger event being the earlier of an Intuitive IPO (initial public offering) or a specified date (9/1/98, which date was delayed to 11/2/98 in Amendment No. 1). This payment combined with the closing payments makes the license fee $5.5 million for the LARS patents and $500,000 for the ROBODOCS patents, for $6 million total.

  - Although not directly a wheelbarrow element, it is interesting to note that closing payments are 20 percent of the respective trigger payments, namely, the deal was 20 percent down with the balance paid on the trigger which was less than one year after the effective date.

  - In addition, there are two payment "kickers," payments which become due upon the achievement of specified milestones. A kicker of $1 million is due after the first year in which sales of all licensed products and services first equals or exceeds $25 million.

  - A second kicker also of $1 million is due after the first year in which sales exceeds $50 million. Thus, in addition to the $6 million paid at closing and on the trigger, Intuitive could owe as much as an additional $2 million, for a total of $8 million, in the event annual sales of licensed products and services exceeds $50 million, something it is reasonable to assume that Intuitive aspires to occur.

- Because there is no royalty provision, all Intuitive sales beyond the second kicker event, namely the first year with annual sales of $50 million, are free of any further payment obligation to IBM. Based upon various revenue scenarios that, each party could estimate the effective royalty rate over the life of the subject patents corresponding to this payment structure. Clearly if the total revenues turn out to be small, these payments would correspond to a high effective royalty rate. In the worst case, Intuitive would have just one year of sales and just reach the $50 million threshold triggering both $1 million payments and then have no further sales. It will then have paid $8 million in "royalties" on a base of $50 million in sales, or an effective rate of 16 percent (ignoring for these purposes the time value of money). On the other hand, if over the lifetime of the patents, Intuitive had cumulative sales of (say) $1 billion, then the effective rate (again ignoring the time value of money) would have been just 0.8 percent. Depending on what actually turns out, one party or the other would have been better off financially by a royalty structure.

- Intuitive essentially bears the cost and responsibility for enforcing the patents (at its election to do so).

The attraction of fixed license payments is that, by their fixedness, both parties understand the financial terms and can more easily plan their businesses. This agreement shows how the parties sought to use the framework of fixed payments to make payments over multiple periods, sometimes for the benefit of the buyer but other times for the convenience of both parties, and to provide conditional fixed payments upon the attainment of future business events which presumably warrant and make affordable such payments.

Becton Dickinson and Selfcare, Pure Royalty License Agreement

A second example agreement obtained through SEC filing is between licensor Becton Dickinson and licensee Selfcare, Inc.. The full agreement is provided at *www.razgaitis.com/ Consulting/Valuation_and_Pricing_of_Technology_Book--Resources/*. Like the IBM-Intuitive agreement this is devoid of redacting and has some interesting provisions illustrating creative use of the Box and Wheelbarrow, as summarized here.

- *Box*
  - A specified patent, so-called Campbell patent [Art 1.2, as given in the agreement identified as Exhibit 10.1].
  - A specified patent, so-called Rosenstein patent [Art 1.2 and Appendix A, as given in the agreement identified as Exhibit 10.2].

- A specified "product" field of use [Art 1.3 of both exhibit agreements and in Art 2.0]

- A nonexclusive license.

- No sublicensing or transferability rights.

- Worldwide license.

- A release from past infringement by Intuitive (although the existence or magnitude of such past infringement is not stated).

- There is limited warranty and representation by Becton Dickinson in Art. 9.

- Becton Dickinson provides a "most favored nations" (MFN) feature in the below described royalty rate [Art. 15]. An MFN provision basically assures a nonexclusive licensee that it will have its royalty reduced to the lower rate that the licensor licenses the same technology to a third party. The language in this article describes a process for enabling Selfcare to receive that protection and benefit.

- *Wheelbarrow*

  - No payment on closing, or other fixed license fee payments (which suggests that there were known, ongoing sales by Selfcare that would be subject to royalties as given below).

  - Royalty payments in a tiered (sometimes called *wedding cake*) structure. For sales covered by the Campbell patent from the effective date of the license until a first fixed date (1/1/99), the specified royalty rate is 6 percent.

  - From the first fixed date (1/1/99), the royalty rate for the practice of the Campbell patent increases to 6.25 percent and is due on all sales up to a cumulative amount of $108,667,100, for a total royalty payment of $6.79 million.

  - For sales after the fixed date in excess of the cumulative amount of $108,667,100, the royalty for the practice of the Campbell patent reduces to 5.25 percent for all remaining sales for the life of the agreement. (A traditional "wedding cake" royalty structure has the royalty rate decreasing with time or sales; this agreement shows first an increase in rate, followed by a decrease).

  - The above royalty terms are also applicable to the practice of the Rosenstein patent with the provision, however, there is a full credit allowed when both patents have been used, meaning, that Selfcare only has to pay the (say) 6.25 percent royalty once. However, if they make, use, and sell a product in one country under only Campbell they pay the full royalty and likewise for the Rosenstein patent.

  - The royalty base is the "net sales" which is defined in Art. 1.4(a) as being all amounts invoiced (which may be termed "gross sales" or revenues) less (1) cash discounts, (2) transportation and shipping charges, (3) taxes and duties paid, and (4) refunds, rebates and returns. There are also provisions in Art. 1.4 for transactions not at arms length or where the product is not sold but "otherwise disposed of."

- Selfcare indemnifies and holds harmless Becton Dickinson under the terms of Art. 10.

As discussed in Chapter 11, royalty "structures," namely royalty rates that adjust with circumstances, can be used by the parties as economic compromises in their respective positions and to increase the perceived fairness of the terms.

Purchase Price Allocation

Another kind of valuation information available in an SEC filing arises from the need for purchase price allocation. As a result of recent accounting rules, companies making an acquisition must allocate what it paid in three categories: tangibles, intangibles (which could include technology-based intellectual property), and goodwill. An example of such allocation calculation is taken from the 2001 annual report of Avaya as shown in Exhibit 4.13 for two Avaya acquisitions in that fiscal year.

COURT CASES/JUDGMENTS AS A SOURCE OF INDUSTRY STANDARDS

Another source of industry data are technology licenses that are the subject of a lawsuit. Many cases settle before final judgment and are thereby usually secret. However, when a judgment is rendered there is the opportunity to study in some detail the specific circumstances that led a court to a subject valuation.

One legal text gives an extensive summary of court imposed "reasonable royalties" ranging from *GM v. Dailey* for supporting rods for automobile curtains (15 cents per car; 1937 case), to a machine for making paper cups (5 percent of selling price; 1948), to a vitamin (10 percent of gross sales; 1960), to CRT oscilloscopes (10 percent of gross sales, 1977), to vehicle suspension systems (30 percent of net sales; 1986).[50] Another example of a survey done by M. Michael Carpenter of legal judgments is given in Exhibit 4.14.[51]

Such data represent the opposite extreme from the survey and expert judgment examples considered earlier: whereas those surveys and judgments were averages and general, sources from legal cases are specific, narrow, and exact. However, legal disputes more frequently pertain to product licensing rather than technology licensing. It is difficult to find a dispute on a directly comparable situation, particularly within a recent time frame. Also one needs to be careful in the interpretation of the finding because there are many factors argued and considered that may or may not be relevant to a pure technology licensing situation.

EXHIBIT 4.13   AVAYA: 2001 ANNUAL REPORT

ACQUISITIONS

The following table presents information about certain acquisitions by the Company [Avaya] during the fiscal year ended September 30, 2001. These acquisitions were accounted for under the purchase method of accounting, and the acquired technology valuation included existing technology, purchased in-process research and development ("IPR&D") and other intangibles. The consolidated financial statements include the results of operations and the estimated fair values of the assets and liabilities assumed from the respective dates of acquisition. All charges related to the write-off of purchased in-process research and development were recorded in the quarter in which the transaction was completed. There were no material acquisitions accounted for under the purchase method in fiscal 2000 and 1999.

		Allocation of Purchase Price[1]					Amortization Period (in years)		
	Acquisition Date	Purchase Price	Goodwill	Existing Technology	Other Intangibles	Purchased IPR&D	Goodwill	Existing Technology	Other Intangibles
VPNet[2]	February 6, 2001	$117	$48	$30	$16	$31	5	5	5
Quintus[3]	April 11, 2001	$29	$3	$9	$3	$1	5	3	3

(1) Excludes amounts allocated to specific tangible assets and liabilities.

(2) Acquisition of VPNet Technologies, Inc., a privately held distributor of virtual private network solutions and devices. The total purchase price $117 million was paid in cash and stock options.

(3) Acquisition of substantially all of the assets, including $10 million of cash acquired, and the assumption of $20 million of certain liabilities of Quintus Corporation, a provider of comprehensive electronic customer relationship management solutions. The company paid $29 million in cash for these assets.

EXHIBIT 4.14	CASE LAW SOURCES OF ROYALTIES		

Product	Royalty	Date	Cite
Rotary Wing Aircraft	2%	1976	192 USPQ 612
Sleeping Bag	5%	1967	156 USPQ 403
Digital Data Transmitter	7.50%	1978	200 USPQ 481
Oscilloscope	10%	1977	193 USPQ 385
Computerized Teaching Aid	12%	1978	199 USPQ 178
Toilet Paper Perforator	20%	1977	195 USPQ 125
Airline Baggage Cart	100%*	1977	196 USPQ 129

*of profit
Source: M. Michael Carpenter, Workshop at the 1979 LES Annual Meeting.

Some other issues involving the use of court-originated royalty data include:

- The patent or know-how involved has been judged as valid and infringed which can make the license more valuable than the case where the validity of patent is unknown and in cases the patent has not yet been issued.

- The data is very situation specific.

- The data can be old because litigation often starts after manufacturing by an infringer has begun and can take many years. By the time it is available to the public it can be many years after the R&D stage.

- The biggest limitation is simply that there are very few cases in which the royalty rates (or other financial information) become publicly known.

Despite these limitations, court cases should be considered as a possible source of industry standard insight.

LIFETIME AND ORGANIZATIONAL LEARNING

One should not neglect an obvious source of industry standards: one's own experience over time. An active licensing professional will eventually develop a record of first-hand valuation experience based upon deals done as well as deals that could not be consummated. This personal database can be expanded through long-term professional relationships and experience sharing that develops through active participation in societies such as the Licensing Executives Society (*www.les.org*) and the Association of University Technology Managers (*www.autm.org*). In addition, there are other societies with significant interest and activities in licensing, such as AIPLA (for IP lawyers), and various pharmaceutical and biotech and other technology/industry specific societies and conferences.

In the health profession there is a parallel concept generally termed "evidence based practice."[52] The parallel to our situation includes the idea of building a database of experience, even evidence, using a structured approach to my encounters and learning. This database, however formal or informal, aggregates my experiences and by diary-like notations can capture learning and systematize what can otherwise be a jumble of memories, often unreliable.[53]

Borrowing another idea from a high school teacher notably successful in developing math skills in his students is creating a valuation equivalent of a "math only notebook." The idea is simply this: start, and no matter what keep, a notebook, in some form, that contains the essence of any valuation event including analyses you have performed, or had performed for you, offers you made or received, or noteworthy deals or deal "nuggets" that you encounter.

A final aspect of lifetime learning is organizational learning. Most of us work as part of an organization with parallel current (lateral) and historic (longitudinal) experiences. In some cases these lateral and longitudinal experiences could be vast, and valuable, and are often not very accessible apart from some systematic effort made to make them so. Shared learnings with peers, and data-mining from files and people, including people who may have retired from active practice, can be a precious source of valuation and pricing insight and experience. With any retrospective analysis there is the caution of being a prisoner of the past way of thinking or doing and current values and terms may simply be different. However, as experimentalists know, all data needs to be scrutinized (scrubbed), digested, and analyzed. The point of historic investigations is not simply to replicate the past, as though that would even be possible, but to learn from it. Likewise, peer-to-peer experience sharing is not about who did better (or worse) but who has learned what from the world and events that surround us.

AVERAGE ERROR[54]

Underlying certain manifestations of the industry standards method is the idea of using averages. For instance, survey results are normally expressed as averages in various categories or segments as we saw previously. Averaging also can occur when one is looking at multiple agreements and one is trying to capture a single, representative value, which may be done by using an arithmetic average (adding them all up and dividing by the total number), or a median value, or even a modal value (the most frequently occurring value).

Do such averages lead us to a more accurate grasp of value? The firm answer is: Maybe.

There are three particularly important aspects of averaging that apply to valuing technology: the law of large numbers, the sensitivity to small distinctions, and the "Tiger Woods phenomenon." To illustrate the first two aspects, consider the following real example. In the early days of commercial aviation, they not only weighed your baggage, they weighed *you*. Today, despite all the precautions we encounter at airports in a post-9/11 world, no one is weighing anyone.[55] Why not? The answer lies in the combination of the law of large numbers and relative insensitivity to small distinctions. In the early days of commercial aviation the number of passengers was relatively small, in some cases fewer than 20, and the performance of the piston engines pulling relatively inefficient (in terms of aerodynamics and structure) airframes the difference between a full load of, say, a women's club and football linemen was the difference between a smooth takeoff and burning rubble at the end of the runway. With modern jet aircraft carrying hundreds of passengers with enormous performance capabilities the law of large numbers and the relative insensitivity to reasonable variations makes the weight worry largely unnecessary. (Yet, if we outfitted even a modern jet to carry, say, metal ingots, it would be important to know whether our cargo on a particular flight were aluminum versus iron versus uranium.)

In valuing technology we can conceive of examples of both early and modern aviation, namely: there could be cases where we were dealing with just a few relevant agreements with significant variation among them and the amount of money at stake appears large, versus another case where we have many relevant agreements with relatively small variations among them and the total value of the deal is not expected to be large. In the first case, taking an average value as characterizing the group is unlikely to be a reasonable single-value to use, whereas in the second case, it would be. Making this concrete, let us assume we have a deal that we perceive to be of total value of about $100,000, and we have found 20 comparable license agreements, all for paid up license fees, scattered between a low of $80,000 and a high of $140,000; taking an average (or median) value as characterizing the industry standard may be a very reasonable act. On the other hand, consider the contrasting situation if we believed that the total deal value over time was going to be in the range of $100 million, and we could only find three relevant, and in this case pure royalty license agreements at 2 percent, 5 percent, and 14 percent (all on some comparable royalty base), taking the average of 7 percent or the median of 5 percent with so much at stake could be seriously misleading. When the numbers are few, and the stakes are high, one is pressed to consider the industry standard method as a collection of individual "comparables" that is not well-characterized by an averaging process.

The third aspect of averaging is what I have called the "Tiger Woods phenomenon." Currently, the professional golfing world is being turned on end by the amazing performance of a still-young man by the name of Tiger Woods. His play is simply on a higher plane than his peers. Lance Armstrong in recently winning his fourth Tour de France; the now semi-retired Michael Jordan in basketball; Cameron Diaz, Mike Myers, and Eddie Murphy, who were the lead voices in the movie *Shrek 2* and received $10 million each for their respective 15 to 18 hours of narration work;[56] and Mike Tyson's household expenses[57] are other examples of performance beyond any normative expectation. It is not likely that any historic averaging would account for these examples. One of the exciting aspects of technology is that a particular invention or discovery could be transforming ("game-changing") in performance or cost reduction. When that happens, historic averages are normally not reliable indicators.

One final, and graphic, example of averaging error is related to us human beings. In many ways one can obtain meaningful averages of the human population, such as the design passenger load on a commercial aircraft just discussed. We can also talk about average life span in some contexts, though that number says nothing about us individually. And in yet other contexts, averaging leads to ridiculous results, such as this: the average U.S. resident has (approximately) one ovary and one testicle and lives in Edgar Springs, Missouri, population 190.[58]

CONCLUDING OBSERVATIONS AND CAUTIONARY NOTES

The power of the method of this chapter is that the valuations are based on market outcomes: real live buyers and sellers reaching agreements by acting in their respective self-interest. This can be very valuable when the point of reference is relevant to a subject valuation.

However, with all sources of Industry Standard information, we need to think about the various factors that could affect how the financial information discovered might be applied to the valuation of our present opportunity. Some of the factors we could consider include:

- *The Box.* What do we know about the Box of the reference agreement(s)? How does the Box of the historic agreement relate to the deal under consideration? Are the differences in the relative Boxes significant in terms of their likely effect on deal value?

- *The Wheelbarrow.* What do we know about the Wheelbarrow? Were there elements in the reference agreement(s) not in ours, or vice versa, that are significant? Were there likely to be financially important payment provisions that affect the valuation?

- *Timeliness.* There is an inherent time lag to historic information because it would not be available to us unless it occurred in the past. Does the difference in time of the discovered historical agreement(s) affect its applicability to our present situation? Was the reference agreement(s) done at a time when such deal values were low (or high)?

- *Bias.* If we are using survey or expert sources of data, is there a significant bias in the data set?

- *Actual outcomes.* If we are using expert opinion or published term sheets or price lists, are the valuation opinions or aspirations close to the finally realized deal value?

- *Special circumstances* Although it is easy for an enthusiastic seller to believe that his or her opportunity is unusually high in value in comparison to some reference agreement(s), is such a belief well-founded? Or, conversely, are we as sellers (or buyers) being too quick to peg our opportunity into a historic value range when in fact we have some extraordinary opportunity before us?

As we discussed at the beginning of this chapter, it is rare to find exact or near-exact comparable agreements with the published or accessible information that will be useful in a subject valuation, but sometimes it happens. And when it doesn't, there is often some useful insight into valuation that comes from the search and study even if there is no close set of comparables. And there are times when we are in a paradigm licensing situation and, thus, even without a specific agreement, we can obtain a useful insight into a valuation range.

Ah, yet, there is this craving somewhere deep inside for norms/standards that can be relied upon. From the time we make selections of what clothes we will wear (is it dress up, or dress down? and if it's down, is really down?), to how we greet one another (hugs for family and special people, definitely and regrettably no hugs in business encounters, handshakes only upon greeting initially or after some absence and definitely not daily with colleagues), to the structure and etiquette of our meals (soup and salad before entrees, absolutely not after), to every aspect of our respective lives, even the most non-conformist of us. One can even say there is a kind of bizarre haiku of standards and norms surrounding each of us: TCP/IP, XML, CDMA, OC-48, Mac OS, MIDI, MP3, AA batteries, 1% milk, kosher, 24 carats, 1 gallon per flush, 0.08 blood alcohol, April 15, July 4th, 16 ounces, 8 to 5, 40 hour workweek, $3^1/_2$ inch floppy, $8^1/_2$ by 11, #2 pencil, QWERTY, 26 letters, king's English, 88 keys, on key, do re me fa so la ti do, $33^1/_3$ rpm, $^4/_4$ time, four-year degree, three-ring binder, three-prong plug, 110 VAC/60 Hz, Sunday, RGB, PG-13, 20/20, 120/80, USDA Prime, shake hands with the right, different fingers in different positions have quite specific communication value, 9 innings, 100 yards, par, .357 magnum, 93 octane, 65 mph, 26 miles 385 yards, 8-track, Betamax.[59] Standards and norms are a kind of safe harbor. There's other people who are already there, it's been predetermined as safe, going there is if not a best practice it's at least a defendable one (akin to the adage in the pioneering computer-decision days, "no one ever got fired for buying IBM"). So the desire and search for valuation standards and norms is a natural one. And, in almost all circumstances, it is a reasonable effort to make. But, in valuing technology one should normally not expect to find the easy comfort of a well-defined, established standard.

The search for the holy grail of an industry standard "pricing book" is not likely to bear fruit (nor does it need to for the search to be valuable). A wide variety of published information is available that will increase the likelihood that examples exist that are reasonably close to your deal. When used cautiously and judiciously, they can usefully contribute to the consideration of value.

In the next chapter we will consider the use of rating/ranking as a semi-quantitative method of making comparisons between a reference (or comparable) agreement and the opportunity being valued. It is a natural extension of the subject addressed in this chapter, particularly for those circumstances when the discovered reference agreements contain enough information that they can be compared to our subject opportunity across multiple aspects that can affect value, as we shall see.

NOTES

1. But, in 2001, the toniest avenues in New York rented for $700 a square foot, according to a *Wall Street Journal* article Nov. 7, 2002, p. C11. This was 25 times the $28 a square foot for the average U.S. shopping mall.

2. Munger, James, P., *What's It Worth? A Guide to Current Personal Injury Awards and Settlements*, 1998 Edition, LEXIS® Law Publishing, 1998.

3. Ibid., p. 95.

4. I invite you to enjoy an especially good such foreign film nominated for an Academy Award in 2002: *Son of the Bride*; it is an Argentine film with many culturally specific events and yet when it is over we can see ourselves and people we know in a similar, yet deeper, way.

5. Thanks for this example belongs to Richard Brown, who for some 30 years has taught various incarnations of "Movies 101" in New York City.

6. There exist comparatively rare situations where one could identify a historical agreement that can approach being essentially the same as one's subject opportunity. For instance, a licensor can offer a bare patent license (such as a non-assert) on a non-exclusive on a one-time payment basis to an industry comprised of very similar actual and prospective licensees.

7. For those of you with some extra money and interested in becoming baseball owners, a consultant's recent valuation of the Mets was less than $450 million, when Doubleday, 50% owner, had been expecting an appraisal in excess of $600 million, noting that the Boston Red Sox had recently been sold for a reported $720 million and Forbes valued the Yankees at $730 million, though such value includes more than just the brand/IP value; according to FutureBrand, the Yankees are the most valuable sports-franchise brand in the U.S. at $338.8 million (according to a *Wall Street Journal* summary, July 8, 2002, p. A20.)

8. Battersby and Grimes, *Licensing Royalty Rates, 2001 Ed.*, Aspen Law and Business, 2001.

9. *New York Post*, June 18, 2002, p. 31.

10. It is probably a powerful indication of unique value when the public associates a person or product by an unusual, single name such as J-Lo, Elvis, Madonna, Bono, Cher, Sting, or Prince (or, now more accurately, by an unpronounceable name of the artist formerly known as Prince). On the other hand the unique name Liberace does not seem to have much traction these days, and "Raz" has not done much for me.

11. Buyers characteristically play a game I've called the "Where's Waldo™ of Licensing?"—shrinking the domain of the licensed technology down to the most microscopic scope possible so that almost any royalty rate, even 100 percent, does not constitute a significant payment.

12. For the moment we are ignoring the issue of how one would determine the appropriate "price" of the base, as in this example the manufacturer is "selling" the chip to itself.

13. "Factors Affecting Royalty Rates," Dan McGavock, David Haas, and Michael Patin, *les Nouvelles*, June 1992, p. 107.

14. "A Survey of Licensed Royalties," Stephen Degnan and Corwin Horton, *les Nouvelles*, June 1997, p. 91.

15. Patrica A. Martone, LES Multimedia Licensing Seminar, Copenhagen, Denmark, September 17, 1995.

16. Ibid.

17. Tom Kiley, *IPH Newsbrief*, April 1990, and published *in Licensing Economics Review*, September 1990, p. 4.

18. George D. Corey and Edward Kahn, "Biomedical Royalty Rates: Some Approaches," *Genetic Engineering News*, July–August 1991, p. 4; also published *in Licensing Economics Review*, December 1990, p. 13.

19. Ibid.

20. This information is based upon a one page summary prepared by IBM in 1993 entitled "IBM Worldwide Patent Licensing Practices." This practice was also cited in a paper by David Guenther and John Wills, "A Survey of PC Technology Royalty Rates," *les Nouvelles*, December 1995, p. 200. It is the author's understanding that this does not constitute IBM's current licensing practices.

21. *Wall Street Journal*, July 27, 1999, p. B5.

22. LXR Biotechnology press release, October 25, 2000.

23. "An Overzealous Defense of Its Patents Hasn't Made Rambus Many Friends," Dan Briody, *Red Herring*, October 15, 2001, p. 92.

24. *Wall Street Journal*, August 21, 1999.

25. "Intel settles patent suit with software makers," *Reuters*, April 15, 2002.

26. *Business Week*, May 22, 2000, p. 136.

27. "Microsoft to pay Inprise $125 million to license products and form alliance," Don Clark, *Wall Street Journal*, June 8, 1999, p. B13.

28. *Wall Street Journal*, May 26, 1999, p. 1.

29. *Wall Street Journal*, November 2, 1999, p. B1.

30. *New York Times*, April 23, 2002 "Celera Genomics in Surprise Appointment," story by Andrew Pollack.

31. *Wall Street Journal*, March 12, 2002.

32. "New Microsoft pricing looms," Rebecca Buckman, *Wall Street Journal*, June 24, 2002.

33. "InterTrust Signs Licensing Deal," *Wall Street Journal*, May 23, 2002, p. B8.

34. "Jury Rules Against Genentech in Research-Royalties Lawsuit," David P. Hamilton, *Wall Street Journal*, June 11, 2002.

35. "Genentech faces $500 million charge," David P. Hamilton, *Wall Street Journal*, June 25, 2002, p. D4.

36. "Knowledge is power, but pills are profits," Stephan Herrera, *Red Herring*, May 2002, p.72.

37. "Listen.com deal to advance effort in music licenses," Nick Wingfield, *Wall Street Journal*, July 1, 2002, p. B5.

38. Bryon, Christopher, "Smart Babies, Dumb Investors, *Red Herring*, July 2002, p. 94–5.

39. "Facing big threat from Microsoft, Nokia moves to share its software," David Pringle, *Wall Street Journal*, May 22, 2002, p. 1.

40. "IBM to Make Patent Payment in Rodime Case," *Wall Street Journal*, Nov. 2, 1990, p. B2.

41. "Microsoft's Earnings Hot Streak Cools," *Wall Street Journal*, July 18, 1997, p. B6.

42. "A Chip Maker's Profit on Patents," *New York Times*, October 16, 1990, p. C1.

43. "Nokia to join with IBM in 2 ventures on software," by Steve Lohr, *New York Times*, July 10, 2002.

44. "Matsushita to Use Nokia's Cellphone Software," story by David Pringle, *Wall Street Journal*, July 11, 2002, p. B6.

45. Reported by SoundScan in Billboard, July 13, 2002, p. 6.

46. "Ron Katz, Enforcer," by Seth Lubove, *Forbes*, August 25, 1997, p. 78.

47. "DuPont Stakes Claim on Superconductor Rights," *Science*, Vol. 241, p. 1156.

48. Although we will discuss the recently publicized problem of confusing and unreliable financial data such problems have not extended to license agreements that have been filed. Companies will regularly redact certain information for competitive (or perhaps embarrassment avoidance or other) reasons, but what is submitted is generally taken as a faithful representation of the agreement between the parties. One always wonders if there are other related agreements, sometimes called *side letters*, which are not filed or otherwise disclosed that exist that have a material effect on the valuation of the deal being disclosed. The problem with side letters is that there is no way to prove their non-existence (short of having access to the complete files of the respective parties, which is not going to happen).

49. Just to state what should be obvious: I am not a lawyer and, accordingly, I am not giving here, or anywhere, a legal interpretation but, rather, a business person's understanding of what is being sold and bought in exchange for what consideration.

50. *Patent Licensing*, Harold Einhorn, Section 3.03, Royalty, 1990, p. 3-11ff.

51. Mike M. Carpenter, "Traditional Royalty," presented at the 15th Annual Meeting of the Licensing Executives Society, 1979.

52. These summary comments derive from a telephone discussion with Dr. Suzanne Bakken, Professor of Medical Informatics, Columbia University School of Nursing, an authority on evidence-based advanced practice nursing, but do not do justice to the vast literature available in that discipline.

53. There is a an epic novel of gargantuan length, such that almost no one on earth has actually finished it, including me, that has as its deep thought that the past is both far more and far less accessible to us than we think. Marcel Proust in *Remembrance of Things Past* expends some 3,000 pages to demonstrate the strangeness of memory and our forming present meaning from it. Creating some system for recording valuation and pricing memories as described in the next text paragraph can help circumvent much of that strangeness.

54. Yes, this is a play on words.

55. Yet even today, in small airplanes, such as four- or six-passenger, single-engine piston aircraft, the pilot is, or should be, doing such weight assessment when approaching a full load for the same reasons discussed in the text. A recent, tragic commuter airline crash may also have been caused by passenger overloading.

56. "An Animated Conversation," authored by Tom King interviewing Dreamworks's Jeffrey Katzenberg, *Wall Street Journal*, May 17, 2002.

57. As reported by Mr. Tyson's accountant and introduced in the U.S. district court in New York (reported by *Sports Illustrated*), his expenditures for the three-year period 1995 through 1997 included: automobiles/motorcycles $4,477,498, pet expenses (pigeons *and* cats) $411,777, lawn care $748,367 (but it was for three houses, so it only "averaged" $249,456 per house), and cash and personal expenses $7,794,103; *Sports Illustrated*, 2002.

58. According to the 2000 U.S. census data, Edgar Springs has replaced Steelville, Missouri as the human center of gravity for the United States, reported in *National Geographic*, May 2002; I am not aware of a specific scientific source of the other statistic cited.

59. Adopted from a sidebar "The Poetry of Standards," *Wired*, January 2002, p. 89.

Negotiating Licenses from Developers

EXHIBIT 4A.1	MULTIMEDIA ROYALTIES & BUSINESS CONTEXT OF "PRODUCERS" NEGOTIATING LICENSES FROM "DEVELOPERS"

1. Producers have the most financial clout and the greatest financial exposure (including substantial distribution costs).
2. Producers want to limit advances and milestone payments and to recoup them as quickly as possible.
3. Producers want to own as many rights as they can, and license only the remainder.
4. Producers want royalties to developers based upon "adjusted gross receipts."
5. Producers are historically unwilling to pay a total royalty (including for development) of more than 10–15 percent. [becomes a "standard"]

Created by: Patricia A. Martone (Fish & Neave, 1995) for the LES Multimedia Licensing Seminar, Copenhagen, September 17, 1995. Reprinted with the permission of Patricia A. Martone, Fish & Neave.

EXHIBIT 4A.2	MORE BUSINESS CONTEXT RE: MULTIMEDIA ROYALTIES

1. High distribution costs—50 percent to 75 percent** of sales (est.)
2. A lot of CD-ROM titles in typical software store (300–500) but few sales (as few as one copy/month*).
3. Average CD-ROM costs $383K to produce and generates $20 in wholesale revenue. Must sell 19,000 copies to break even.*
4. Consumer pressure for low retail prices for products containing digitized information.
5. Current problem: out of 912 developers in one survey, 96 percent were unprofitable.*.
6. Growth of sales in CD-ROM players provide hope for future—about 27 million CD-ROM players worldwide as of 1994; expected to increase by 80 percent in 1995.**

*Source: Don Clark, "Slipped Disks," *Wall Street Journal*, March 1, 1995.
**Source: James M. Kennedy et al., "Structuring Multimedia Transactions," University of Southern California Law Center Sixteenth Annual Computer Law Institute, Sect. I, May 1995.
Created by: Patricia A. Martone (Fish & Neave, 1995) for the LES Multimedia Licensing Seminar, Copenhagen, September 17, 1995. Reprinted with the permission of Patricia A. Martone, Fish & Neave.

EXHIBIT 4A.3	TYPICAL MULTIMEDIA ROYALTY RATES

Text (usually separate licenses for North America and Europe)
- small segment (up to several pages), $500–$1500, nonexclusive use
- majority of books, 5–20 percent royalty. (National Writers Union paper recommends no less than 50 percent of list price!)

Still Images
- unique photographs, $200–$650 ("editorial" use, per Timestream, Inc.)
- multiple generic photographs (50 to 100), $50–$75 each
- for more information, see "Licensing Still Images," Timestream, Inc., http//www/timestream.com/web/, September, 1994.

Motion Pictures
- $3,000 to $10,000 per minute
- Often need to license publicity rights through screenwriters and Screen Actors Guild

Music
- each, as appropriate, get a royalty of $.05–$.13 per song
  - recording company (not needed if developer creates its own recording)
  - publisher of musical work

Created by: Patricia A. Martone (Fish & Neave, 1995) for the LES Multimedia Licensing Seminar, Copenhagen, September 17, 1995. Reprinted with the permission of Patricia A. Martone, Fish & Neave.

Outline of Agreement Between DuPont and University of Houston (UH)

1. Important Definitions
   a. "Patent Rights"—(1) rights in any patents which the U.S. or any foreign country might grant covering claims to superconductive materials applied for by UH as of execution date, and (2) any certain filed applications.
   b. "Licensed Products" and "Licensed Processes"—products and processes covered by an allowed or issued claim included in any of the Patent Rights. Also includes products, the sale of which would result in contributory infringement.
   c. "Net Sales"—the amount invoiced on sales of Licensed Products or Licensed Processes less certain discounts, return credits, taxes, transportations costs, and insurance premiums.
   d. "Field of Commercial Interest"—any commercial field in which DuPont can demonstrate financial commitment to research, capital expansion, marketing plans, and so forth.
   e. "First Commercial Sale"—can include a sale to U.S. government pursuant to a contract awarded without a competitive bid by a third party.

2. Grant of License
   UH grants DuPont an exclusive, world-wide license to make, use, and sell Licensed Products and Licensed Processes, subject to the following:
   a. UH may make materials for its own research.
   b. DuPont will use its best effots to introduce Licensed Products and Licensed Processes into the commercial market as soon as possible.

c. Includes the right to sublicense; all sublicenses will include a "best efforts" clause.

d. U.S. government rights.

3. Sublicenses

DuPont may grant sublicenses under the following conditions:

a. At UH's request, DuPont will grant a restricted sublicense to a TCSUH (Texas Center for Superconductivity at the University of Houston) consortium member, who shall pay a reasonable royalty therefor. DuPont will pay UH 75% of sublicense royalties in fields of no commercial interest to DuPont and 50% of royalties in fields of commercial interest to DuPont.

b. At UH's direction, DuPont will grant a sublicense to a third party, regardless of TCSUH membership, in any field of no commercial interest to DuPont. DuPont will pay UH 75% of royalties in such cases.

c. After the earlier of (i) three years after DuPont's first commercial sale (unless DuPont is proceeding diligently toward commercialization) or (ii) eight years after date of patent issuance, UH may direct DuPont to grant a sublicense to a third party in a field of commercial interest to DuPont at a royalty rate no less favorable than DuPont is paying in that field. DuPont will pay UH 50% of royalties so received.

[NOTE: These features, i.e., 2(d), 3(a), (b), and (c) render the license, in some respects, a "non-exclusive" license.]

d. DuPont may grant sublicenses on its own initiative and will pay UH 75% of all royalties received by DuPont.

4. Payments

In return for the grant of license and rights associated with it, DuPont will pay UH:

a. $1.5 million upon execution of the agreement

b. $1.5 million upon the issuance of a U.S. patent covering the "1–2–3" phase material claimed in the patent applications.

c. At DuPont's option, $1.5 million two years following the date of patent issuance. If DuPont does not execute this option, the agreement terminates with no obligation by UH to refund any previously-paid money.

d. DuPont will pay royalties on net sales as determined by agreement between UH and DuPont at the time of commercialization, or in the event UH and DuPont cannot agree, by a third-party arbitrator experienced in the field of industrial licenses and royalty arrangements. Added value-in-use by licensed technology is to be a prime factor in determining royalty rates.

e. In the event of cross-licenses, trades, single-payments, or receipt of property, UH and DuPont will agree on the appropriate royalty value, or, failing agreement, submit to arbitration.

f. DuPont will pay the greater of earned royalties or a minimum royalty of $100,000 per year. The minimum is not required until the earlier of (i) the expiration of three years following the first commercial sale (but not before patent issuance), or (ii) five years following patent issuance.

g. Despite U.S. government rights, if DuPont is the supplier to the U.S. government of Licensed Products, based on a contract awarded without DuPont's having to match or overcome a competitive bid, DuPont will pay UH a reasonable royalty.

h. DuPont will require sublicensees to pay royalties on sales even before the grant of patent, provided there is no third-party competitor who is not paying a royalty.

i. DuPont is entitled to credits against earned royalties due UH, but only for the third $1.5 million payment and for reimbursement of legal expenses associated with patent filing and prosecution.

5. Patent Filing and Maintenance

UH will prepare, file, and prosecute patent applications. UH will cooperate with, and consider the opinions of, DuPont with respect to such applications. DuPont will pay all expenses relative to such applications, retroactive to the filing of the first application. In the event DuPont decides to cease paying expenses (after the expenditure of $1,000,000) with respect to particular applications, its rights in such applications will terminate.

6. Records and Reporting

DuPont and its sublicensees will keep accurate records and permit a UH-designated CPA to inspect them upon demand. To the extent permitted by law (e.g., Texas Open Records Act), UH will keep confidential information obtained from such inspections. DuPont will submit semiannual of sales and royalties due.

7. Improvements

a. Any inventions which are "improvements" of the licensed technology will be included in the Patent Rights. For purposes of the agreement, "improvements" are considered additional filings or new applications that would be dominated as matter of patent law by the existing applications.

b. UH will continue to file patent applications on inventions resulting from Chu-directed work. For three years, DuPont will have a right of first refusal on new patent applications (as opposed to "improvements") covering superconductive materials resulting from Chu-directed work. Other research and researchers at UH are not covered by this right.

c. DuPont and UH will encourage and promote exchanges of information between Chu and Chu-directed researchers and DuPont's Wilmington Experimental Station. Any contribution of a UH researcher at DuPont will be subject to DuPont's right of first refusal.

8. Infringement

Both parties have the right to pursue legal action against infringers or to otherwise protect the Patent Rights, and either may bring action in the name of the other if the other is an indispensable party. Funding of legal expenses may be derived partially from royalties, and recoveries will reimburse such expenses, then cover royalties, then be shared equally. Royalties may be partially reduced during the period of an infringement if it has not been successfully abated within six months after it is discovered.

9. Termination

a. Unless earlier terminated, the agreement will automatically terminate on the expiration of all Patent Rights.

b. If either party defaults, the other party may terminate by giving notice and the defaulting party does not initiate action to cure the default within 90 days.

c. DuPont may terminate if it decides not to make the payment provided in 4(c) above.

d. DuPont may terminate without making the payments provided in 4(b) and (c) above if the patent is not granted in 10 years. UH need not refund the initial payment, and all rights revert to UH. DuPont is relieved of any remaining obligations to pay legal costs.

e. UH may terminate without refunding any payments and all rights revert if DuPont does not make a royalty-bearing sale with eight years after grant of patent and DuPont is not proceeding diligently toward commercialization.

f. After DuPont makes all of its payments required by 4(a), (b), and (c), it may still terminate by giving 30 days notice. All rights revert to UH.

10. General

a. UH warrants that all interest in the Patent Rights have been assigned to it, and that UH has the authority to license those rights. UH does not warrant that the Patent Rights are valid, that they have any particular scope, or that DuPont may exploit them without infringing other patents.

b. DuPont indemnifies UH from personal injury and products liability claims.

c. DuPont may not assign the agreement without UH approval.

d. UH and DuPont agree to attempt to settle all disputes, claims, etc., amicably between themselves. If they fail, they will submit the matter to binding arbitration.

R18/18.11.03.1,2

CHAPTER 5

Method Two: The Rating/Ranking Method to Determine Valuation

$\mathbf{I}$n this chapter we will consider the second of six valuation methods, that of Rating/Ranking. This method requires the pre-identification of a reference or comparable agreement or cluster of agreements. For this reason this method is closely associated with Industry Standards, the method described in the preceding chapter.

INTRODUCTION: WHAT IS MEANT BY RATING/RANKING AND WHY IS IT HELPFUL?

Rating/ranking approaches are one of the most widely used tools when dealing with hard-to-quantify issues. They regularly appear hidden behind newspaper stories of "the best city in America" or some other "best of..." story. There is even at least one web site that is dedicated to such method and its applications: *www.bestplaces.com*. At this site one can find rating/ranking examples and results on all sorts of decision-making. They even provide their rating/rankings of third party rating/rankings (such as might be published by *Forbes*, and *Money* magazine). There are many more everyday examples of the use of rating/ranking. *U.S. News and World Report* regularly publishes its rating/rankings of academic programs offered by colleges and universities, and hospitals by specialty. In a specialized and emerging form of rating/ranking, hospitals themselves are now widely using a 10-point pain rating/ranking, the so-called fifth vital sign,[1] using graphics to assist patients in self-analysis: from smile faces ("0" for "no hurt") to crying frown faces ("10" for "hurts worst"). Edmunds (www.edmunds.com) provides a ranked valuation of every automobile, new and used. In the wake of terrorist attacks of 9/11 there now exists a Transportation Security Agency (TSA). One of its actions is to develop a screening tool for risk potential. In response to another kind of adversity, Charles Schwab, the financial services company, has developed a proprietary rating/ranking tool that groups some 3,000 publicly traded stocks into five categories: 20 percent top ranked stocks as "A" stocks, 20 percent high ranked stocks as "B," 20 percent as "C,", 20 percent as "D," and 20 percent as "E." According to the company, it uses a computer program to automatically assess these stocks based upon 24 different criteria. Morningstar rates some 10,000 mutual funds now (since July 1, 2002) in 48 distinct sectors by the assignment of stars: the top 10 percent receive five stars, the next 22.5 percent get four stars, the next 35 percent three stars, the next 22.5 percent two stars, and the bottom 10 percent one star. Value Line® has for many years used its own proprietary rating/ranking approach enjoined with some measure of human judgment. Clearly the Schwab approach is an attempt to assist investors who seek advice from someone, anyone, who is not shamelessly promoting their own self-interest by the individual recommendations.[2] How could such ranked determinations be made? Within the body of such "best" stories is usually embedded a description of how the results were obtained. Generally, a series of criteria (or issues) was prepared by an individual or panel together with some form of a prescribed numerical scoring scale for each criterion. This information was then supplied to a panel of experts who solely or in committee fashion developed scores for each of the criterion; the purveyors of the survey then tabulate the scores and rank the winners. (See Exhibit 5.1.)

EXHIBIT 5.1   METHOD 2: RATING/RANKING

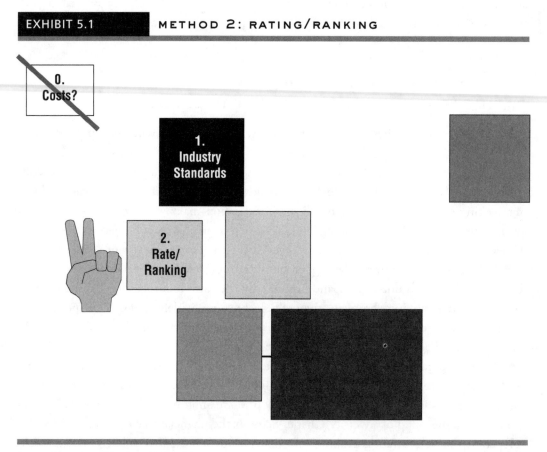

Source: ©2003 Razgaitis, richard@razgaitis.com.

A variant of such an expert panel scoring system is using a prepared look-up table, such as: if the city has one or less libraries per 10,000 people, then the score on this criteria is "1," if two to four libraries then it is "2," and so on; usually in such instances, an expert panel was initially used to create the look-up table.

Another example of a Rating/Ranking method is Benjamin Franklin's "decision algebra." He is reported to have developed this decision-making tool over his life and used it in many contexts. When faced with a decision he would create two columns, one for the "yes" outcome and one for the "no" (he lived in simpler times). Then in each column he would list every reason or argument that would support the respective outcome. (Presumably he did some compression so that he did not end up with the same reason expressed multiple times in different ways). Then he would select one idea from, say, the "yes" column and cross it off and at the same time cross off as many "no" entries as needed to be of equal "weight" to the "yes" entry crossed off. He would continue to cross off equal weights of reasons until one column had no more reasons left. Then he would examine the other column to find at least one good, un-crossed-off reason supporting that decision (say, "yes"), unbalanced by any entries supporting the opposing decision ("no"), and chose "yes". In these times of "paralysis by analysis" one can truly appreciate Mr. Franklin.

Moody, and Standard and Poor's (S&P) ratings of commercial bonds are examples of the use of Rating/Ranking as a valuation method. In such context, the higher rated/ranked bonds are associated with lower risk. In the middle of the rating/ranking categories there is a demarcation between the upper categories, which are generally termed "investment grade," and the bottom categories, which are popularly known as "junk bonds" but are more accurately simply high risk/high (potential) yield bonds. The market in response to such scoring, and accounting for any other factors, then accepts lower expected rates of return (yield) on such highly rated/ranked bonds. It is, however, important to recognize that lower rated/ranked bonds, even so-called junk bonds, have value in the marketplace. Indeed investors can make very attractive returns from portfolios of high-risk bonds providing they have been acquired with an appropriately high rate of return potential. For instance, Angelo Gordon, a distress-debt investor managing more than $8 billion, has recently acquired both Enron and *Excite@Home* bonds, a presently precarious pair of debt issuances; but such purchases, like others in Angelo Gordon's portfolio, were at significant discounts to nominal value of the bond (not pennies to the dollar, but more typically dimes to the dollar); previous 'bottom fishing' investments has enabled it to deliver returns of more than 20 percent to its investors.[3] In fact, according the standard dictum of capital asset pricing theory, a portfolio of high risk bonds should, over time, provide a *greater* reward to investors than a portfolio of low risk bonds. Risk can be good (though, it is risky to simply say: risk is good).

Finally, rating/ranking is conceptually related to a current best practice for new product development, namely the "stage gate process." As in stage gate product development there is an undergirding belief that systematic analysis, especially by expert panels using prescribed tools and methods, leads to wisdom (better choosing). Specifically, in rating/ranking valuation, and stage gate product development, we have:

- Our key assumptions/beliefs are overtly articulated.
- Biases are brought out into the light and tested.
- Systematic process using established tools enables the use of structured panels, even with changing membership.
- A track record/history is created that can be very useful in future exercises.
- One is prepared for next step decision-making (in the context of valuation the next steps are normally pricing and negotiation readiness).

Although our focus is on technology valuation, rating/ranking is also effectively applied to two related processes: deciding which opportunities to pursue (portfolio selection), and deciding on the "best" commercialization path. These three uses are shown in Exhibit 5.2 below.

Shown in Box 1 is the opportunity choosing process; which opportunities represent the best use of my precious time? At the end of this chapter we will return to this choosing process. In Box 2 is the determination of the best commercialization path; given the opportunity, what is the best way to exploit it considering risk, investment, and reward? This

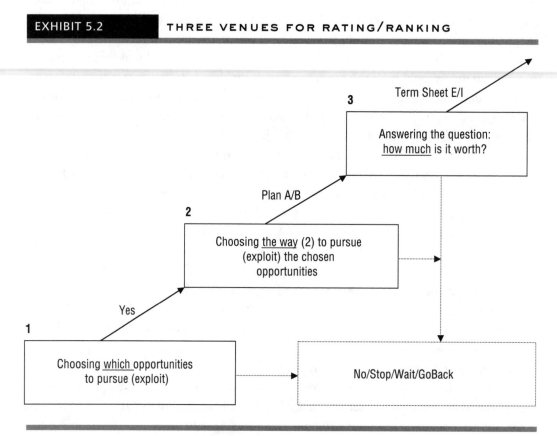

EXHIBIT 5.2   THREE VENUES FOR RATING/RANKING

Source: ©2003 Razgaitis, richard@razgaitis.com.

issue was discussed in Chapter 4 in regard to exclusivity and licensee. Finally, in Box 3 is the present issue of determining a value; how much is this chosen opportunity pursed in the best way worth? The output of this step is normally an internal and external valuation term sheet.

The five elements that comprise the Rating/Ranking Method are as follows:

1. Scoring criteria
2. Scoring system
3. Scoring scale
4. Weighting factors
5. Decision table

Scoring Criteria

Examples of criteria that are used in licensing valuations are market size, patent protection, and stage of development. A further discussion of useful criteria is given later in this chapter in the section entitled, "Developing Criteria for Using Rating/Ranking for Valuation of Technology."

Scoring System

Many different kinds of scoring systems are used, and the choice is a matter of taste and experience. Perhaps the most common system is the 1 to 5 point system, with 5 as the best, 1 as the worst, and 3 representing equivalence to the reference condition or standard. Its appeal may be related to people's familiarity with college GPAs. It is also very simple as there are only two levels "better" and two levels "worse" than the reference condition.

For those preferring more distinctions or levels, there is the 1 to 7 scale, sometimes known as the Likkert Scale. Here a 4 represents equivalence to the reference condition, 5 is "better," 6 is "much better," and 7 is "outstanding" (and vice versa for 3, 2, 1), thus permitting three levels of "better" and "worse."

Others, more digitally inclined, seem to prefer the 0 to 10 point scale. For obsessive compulsives, a 0 to 100 point scale is a possibility.

Right-hemisphere people seem to lean toward non-numerical methods. The simplest such approach used is H/M/L for high/medium/low (i.e., better, same, or poorer) which forces the decision to one level better and worse. A variant of this approach is to use symbols such "+" for "better," "++" for much better, "=" for comparable, and similar negative signs for worse and much worse; this has the same effect in terms of levels as the 1 to 5 scale but avoids attaching numerical significance to the outcome. A finding with the "+" approach would be expressed as "somewhere between a + and ++" whereas in the 1 to 5 scale the result would be "4.5."

For the Crayola regressives there is even the possibility of colors: green for "better," blue for "much better," yellow for "worse," and red for "much worse" (no color, or white, for equivalence to the standard). Colors can be useful when presenting findings to either young children or management (there's a Dilbert cartoon yet to be written here).

Although there is some arbitrariness about the choice of a scoring system, it is actually important and serious to select one and to standardize it. The power of rating/ranking increases with experience and a database of previous determinations. It would defeat some of the value of the method to make ad hoc selections of scales.

The advantages of a Likkert Scale are:

- Clearly scores opportunities above and below a reference point (such as a comparable), which is the essence of the rating/ranking method

- Can create any number of levels above and below the reference point (a 5-point scale has two above and below, a 7-point has three above and below, etc.), allowing any level of precision desired or warranted

- Numerical normalized result can be used to create priorities when evaluating a portfolio of opportunities.

- The individual scores on each of the factors can be used in preparing for negotiation.

- It just looks like a serious process, perhaps because of the echo of college grading.

Some issues with the use of Likkert Scale are:

- Quantification can be misleading ("exactly what do I do with a 4.0?").

- It does not overtly reflect the catastrophic effect a fatal flaw can have on value. Suppose on an IP protection score, an opportunity receives a "1" because it has none, but it scores high on all other factors. Just determining a weighted average score will obscure the fact that the opportunity is likely to have no (or little) value.[4]

- It can too easily let mediocrity slide by on each of the factors so that the results are commonly "better than average" (like Garrison Keillor's *Lake Wobegon*, where all the kids are above average), something like "gentleman's C's."

One of the advantages of the four-color (Crayola) scheme is that it overcomes some of the previously listed disadvantages:

- Fatal flaws are red and obvious.

- Drives one to focus on the opportunities with benefits that are truly outstanding (blues).

- Avoids quantification battles (but does not avoid the need for making distinctions).

- Highlights by "yellow" the factors that need to be analyzed carefully to understand why they're negative or what key information is missing.
- It is a great management communication tool.

Scoring Scales

Two types of scoring scales can be used: subjective and objective. Subjective scales merely ask an expert or expert panel to consider the described circumstance through the "eyes" of each of the criteria and assign a score based upon the selected scoring system (i.e., 1 to 5). Objective scales can be created when enough experience has been gained with predicting values using rating/ranking and comparing such predictions with actual outcomes. After numerous experiences, it is possible to estimate (or in some cases derive) numerical scales; when derived scales can be created they are commonly known as influence coefficients. It is possible to use a mixture of subjective and objective scales for any given rating/ranking valuation.

When subjective scales are used, an expert panel of some sort has to be established. Setting up such a panel requires some thought and planning. If the number of people on the panel is small, say two to four, the panels tend to operate by consensus rather than by vote. This seems to work best when all the parties are in the same room and participate in an active discussion and debate before proposing scores and reaching consensus. If a large number of people are involved, then voting and averaging seems to work better. In such cases it may be difficult to assemble everyone in the same room and commit the time to hear all opinions and debate. However, when voting remotely, it is possible, even likely, that such voters will not have considered important aspects of certain matters, calling into question how much weight to attach to their vote. Sometimes political necessity requires the larger panel. Decision-making in large groups has been the subject of much research, though none known in the context of technology valuation. The recommended approach would be a panel of three to five persons, at least half of which (two to three) are regular participants in such technology valuation processes, and the balance are other needed experts and stakeholders. The optimal result is a weighted opinion of the regulars over the experts and stakeholders.

Weighting Factors

The weighting factor is used as a means of assigning a higher importance to some criteria and a lower importance to others. For example, one could choose 10 criteria to be scored and deem that one particular criterion (say, market size) is twice as important as any of the other nine; in this case, the score for the market size criterion would be doubled, effectively (but intentionally) counting it twice. What should be carefully avoided is unintentionally counting the same idea or criteria multiple times. This might happen if one criterion was "market size," another was "projected sales," another was "likelihood of use for other applications," and another was "likelihood of sales in other countries"; this is tantamount to scoring "market size" four times.

Decision Table

The end result of a rating/ranking process is a column of raw scores entered by the expert(s) next to each criterion, which is then multiplied by the respective weighting to obtain a weighted score, and then all the weighted scores are added to determine the rated/ranked score. For convenience, often the rated/ranked score is normalized so that, for example, on the 1 to 5 score system, an "average" score would yield a "3.00." This simply makes interpretation easier.

The issue then becomes this: How does one actually put a result to use and aid a valuation? It is helpful to consider what is being accomplished by the Rating/Ranking Method. In essence, we can visualize the process as creating an "industry standard" in the following sense. The method requires a comparable or reference agreement or cluster of agreements in order for the scoring to take place because each score is always in the context of a point of reference. A comparable deal could be one specific technology which was licensed under known terms, or a general understanding of a population of related (in the sense of belonging to a category) technologies licensed. In effect, this method assumes that the technology being valued "belongs" to the category of the comparable deal. The scoring and calculations are means of creating quality or value differences from the comparable deal. The result is similar to saying the technology being valued is "like" a 1995 Ford Taurus, but its overall quality differs from the norm of that category by the rating/ranking score.

At one level, this approach can appear to be so ad hoc and so subject to intentional and unintentional biases that it is a pointless exercise. However, this is how decisions are often made in many highly complex situations. In Chapter 4, some New York City office rental rates were quoted, which might seem a comparatively simple decision domain but how would one decide whether to pay $33.56 for "Grand Central," or move up to $41.01 for "Sixth/Rock," or go for $45.68 on "Park Avenue?"[5] There is no differential equation or computer program that can answer such a question.

Here are some reasons why the Rating/Ranking method is used and valued:

1. It causes one to prepare for negotiation by thinking through the relevant factors that make up licensing value.

2. It facilitates discussions with other valuation experts as it focuses on the key components of value and what is known (and not known) and good (and not good) about the subject technology.

3. It can be useful in explaining to non-expert stakeholders how the valuation was reached.

4. With experience, the method increases in value. As one sees more and more outcomes and develops more experience with rating and ranking, the structure of the

method enables one to make more insightful comparisons. The method becomes a tool for creating a storehouse of one's own licensing experience.

5. It is easy to use and can, with a good benchmark(s) and appropriate criteria, yield useful results.

6. For all its subjectivity, it is a tool in the toolkit of the licensing professional and no tool should be ignored (and, in this regard, it complements the more quantitative methods considered in Chapters 7 and 8).

7. It can lead to strategies for increasing the value of the technology by identifying important missing components of a potential deal, or reducing the risk (uncertainty) by further research or inquiry to improve a low score on a particular criterion.

8. During or after negotiations, an already-completed Rating/Ranking valuation can be useful in assessing the need for a re-valuation, or a "Plan B."

DEVELOPING CRITERIA FOR USING RATING/RANKING FOR VALUATION OF TECHNOLOGIES

One of the critical steps in employing the Rating/Ranking Method is selecting appropriate criteria. Like other aspects of this method, the identification of such criteria is a matter of judgment. For the method to be effective, one generally needs at least five criteria.

A set of criteria widely cited in legal context is the 15 "Georgia Pacific Factors."[6] These were developed by a court for the purposes of determining a reasonable royalty. These factors are presented in Exhibit 5.3. Bob Goldscheider has written an extensive review article on the use of such factors in litigation contexts.[7]

Factors 1 and 2 are expressions of the first method considered, the Industry Standard Method. Factor 8 is applicable to rating/ranking and will be also considered in the Discounted Cash Flow Method and the Monte Carlo Method (Chapters 7 and 8, respectively). Factor 11 is primarily relevant in the context of a litigation matter. Aspects of Factors 12 and 13 will be considered in Chapter 6 under the Rules of Thumb Method, although these are also legitimate matters for use in the Rating/Ranking Method. Factor 14 is itself a summary statement of the use of this Rating/Ranking Method. Factor 15 is the outcome of the valuation process and so can for our purposes be considered as the objective, not a criterion. From this perspective, that would leave 10 of the 15 Georgia-Pacific Factors that could be directly applied in a rating/ranking approach: numbers 3, 4, 5, 6, 7, 8, 9, 10, 12, and 13.

In the Degnan and Horton survey cited in Chapter 4,[8] one of the surveyed questions was directed toward the use of such Georgia-Pacific Factors in performing valuations. The respondents were asked to rank each factor on a 1 to 5 scale with "5" designating very important and "1" not important; this in itself was a rating/ranking exercise. The results are shown in Exhibit 5.4. The two columns deal with the two licensing situations: selling and buying. The factors are ranked from highest to lowest, so the factor numbers do not correspond to the numbering of Exhibit 5.4.

EXHIBIT 5.3   GEORGIA-PACIFIC CORP. V. U.S. PLYWOOD CORP. FACTORS APPLICABLE TO THE DETERMINATION OF REASONABLE ROYALTIES

1. The royalties received by the patentee for the licensing of the patent in suit, proving or tending to prove an established royalty.

2. The rates paid by the licensee for the use of other patents comparable to the patent in suit.

3. The nature and scope of the license, as exclusive or non-exclusive; or as restricted or non-restricted in terms of territory or with respect to whom the manufactured product may be sold.

4. The licensor's established policy and marketing program to maintain his patent monopoly by not licensing others to use the invention or by granting licenses under special conditions designed to preserve that monopoly.

5. The commercial relationship between the licensor and licensee, such as, whether they are competitors in the same territory in the same line of business; or whether they are inventor and promoter.

6. The effect of selling the patented specialty in promoting sales of other products of the licensee; the existing value of the invention to the licensor as a generator of sales of his non-patented items; and the extent of such derivative or convoyed sales.

7. The duration of the patent and the term of the license.

8. The established profitability of the product made under the patent; its commercial success; and its current popularity.

9. The utility and advantages of the patent property over the old modes or devices, if any, that had been used for working out similar results.

10. The nature of the patented invention; the character of the commercial embodiment of it as owned and produced by the licensor; and the benefits to those who have used the invention.

11. The extent to which the infringer has made use of the invention; and any evidence probative of the value of that use.

12. The portion of the profit or of the selling price that may be customary in the particular business or in comparable businesses to allow for the use of the invention or analogous inventions.

13. The portion of the realizable profit that should be credited to the invention as distinguished from non-patented elements, the manufacturing process, business risks, or significant features or improvements added by the infringer.

14. The opinion testimony of qualified experts.

15. The royalty that a licensor (such as the patentee) and a licensee (such as the infringer) would have agreed upon if both had been reasonably and voluntarily trying to reach an agreement; that is, the amount which a prudent licensee—who desired, as a business proposition, to obtain a license to manufacture and sell a particular article embodying the patented invention—would have been willing to pay as a royalty and yet be able to make a reasonable profit and which amount would have been acceptable by a prudent patentee who was willing to grant a license.

Source: 318 F. Supp. 1116 (S.D. N.Y. 1970).

| EXHIBIT 5.4 | FREQUENCY OF USE OF GEORGIA PACIFIC FACTORS BY LICENSING PROFESSIONS ACCORDING TO A SURVEY |

Importance of Factor	Licensing In	Licensing Out
1. Nature of the Protection	4.3	4.2
2. Utility Over Old Methods	4.2	4.2
3. Scope of Exclusivity	4.1	4.1
4. Licensee's Anticipated Profits	3.0	3.4
5. Commercial Success	3.7	3.7
6. Territory Restrictions	3.7	3.5
7. Comparable License Rates	3.6	3.7
8. Duration of Protection	3.3	3.1
9. Licensors' Anticipated Profits	2.6	3.1
10. Commercial Relationship	2.6	3.6
11. Tag Along Sales	2.1	2.1

Source: Stephen A. Degnan and Corwin Horton, "A Survey of Licensed Royalties," *les Nouvelles*, June 1997, p. 91–96. Reprinted with permission from *les Nouvelles*.

The McGavock survey discussed in Chapter 4[9] also asked its participants similar questions. The findings on this matter are presented in Exhibit 5.5.

One massive list of 100 factors was developed by Tom Arnold.[10] Although Mr. Arnold did not present his list in the context of employing a formal rating/ranking approach, he did enumerate a comprehensive list of points to consider. Mr. Arnold's paper is provided in Appendix 5.A and summarized in Exhibit 5.6. In this author's experience, 100 criteria are simply too many. Such a large number makes it difficult to grasp and adequately characterize a reasonable predictive value. However, the list and article are commended as a reference in the consideration of which criteria are to be selected.

For many licensing situations, the most important criteria include:

- *Estimated attainable market size and overall product profit margins.* Together, these two factors will strongly influence the earnings (EBIT, as will be discussed in Chapter 7), which has a very strong influence on the value of a license.

- *Strength of the IP protection (patents, trade secrets, copyrights, and trademarks).* For exclusive licenses, this criterion plays an important role in creating defendable, unique products (and, thereby margins higher than commodity levels). For nonexclusive licenses, buyers consider this criterion because it affects what they would have to do if a license agreement is not entered into.

EXHIBIT 5.5   IMPORTANCE OF VARIOUS FACTORS ON ROYALTY RATES

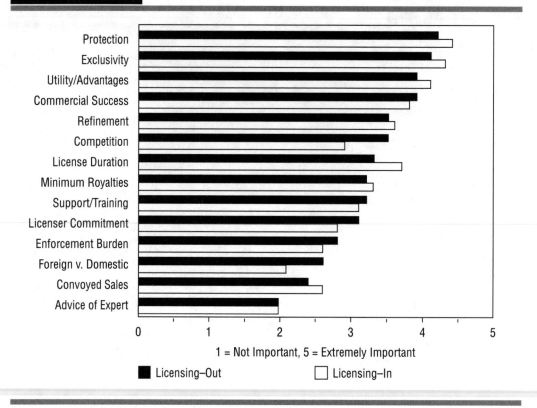

Source: McGavock, et al., "Factors Affecting Royalty Rates," *les Nouvelles*, June 1992, p. 109. Reprinted with permission from Daniel M. McGavock, Managing Director, InteCap, Inc.

- *Breadth of the IP protection.* This criterion addresses the economic impact of working just outside the patent or other IP protection. It is important to know, for example, that even in the case of a strong patent, one can operate outside the boundaries of the claims at (say) only a 1 percent performance or cost penalty; such a situation would clearly lower the value of a license in comparison to a circumstance where such a penalty were 100 percent, or practical operation was impossible.

- *Stage of development.* This criterion addresses three interrelated issues: How long will it be until the licensed invention will be producing profits? How much additional investment will need to be made prior to commercial introduction? What is the overall development risk?

- *Market environment.* Any invention being developed for commerce enters some kind of business environment. Is it in a generally growing market (or not)? Are there strong and aggressive competitors? Are there existing channels of delivery or will en-

| EXHIBIT 5.6 | A CHECKLIST OF 100 FACTORS IN SETTING THE VALUE OF A LICENSE: A SUMMARY OF THE 100 FACTORS |

	Category	Example Factors	
I.	Intrinsic Quality	Stage of development Marketability	Significance of the invention Type of license
II.	Protection	Scope of protections Contractual commitments	Enforceability issues
III.	Market	Market size	Distinctiveness of market
IV.	Competition	Scope of protected market niche	Third party alternatives
V.	Licensee Values	Grant-backs	Manufacturing, market, capital
VI.	Finances profit	Manufacturer's margin	Costs of warranty negotiation
		Degree of design-around possible	Expected follow-on sales
VII.	Risk	Exposure to liability suits	Technical obsolescence
		Exposure to patent validity suits	
VIII.	Legal	Force majeure clauses	Favored nation clauses
		Duration of license	
IX.	Requisition	Government restrictions on royalty and other terms	Currency movement restrictions

Source: Howrey, Simon, Arnold, & White LLP, Houston, Texas; paper presented at workshop at LES U.S.A./Canada Annual Meeting, Los Angeles, California, October 1986; published in *les Nouvelles*, March 1987, p.34. Reprinted with permission from *les Nouvelles*.

tirely new infrastructures have to be developed (for instance, to create value for a hydrogen burning auto engine technology, one would also need hydrogen "gas" stations, hydrogen mechanics, etc.).

Referring again to the McGavock survey in Exhibit 5.5, although there is some variation in perspective between seller and buyer, overall both sides appear to place the highest importance on "protection," "exclusivity," and "utility/advantages," and lowest importance on "advice of expert," "convoyed sales," and "foreign versus domestic."

The selection of specific criteria, the scoring system, and weighting should be tuned for the particular industry in which the valuation is being made. Thus, there are multiple levels of expert judgment required with the Rating/Ranking method:

- Selection of benchmark agreement or category of agreements
- Selection of criteria to be used
- Scoring system (what warrants a score of "4"?)

- Weighting factors for each criterion which are used to multiply the raw scores
- Interpretation of the result (discussed later in this chapter).

This may appear daunting. Yet, with experience and expert help inside and outside the organization, this method can be very useful.

AN EXAMPLE OF APPLYING THE RATING/RANKING METHOD

Consider an instance where one is attempting to value a new laser device for optical communications. The first step is to find a "comparable," or an individual license agreement or group of agreements to which such a device generally "belongs." One would conduct reviews of one's own company files, search for published information (as discussed in Chapter 4), look for SEC filings (also Chapter 4), network with colleagues, and/or hire consultants who have developed license agreement databases or who are expert at conducting searches for finding comparable agreements. By some means, one must find at least one comparable in order to begin.

For the sake of this example, let us consider that this search has found an excellent comparable: a different technology for making a comparable laser device was found to have been licensed for $1 million upfront, and 5 percent royalty on the sale price of the entire laser device, with no rights to improvements, no grant-back rights, and no other significant financial factors. Further, let us assume that the criteria selected are as shown in Exhibit 5.7. As shown, it was determined that there were three different levels of weighting, 1, 2, or 3. For this marketplace, the experience and expert opinion was that factors 2, 4, and 5 were notably more important than 1 and 3, and significantly more so than 6. Also as shown, the scoring system used was the 1 to 5 scale. Multiplying the score times the weighting determines the rightmost column, the weighted score.

By adding all the weighted scores, the result is 47. However, the result needs to be scaled in comparison to the benchmark with all the weightings. Had all the scores been "3," the total weighted score would have been 42. In other words, based on this scale and

EXHIBIT 5.7	EXAMPLE USE OF RATING/RANKING METHOD		
	Weighting (1–3)	**Score (1–5)**	**Weighted Score**
1. Market Size	2	3	6
2. Product Margins	3	5	15
3. IP Strength	2	4	8
4. IP Breadth	3	3	9
5. Stage of Development	3	2	6
6. Market Environment	1	3	3
TOTALS	-	-	47 [1.12]

score, the subject opportunity was perceived to be only a little better than the comparable (12 percent to be exact, though this is not an exact process, corresponding to an average score of 3.36). Allowing for the uncertainty of the process, this finding would suggest that the subject opportunity should be worth only a modest amount more than the reference agreement or category.

ISSUES IN INTERPRETING VALUE FROM A RATING/RANKING SCORE

In Exhibit 5.7, the result of the rating/ranking method was essentially parity with the benchmark. What if the result had turned out to be much higher? Suppose the total score had been 4.0. What should one do with such a value?

One approach is to do a simple linear normalizing ratio: 4.0/3.0 = 1.333. Multiply each of the economic terms of the comparable agreement by the ratio 1.333 to yield a valuation. So, in this example, such an approach would yield a valuation of $1,333,333 as a market-based upfront payment, and 6.67 percent as the corresponding running royalty.

The reality of using such a ratio as a direct multiplier depends upon the reasonableness of the assumption of a linear scale. Does a score of 4.0 compared to the comparable reference of 3.0 really mean that the subject technology is four-thirds as valuable? What would a score of 1.0 mean? (Remember a score of "1" was effectively a zero; it was the lowest possible outcome). It could be argued that 1.0 scoring technology would be worth nothing, not 33 percent of the comparable. On the other hand, a 5.0 on this basis could only be worth 67 percent more than the comparable license value.

It is often helpful when translating a rating/ranking score to a value to go through each of the criteria that was scored and look at how it affects value. For example, if the total gross profitability of a deal (defined as market size multiplied by average margins summed over the commercial life of the products made from the technology) is estimated to be one-half of the comparable, and if the other criteria are scored as good or even somewhat better than the comparable, then a deal is likely to be doable with an upfront payment of approximately half as much, namely $500,000 and likewise for the royalty. This translation between score and value will be considered in detail in Chapter 7, once discounted cash flow analysis has been introduced. As we shall see, the use of the Discounted Cash Flow Method is a very powerful technique for assessing the impact of market size, margins, timing, and risk upon license value. This is another example where two valuation methods can work well in combination.

However, if one were to try to resolve this question without resorting to other methods, how would one convert a "4" into, value compared to a "3?" Like many of these matters, there is no simple answer. If there had been a benchmark license of a comparable technology that had been a "4" itself, then it would have been used and the subject technology would have shown a parity score suggesting that the value of the "4" benchmark license was an appropriate place to start. However, by definition, the best we could find in this example is the benchmark that led us to score this opportunity as a 4. What is needed is some combination of license agreements in other areas, or equivalent experience and expertise with another panel, that can begin to characterize the sensitivity to the value of such scores. With study and experience, one can begin to grasp, at least qualitatively, how the market reacts to opportunities that are "better" or "much better" in various criteria. A valuation expert panel could be convened to examine a series of published agreements using an established rating/ranking method for the purpose of sorting them out by score from low to high. Then by comparing their rating/ranking scores to their actual valuations (recall that one chooses the benchmarks because one has the data needed), it is possible to develop a correlation, however approximate, between rating/ranking score and value, at least with respect to the selected family. In the absence of other information, such correlation would be a useful place to begin to assess the value of a "4" in the subject case.

A caution is needed on the use of numerical scoring approaches for the special case of a fatal flaw. If one critical rating/ranking factor has a fatal flaw, say patent protection has been irretrievably lost and there are no other forms of protection, then one can obtain a misleading result by assigning a value of "1" to such factor. For this situation, some modification to the approach is needed. One way this can be treated is with a color-scoring system where a "red," for example, eliminates any value to the opportunity being analyzed. Another approach is to multiply the scores, rather than add them so that the effect of a "1" or a "0" can be dramatic. Yet another approach is to discard the analysis when confronted with a genuinely fatal flaw.

RATING/RANKING AS A MEANS OF CREATING CATEGORIES AND PORTFOLIO ANALYSIS

Because technology valuation is normally performed in the context of multiple opportunities, either simultaneously or sequentially available or both, it is useful to consider how rating/ranking can be used in portfolio analysis.

How might rating/ranking help us with both valuation and deciding what to do with a portfolio of opportunities? Put another way, how can this method be used for both valuation of a specific opportunity and for sorting and categorizing many opportunities presently available to us or as will become available to us over time?

We are already well familiar with one such application of rating/ranking for portfolio categorization, and that is academic performance. As a general rule, one would imagine, or like to believe, that A and B high school graduates are candidates to become college students, and C (and lower ranked) students are candidates for something else, with notable exceptions which tend to establish the rule. Similarly, A and B college graduates tend to be good candidates for graduate school, and C students not. Prospective employers make similar ranking categorization when they seek top 10 percent students, or any other range specification based upon academic performance. We even tend to label top students by "he (or she) is a top student" ("top" being a ranking outcome) or "an A student" or "just a C+ student."[11] We even resort to poker chip measures by talking about a "blue chip [i.e., highest value] student."

In commercializing IP a common difficult choice is which of many disclosures do I take action on and file patents, or take steps to preserve as trade secrets, and subsequently to commercialize by manufacture or licensing. Another common context is choosing a particular commercialization path for already selected projects (IP/technologies). This choice might be forming a startup versus licensing, or licensing non-exclusively to the industry versus exclusively to a strategic partner, or licensing for all fields of use or licensing separately for each field. In such circumstances, Rating/Ranking can be systematically used to ascribe perceived value to each alternative under consideration. Although such purposes are outside the scope of this book, the tools and approaches described above can be readily adapted for making choices. As with the qualifications given above for its use with valuation, Rating/Ranking does not lead to certifiable "right answers." Subject to the assumptions and the judgment of the raters/rankers, it leads to generally better choices. In the context here of choosing a "best" path, the ultimate realization is also dependent upon the implementation skill and industry. Returning to a baseball metaphor, Ted Williams, who is generally attributed to be one of the greatest hitters of all time and one of the greatest students of hitting, claimed the deepest secret of hitting he got early in his career from a conversation with another outstanding hitter, Rogers Hornsby (1897–1963), and it is simply this: "Get a good pitch to hit."[12] Choosing by Rating/Ranking is just this simple: grasping what a "good pitch to hit" looks like, and doing everything one can to get opportunities to hit one. Neither Hornsby nor Williams ever batted 1000 (100%), but their averages would have been a lot lower, even with their prestigious talent, had they been swinging at everything that came their way or swinging without purposeful choosing.

Some examples of non-Likkert rating/ranking approaches to opportunity selection are shown in Exhibit 5.8.

The most important idea in this busy, and somewhat fanciful chart is the divided line: opportunities to the left are worth pursuing (at some level of effort) and those to the right are not. Creating the divided line is one of the most difficult tasks in licensing. The Osterizer example is intended to illustrate the simple ten-point scale where every opportunity is given a number and that number determines its fate in terms of internal priorities and resources and ultimately valuation.

The Wong Baker scale is a six level scale for pain often used with children or developmentally disabled persons. For those of pessimistic orientation, choosing the least painful opportunities may be easier to do.

The "A-List" example occurs in many settings. Among the most well known are so-called movie "stars." Within that broad category, there is the "A List," the "B," and so forth. Denzel Washington and Halle Berry, 2002 Academy Award winners for best male and female actors, would typify A-List membership.

The Crayola example is yet another way to characterize opportunities. For those with multiple "blue" (top 5 percent) scores in the factors analyzed, can be considered "blue" (great) opportunities. And so forth with green and yellow and red.

As yet one more example that has an interesting scientific corollary, and presented for those readers with a science background, consider Exhibit 5.9.

EXHIBIT 5.8   NON-LIKKERT SCORING/
CLASSIFICATION SCHEMES

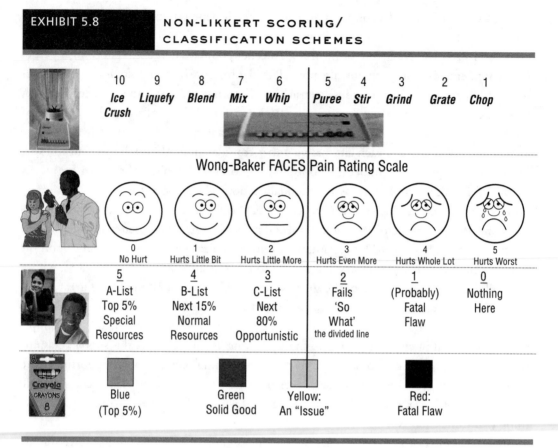

10	9	8	7	6	5	4	3	2	1
Ice Crush	*Liquefy*	*Blend*	*Mix*	*Whip*	*Puree*	*Stir*	*Grind*	*Grate*	*Chop*

Wong-Baker FACES Pain Rating Scale

0	1	2	3	4	5
No Hurt	Hurts Little Bit	Hurts Little More	Hurts Even More	Hurts Whole Lot	Hurts Worst

5	4	3	2	1	0
A-List	B-List	C-List	Fails	(Probably)	Nothing
Top 5%	Next 15%	Next	'So	Fatal	Here
Special	Normal	80%	What'	Flaw	
Resources	Resources	Opportunistic	the divided line		

Blue (Top 5%)	Green Solid Good	Yellow: An "Issue"	Red: Fatal Flaw

Source: ©2003 Razgaitis, richard@razgaitis.com.

All stars are classified into the seven categories shown by the letters at the top of the chart: O, B, A, F, G, K, M, going from hotter stars to cooler stars; our sun is a "G," on the edge of a white star and near the orange/red categories. The temperature of approximate mid-point of each class is shown in thousands of degrees Kelvin. Shown in the graph below these letters is the respective luminosity (brightness) of the star. The broad line, which is shown for our purposes as three segments, is among the most famous relationships in astronomy and is known as the H-R line (for Hertzsprung-Russell, the co-discoverers of the relationship). What it shows is that the highest temperature stars are the ones with the brilliant and amazingly high luminosity, which, by metaphor, I take as representing great commercial success. The coldest stars (relatively speaking), the K and M categories, have extremely low luminosities and are not observable unless one is not far away. The metaphor is this: based on the attributes assessed of each opportunity, this leads to an overall belief as to its "temperature" (potential value); the really high temperature ones are the ones that can have dramatically observed commercial success (luminosity). However, as the H-R diagram shows, there are some stars that, though they are hot, they do not illuminate brightly; these are the white (or, say, blue) dwarfs at the lower left. Likewise, there are some red giants as shown at the upper right. So although most stars fall on the so-called "main sequence"

| EXHIBIT 5.9 | FAMOUS STAR CLASSIFICATION SCHEME |

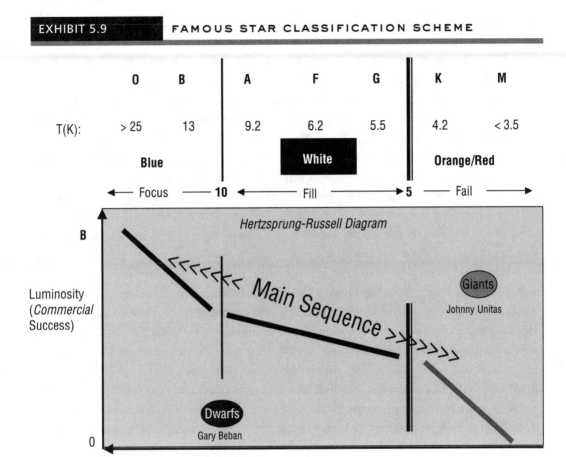

Source: ©2003 Razgaitis, richard@razgaitis.com.

(shown by the three-segmented line used here), even in astrophysics there are notable exceptions and so there will be in technology commercialization: some opportunities that looked like they would turn out phenomenally well become only white dwarfs, and others that looked like they had no potential could become red giants, but most of the time, one should follow the main sequence.

Whatever rating/ranking choosing structure is used, the key is to focus one's limited energies on the highest (and few) opportunities, be they 10's, "no hurts," A's, or blues. The next lower group can be pursued opportunistically, and beyond that is that painful, divided line. Closing this thought with two baseball anecdotes. Ted Williams, cited previously, and recently deceased (though as of this writing still frozen awaiting legal resolution in a battle among his heirs), plotted his prospective batting average for each possible pitch in his strike zone. The home plate is approximately 7 baseballs wide and Ted Williams's vertical zone was 11 baseballs high, making 77 possible pitch locations that could count for strikes. Mr. Williams computed his prospective batting average for *each* of those 77 locations from a fabulous high of 400 in the middle of the plate down to a poor 230 for the farthest "low and away" strike.[13] Even as great a hitter as Williams was, perhaps the very best, he would have had a short and uninspiring career if he swung at many of those low and away strikes; and he never hit 100 percent even on his best-located pitch.

A final baseball example of the difficult process of deciding on which players have a chance to make it at the highest level of the profession: "Major-league teams scout about 500 amateur players a year, sign 40 [ca. 10%], and hope 4 to 6 make the bigs [ca. 10% of 10% = 1%; 'bigs' is baseball slang for The Major League]. It's the hardest job to do in all of baseball except playing the game."[14] So it is in managing technology opportunities.

When assessing outcomes from a portfolio of technology investments one can expect a notable number of failures. But the word *failure* conveys a mental image that it should have been otherwise, namely that failure is non-realization of what should have been. But when investing in a portfolio of opportunities, particularly technology, it is so highly probable that such non-realization will occur that it is not appropriate to consider "such" outcomes as something less than what they should have been. From any portfolio of investments in R&D, or investments in technology marketing and licensing, it is expected that some individual opportunities will be more valuable than had been anticipated, some about as valuable as anticipated, some less, and some will become *non-performing assets* (NPA), not *failures*; for some reason it helps to be able to say: "Well, that blue-green laser invention appears to have gone NPA." Even airlines use "hull loss" as a euphemism for "crashed."

Developing and applying a rating/ranking opportunity selection tool can be strategically valuable and itself proprietary. Exhibit 5.10 shows a "Technology Evaluation Worksheet" developed at regional meeting of the Association of University Technology Managers (AUTM).[15]

PERSPECTIVES ON RATING/RANKING AS A BUSINESS METHOD

There are two common reactions to the use of rating/ranking as a valuation method. The relativism inherent to the approach leads some to conclude that the use of the method merely reflects underlying biases rather than some rational, defendable approach to value. Although to be sure, rating/ranking can be used as a construct for making "the answer" come out as one wants, such a criticism can be leveled against essentially every valuation method in that they all to some degree rely on an assumed model of an envisioned future and assumed values. So in this respect, even the use of discounted cash flow models expressed in spreadsheets, as we shall see with Method Four, is not immune from bias.

In fact, the presence of bias is actually a benefit of rating/ranking because it should become apparent and in some way characterized by virtue of the articulation of the key valuation characteristics, as we shall see later in this chapter. Rating/ranking is based upon the determination and assessment of the key assumptions that are expected to affect valuation. In this respect it is similar to the stage gate product development process, which is presently taken as the best-in-class approach to new product development. In the stage-gate process,

EXHIBIT 5.10   TECHNOLOGY EVALUATION WORKSHEET

Invention Title: _____

Inventors: _____

Docket # _____ Date: _____ Associate: _____

Commercial Potential	(+)	(0)	(–)*
• Ability to define product (i.e. what is for sale?)	—	—	—
• Perceived need	—	—	—
• Identity of end user	—	—	—
• Market size	—	—	—
• Maturity of market	—	—	—
• Competitive advantage/product differentiation	—	—	—
• Prospective licensee(s) identified	—	—	—
• Liability considerations	—	—	—
• Predisposition of industry to licensing	—	—	—

Inventor Profile			
• Cooperative/will serve as champion	—	—	—
• Industry contacts	—	—	—
• Realistic expectations	—	—	—
• Success with previous disclosures	—	—	—
• Credibility/recognition in field	—	—	—
• Research funding and direction	—	—	—
• Conflicting obligations	—	—	—

Scientific/Technical Merits			
• Invention is adequately defined in disclosure	—	—	—
• Supporting data are available	—	—	—
• Utility shown (i.e., solves a problem)	—	—	—
• Core technology versus improvement	—	—	—
• Features of invention versus limitations	—	—	—

Proprietary Position/Patentability Issues			
• Patentability of invention (new, useful, non-obvious)	—	—	—
• Breadth and strength of claims	—	—	—
• Freedom to practice (i.e., other dominant patents?)	—	—	—
• Possibility of reverse engineering	—	—	—
• Ability to detect infringement	—	—	—
• Ability to withstand litigation	—	—	—
• Known prior art exists	—	—	—

(Continued)

EXHIBIT 5.10   *(Continued)*

Stage of Development	(+)	(0)	(−)*
• Only a concept	—	—	—
• Reduced to practice/prototype available	—	—	—
• Manufacturing feasibility (facilities, equipment, etc.)	—	—	—
• Clinical data available	—	—	—
• Inventor cooperation required	—	—	—
Avenues of Commercialization			
• License to established company	—	—	—
• License to start-up company	—	—	—
• Access to venture capital	—	—	—
• Package with other technologies	—	—	—
• License to inventor	—	—	—
Financial Analysis			
• Cost of patenting	—	—	—
• Financial support from licensees	—	—	—
• Possibility of sponsored research	—	—	—
• Anticipated license/royalty income	—	—	—
Total:	—	—	—

Comments:_____

_____

_____

_____

_____

_____

_____

Recommendation: _____ Needs further research

_____ Return to Sponsor/Inventor(s)

_____ Patent application

_____ Market without patent

*Ranking Codes: (−) unfavorable   (+) favorable   (0) neutral
Source: Reprinted with permission from Stanford University, 1995.

a critical element of managing new product development is articulating the assumptions about what will be achieved in the future as specifically as possible with respect to the key aspects that will affect performance and value.

Another criticism that is waged against rating/ranking is its relativism. By definition, rating/ranking requires a comparison. So, rating/ranking cannot be done on a blank page. But this requirement of a reference point, or points, is by no means a flaw of the method; the method is intended to make as rational as possible a comparison between a subject opportunity and one or more reference points. As we shall see in this chapter, such comparison extends the value of Method One, the use of industry standards. Later, we shall see where it can be used to increase the value of other methods.

Returning to the issue of bias, rating/ranking is frequently used with expert panels where multiple perspectives can uncover defendable and weak biases, as will be discussed later.

So, my response to those who might contend that this method is so inexact and ungrounded as to be valueless, is that in general it can be done systematically and skillfully to provide valuable insight on relative value.

At the other extreme, there could be some who expect more of rating/ranking than they should. Holders of this view could become paralyzed by analysis and argument seeking a level of precision or confidence that is unreasonable (recall the Aristotelian admonition not to seek more from a method of searching for truth than it is capable of giving). Although as we shall see, rating/ranking can lead to a numerical value, the source of the value is an accretion of judgments. So, we should not be lured in calculating as many significant digits as possible in the hope that this will lead to greater valuation utility.

Between these two extremes is our Greek idea of FRO-knee-sis (phronesis = judgment). It requires phronesis to perform rating/ranking, and to determine when enough (analysis) is enough, and to apply the result to determine value.

Looking at this from another perspective, consider a world that I will call "Certainty World" (CW). CW is that environment where I can anticipate outcomes with certainty. Consider arithmetic and geometry. When we proceed with the addition of a column of numbers, we proceed with the mental framework that we are in CW: the addition will lead to a result which we *a priori* believe will be the value representing the sum of the numbers added; if it turns out not to be so, we immediately recognize the situation as a correctable mistake, and it is our aspiration and expectation that such mistakes would be, apart from inadvertent human error, unexpected. Similarly, if we are trying to determine the hypotenuse, C, of a right triangle of sides A and B, we expect it to be determined by the relationship $C^2 = A^2 + B^2$, namely the Pythagorean Formula. CW can be diagrammatically illustrated as shown in Exhibit 5.11.

The top row of this figure reflects the condition when we *a priori* believe that a specific opportunity will turn out to be favorable. In CW, what actually transpires, like the calculation of the hypotenuse, is what we expected, commercially favorable outcomes. In other

EXHIBIT 5.11   CERTAINTY WORLD

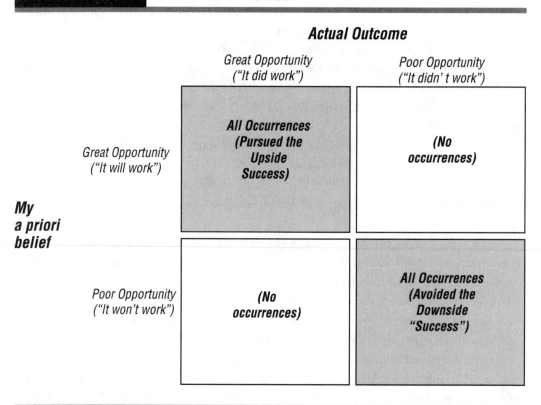

Source: ©2003 Razgaitis, richard@razgaitis.com.

CW cases, we will find those opportunities where we hold the *a priori* conviction that an unfavorable commercial outcome will occur and, in CW, so it is; so we have the favorable result of avoiding just those opportunities as shown in the bottom right hand cell. The other two cells, top right and bottom left, never occur in the crystalline certainty of CW. Rating/ranking is not like CW. Most of life is not like CW.

At the other extreme is "Uncertainty World" (UW). This is shown in Exhibit 5.12.

In UW, no matter what gymnastics we go through in an *a priori* analysis, the results turn out about half the time as we expected and about half the time the opposite of what we expected. Coin flipping is a perfect illustration of UW. If I am trying to conjure up an *a priori* perspective on how your coin flip will turn out, and you are using a trusted coin, no matter what differential equations I use, experts or mystics I consult, I will discover about half the time I will be right and the other half wrong. A more interesting illustration of UW is the stock market. Because the stock market represents, at least in theory, a perfect expert system, each stock is priced perfectly at its true present value, though almost no one seems to believe this. Here is a test I shall call the SUW, for Stock Uncertainty World, Challenge:

EXHIBIT 5.12   **UNCERTAINTY WORLD**

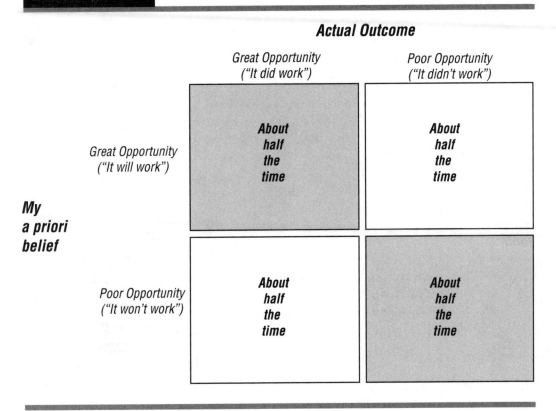

Actual Outcome

	Great Opportunity ("It did work")	Poor Opportunity ("It didn't work")
Great Opportunity ("It will work")	*About half the time*	*About half the time*
Poor Opportunity ("It won't work")	*About half the time*	*About half the time*

My a priori belief

Source: ©2003 Razgaitis, richard@razgaitis.com.

pick ten publicly traded stocks for which you hold an *a priori* belief, on whatever basis, represent a good opportunity relative to their price, meaning that you believe they will outperform on average, then pick ten more for which you hold the opposite *a priori* belief, namely that they will be poor performers, and ten more that are randomly selected. Track these three tens of stocks for say ten years and my prediction is that their financial performance will be indistinguishable as a portfolio because of stock picking on a price-weighted basis in UW.

The underlying belief in the value of rating/ranking is that it can be applied to technology valuation because such an activity is neither CW nor UW but, rather, "Probability World," PW, as shown in Exhibit 5.13.

Rating/ranking, like many human activities, is about making reasoned, systematic *a priori* judgments with the belief that such choosing is justified over time that most of the time, or at least an economically significant percentage of the time. The key attribute of PW, which drives people who love CW crazy, is that there are times when despite the most careful of analysis some of our *a priori* positive outcome choices turn out to be duds and vice versa;

EXHIBIT 5.13	PROBABILITY WORLD

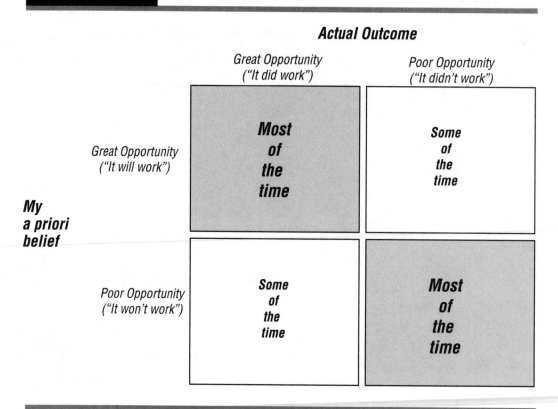

Source: ©2003 Razgaitis, richard@razgaitis.com.

CW lovers tend to say that rating/ranking "failed" in such circumstances. Actually rating/rankings does not fail when exceptions occur because it, and we, live in PW; it fails when our rating/ranking process is either so flawed that there turns out to be no economically valuable correlation between *a priori* analysis and actual outcomes or the process has been applied to a UW context, such as coin flipping or stock picking. Technology, markets, and IP protection normally reflect PW conditions.

Returning to the rating/ranking example of corporate bonds by S&P, this table shows the default rate on the payment of such bonds over the past 15 years as function of the original S&P bond rating, where those rated BBB or better are "investment grade":[16]

Original Rating	Default Rate
AAA	0.52%
AA	1.31
A	2.32
BBB	6.64
BB	19.52
B	35.76
CCC	54.38

There are several points to make in conclusion. Rating/ranking does not eliminate defaults (failures to perform as promised); in the above example every rating experienced defaults. A well done rating/ranking process of a portfolio of opportunities (a statistically meaningful number in each rating class) should show, as in the above table, the risk increased as the ranking declined. And even with "investment grade" investments (BBB), more than 1 out of 20 rated bonds goes into default; but nearly 19 out of 20 perform as promised.

CONCLUSION

The Rating/Ranking Method is the most overtly subjective of the six methods we will consider. However, as we shall see, all methods contain a certain amount of subjectivity because they deal with the unknowable future. Because the application of a rating/ranking method must be fact and content specific, it is not possible to identify a universal set of criteria that can be applied in all circumstances.

Rating/Ranking works best when it is systematized and applied by a panel of "regulars" who develop a history of making such judgments. It is greatly aided by feedback from actual values received (favorable and not). Over time, an organization can develop a very powerful set of enabling tools for expert panels to apply.

It should be recognized that this process is very similar to that followed by focus panels and other formats that companies use to test market acceptance and enthusiasm for new drugs. It is also used with proxy juries in preparation for trial before the actual jury. It is used with prospective voters on issues as well as candidate subjectives. It is even used on odors. It turns out that for many purposes, the human nose is the most appropriate instrument to assess favorable and unfavorable odors. Companies concerned about such matters work very hard to develop an expert "smell panel" that is used again and again to perform similar rating/ranking exercises. So, rather than thinking of the Rating/Ranking Method as a "smelly business," it should instead be considered as a structured way to "scent opportunity."

To gain a more elevated appreciation of the Rating/Ranking method, we can rightly claim it as an expression of an important philosophical concept which is succinctly expressed in Latin as *mutatis mutandis* (derived from the word *mutate* and means, literally: "things having been changed that need to be changed," namely, we have adjusted, or mutated, as needed to make things applicable); so if someone reacts to this method as being *ad hoc*, you can reply, "ah, contrare, *mutatis mutandis*."

The method has to commend it three important values: It directly links to market value while characterizing the differences; it is useful preparation for marketing and negotiation by causing one to sharpen thoughts about strengths and weaknesses, and it is a useful way of defending both a valuation and a process to internal stakeholders.

In the next chapter we will consider another powerful technique: the use of rules of thumb. In many respects this method will be based on a subjective judgment because the "rules" are guidelines and need to be applied case-by-case. In this respect, the Rating/Ranking Method will apply in the next chapter as well.

NOTES

1. The common four vital signs are temperature, blood pressure, breathing, and pulse, all readily quantifiable by conventional means, which is probably why attention to pain levels has come late to medical practice.
2. It could be argued, however, that Schwab is promoting its self-interest by creating such an ever-changing recommended list of stocks which will, or should, encourage stock trading and from which Schwab will make money.
3. "Enron Bets May 'Bite' Vulture Firms," *Wall Street Journal*, May 23, 2002, p. C4.
4. This can be overcome, to a degree, by multiplying each of the factor scores instead of adding them. This has the effect of splaying out the differences and rightfully punishing an opportunity that scores only a "1" on one or more factors. However, the numerical result is not easy to normalize and visualize meaning.
5. Apologies to those unfamiliar with New York City. For our purposes all one needs to know is that if money were no object, "Park Avenue" would be the answer, and for those who like the ambiance of industrial parks, they would probably actually prefer "Grand Central."
6. *Georgia-Pacific Corporation v. U.S. Plywood Corporation*, 318 F. Supp 1116 (S.D. N.Y. 1970).
7. Robert Goldscheider, "Litigation Background for Licensing," *les Nouvelles*, March 1994, pp. 20-33.
8. Stephen Degnan and Corwin Horton, "A Survey of Licensed Royalties," *les Nouvelles*, June 1977. p. 91.
9. Dan McGavok, David Haas, and Michael Patin, "Factors Affecting Royalty Rates," *les Nouvelles*, June 1992, p. 107.
10. Tom Arnold, "Factors in Pricing License," *les Nouvelles*, March 1987, pp. 19-22. Adapted from a paper presented at a workshop at LES U.S.A./Canada Annual Meeting, Los Angeles, CA, October 1986.
11. This discussion brings to mind the advice given by one retiring small college president to her replacement, a first-time president: "Be nice to your 'A' students because one day one of them will return and head your physics department; but also be nice to your 'C+' students, because one day one of them will donate ten million dollars to this college so you can have a physics department."
12. Williams, Ted, *The Science of Hitting*, quoted in *Sports Illustrated*, June 21, 2002, Scorecard.
13. Taken from a chart originally published in a series of article written by Ted Williams and John Underwood published in *Sports Illustrated* in 1968 and the basis of Williams' book, *My Turn at Bat*, 1969.
14. Allard Baird, General Manager of the Kansas City Royals Major League Baseball team, quoted in the *New Jersey Star Ledger*, March 25, 2001.
15. At the Western Regional Meeting of AUTM in August 1994 the focus was on methods for technology assessment. The chart given in Exhibit 5.10 was developed from this meeting. Kathy Ku, Director, Office of Technology Licensing, Stanford University, was the source for this document originally published in *Technology Access Report*, December 1994. Reprinted with permission from Stanford University, 1995.
16. Data is Standard & Poor's Corp, reported in *Business Week*, April 8, 2002, p.40.

Factors in Pricing License

A checklist of 100 important considerations in setting value of technology license

By Tom Arnold and Tim Headley

There is cost, risk of (i.e. hope for) profit and risk of loss involved,

- in licensing early or concept-only technology vs. matured and proven technology development;
- in scale-up from prototype or pilot plant to production model or commercial plant;
- in commercial manufacture and marketing;
- in patent or know-how litigation and commitments to enforce rights;
- in license nonexclusives and in license exclusions;
- in licensee competition with the licensor;
- in third-party competition and new leap-frogging developments;
- in guarantees of costs, quality or production rates of the licensed operation;
- in favored-nations clauses;
- in the cost and quality of the technology transfer itself;
- i.e. in everything in the license.

The total price for a technology may be structured in the forms of commitments and guarantees plus total or partial payment in equity, debt, front money, postponed sums certain, minimum royalties, running royalties, etc. But in the ultimate sense the total price is primarily a balance in the hope/risk of profit and loss by the two license parties.

Each of the following-listed considerations affecting the setting of the price on a technology, should be reviewed by both sides in the context of hope/risk, in arriving at that balance.

If reviewed before and during a negotiation, these considerations will help a party put his own value on the technology and will forewarn him of the thinking on the other side—thinking for which he should be forearmed when entering the negotiation.

Because many of the considerations are a mixture of intrinsic quality, strength of protection, market niche, financial and other factors, grouping them under headings can be misleading and beget redundancy. We feel, however, the headings and groupings help the reader a bit in spite of such inherent shortcomings.

Intrinsic Quality

1. The stage of the technology's technical and market development. Barely conceived? Reduced to practice? Commercially proven?

2. The intrinsic quality of the technology as a marketable quality, reliable technology.

3. The *perceived* utility by the buyer or user of the technology or its product.

4. The value to the licensee or its country of educating the licensee employees in the technology. Often developing nations will subsidize a technology-transfer or a licensee-research clause in a license in order to get their citizens technically trained and gainfully employed in a technology.

5. Perceived value of continuing access to technical help and ongoing research and development by the licensor and/or other licensees, including reputation of the seller for innovation and technical development.

6. The possibility of profiting from the good reputation of the licensor.

7. The need for the licensor's technology in the licensee's operations.

8. Pioneering invention or mere slight improvement?

9. Ongoing technical services by the licensor.

10. Whether the technology arose as a byproduct of other R&D. (This does not truly change the intrinsic value of the licensable technology, but it seems to have a psychological influence which, when properly advocated, does sometimes affect what a licensor will take.)

11. The type of license (patent, know-how, trademark, copyright, mix, etc.).

Protections and Threats of Protection

1. The scope and reliability of the protections of the technology, be it patent, trade secret, trademark, copyright or chip protection, etc.

2. Whether there is a favored-nations clause.

3. Precedent, the value in money and other considerations being paid by, or offered as acceptable from, other licensees, particularly if they are likely to be partly competitive.

4. Reputation of the seller for defending its invention and for technology protection.

5. Contractual commitment of either party to protect the technology, or risk of nonprotection.

6. Can the offered patents or secrets be designed around (and at what cost in time, money, legal risks or technical risks)?

7. Enforceability of capacity, volume, location, geographic restriction or field-of-use clauses or other restrictions against competition.

8. Is this license a compromise of a suit for patent infringement or misappropriation of trade secrets, etc.?

Market Considerations

1. Size of the total relevant market and licensee's likely share.

2. Distinctiveness of the market niche of the licensed subject matter; differentiation of licensed product (e.g. if 10 companies are making a soft, stretchable quality of polyethylene as commonly used for garment bags, would a licensee pay more for a license for a nonstretchable film strong enough for use as shopping and grocery bags?)

3. Demand for the product of the technology in the licensee's potential market at various potentially available prices and product quality and styles (e.g. the same invention may have a bigger market in a Cadillac than in a Volkswagen or vice versa).

4. Geographical location of licensee's manufacture or sales base.

5. The importance of a second source of supply in the market. Many is the market where two quality competitors will sell nearly three times as much as one alone.

6. Changing market trends in competition.

7. Dynamism of the market.

8. Trade cycles.

10. General state of the economy.

11. The possible extent to which the demand for the licensed product may be depressed by unemployment, union attitudes, etc. in the primary marketing area of the licensee.

Competitve Considerations

1. The nature and extent of the third-party competition with the licensee.

2. The nature and extent of licensee competition with the licensor and/or reaching markets not served by the licensor.

   a. Will the licensee serve markets the licensor cannot effectively serve or will the licensee serve competitively the licensor's own markets, etc.?

   b. Whether and to what extent gray-market goods of the licensee will compete with the licensor's products.

3. The scope of the market niche which is protected, and the cross-elasticity of the market within and without the protected niche (i.e. the degree of exclusivity of the license of the inherent market niche).

Value Brought to the Table By the Licensee

1. Capital, marketing talent, and other values brought to the table by the licensee.

2. Grant-backs of research and development by the licensee.

3. The possibility of acquiring an equity interest in the licensee.

4. Manufacturing and marketing capability of the technology recipient: Whether the licensee has greater talent and capacity effectively to make or to market the invention in the subject market, or to use the technology, than the licensor.

5. The degree of economic and industrial development, the labor and capital availability and cost, etc. in the licensee's country.

Financial Considerations

1. Manufacturer's margin. For example, a unique agricultural chemical, medical device or pharmaceutical may often be priced in response to value to the customer, independently of cost of manufacture and sale or competitive prices. Perhaps the farmer can be given a three dollars return in increased crop yield for one dollar of cost to buy the product, and the manufacturer can still sell such a chemical, if protected, at eight or eighteen times its manufacturing plus sales costs. A much higher royalty (33% of retail price in one of my cases) is justified in such a case than when the manufacturer's margin is forced to be one or two percent.*

2. Cost of the license negotiation and the technology transfer itself, and profit on that cost. Licenses for small markets often cost more to negotiate than the license is worth.

3. Potential for profits at royalties at X%, Y%, and Z%, each to the licensor and the licensee.

4. Availability and cost of capital and labor.

5. Tariffs.

6. Taxes and related considerations—capital gains vs. ordinary income. But "capital gains" as such seems destined to disappear under U.S. Tax Reform Act of 1986.

7. The amount of the licensor's expected cost savings, risk savings, and other burden savings, which follow from licensing a given market in lieu of developing it himself.

8. A comparison of the projected license net income against the potential for profit by the licensor's service of the same market.

9. Can the offered patents be designed around? Or the secrets be independently duplicated?

10. The burdens on the licensee inherent in its developing the same or competitive technology by its own effort:

   • Cost of licensee R&D.
   • Time for licensee R&D.
   • Quality of licensee R&D result.
   • Unresolved infringement, environmental and other legal risks involved in likely licensee R&D result.
   • Technological risks in likely licensee R&D result.

11. What did the technology cost the licensor to develop? This should be disregarded except insofar as it helps evaluate the cost of the licensee's competitive development of the same technology.

12. Cost and risks of enforcing patents or trade-secret rights.

13. Cost of warranty service.

14. Cost savings in avoiding litigation to enforce a patent.

---

*As with many of the considerations, manufacturer's margin is a mix of the considerations of intrinsic quality, strength of legal protection, uniqueness of market niche, competitive, financial and other considerations, so it could be classified many places.

15. Costs of obtaining and maintaining local or foreign patent and trademark protection. (Really, not relevant.)

16. Cost of training the licensee's employees; risk that the planned training may prove inadequate.

17. The seller's cost of continually upgrading the project.

18. The nature and type of obligations to be assumed by the licensee under the contract; e.g. books to be audited by the competing licensor, licensor quality control burdens, royalties to be made on sales before goods paid for, force majeure clause.

19. Policing costs: accounting audits, quality control tests/inspections.

20. The *probability* of the license being profitable for the licensee.

21. The *amount* of expected profit or saving incurred by the licensee, including any likely monopoly profit.

22. Different costs in the different countries involved,
   • of capital (either equity or debt capital),
   • of labor,
   • of raw materials.

23. Traditional royalty rates in the industry—a factor relevant more to negotiating tactics and psychology than to what is fair or economically reasonable for the subject technology. Be imaginative in developing reasons for departing from tradition. Precedent-priced technology is often wrongly-priced technology.

24. The profit plan; the traditional profit margins in the industry. But again, be imaginative in finding reasons for departure from tradition.

25. Estimated cost of adapting the technology to planned applications like 220-volt power in lieu of 110, etc.

26. The structure and time spread of payments of equity, sums certain, royalty minimums, running royalties, payments to be of large sum certain in spite of market failure by licensee, etc.

27. Accounting simplicity.

28. The potential for and availability of barter and local manufacture arrangements to cover currency control problems and the like.

29. Follow-on related sales, the profits thereon.

31. The buyer's right to duplicate the seller's technology in subsequent projects.

32. Inflation, in some countries running at 400% annually.

33. Varying international exchange rates.

34. The prices (equity, sums certain, royalties) being asked by sellers of competitive or similar technology. Recent industry licensing rates and practices for similar products and processes.

35. Anticipated sales volume of licensed products.

36. Contract administration costs, comfort, and convenience.

37. Division of projected profits, as for example 25% to 50%, which is common for the licensor, and perhaps 50% to 75%, which is common for the licensee who usually has much more at risk.

Particular Risk Considerations

1. Exposure to product liability suits.

2. The licensor's risks and costs of litigation against the licensee, in lieu of license, e.g. risk of loss of royalties from existing licensees if the patent is held invalid.

3. The risk of cost and other burdens upon either party who assumes to police patents and sue infringers.

4. Risk of having to perform uncompensated technical study or training services to verify performance guarantees and specifications.

5. The risk of loss or prior license royalties if the patent is litigated and held invalid. The potential for this risk biases toward an early litigation—which in turn puts at risk all the royalties that might have been collected, usually at lower rates, had the patent never been risked in court.

6. Licensee's credit position.

7. Licensee's willingness to be audited—perchance by a competitor.

8. The risk of a diminished quality of future R&D if the licensor does not manufacture.

9. The reliability of clauses protective against product liability law suits, particularly in connection with trademark licenses.

10. Exposure to charges of infringement of rights of others.

11. The risks of the licensee's developing the same or competitive technology by its own effort.

12. The risks of the licensee's developing the same or competitive technology by its own effort.

13. Uncertainties in cost, time, legal quality and technological quality of licensee R&D result, if independent development is selected in lieu of license.

14. Risk to the licensor and value to the licensee of the licensor's guarantee of performance in

- time of plant erection,
- quality of product,
- production capacity,
- cost of product,
- enforcement of patent and know-how protections and exclusivities,
- indemnity against infringing 3rd party patents,
- etc.

15. Apart from the guarantee (which is often an incomplete remedy for failure of performance), the licensee's perception of the true reliability of the

- time of performance,
- quality of product,
- production capacity,
- cost of product,
- enforcement of protections and exclusivities,

• indemnity against infringements of third-party rights,

• etc.

16. The potential licensee's

• cost of defending an infringement suit,

• risk of damages,

• risk that the license price if any will go sharply up after a litigation.

• risk of injunction with no license available at all.

17. The term of licensee lock-in (as by a plant design frozen in steel and concrete).

18. The risks of technological obsolescence.

19. Can the offered patents or secrets be designed around (and as aforesaid, at what cost in time, money, legal risks or technical risks)?

20. Risk of erroneous estimates of licensee employee training.

Legal Considerations

1. Force majure clauses.

2. Legal enforceability of restraints on competition.

3. Whether the patent value has been or will be enhanced by a judicial reexamination and decree. Patentees frequently should decline to license or price a license very high before the first litigation, hoping to precipitate an early litigation with respect to an infringer suffering poor litigation equities, thereby to enhance the subsequent license value of the patent(s).

4. Duration of the license, of payments of sums certain, of the royalty payments, of the obligation of confidence—all of which commonly should be different terms.

5. Favored-nations clauses.

6. The risk of, or opportunity for, suit by the licensee to invalidate patents at times and forums of his choice—he may not stay hitched.

Government Regulatory Considerations

1. Licensee's government's restrictions and law on royalty rates, royalty terms, etc.

2. Legal restrictions on currency movement.

BIBLIOGRAPHY

T. Arnold, "Basic Considerations in Licensing," in *The Law and Business of Licensing: Licensing in the 1980s* 2A-73 (1984).

Bayes, "Pricing the Technology," 1977 *Current Trends in Domestic and International Licensing* 369.

J. Bowler, "Payments for Technology," 1980 *Les Nouvelles* 241.

D. Cruver, "The International Marketplace" (September 16, 1983)

(Handout at The Society for Marketing Professional Services, Tenth Anniversary Convention, Dallas, Texas).

Evans, "Packaging and Pricing Technology," 1984 *Domestic and Foreign Technology Licensing* 77.

Evans, "Pricing the Technology," 1977 *Current Trends in Domestic and International Licensing* 361.

L. Evans, "Turning Patents and Technology Into Money" (Handout at The First Annual Licensing Law and Business Institute. February 26-March 2, 1979).

Farley, "Price Fixing and Royalty Provisions in Patent Licenses," 34 *J. Pat. Off. Soc'y* 46 (1952).

Finnegan & Mintz, "Determination of a Reasonable Royalty in Negotiating a License Agreement: Practical Pricing for Successful Technology Transfer," Vol. 1, No. 2 *Licensing Law and Business Report* 13 (1978).

R. Goldscheider, "The Art of 'Licensing Out'," 1984 *Les Nouvelles* 84.

R. Goldscheider, *Technology Management Handbook* (1984) (In particular, see Chapter 9, "Royalties and Other Sources of Income from Licensing").

S.B. Hadji, "Licensing as a Proft Center," 1985 *Les Nouvelles* 193. Interview with Donald R. Cruver, Partner, Blask, Cruver & Evans, Houston, Texas (July 17, 1986).

H. Janiszewski, "Licensee Evaluation of Payments," 1978 *Les Nouvelles* 248.

P. Leprince, "How Evaluation of Process Technology Affects Licensing," 1974 *Les Nouvelles* 182.

R. Marlow. "Matrix Approach to Pricing." 1978 *Les Nouvelles* 11.

Y. Matsunaga, "Determining Reasonable Royalty Rates," 1983 *Les Nouvelles* 216.

McKie, "Pricing and Packaging the Technology," 1984 *Domestic and Foreign Technology Licensing* 93.

G.P. Orleans, "Pricing Licensing of Technology," 1981 *Les Nouvelles* 320.

R.W. Rahn, "Determining the Royalty—What is Done and What in Fact Should Be Done." in 2 *The Law and Business of Licensing* 657 (1980). (Excellent! He lists 46 factors ranked by usage by licensing executives.)

Root & Contractor, "Negotiating Compensation in International Licensing Agreements," Vol. 22 No. 2 *Sloan Management Review* 23 (1981).

P. Scaglione, "Licensor View of Royalty Rates," 1981 *Les Nouvelles* 231.

Source: Arnold, White & Durkee, Houston, Texas: paper presented at workshop at LES U.S.A/Canada Annual Meeting, Los Angeles, CA, October 1986. Reprinted with permision from les Nouvelles.

CHAPTER 6

Method Three: Rules of Thumb to Determine Valuation

INTRODUCTION

This chapter will consider another approach for using market data to value a technology. The focus will be on identifying and using suitable market-based "rules of thumb" as a tool in value assessment (See Exhibit 6.1.).

The term "rule of thumb" has come to mean a useful guideline for decision-making based on numerous experiences. A simple example used with first-year college students is: two hours of study outside of class for each hour spent in class. There are similar such rules in every walk of life that serve as useful simplifications of complex phenomena and behaviors. They tend to be reasonable approximations, not unbendable laws, so "rules" is probably a poor though well-established term; "guidelines" may be a better word as it more accurately reflects the idea behind the method.

Rules of thumb are closely related to a more formal idea known as a *heuristic*. A dictionary definition of a heuristic is: "involving or serving as an aid to learning, discovery, or problem-solving by experimental and especially trial-and-error methods."[1] The idea of a heuristic as used here is the desire to develop a simple valuation principle that can be conveniently and quickly applied to many different types of specific situations and one that can be flexibly applied to publicly-available data. The origin of such an idea is the belief that negotiations between numerous willing buyers and sellers have some rational, underpinning principle that can be discovered and applied.

Financial rules of thumb become everyday obvious once one begins thinking about them, much like buying a particular automobile and then seeing the same model everywhere. In house rentals, the monthly rent is (typically) about 1 percent of the house's value.

EXHIBIT 6.1   **METHOD 3: RULES OF THUMB**

Source: ©2003 Razgaitis, richard@razgaitis.com.

One's personal investment percentage in equities, versus fixed income securities such as bonds, should be determined by subtracting one's age from 100.[2] One should not borrow more than 2.5 (2 to 3) times one's annual income for a house. Commissions paid to selling agents range from 5 to 10 percent (realtors historically at 6–7 percent, investment bankers at 3–7 percent). Stocks of publicly traded companies sell for price/earnings ratios of (on average) 15 (historically) to more than 20 (more recently, and with notable exceptions, and apparently declining to more historic levels). In retail businesses, a 10 to 15 percent unexpected decline in sales will eliminate 100 percent of the store's planned profits. Acquiring ownership of a company typically costs a "control" premium of 30%.[3] Consulting firms sell for one to 1.5 times annual sales, though IBM recently acquired PricewaterhouseCoopers, shortly before it was to be spun off as a company called Monday, for 0.7 of annual sales.[4] Corporate software annual maintenance agreements cost 15 to 20 percent of the upfront license fee. An employee's benefits package costs 20 to 30 percent of the employee's salary. Area managers of music concerts typically get 30 to 40 percent of T-shirt dollars. Movie studios are reported to allocate up to about 40 percent of gross receipts for the combined costs of the producers, directors, and stars. When N couples have dinner, they'll split the check 1/N, regardless of who ate or drank more (exception: if one of the couples are particularly slender and fastidious bookkeepers; then the bill will be itemized by person, including the weighted sales tax and tip, and who will not be invited the next time).

The most famous heuristic, or rule of thumb, for licensing valuation is known as the *25 Percent Rule*, or the *25 to 33 Percent Rule*. In this chapter such rule, the 25 Percent Rule, will be defined, the rationale behind the rule will be analyzed, specific examples will be considered. Situations that require values other than 25 percent also will be discussed.

FOUNDATIONS OF RULES OF THUMB

The existence and wide use of a term such as the 25 Percent Rule is itself an indication of an important fundamental idea. The undergirding idea of a valuation rule of thumb is that the total value created from a deal (license) should be equitably apportioned between the seller and buyer; the DE of *TR R A DE™* can also be thought of as *Deal Equity*.

An agreement reached by a willing seller and buyer is a value-creating event. For the moment, without considering who keeps what portion of the value created, it is important to recognize that a deal necessarily creates the expectation of a gain. Were this not so, neither the buyer nor the seller would be willing to enter the agreement. (Presently, we are not considering the case of involuntary licensing, such as in the settlement of a lawsuit, where a gain unjustly realized is being reapportioned between the parties).

How Is "Deal Equity" Determined by Rules of Thumb?

The question arises, is there a general observation, (or rule-of-thumb) that can be made about how sellers and buyers seem to reach agreement on splitting such gain? Put another way, on average what do buyers *and* sellers both agree is deal equity? Clearly cases where either the buyer or seller claims "it's all mine" can be dismissed. We are considering values for which the seller will receive more than 0 percent and less than 100 percent of the total gain resulting from a deal. Well, how about 50 percent, where the seller and buyer split the gain 50:50? Except for some unusual circumstances, this rarely happens. In order to understand why, it is useful to analyze four elements behind the idea of rule of thumb.

- Total value (or gain)
- Apportionment (split)
- Investment
- Risk

Total Value   As a result of the transaction, the buyer will be able to create a product(s) or provide a service(s) that will produce a stream of revenues and a profit. (The presumption throughout this book is that the "buyer" of the license becomes the "seller" of the products made from the technology and, so, receives all the proceeds from all the sales, a portion of which must then be re-distributed to the licensor/seller.) Generally such profits will occur over a period of many years.

Apportionment   The second element is apportionment, or in colloquial terms, the split. This is the heart of the rule of thumb as applied to valuation. For the 25 Percent Rule, the apportionment is 25 percent of the total gain to the seller, and 75 percent to the buyer. This particular value seems to be arbitrary so it leads to the logical question: on what basis is 25 percent fair? For the moment, we will only assert that enough buyers and sellers believe that this particular value is fair that it has risen in stature to a commonly used guide; a deeper discussion of this issue will take place later.

Investment   The third element is investment. The seller has made the investment in order to bring the technology to its current state. From this state, the buyer alone, or in some circumstances with participation from the seller, must make subsequent investments to create a product and business. When two parties to creating a business begin at the same point, it is common to apportion the rewards in the same manner as the total investment: Whoever does most of the work gets most of the reward—it is a principle as old as antiquity. Because in a licensing transaction the two parties by definition did not begin at the same point, there was a period when only the seller was investing and there will be a period when only the buyer is investing. In addition to the timing of the investments being different, the magnitude of the investments is almost certainly going to be different, as will be the risk undertaken in making such investments. Therefore, it should not be a surprise that a 50:50 split rarely occurs.

Risk   The aforementioned sentiment brings us to the fourth and final element: risk. Not all investments deserve the same return. Although this principle will be examined in quantitative detail in Chapter 7, the relevant point here is that higher risk investments, typically borne by the seller, deserve a greater return in proportion to the magnitude of such investment than the lower risk investments that will be borne by the buyer, all other factors being the same. There is a prevailing failure rate of all new technology projects that begins at conception. Although failure can and does occur at all phases, including after market introduction, it is generally the case that the fallout rate of new ideas is highest during the research and development stage, which normally precedes a licensing event.

Practical Application of the 25 Percent Rule

In order for any valuation rule of thumb to be of use, there has to be a way that both the buyer and seller can compute the first two elements: gain (value created) and apportionment. In general, there are two ways "gain" arises, cost savings and new profits. The cost savings type is realized because the licensed technology enables the buyer to make a product or provide a service more cheaply than without the technology. In the new profits case, the buyer will be able to charge more for a product already being made (because it has some new performance benefit as a result of enabling the licensed technology) or it will create an entirely new product or even product category. We will first consider the cost savings application.

COST SAVINGS EXAMPLE OF THE 25 PERCENT RULE

Although the cost savings situation occurs less frequently than the new profits case, it is easier to understand and apply, so it will be presented first.

Consider a seller offering to license technology that will enable the buyer to operate a factory (or some other business process) at lower cost. For simplicity, let us assume that both the seller and buyer agree that if the technology can be successfully deployed in a factory floor environment, it would save the buyer-manufacturer $100 per unit made.

Setting aside temporarily the issue of upfront payments or other forms of non-royalty compensation, what would be an equitable apportionment of this $100 savings? If the seller argues for receiving 100 percent of the $100 benefit per unit made, the buyer will rightly point out there is zero (or negative) incentive to incorporate the technology. Likewise if the buyer argues for keeping the entire savings, there is no incentive for the seller to transfer a rightful possession. What about a 50:50 split of the savings? From the point of view of the buyer, this is unlikely to appear reasonable as there are numerous costs commonly borne solely by the buyer:

- Making the technology fully design-ready for manufacturing
- Purchasing, installing, and conducting shake-down of manufacturing tooling
- Sample making and test marketing
- Creating and maintaining finished goods inventory
- Creating specialized products for specific customer requirements
- Marketing the product (advertisements, collateral materials, trade shows)
- Selling the product (salespeople, 800-numbers, processing orders)
- Shipping and distributing the product (warehousing, tracking, reordering)
- Handling returns and allowances
- Collecting payment (that's why it is called accounts *receivable*)
- Performing the accounting, paying the royalties

If two parties decided to go into business and split the profits 50:50, it would be expected that they would likewise split 50:50 all the investment, risk-exposure, and day-to-day work to make the business successful. In the above licensing example, it is perfectly legitimate to consider the seller and buyer as going into a business to produce $100/manufactured unit of gain. Thinking of the transaction in this way, are the seller and buyer making equal contributions to creating this new $100/unit? In most circumstances, the situation is that the buyer is recognized to contribute more than the seller to the $100 real-ization. (Later in this chapter, circumstances will be considered where the seller deserves 50 percent or even more, but these are not common situations.)

The 25 Percent Rule states that an equitable split of the $100 savings is $25 to the seller and $75 to buyer. Thus, in this simple example, the royalty rate would be $25 per item man-ufactured, with some terms to account for the effects of monetary inflation and perhaps changes in the savings benefit over time.

Before going further in the use of the 25 Percent Rule, it is useful to think through the rationale for the specific apportionment of 25:75. The following are six different ways of looking at why this apportionment could be perceived as fair to both the seller and buyer.

"That's The Way It Is" Perspective

One simple way to look at the 25 Percent Rule is to simply say this particular apportion-ment is what numerous sellers and buyers have agreed to, or appear to have agreed to, in many different transactions and there is nothing more to be learned by thinking about it. This perspective is exactly the how technical analysts, sometimes called "elves," look at stocks and the overall stock market: The market has spoken, deal with it.

The Going Concern Perspective

As enumerated above, there is a long list of business processes that the buyer must possess and apply in order to realize the benefit from the technology. Many if not all of the processes are business assets that the buyer has developed prior to the transaction and which will be leveraged to create value out of the technology. The 25 Percent Rule then asserts that 75 percent of the work that has to be done to go from a raw idea to the cus-tomer's cash in hand will be done by the buyer using extensive business assets it has pre-viously and independently developed, which are also necessary to commercialize the subject technology.

The Golden Rule Perspective

In a famous and lighthearted re-statement of the Golden Rule, "He who has the gold makes the rules," there is the recognition that in many transactions a willing buyer can ex-ert considerable leverage in a transaction. This is generally because there are more goods, services, and technologies seeking buyers than there are buyers seeking goods, services, and technologies. The money in the hand of the buyer is readily transformable into many dif-ferent kinds of assets and opportunities. From this perspective, the deal will have to look at-tractive or buyers will look elsewhere to make their investments. This perspective suggests that buyers will look for opportunities where they can realize *most* of the gain in their own pocket, and they will continue to scan for sellers until they can find a suitable opportunity in which this will be true. Put simply, if a buyer is considering the subject technology (Plan A) and an alternative (Plan B), and the seller of Plan A insists on a 50:50 split of the future gain, and the seller of Plan B will settle for a 25:75 split, the buyer will have no difficulty in deciding which deal to pursue (all other factors being the same).

The 3-Times Impetus Perspective

Buyers tend to include payback multiple in their decision-making. Buyers (in business) think in terms of every one of their payments resulting in a multiplied return. The more complex the circumstances, the more unclear the timing and likelihood of the return, the higher the multiple has to be in order to be worth making the deal. It has been observed in other contexts that buyers frequently need to be convinced that they will benefit at least about three times the cost of getting the benefit (although the author is not aware of any formal study of this phenomenon). However, it has been observed in diverse settings that to induce buyers to proceed with projects, they need to be convinced (if only by an introspective mental calculation) of a 3-times return on the immediate costs, assuming all goes according to plan. Applied in this context, the commitment to pay a royalty equivalent to 25 percent of the cost savings is another way of saying that the buyer is getting back 3 times what it is committing to pay on each unit being manufactured.

The One-Quarter of the Way Perspective

Yet another way of looking at the 25 Percent Rule is that it is the recognition that "technology" is only about one-quarter of the way to a product.[5] How might this be? One could assert that creating the technology of a new product or service is one big step. Making it manufacturable is a second big step. From this perspective, then manufacturing and selling the product are the third and fourth big steps. Therefore, creating the technology is one of four big steps to commercialization and, thereby, receives one quarter or 25 percent of the gain. From the perspective of a 33 Percent Rule, the argument is that the technology has already accomplished a portion of the manufacturing component. Therefore, the making and selling yet to be done are two big steps out of three, so the "technology" is actually one-third of the way.[6]

The R&D Tax Perspective

One can think of technology as the product of a research and development (R&D) organization. When a company's own R&D department creates technology, normally there is no license payment or royalty made by the manufacturing group or the respective business unit that puts the technology into commerce. However, on average there has been a payment made by all the business units for such R&D technologies. This is commonly done by "taxing" a company's sales in accordance with industry norms and the company's strategy (being the lead innovator justifies more spending; being a follower requires less R&D spending). *Business Week* used to publish an annual "R&D Scorecard." The last such version known was published June 27, 1994 and covered the year 1993. *Business Week's* "all industry composite" covers public companies with annual sales exceeding $75 million and R&D expenses of at least $1 million. The total annual R&D spending for 1993 was $83.023 billion and compared to pretax profits of $129.501 billion. Using a strict interpretation that R&D is usually for long-term benefit, it can be argued that all such R&D spending could have been added to the current-year profit increasing such profits to $212.52 billion. In other words, in aggregate all these many companies elected to spend $83 billion of their potential total profit of $212 billion on the prospect of future economic benefits. The ratio of $83 billion into $212 billion is 39 percent. So in terms of discretionary corporate investment, it appears that companies elected to follow a 39 Percent Rule. However, companies did so because there was the expectation that the current-year R&D spending was going to increase annual profits when such R&D began to be commercialized. Therefore, in forward-looking profit terms, the R&D Rule was actually less than 39 percent. Also, some of the R&D was really non-discretionary, such as designing a costly operating process to comply with environmental regulations; so it wasn't all really elective or profit-enhancing. Taking this into account would further reduce the R&D ratio. Without resorting to a research process it is possible to envision that companies choose to invest something in the range of 25 to 33 percent of their profits to acquire the fruits of their own R&D department. Put another way, if an external organization could provide all the technologies otherwise produced by a captive R&D department, management should be willing to pay such an external organization (the seller) approximately 25 to 33 percent of its profits and be in the same financial situation as when funding its own R&D operation.[7]

PERSPECTIVES ON THE 25 PERCENT RULE

Regardless of the validity or weight of the previous arguments as to why 25 percent (or 33 percent) has emerged as a commonly cited rule, the fact is that the phrase 25 Percent Rule (and the idea behind it) is widely recognized in the licensing community. It appears in almost every article about valuation. It has been cited in court cases: "As a general rule of thumb, a royalty of 25 percent of net profits is used in license negotiations."[8]

Bill Lee has written a very succinct summary of the history of the 25 Percent Rule.[9] It has a long history, with many claimed fathers. His paper summarizes values ranging from 25 to 33-1/3 percent and it is cited in an "authoritative treatise on licensing,"[10] in an article by Larry Evans,[11] and by a Japanese author, Yoshio Matsunaga,[12] and in an article by Edward P. White, who cites the value range as 25–35 percent.[13]

In a recent paper by Goldscheider, Jarosz, and Mulhern, the authors provide a history of the 25 Percent Rule going as far back as 1938 where the Sixth Circuit Court of Appeals heard expert testimony that asserted the inventor was entitled to a proportion ranging from 10 to 30 percent of net profits.[14] It is likely that examples of 25 percent profit sharing arrangements with the asset owner can be found dating back to the Middle Ages in feudal times where the serfs had to dedicate two days a week (29 percent, which is nicely midway between 25 and 33) of farming service to the feudal lord.[15]

However, it is important to note that there are other points of view. Buyers can argue, especially when dealing with very early-stage, speculative technology that 25 percent is simply too high to make business sense. Such reasoning is this: (1) the seller has not moved the technology even to the end of the R&D stage, and/or (2) the costs (and risk) of getting through "manufacturability" are huge (especially in comparison to the R&D), and/or (3) the costs (and risk) of marketing and sales are large, and/or (4) this is a low margin, competitive business that does not provide the profitability to support a 25 Percent Rule.[16] The net result of such an argument could be a proposal from the buyer that amounts to a split smaller than 25 percent.

On the other hand, sellers can, in some circumstances, argue: (1) this technology is ready to manufacture (or nearly so), and/or (2) there will be almost no incremental costs or risks in marketing and sales, and/or (3) this is or will be a very high margin (high profitability) business in an exploding market. The net result of this point of view could be a proposal that reflects a 33 percent split or even higher.

The key point here is that 25 percent, and to a lesser extent 33 percent, has emerged as a commonly-cited number that appears to be helpful in many negotiations. However, it is not a rigid "rule," despite the use of the word next to "25 percent." The specific circumstances of each valuation should be analyzed to determine whether it deserves more, the same as, or less than that given by the 25 Percent Rule. One useful tool for conducting such an analysis is the Rating/Ranking Method (discussed in Chapter 5). An effective way of using rating/ranking for this purpose is to use as a comparable agreement one which is known (or believed) to have resulted in a valuation and agreement that reflects the use of the 25 Percent Rule. Then by conducting a rating/ranking scoring process, one can develop a perspective as to whether the present valuation is wisely guided by 25 percent or by some other number.

USE OF THE 25 PERCENT RULE FOR APPORTIONING NEW PROFITS

In the preceding discussion of the 25 Percent Rule, the example used was a cost savings of $100 per unit. In most licensing situations, what is being licensed is more appropriately considered as creating new revenues rather than reduced costs. How would one apply the rule to such a situation? The 25 Percent Rule for this case can be stated as follows: The royalty in percent of net sales price should be one quarter of net sales after deduction of (1) cost of goods sold (including depreciation of relevant plant and equipment), (2) appropriately allocated general and administrative cost, (3) appropriately allocated marketing and sales cost, and (4) any other appropriate costs (but not including interest, taxes or dividends). Let us now consider each of these elements.

Net Sales Price

Why, after all the discussion of dividing profit or gain, does one base the royalty on sales? Rather, it would seem convenient for the buyer and seller to agree that the buyer will simply pay the seller a royalty of 25 percent (or 33-1/3 percent) of its pre-tax profit, as such a figure includes the deduction of the appropriate costs. This actually is a bad idea. Companies pay taxes on their pre-tax profit.[17] So there are (well) paid people at such companies to make every effort to reduce the taxable exposure. Further, companies of any reasonable size create operating groups onto which costs are allocated with wide discretion and such allocations determine profitability for such groups and individual products. Basing a royalty on a number that is calculated "low" (i.e., below the top line, namely that of sales) on the income statement is just not a good idea. For this reason, almost without exception sellers insist that the royalty be based on the easiest-to-measure number: sales revenues. The term "net sales" will be discussed in Chapter 11, but "net" in this context does not refer to net of operating costs but of certain direct costs associated with delivering the sale, such as shipping and insurance.

Appropriately Allocated Cost of Goods Sold

Cost of goods sold (commonly designated COGS) refers to the direct costs of producing the product or service. It typically includes the cost of raw materials, the direct labor of converting the materials to the product, the depreciation cost of the necessary manufacturing equipment, and so forth. A portion of all such costs are unambiguously connected to the making of the product from the technology. Some of the costs are calculations derived from many circumstances, such as two products, one based on the licensed technology and one not, being made on the same machine in the same building. How should the depreciation costs of machine and building be allocated between the licensed product and all other uses? Like all cost allocation issues, there is some degree of interpretation and opinion involved.

The number that results from subtracting COGS from net sales is called the "gross margin." It is a very important barometer of profitability and, as such, is widely reported and studied. However, the reported values for gross margin are not always to be relied upon. It is believed that some companies engage in reporting lower gross margins by finding ways to increase the calculated cost of goods sold so as to dissuade competitors from entering a business because of the attractiveness of high reported gross margins; another example of a rule of thumb is that if your gross margin is more than 50 percent you will be attacked by competitors. Also, upon seeing "juicy" gross margins a company's customers are likely to become more aggressive in their purchase negotiations. Finally shareholders, who always want to see costs minimized, are especially vigilant for overhead (SG&A, discussed below) costs, so some companies interpret certain gray-area costs as being COGS. There are also motivations to overstate gross margins as we have recently learned in the postmortem of various company collapses. Companies reporting high gross margins tend to be more attractive to investors, even for the same value of EBIT, because of a belief that the present SG&A costs can be reduced as a percentage as the company grows and after incurring certain one time expenses such as a new launch of a major new product. These uncertainties in real gross and other margins are serious complications to valuation because the gross margin is a very useful measure of the profitability of a technology or business. Sellers are at a valuation and pricing disadvantage if they are unable to make accurate estimates of the potential gross margin of a product.

Conversely, buyers who are likely to have a much better estimate of their potential gross margins are motivated to understate them.

Two points should be made here: (1) basing royalties on gross margins, rather than net sales, is fraught with accounting (and other) perils and should rarely, if ever, be done, and (2) there is some inherent uncertainty (putting it charitably) when surveying gross margins data on public companies.

Other Allocated Costs

As one goes lower on the income statement, there is increasing room for, shall we say, discretion in allocating costs. Below the gross margin line are the general overhead (sometimes known as SG&A for sales, general, and administrative) and other expenses of running a business such as paying loans to lenders of operating capital. Considering an appropriate allocation of sales cost for, say, a drug being licensed, the result can be very different if the drug will be sold through an existing sales force, or whether an entirely new sales force has to be created, or through some combination of the two. Other issues relating to general allocations will be considered in the next section, which covers specific examples.

EXAMPLES OF APPLYING THE 25 PERCENT RULE TO NEW PROFITS LICENSING

Considering first a generic example, let us take the following "data" from the marketplace and apply the 25 Percent Rule. Considering the case where the buyer has revenues of 100, and "profits" of 7.54, what would be an appropriate royalty from the application of the 25 Percent Rule? We will assume for this example that the appropriate costs have been included in the income statement leading to the reported profit figure.

The calculation of such "profit" number begins with the revenues, deducts all the direct costs (COGS, as defined above), indirect costs (SG&A), and other costs (such as interest expense and restructuring or other extraordinary costs), and finally provision for taxes (both federal and state/local). The final number, often referred to as EAT for earnings after tax, represents the net gain from operations after all bills have been paid. It is the figure to be distributed to the shareholders (the owners) or to be retained by management for reinvestment in the company, or any combination of the two.

One way to apply the 25 Percent Rule is to start with such after-tax profit and work backward. The 25 Percent Rule should be based upon a pre-tax profit which is known by a variety of terms: EBIT (Earnings Before Interest and Taxes),[18] operating profit, even "gross profit;" here we shall use EBIT. The immediate question is why the 25 Percent Rule should be applied to pre-tax profits. The answer is that the royalty is an expense of operations and like any other expense of operations it is a deductible business expense that reduces taxable profits. Further, the seller receiving such royalties will have to pay tax on such moneys (depending, of course, on the kind of entity the seller is and its particular tax situation in any year in which it receives such royalties). In addition, the value "25" (or "25 to 33") in the 25 Percent Rule has evolved because parties used such EBIT value as the basis for the calculations.

To convert from after-tax to pre-tax dollars, one divides by the factor: $1 - T$, where T is the effective tax rate of the reporting organization as a decimal value. Although the value of T depends upon specific circumstances, including the effective tax rate of the respective state/local government, for illustration purposes the factor 0.40 will be used. Thus, dividing 7.54 by 0.6 (which comes from $1 - 0.4$) results in 12.57 percent pre-tax earnings.

Using the 25 Percent Rule on these data, taking 25 percent or one quarter of the value of 12.57 percent, would result in a royalty of 3.14 percent of sales.[19] Such payment would become a revenue line to the seller and an expense line to the buyer, reducing the buyer's pre-tax profit to 9.43 percent (by simply subtracting 3.15 percent royalty from the 12.57 percent EBIT) which results (by multiplying 9.43 percent by 0.4, the assumed effective tax rate) in an after-tax profit of 5.66 percent. Thus in this example, the seller would receive 3.14 percent of sales, and the buyer's after-tax income would be reduced from 7.54 percent of sales to 5.66 percent of sales for those sales subject to the royalty.

So, on an after-tax basis, the 3.14 royalty "cost" the licensee 1.88 points of profit because such 3.14 was a deductible business expense.

Performing such a calculation on a company's total profits on which to apply the 25 Percent Rule does not normally produce an appropriate result. This is because in this example the gain has included businesses with widely varying profitability, as well as those that do not use technology to any appreciable degree and those that have a high reliance on technology. Also, the above calculation did not take into account the marginal costs (COGS and SG&A) of adding the licensed technology into the product mix of the licensee. A much more useful result is obtained when the reference profit numbers are closer to the technology being valued, as will be shown.

Applying the 25 Percent Rule to Specific Companies

In any specific valuation, one should attempt to perform the calculation on an income statement that most closely approximates the expected profitability of commercializing the subject technology. There are two general ways of doing this: *bottom's up* or *benchmark*. Bottom's up means that all the terms of the income statement are estimated from first principles. So the COGS would be calculated by considering the actual costs of raw materials required, the labor costs required, the capital equipment and the associated life of such equipment, the number of salespeople and related non-personnel costs, and so on. For new technologies it can be quite difficult to make accurate estimates of such costs. Also, in many circumstances the seller is somewhat unfamiliar with the licensed application, which is why the seller is licensing rather than going into manufacturing.

The other approach is to find benchmark data from published sources. This is very similar to what was done in Chapter 4 to find a published agreement approximating the subject valuation and then using the Rating/Ranking Method of Chapter 5 to estimate valuation differentials based on the particular situation.

Thus, the first task is very similar to what was done in performing the rating/ranking method, namely, finding a benchmark or comparable. Rather than using an all-industry composite as was done in the preceding section, it would be much better to be focused on the industry and companies that typify those that will be commercializing the subject technology. Using the *Business Week* data for the first six months of 1998 and the laser example, consider the following data for two companies, both of which make lasers and many other things:

HP (Hewlett Packard)	6.77 percent (after tax profitability)
AMP	5.72 percent

For reasons to be discussed, it is also useful to examine the industry groups to which these companies belong. These two companies belong to two different industry groups in the *Business Week* data: HP is in "Computers & Peripherals, within "Office Equipment & Computers." Computers & Peripherals composite had a net profit of 1.08 percent. Office Equipment & Computers composite was 3.66 percent.

AMP is in "Semiconductors & Other Components" within "Electrical & Electronics." Semiconductors & Other Components as a composite had 8.72 percent. Electrical & Electronics had a composite of 3.56 percent.

Just considering these two companies and the immediate and larger categories to which they belong results in net profit numbers ranging from 1.08 percent to 8.72 percent. Performing the 25 Percent Rule calculation using an effective tax rate of 45 percent[20] results in a royalty range of 0.5 percent to 4 percent, a range spanning a factor of 8, a very wide variation. If one considers just the two company's individual earnings performance, the range would be narrower: approximately 2.5 to 3.0 percent (exactly 2.6 to 3.1 percent).[21]

So what is the right answer? Unfortunately, there is no easy answer to this question. HP and AMP both make many products besides lasers. Normally companies do not report their profitability by product line. Their reported earnings are the smeared out average on all their products. It is possible then, that their laser profitability could be substantially larger or smaller than the average number used above.

Because the buyer's use of the licensed technology will extend over a period of years, it is important to look at profitability data over a period of time. There could be, and are, "down" years in individual companies and even entire industry groups. So it is prudent to consider trends in profitability over at least several years. Many companies and industries go through regular boom and bust cycles. Unless something extraordinary is happening with a comparable company or its industry, going back five years or so is probably sufficient to capture the important time variaiabilities. However, since the whole point of the 25 Percent Rule is a prospective calculation, it must be realized that it is the future profitability that is important, not the historical performance. Unfortunately, no data for the future profitability of companies or industries exists so there is a forecast issue involved. This is one good reason to use the 25 Percent Rule on the profitability of industry groups rather than a specific company: because groups are averaged by definition, the historical data will show less dramatic swings and the future will as well. The difficulty with using groups of companies is the same one encountered in the discussion of industry data and benchmarking for rating/ranking: groups include both high performers and low performers.

Should One Just Use the Average Value?

Businesses have upturns and downturns that may or may not be related to the specific technology/product area being valued. In either case one needs to consider several different time periods to appreciate the effect of year-to-year variability.

Another important factor to consider is the maturity of an individual product within the product family. Let us suppose that the profitability of the division that makes lasers and only lasers was identical to the 2.5 percent figure considered earlier. This number is a smeared out average of all the laser products being sold, including some old, low-margin products and some high-margin products.

Analyzing the Profitability of a Benchmark Category

One reasonable way to approach this issue is to decide on a percentile performance of an industry group as the benchmark: Percentile performance is defined as follows: taking the median is taking the 50th percentile performer; selecting the highest performer in the group would be taking the 100th percentile performer. Consider the laser example calculated previously. There were four groups identified: semiconductors and other components within electrical and electronics, and computers and peripherals within office equipment and computers. What would be the most relevant category to consider for the making of lasers? There are two other groups that could be considered: equipment and services within telecommunications (because lasers are widely used in telecommunications), and medical products within health care (because lasers are also used in medical diagnostics and therapy). Lasers are also used in instrumentation for manufacturing and in certain manufacturing operations (such as laser cutting) so companies that make lasers for use in these areas could be relevant as well. The point here is that one needs to identify as closely as possible the business of the technology being licensed. Is this a high-powered laser that will be used (primarily) for cutting steel? Alternatively, is it a highly reliable, high speed monomode laser that would be used in telecommunications? Is it most suited for low power level diagnostics? Or is it a revolutionary new laser method that could be used in multiple industries? The closer one can come to the most likely use, the more accurately one can identify a data set on which to apply the 25 Percent Rule.

For illustration purposes, let us assume that the laser technology being valued would be used by semiconductor manufacturers to create lasing components which would subsequently be used by various manufacturers to create a "box" that has, as one of its devices, a laser. At this stage, it is not known or predictable how the technology will be used beyond these assumptions. In this case, it would make sense to focus just on the industry group "semiconductors and other components." The 14 companies in the *Business Week* index for this category are shown in Exhibit 6.2. Clearly the average profit figure of 8.7

percent (6 months' profits of 2,621 divided by corresponding revenues of 30,052.8) used previously results from a very non-uniform group: four of the 14 companies lost money during the period, a lot of money, with losses ranging from 11 percent to more than 16 percent. At the other extreme is Intel which had an after-tax profit of more than 20 percent (2,445/11,928).

No buyer is going to license technology from a seller for the joys of losing money. So the four companies showing a loss should not be used in characterizing this industry group.[22] (One could also argue for deleting TI, which had unusually low earnings because of the same adverse business climate affecting the four companies with losses.) Of the remaining 10 companies, the average profitability was 12.2 percent, significantly higher than the 8.7 percent average. Using this figure as the basis of the 25 Percent Rule results in a calculated royalty of 5.6 percent versus the 4 percent calculated previously with all 14 companies in the equation. If one discards TI, because of its unusually poor performance, and Intel, simply because it is (at that period) the Michael Jordan of companies making devices, then the 25 Percent Rule for the remaining eight companies results in a royalty of 3.1 percent. (One question is this: Does one compute the average profitability by adding up all the profits and all the revenues or by averaging the profit percentages? The difference is that the former approach weights the calculation to the large companies, whereas the latter calculation averages the performance of the companies regardless of size. Unless there is some particular reason why the technology being valued is better utilized by larger companies, a more representative measure of company profitability is obtained by calculating the average of the profitabilities directly).

A further refinement of the calculation is derived from realizing that most companies do not embark on new business ventures with the goal of replicating their average performance. A key step in the decision-making of the buyer is how much can the subject opportunity *boost* its average performance. How might this be taken into account? One way would be to apply another kind of 25 Percent Rule: use the 75 percentile profitability (25 percent from the top) of the category. Again, referring to the 10 companies in Exhibit 6.2, the profit percentages vary from 1.2 percent to 20.5 percent and the 75th percentile profitability would be 10.5 percent. Dropping TI from the calculation would boost this to 11.0 percent and dropping both TI and Intel (because of its extraordinary performance) would decrease this to 9.5 percent. The corresponding royalties to these three possibilities as computed by the 25 Percent Rule would be 7.1 percent, 7.4 percent, and 5.2 percent, respectively.

Further Refining Benchmark Categories

In the above example, the benchmark category was obtained by selecting the most appropriate *Business Week* grouping. A better benchmark could be obtained by creating one's own grouping based upon an analysis of the subject technology. This could be done by identifying about 10 specific companies that appear to be closely related in technology, industry, and business model to the deal being valued. Start by identifying (1) companies to

EXHIBIT 6.2 SEMICONDUCTORS & OTHER COMPONENTS

| | Sales | | | | Profits | | | | Margins | | Return on Common Equity | Price-Earnings | 12 Months' |
	2nd Quarter 1998 $Mil.	Change From 1997 %	6 Months 1998 $Mil.	Change From 1997 %	2nd Quarter 1998 $Mil.	Change From 1997 %	6 Months 1996 $Mil.	Change From 1997 %	2nd Quarter 1998 %	2nd Quarter 1997 %	12 Months Ending 6-30	Ratio 7-24	Earnings Per Share
Group Composite	**14875.8**	**-5**	**30052.8**	**-3**	**1094.0**	**-54**	**2621.0**	**-49**	**7.4**	**15.1**	**15.0**	**31**	**1.74**
Advanced Micro Devices	526.5	-11	1067.4	-7	-64.6	NM	-127.3	NM	NM	1.7	8.9	NM	-1.20
AMP	1352.8	-8	2747.7	-4	54.8	-49	157.4	-25	4.1	7.3	14.0	16	1.85
Analog Devices (2)	333.1	11	663.8	12	48.4	15	92.7	14	14.5	14.0	15.9	20	1.10
Atmel	288.2	28	548.6	15	44.5	NM	-70.5	NM	NM	12.2	-19.9	NM	-1.37
AVX (9)	292.0	-7	597.0	-3	17.4	-50	47.1	-28	6.0	11.1	13.8	12	1.33
Intel	5927.0	-1	ll928.0	-4	1172.0	-29	2445.0	-33	19.8	27.6	26.5	26	3.24
Jabil Circuit (4)	309.6	25	640.3	36	17.3	19	37.4	46	5.6	5.9	30.2	17	1.94
LSI Logic	330.1	-1	655.0	2	32.0	-30	62.5	26	9.7	13.8	8.6	21	0.97
Micron Technology (4)	609.9	-37	1365.3	-26	-106.1	NM	-154.2	NM	NM	10.0	-2.6	NM	-0.36
Molex (6)	398.1	-4	807.3	1	45.8	-3	92.2	2	11.5	11.4	14.4	23	1.15
National Semiconductor (7)	510.0	-24	1160.0	-16	-212.4	NM	-190.1	NM	NM	NM	-5.3	NM	-0.62
Solectron (4)	1278.2	30	2465.0	34	49.2	18	98.0	24	3.8	4.2	17.5	31	1.58
Texas Instruments	2167.0	-15	4353.0	-10	43.0	-81	54.0	-83	2.0	8.8	0.5	NM	0.07
Thomas & Betts	553.3	-5	1054.6	-7	41.5	3	76.8	7	7.5	6.9	15.6	15	2.91

Source: Reprinted from August 17, 1998 issue of Business Week by special permission, © 1998 by The McGraw-Hill Companies, Inc.

which the technology is being marketed, (2) competitors of such companies, (3) companies of like SIC code (a government code used to index companies), (4) companies found from Internet or library searches that make products like or similar to those produceable by the technology, and (5) companies from lists such as those compiled by *Business Week* and others.

All such data should consider multiple time periods (if available). Certainly whole years should be used, because there are seasonal effects. Multiple years should be considered to average out unusual fluctuations.

The data should then be analyzed to see if some companies should be dropped from the calculation because, for example, they had losses or their business performance was suppressed because of other factors. There may also be cases where the top performers might be excluded: the "Michael Jordan" effect. Other reasons could include extraordinary performance due to a huge new marketing initiative, or the realization of profits from the sale of a division, and so forth.

The result is a list of at least two or three and ideally five or more companies. The average profitability of the group is one indicator of profitability. A better indicator is to consider the 75th percentile performer, or even higher, because all companies are buying and selling with the aspiration of increasing their profitability performance, not just holding steady (again, perhaps, the extraordinary performance by one company, such as Intel in the previous example, could warrant it being excluded).

All of this can consume a significant amount of time and requires critical thinking. For this reason it is common to employ consulting experts to develop some or all of this type of information or to provide an expert pair of eyes to review an internally-prepared analysis. The economic significance of the valuation in question has to be used to determine how much effort should be expended. If a particular opportunity cannot conceivably be worth more than, say, $100,000 in total, then it is not prudent to spend $25,000 worth of time or consulting to develop a ten-member benchmark category. On the other hand, if the opportunity could be worth $10 million, it is worth making a serious effort to develop a thorough economic framework in preparation for negotiation.

Using a Specific Company's Profitability for the 25 Percent Rule

Another approach to finding a benchmark for the 25 Percent Rule calculation is to identify one single company instead of looking at a category. In this section, two examples will be considered: Raychem and Morgan Matroc.

In Exhibit 6.3, the income statement for Raychem for the year 1991 is presented. In previous examples, the starting point was the after-tax profit numbers. A more accurate method is to look at the income statement and examine how the profitability number was reached. Recall that the definition of the 25 Percent Rule introduces the ideas of "appropriate" deductions from the sales number. In the Raychem example we see the following deductions from sales: COGS (Cost of Goods Sold) of $643 million or 52 percent of sales, SD&A (Sales, Distribution, and Administrative) of $448 million or 36 percent of sales,

EXHIBIT 6.3	EXAMPLE APPLICATIONS OF THE 25 PERCENT RULE

	Raychem Annual Report, 1991			Morgan Matroc Annual Report, 1991 European Company	
	$K	%		£M	%
Sales	1,249,512	100	"Turnover"	454.0	100
COGS*	643,357	52	Other Inc.	2.2	
Gross Margin	606,155	48		456.2	
SD&A	447,607	36	"Operating Costs"	405.0	89
R&D	140,196	11	EBIT	51.2	11
EBIT**	18,352	1			
Interest	8,090		"Investments"	(1.4)	
Restructuring	3,697		"Finance Charges"	8.7	
Other	9,674		EBT	43.9	10
EBT†	(3,109)	(0.25)			
				Now what?	2.5%?
Now What?		0.25%?			
		(0.06%)?			

*Cost of Goods Sold (all "direct" costs of making the product).
**Earnings Before Interest and Taxes.
†Earnings Before Tax.
Source: Raychem & Morgan Matroc Company Annual Reports. Reprinted with permission.

R&D of $140 million or 11 percent of sales, leaving an EBIT (Earnings Before Interest and Taxes) of just $18 million or 1.5 percent of sales.

Below the EBIT line, there are two other deductions: interest expense (paying lenders of capital employed by Raychem) and "restructuring costs" (presumably non-recurring costs associated with some significant change in business operations). Together, these two additional charges result in a net loss for the year of $3 million, shown as EBT (Earnings Before Tax).

Now, assuming that Raychem 1991 is the appropriate benchmark, how would one apply the 25 Percent Rule? Clearly, applying the 25 Percent Rule to the EBT line would result in no royalty at all, which makes no sense. However, one cannot just arbitrarily pick a favorite line on the income statement and take 25 percent of that number as the appropriate royalty calculation.

What about the appropriateness of the interest and restructuring cost deductions? Restructuring costs, like other extraordinary costs, are by their nature not reflective of normal business operations. Although they may be a legitimate deduction for tax computation purposes, it is not reasonable to deduct these costs from the profitability calculation for computing royalties. Adding such costs back increases the EBT line to $10 million or 0.8 percent of sales.

What about interest costs? Generally it is not appropriate to deduct such costs before applying the 25 Percent Rule. The idea is that a company obtains capital from lenders and equity holders in accordance with its financing strategy. However, the corporate financing strategy should not be used to affect the profitability calculation for use with the 25 Percent Rule.

Also shown in Exhibit 6.3 is shown the 1991 financial data for Morgan Matroc, a UK company. This is an example of a sparse income statement. "Turnover" corresponds to sales. "Operating costs" encompasses COGS, SG&A, and R&D. The lack of detail shows how difficult it can be to use financial reports to analyze the real operating economics.

By studying an income statement, judgments can be reached about the appropriateness of the charges against profitability in the context of the subject valuation. For example, the COGS shown is 52 percent. If estimates can be made of the COGS that will occur for the subject technology, then this figure could be adjusted upward or downward to more accurately reflect the prospective situation. Although adjustments could also be made for SD&A (more commonly termed "SG&A"), and R&D, it is more difficult to rationalize. One could argue that R&D costs are really being incurred to develop other products for the company—products which will not be subject to the royalty and so will not benefit the seller. From this perspective, R&D costs should not be deducted. On the other hand, R&D covers a bundle of activities associated with keeping products up to date with enhancements, new models, and so forth, and such costs will benefit the seller because they will tend to keep the technology up to date and commercially useful. So, generally speaking, it does make sense to allocate some R&D costs prior to using the 25 Percent Rule. Further analysis could reveal appropriate adjustments in such costs if the company is incurring extraordinarily lower- or higher-than-average costs in those business segments that make products closely related to the technology being licensed.

Likewise, adjustments in SG&A could be made because, for example, the company incurs very large sales costs on average, but will not incur them for the subject technology (or vice versa). Again, a detailed analysis should be performed to determine norms for such costs and to compare them to the specific income statement being analyzed.

If we conclude that the COGS, SG&A, and R&D are appropriate allocations, and the restructuring is not, then the bottom line EBIT is 1.5 percent of sales, so the 25 Percent Rule suggests a royalty of 0.37 percent. However, such a low value of EBIT would not be credible to an opportunity licensing situation: why would a buyer aspire to enter such a low-performing business?

Considering a pharmaceutical example, in Exhibit 6.4 is the income statement of Eli Lilly for the year 2000.

As is characteristic of pharmaceutical companies, the value of COGS (shown by Lilly as "cost of sales") is very low as a percentage because the direct cost of the chemicals and packaging in making a drug is (like perfume, beer, and boxes of Crayolas) quite low (in the latter three examples, the cost of the packaging is frequently greater than the cost of the contents). What is very costly are the selling and marketing costs, because of the high cost of

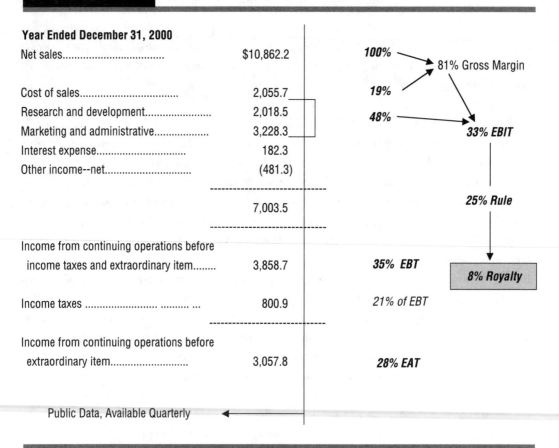

EXHIBIT 6.4   ELI LILLY INCOME STATEMENT

Year Ended December 31, 2000

Net sales..................................	$10,862.2	100% → 81% Gross Margin
Cost of sales.................................	2,055.7	19%
Research and development.......................	2,018.5	48% → 33% EBIT
Marketing and administrative..................	3,228.3	
Interest expense..............................	182.3	
Other income--net............................	(481.3)	
	7,003.5	25% Rule
Income from continuing operations before income taxes and extraordinary item........	3,858.7	35% EBT 8% Royalty
Income taxes	800.9	21% of EBT
Income from continuing operations before extraordinary item..........................	3,057.8	28% EAT

Public Data, Available Quarterly ←

Source: ©2003 Razgaitis,richard@razgaitis.com.

"detailing" drugs to doctors and hospital formularies and advertising, and because of the high cost of developing new drugs (as shown in the R&D expense of more than $2 billion or 18.6 percent of sales). If all such costs were included in calculating an EBIT for licensing purposes, and a 25 Percent Rule applied, the resulting royalty would be, as shown, approximately 8 percent. However, for such a licensing situation a number of substantial adjustments would need to be applied. As discussed elsewhere, the R&D cost in large part can be reasoned not to belong as a deduction for 25 Percent Rule calculation because it is an expense Lilly is incurring to develop other, non–royalty-bearing products; arguably, some of such costs would or could be relevant to enhancing and sustaining the licensed product and as such should be included. The marketing and sales costs are another matter requiring careful attention. It would be normal for a licensor to approach candidate licensees who are already established at selling into the markets relevant to the technology opportunity. So, for instance, if the seller has a new wonder drug for heart disease, it would make sense to target pharmaceutical companies who already have an established sales and marketing force targeted to cardiologists. This being the case, the seller can then reason that the only cost that should be deducted from the gross margin should be the *incremental* cost of marketing and selling the drug, not the apportioned total cost of the existing marketing and selling infrastructure. Eli Lilly would argue, with some justification, that *someone* has to account for the basic infrastructure; for example, one cannot expect to hop on an airplane by paying only the small incremental cost of the fuel consumed to carry your additional weight to the destination under the argument that the airplane and pilot would have been there anyway and so should not be allocated to *your* ticket.

There are additional factors that should be considered in applying the 25 Percent (or other valued) Rule. One large factor is the stage of development, or degree of completion, of the technology at the time of the license. Licensing in the pharmaceutical industry is a perfect example of this issue. There is a long and very expensive process required by companies and the FDA of the U.S. Government to obtain government approval to sell a drug to the public. In a 1994 interview with Merck's CFO published in the *Harvard Business Review*, Judy Lewent characterized in general terms that "roughly 1 in 10,000 explored chemicals become a prescription drug" and "we need to make huge investments now and may not see a profit for 10 to 15 years."[23] If the license valuation is occurring prior to even the first phase, then Lilly would rightly argue that the cost, time-to-market, and risk (FDA satisfaction as well as market risk) do not warrant 25 percent.

Another factor that can arise is commonly termed royalty "stacking." Staying with the Lilly example, suppose the seller is licensing a proprietary time-release drug delivery system for a pharmaceutical that Lilly has already licensed from a third party. When Lilly sells the drug in the marketplace, it is going to receive one revenue payment for the drug in the bottle, which includes the chemical composition and the delivery means. Accordingly, even if Lilly agreed to pay a 25 Percent Rule royalty, it could not do so to each of the two licensors. An even more compelling situation can be envisioned by considering a telecommunication switch or a computer that has perhaps dozens or hundreds of patents governing its operation. If such a manufacturer had to pay 25 Percent Rule royalties to four licensors, it would be left with no profits. Accordingly, the application of such Rule has to generally consider 25 percent, or whatever is the appropriate apportionment, in the context of all the enabling technology. This does not mean that all relevant licensors share equally (*pari passau*), because their economic contributions are very unlikely to be equal. Nor does it mean that any one needed licensor can justifiably command the full 25 percent in a standoff situation.

Another factor in income statement analyses is shown in Exhibit 6.5. These data are from a publication by Robert Morris Associates (www.rmahq.com) that gives aggregate percentages of SIC coded companies.[24] The data are available by company size, as shown in the left two columns, and by year, as shown in the right three columns. These data tend to be for smaller companies that are seeking commercial loans from banks, so for many purposes they do not accurately reflect profitability for technology-based companies. Using the data as shown is a judgment call. Does one simply take the average of all five data points and take 25 percent of this value to obtain a royalty of 1.8 percent? Generally, this is not a good idea because it completely smears out the beneficial distinction that may be a consequence of exploiting the technology.

EXHIBIT 6.5	ANOTHER EXAMPLE APPLICATION OF THE 25% RULE

Minerals and Earths, Ground or Otherwise Treated* (SIC #2395)

	11 Co's $500K–$2M Assets	17 Co's $2-10M Assets	All 1991	All 1990	All 1989
Net Sales	100.0	100.0	100.0	100.0	100.0
Gross "Profit"	29.9	21.8	25.4	33.8	32.5
"OP-Exp"	21.5	17.7	20.7	26.0	22.1
"Op Profit"	[8.4	4.1	4.7	7.8	10.4]
"Other"	1.2	0.8	1.0	1.8	1.6
"Profit Before Tax"	7.2	3.3	3.0	5.9	8.7

Now What? 1.8%? ◄——————————— Average

*Operating without a mine or quarry crushing, grinding, pulverizing, or otherwise preparing clay, ceramic, and refractory minerals; barite, and miscellaneous minerals, except fuels. Also includes crushing slag and preparing roofing granules.

Source: © 1991 by Robert Morris Associates. All rights reserved. No part of the table may be reproduced or utilized in any form or by any means, electronic or mechanical, including photocopying, recording, or by any information storage and retrieval system without permission in writing from Robert Morris Associates.

There are multiple sources of EBIT information available. Every public company must report such information quarterly (so-called 10-Q's) and annually (10-K's) to the Securities and Exchange Commission (SEC) of the U.S. government. However, as recent events have shown, these numbers that are already difficult to interpret because, for example, of the different ways companies treat extraordinary costs, have been in certain cases simply invented fraudulent values designed to mislead investors. In currently unfolding events, Worldcom is accused of falsely reducing nearly $4 billion in current expenses by treating them as capital costs for the apparent purpose of portraying a higher gross margin and net income to investors; if one were licensing to them, such a maneuver would actually work to their detriment because it would argue for a higher royalty. It is expected that over the next year or two there could be substantial restatement and correction of recently filed income statement and over time improved uniformity of how revenue and costs are interpreted and applied. In the meanwhile, it makes an accurate determination of licensing EBIT more challenging.

One source of EBIT information is Ibbotson Associates (www.ibbotson.com). An example of their data is shown in Exhibit 6.6.

Shown here are the quartile EBIT values ("operating margins") for 1995 and for the five-year period ending in 1995 for three categories of company sizes based on market capitalization. As discussed here and elsewhere, normally the licensed subject matter is intended to improve the operating performance of the licensee. In such case, the appro-

EXHIBIT 6.6 OPERATING MARGIN DATA (IBBOTSON ASSOCIATES)

Operating Margins

Average Sales	Small Cap $320M	Mid Cap $780M	Large Cap $2.9B
Latest (1995)			
90th Percentile	34.38%	38.36%	40.48%
75th Percentile	21.91%	29.17%	31.29%
Median	13.15%	17.69%	20.51%
25th Percentile	8.12%	11.18%	13.64%
10th Percentile	3.87%	7.14%	9.18%
Industry Composite	11.22%	14.69%	18.80%
Five Year Average (ending 1995)			
90th Percentile	31.35%	35.40%	39.23%
75th Percentile	20.07%	25.89%	27.64%
Median	2.33%	16.50%	18.50%
25th Percentile	7.65%	10.59%	12.91%
10th Percentile	4.29%	6.61%	8.32%
Industry Composite	11.00%	13.69%	17.35%

Source: *Ibbotson Cost of Capital Yearbook*, Ibbotson Associates, 1995. All rights reserved, used with permission.

priate EBIT is not the median of the respective industry, or even that of the licensee, but some higher value reflecting a realistic expectation of the economic advantage expected. Shown in this chart is the 75th percentile as a proxy for such higher than average performance expectation. So, using 75th percentile, and the five-year average for the small cap company, the corresponding EBIT is 20 percent and the 25 Percent Rule would then suggest a 5 percent royalty rate. However, Ibbotson bases their operating margins on revenues less costs but not less the cost of depreciation and amortization, which tends to inflate the resulting value. If the licensee has to build an expensive facility to practice the technology, the depreciation cost is a legitimate deduction from their projected revenue.

Other sources of EBIT value include Bloomberg, which publishes a wealth of current and historic information on company financials, the *Almanac of Business and Industrial Financial Ratios*[25], and Schonfeld & Associates[26], both of these latter organization publish corporate financial ratios by industry as determined from more than 4 million tax returns (schedules C and S) filed with the U.S. Internal Revenue Service (IRS). As a point of interest, for 2000, the total of such reported revenues was $15.5 trillion and EBIT $806 billion. So a 25 Percent Rule applied to such IRS EBIT would yield $201 billion, which would correspond to a royalty rate of 1.3 percent of revenues.

The "Pure Play" Analysis

All of the above examples were based upon public data for companies making multiple products. Although some useful information can be obtained by analyzing clusters of related companies, it would be better to find financial data on companies that make essentially only products similar to those being planned under the subject valuation. This is the notion of a "pure play."

The approach is similar to the previous discussion except that the search for benchmarks (comparables) is confined to just the products in question. In many cases this search yields very small companies.

Although such examples exhibit the usefulness of pertinent costs, there are other issues that require interpretation of the data. First, such companies can be rapidly growing which causes significant growth costs of funding inventory, advanced sales and marketing, and so forth. This can bias the profitability to lower values. Also, because they are small, such companies can be subcritical and are thereby incurring a higher percentage of SG&A and R&D than a larger, more established company might incur. Finally, many smaller companies are privately held and their financial data can be harder or impossible to find.

Nevertheless, even with these cautions, it is a good idea to find some examples of pure plays to supplement the analysis.

The Use of a Bottom's Up Income Statement Estimate

All of the approaches to finding EBIT values and applying the 25 Percent Rule rely on data available from existing companies. Another, more complex approach is to prepare an income statement for a hypothetical business unit (or company) created solely to make products from the subject technology. This process is sometimes referred to the making of a pro forma, that is, a forward-looking estimate of business performance.

Preparing such a pro forma would require a mature understanding of how manufacturing, marketing and sales, R&D, and overall administration of such a new business would operate. If the technology is at an early stage, there may need to be substantial assumptions about how the product would be manufactured. Often this leads to a scenario approach to financial modeling: namely, two or three different models are developed (such as optimistic, pessimistic, and most likely) based upon different manufacturing approaches and efficiencies. Similar assumptions would likely need to be made about pricing and other elements of an income statement.

Outside experts knowledgeable in the industry are frequently necessary to be able to determine usable numbers. Depending upon the potential significance of the licensing deal, such an expenditure may or may not be warranted. When such an investment is made, it can provide a very useful cross-reference to the EBIT data obtained from industry analysis.

Technology buyers typically have an important valuation advantage as they are more likely to have good estimates on the costs of making the technology into a business, although they may likewise have to use a scenario approach because of substantial uncertainties.

One potential benefit of both buyers and sellers performing this type of analysis is that it can lead to creative ways of structuring a license so that the royalty rate could be adjusted based upon future events. For example, this can happen through the use of a royalty or lump-sum "kicker." A baseline royalty (fixed payment sums) is calculated assuming a more conservative outcome for manufacturing cost (for example). Then, if it happens that the more optimistic manufacturing costs come true, because the yield is higher or the process is faster or the raw materials are cheaper, then there is an additive royalty (or payments) known as a kicker. Thus, an agreement could be structured with a 3 percent royalty on all sales providing that the product is made in accordance with Scenario A (the more conservative scenario); however, if Scenario B results, then the buyer agrees to pay a kicker royalty of an additional 2 percent (making it a 5 percent royalty) to reflect the added profitability resulting from the more favorable outcome.

Such approaches can be creative ways of dealing with highly uncertain situations by sharing risk. However, to avoid subsequent disputes it is critical that the provisions are carefully specified so that it is clear when the kicker becomes effective.

A UNIVERSAL RULE OF THUMB CHART

A graphical portrayal of the 25 Percent, and any other, Rule and the related valuation adjustments is shown in Exhibit 6.7.

Shown along the inside left scale are percentage values for the rule of thumb starting at 5 percent, in 5 percentage point increments to a maximum of 50 percent. The highlighted value for 25 percent merely illustrates the starting point concept of the 25 Percent Rule.

Shown along the top axis are the projected EBIT values of the commercial use of the subject technology starting at 10 percent, then 15, 20, 30, 40, and 50. Using the "rule" and "EBIT" values fixes a royalty rate because, by definition, the royalty rate is simply equal to the "rule" multiplied by the "EBIT." So, for example, looking at Exhibit 6.7 for the row corresponding to the 25 Percent Rule and below the column headed by the project EBIT of 20 percent we would expect that 25 percent payment to the seller of a 20 percent EBIT realized by the buyer corresponds to a royalty of 5 percent, which is just what is seen within the highlighted box. That is, a royalty of 5 percent paid by the buyer-licensee to the seller-licensor acts just as an additional cost of manufacture for the licensee of 5 percentage points, reducing its EBIT from what it would have realized, namely 20 percent, to what it now realizes, namely 15 percent; thus it has "shared" with the licensor, 25 percent of its EBIT, which is precisely what the 25 Percent Rule assumes.

All the other values within the outer frame are similarly just the product of the rule percentage on the left axis and the EBIT percentage across the top. So, for example, a 4 percent royalty would be appropriate if (1) the appropriate rule was a high 40 percent on a low projected EBIT of 10 percent, and (2) the appropriate rule was a low 10 percent on a high projected EBIT of 40 percent, and (3) for the case of a 20 percent rule with a 20 percent EBIT. Clearly there are an infinite number of combinations of rule and EBIT that would yield a 4 percent (or any other) royalty.

EXHIBIT 6.7   **UNIVERSAL RULE OF THUMB CHART**

Source: ©2003 Razgaitis, richard@razgaitis.com.

Shown along the right axis are various rules that have been cited as discussed previously in this chapter, namely: the 33 percent rule, the 15 to 35 percent range, and the 50 percent rule. Along the very left of the chart is shown how sellers and buyers would reason such rule value up or down in consideration of relative additional contributions by the seller or the buyer (the latter is sometimes referred to as the stacking issue), the stage of development, unusual risks, and any other relevant factors.

Shown along the bottom of the chart are the corresponding licensee earnings after tax (EAT) corresponding to the commercialization of the project. For illustration purposes, a nominal tax rate of 40 percent[27] has been used in making the calculation so that:

$$EAT = (1.0 - 0.4) \times EBIT = 0.6 \times EBIT$$

Noted by the EAT value of 9 percent, for a price/earnings ratio of 22, which was what the S&P 500 showed in 2001, the market value would correspond to twice the annual revenues. This is determined simply as follows:

Market Value/Annual Revenues = (P/E Ratio) × EAT = 22 × 0.09 = 2 (approximately)

Put in words, if investors are willing to pay a so-called P/E multiple of 22 for a company whose EAT was 9 percent (which would correspond to an EBIT of 12 percent for a tax rate of 40 percent), then they are valuing the company at the equivalent of twice its annual revenues.

Finally, on Exhibit 6.7 is shown a diagonal line between the upper right corner and the lower left corner. Sellers clearly hope that their licensing opportunities are toward the upper right corner, justifiably large rules of thumb, because of the specific circumstances, for opportunities that will be very high in EBIT, again because of the specific circumstances. Although buyers are generally also seeking high EBIT opportunities, their perspective of the value may well be more toward the lower left corner as they see less of a relative contribution by the seller than the seller perceives and may be more pessimistic about its EBIT potential in the face of all the costs of doing business, the power of their customers to push down prices, and the general competitive environment. Some of the pushing back and forth along this diagonal can be just the respective posturing of buyers and sellers in their negotiation assertions. However, there is, by this Rule-of-Thumb Method a basis for making a reasoned defense of the advocated, reasonable royalty rate.

OTHER PERCENT RULE VALUES

The 25 Percent Rule, though widely cited, may not be appropriate in many licensing situations. One can easily conceive of circumstances where the technology being sold is very far from commercialization, in terms of investment and time required, for an outcome that is not predicted to be commercially significant; it is unlikely that a buyer, under such conditions, would be willing to pay as much as the 25 Percent Rule computation. The Rating/Ranking Method could be used to scale the 25 Percent Rule downward.

On the other hand, there are also circumstances whereby the seller deserves and should receive more than the 25 Percent Rule (or the 25 to 33-1/3 Percent Rule). Software licensing can easily involve significant contributions by the seller in creating something more akin to a product. Further, a seller could agree to completing the software that expresses the technology (invention) complete with documentation and training manuals and activities, and provide ongoing telephone hot line support for the buyer, and perhaps, even commit to providing upgrades. Such seller-buyer relationships can approximate wholesale-retail sales: the wholesaler provides the finished product and the retailer owns and manages the storefront and the direct one-to-many retail selling environment. Under these circumstances, the appropriate split of the gain may be a 50 Percent Rule, or even more than 50 percent.

The Rating/Ranking Method used on one or more benchmark agreements, or clusters of agreements, can guide both the seller and buyer in determining a fair split of the gain. The closer the benchmark agreement is to the subject valuation, the more accurately the Rating/Ranking Method can be used. In Chapter 7, an additional tool will be presented.

OTHER VALUATION RULES OF THUMB USED (OR HAVE BEEN PROPOSED)

As in any other profession, there are used or proposed various heuristics (rules of thumb) for various situations. In this section we will consider several such examples. First, I must offer an apology and a caveat. I seek to credit the source of any specific insight or suggestion to recognize the contributions of others; for the examples given here, I simply do not recall where or how I first became aware of them and know of no written citation. The caveat is this: these rules of thumb do not have the widespread agreement that the above described 25 Percent Rule (and its variants) has. In fact, as I argue below, in some cases these "rules" many not be economically supportable. So, my inclusion here is not necessary to endorse them but to codify what has been sometimes asserted.

Upfront Fees as a Royalty Downpayment

As will be discussed in Chapter 7, a down payment of 5 to 10 percent of the total value is a widely used criterion in non–risk-averse situations, such as home or car purchases with a reasonable credit history and ability to pay. Such a value provides some assurance to a lender that the borrower has some capacity to pay in proportion to the amount borrowed (5 to 10 percent), that such down payment will be large enough in proportion to what is borrowed to dissuade a borrower from abandoning the purchase and walking away, and that in the event that the borrower does abandon the subject item the lender has some cushion that it can use to regain at least full value of what was lent. In application to licensing when The Wheelbarrow is primarily a running royalty return, it is common that the licensor will require and the licensee accept a license fee that acts as a down payment on such future stream of royalty payments in the range of 5 to 10 percent of their net present value (NPV), a concept that is developed in the next chapter. Although our context is clearly distinct from a lender-borrower situation, the underlying motivations have some similarity. The licensor reasonably wants to see some initial investment capacity by the licensee that is evidence of and in proportion to the ultimate projected royalty payment. Also, the licensor normally wants the licensee committed to the commercial success of what is licensed and, so, seeks some "skin in the game" in the form of license fee as evidence of the licensee's commitment.[28] Finally, in the event of the licensee's termination, the licensor logically wants the opportunity to recover the originally projected NPV by having received such upfront fee and possibly other fees, particularly when the licensee has terminated for reasons unrelated to the commercial merit of the opportunity.[29]

Another upfront fee rule of thumb is one year's mature royalties. In this manifestation, a forecast is made of future revenues subject to royalties and the royalty amounts year by year. Typically, there is an initial period of no revenues, followed by a ramp-up period reaching maturity where the subsequent projected growth corresponds to overall market growth at steady market share. The royalty amount of one of the early years of steady, market growth at its equilibrium market share is then used as the upfront license fee. As will be shown in the next chapter, depending upon the timing and risk of such maturity, the one year's maturity royalties could easily fall within the same range as the 5 to 10 percent rule of the preceding paragraph.

Exclusive versus Nonexclusive Royalties

As discussed earlier, when The Box is an exclusive deal, The Wheelbarrow royalties are normally higher than if The Box had been a nonexclusive deal. One rule of thumb that has been used is that market-appropriate exclusive royalties are double the non-exclusive royalties, all other things being equal (which they rarely are).

Referring back to the Deghan and Horton survey in Chapter 4, we saw data based on a survey that compared exclusive versus non-exclusive royalty rates. It is difficult to make a generalization based on these results because of the range of overlap, but it is reasonable to see how 2 to 1, exclusive to non-exclusive, could be consistent with these data.

Considering the application of the 25 Percent Rule, such 2:1 rule of thumb suggests that the margins associated with an exclusive right are double those associated with a non-exclusive right. Referring again to Exhibit 6.7 showing the general application of the 25 Percent and other Rules to various EBIT levels, one can envision pairing EBIT columns that differ by a factor of two to yield royalty calculations corresponding to exclusive and non-exclusive terms.

This interpretation of margin doubling by exclusivity is a simplification, and possibly an erroneous one, of various possible business situations. Consider the following situation. Licensee A sells its products only to Customer 1, with whom it has a special relationship. Prospective Licensee B sells its products broadly into the same market as A, to Customer 2 through 10, but none to Customer 1. Under these facts, it is possible that Licensee A's margins could be unaffected by the presence or absence of Licensee B and, accordingly, would have the same capacity to pay a royalty under a non-exclusive license.[30]

Conversely, one can conceive of a situation where Licensee A is a high end product provider (a kind of Lamborgini or, now, Maybach), and Licensee B is an aggressive competitor whose corporate strategy and culture is to be the lowest cost, low margin market share usurper (think Wal-Mart). In this circumstance, the non-exclusive license to A and B could result in a drastic reduction in (or complete elimination of) A's margin and ability to sell any product and thereby pay royalties.

So, this 2:1, exclusive: non-exclusive, "rule" is a gross simplification that presumes, according to a 25 Percent Rule model that there is a halving of margins by the presence, or potential presence of a directly competing licensed product.

Minumum Royalties

As will be discussed in more detail later in this book, minimum royalties are fixed dollar sums payable quarterly or yearly for the term of the license. They may begin in the initial year of the license or they could be deferred to some later time. As the term is generally used, such royalties are scaled in some way on the party's expectations of the running royalties, sometimes termed earned royalties to distinguish them from minimum royalties. The magnitude of such minimums is less than the expected earned royalties in the corresponding year.

The rule sometimes proposed for settling on a minimum royalty structure is that they should be 25 to 50 percent of the anticipated earned royalties for the corresponding year with the observation that licensees strongly prefer the 25 percent and licensors the 50 percent, but that establishes the range of negotiation. The idea behind the rule is that the licensor deserves some protection against a less than stalwart market introduction by the licensee and the licensee needs some cushion of less than full royalties as a fixed obligation because things may not go as smoothly as projected for reasons outside its control.

In some cases such a rule, and minimums in general, are inadequate to protect the reasonable licensor's interest. One example would be in pharmaceutical licensing. By any reasoned projection, the minimum royalties scaled on projected earned royalties could be quite distant because of the regulatory hurdles. A licensor entrusting a blockbuster opportunity to a licensee would reasonably want some form of significant milestone, progress, and/or annual payments (subjects to be discussed further in Chapter 11) to not only assure licensee due diligence but also to obtain an earlier return on its having-been-earlier investment. Such payments could be so significant, that the minimum royalty provisions could be negotiated at much lower rates than suggested by this rule.

Another factor affecting the reasonableness of this rule is the reasonableness of the projected royalties on which the 25 to 50 percent minimums rule is applied. As will be discussed in the next chapter, revenue and royalty forecasts are frequently done under multiple assumption sets, called scenarios. The parties may, in the alternative, agree to minimum royalty amounts corresponding to the projected earned royalties for a most conservative, or minimum outcome, case under the reasoning that if the licensee is not making at least this royalty payment it will not want to even retain the license, which is a reasonable way of dealing with a future uncertainty. Harmonizing these two approaches, such 25 to 50 percent minimums rule is equivalent to saying that the most-likely forecast of royalties is two to four times greater than the most conservative scenario.

Payment for Uncovering Underpayment of Royalties

License agreements are normally self-policed. Licensees compute on an agreed-upon frequency, quarterly, semi-annually, or annually, what they think they owe the licensor and submit a payment with a brief report. Most license agreements provide for audit rights of licensors of licensee's records to confirm that such payments were in accordance with the terms of the license. The cost, at least initially, of such audit is borne by the licensor. It is not uncommon, for various reasons, some pure and some not, for such audits to lead to the discovery of an underpayment by the licensor.

An audit rule for underpayments greater than 5 to 10 percent is that in the event of the discovery of such underpayment the licensee must pay for the cost of the audit in addition to making up such underpayment. The concept behind the provision is that the licensee should have the business skills and processes in place to accurately pay under the terms of the agreement since it negotiated with the licensee the agreement itself and it has access to all the business records associated with its own operations. Besides, as they say, this is not rocket science. So, when anything other than a trivial underpayment occurs, then it is only reasonable that the licensee whose fault it was then be required to pay the audit cost as a kind of tuition in learning how to manage its accounts payable function properly and reimburse the licensor for its investment and trouble. For this reason, licensors strongly favor the 5 percent figure.

Late Payment Penalties

Agreements should have very clear dates when royalty and other payments are due to the licensor. Most agreements establish a late fee penalty in the event of late payment, perhaps as part of broader provisions defining licensor termination rights.

Typically, such late fee penalties are expressed by reference to a prime rate established by some publication or source, plus points. A late payment penalty in the amount of 2 to 4 points above the defined prime rate may be used (so, for a prime rate of 4 percent, such rate applied to the magnitude of late payments would then be 6 to 8 percent).

The logic behind the provision is clearly to encourage timely payments in accordance with the agreement. From a licensor's perspective, such provision is to avoid becoming a technology provider *and* commercial bank to the licensee.[31] A licensee, particularly a financially troubled one, may resort to viewing all its accounts payables as potential sources of short-term financing, an action which could be quite adverse to the licensor's business interests even with the 2 to 4 points premium. (In such instances, the licensor may invoke its termination rights under some provision of a material breach, a subject outside the scope of this book.)

SUMMARY POINTS ON THE USE OF THE 25 PERCENT RULE

In the previously cited paper by Goldscheider, Jarosz, and Mulhern[32], the authors seek to find experimental evidence of the 25 Percent Rule. They were able to obtain *average* royalty rates in each of 15 industries using the database of RoyaltySource.com, and used such data to compare to the *average* operating profits of the corresponding 15 industries using data from Bloomberg. By ratioing the average royalty rate (say 5 percent) by the average operating profit (say 20 percent), both expressed as percentages, one can calculate, within the framework of such approach, the inferred Rule (so, using my example, 5% / 20% = 25 Percent Rule). Then the authors *averaged* each of the 15 industry inferred Rules, and found the result close to the value of 25 percent, which is a comforting finding. However, I am compelled to have the reader recall the discussion on risks of averaging at the end of Chapter 4, and the discussion of the Box and Wheelbarrow in Chapter 2, to realize that such approach is interesting but does not itself give empirical proof. Such empirical evidence would require a large sample of directly correlated (paired) royalty rates with expected (or actual) operating profit at the time of the concluded deal. Developing such an empirical understanding would be very useful to valuation practice, but, regrettably, there does not presently appear to be a practicable means for developing such empirical evidence.

Nonetheless, the existence and use of the 25 Percent Rule gives credence that at least many people hold to the view that it is a starting point for valuation in many licensing situations.

Some cautions in the use of the 25 Percent Rule:

- *The appropriate number is not always 25 percent.* The figure "25" (and 33-1/3) has emerged as a common generalization and is almost always a useful initial calculation. However, one should always consider whether more or less than 25 percent of the gain is the appropriate reward for the seller.

- *The base against which the 25 percent is applied is subject to interpretation.* The idea of the base against which 25 percent is applied is that the gain (profit) should be divided 25:75 between seller and buyer. However, determining the gain requires analysis. In the cost savings approach, it is important to determine the costs of operations without the benefit of the subject technology, and the costs with the technology or as compared to the next best alternative.

- *A pro forma income statement needs to be created.* In the case of new sales, the result of the 25 Percent Rule should be expressed in terms of a royalty against sales so as to create an auditable system. Likewise, in the case of cost savings, some conversion is necessary so that the royalty can be paid on something that is counted in an accounting sense and adjusts for inflation.

- *The 25 Percent Rule does not provide guidance on upfront payments.* The 25 Percent Rule suggests how future savings or profits should be divided between seller and buyer. In normal circumstances there is an upfront license fee paid by the buyer. In order to determine what an appropriate upfront figure should be, some additional methodology is needed. In Chapter 7 some tools for doing this will be reviewed.

Some positive aspects of the 25 Percent Rule that make it popular and worth using are as follows:

- *It gives a feeling of fairness.* Because it is based on apportioning anticipated gain, it creates a basis for considering the respective contributions of the seller and buyer.

- *It is based directly on resulting benefits.* The 25 Percent Rule is focused on the EBIT line in the income statement, which is an appropriate measure of the direct benefit of the subject license (subject to potential adjustment in allocated costs).

- *It can be the basis of an early agreement.* Parties beginning a negotiation can sometimes agree to agree that their negotiations will be governed by the 25 Percent (or some other) Rule. This can be helpful in determining mutual expectations at any early stage and in reaching closure.

CONCLUSION

Rules-of-thumb and specifically the 25 Percent Rule are widely used in valuation situations. Like the previous two methods, Industry Standards and Rating/Ranking, it requires judgement in its use and is situation specific. The next chapter continues the analysis of the income statement but with more sophistication. Estimates of the actual cash flow of a business will be made. Then, by using certain simple accounting equations, such future cash flows will be discounted to reflect their timing and risk.

NOTES

1. Merriam Webster's Collegiate Dictionary, Tenth Edition, 1994.
2. According to Charles P. Kindleberger, a retired MIT economist and author of a classic economics text: *Manias, Panics, and Crashes: A History of Financial Crises*, 1978, as quoted in the *Wall Street Journal*, July 25, 2002, p.1.
3. "Let's Talk Turkeys" [in an article about the numerous difficulties of mergers and acquisitions], *Business Week*, December 11, 2000, p. 44.
4. "IBM Boosts Consulting Service with $3.5 Billion PWC Deal," article by William M. Bulkeley and Kemba Dunham, *Wall Street Journal*, July 31, 2002.
5 Duke Leahy has made this point in talks he has given.
6. This discussion should not be confused with relative magnitude of investment made at these various stages. The timing and risk of investments need to be weighted along with magnitude.
7. This example leads to the same definitional ambiguities encountered in Chapter 1 as to what is "R&D." Because this discussion is intended to be only illustrative, one should not attempt to be precise on the appropriate fraction of R&D that corresponds to "technology" as used here.
8. *W.L. Gore and Associates v. International Medical Prosthetics*, 16 USPQ 2nd, p. 1257.
9. William Lee Jr., "Determining Reasonable Royalty," *les Nouvelles*, September 1992, p. 24.
10. "The Basics of Licensing," *The Licensing Executives Society*, 1982.
11. Larry Evans, "Turning Patents and Technology into Money," *Licensing Law and Business Report*, Clark Boardman Company, 1979.
12. Yoshio Matsunaga, "Determining Reasonable Royalty Rates, *les Nouvelles*, December 1983.
13. Edward P. White, *Licensing—A Strategy for Profits*, Licensing Executive Society, 1990.
14. Goldscheider, Robert; Jarosz, John; and Mulhern, Carla; "Use of the 25 Percent Rule in Valuing IP," *les Nouvelles*, December 2002, p. 123n13. The 1938 citation in their paper is: Horvath v. McCord Radiator and Mfg. Co. et al., 100 F.2nd 326, 355 (6th Cir. 1938).
15. An even older, and weightier, example can possibly be traced to the Old Testament of the Bible. In Egypt (ca. 1800 B.C.), Joseph on behalf of Pharaoh used the storehouses filled during the seven years of plenty to acquire the life stock and land of the people, which was then "licensed" based on 20% of seed (profit) obtained from its farming (Genesis 47:23). In the Mosaic Law (ca. 1400 B.C.), God instructed the people that the crop land, which all belonged to God, was to lie fallow (a Sabbath year) after every six harvest years and after seven Sabbaths there was to be a two-year Sabbath rest. So in 100 years, there would be 14 regular Sabbath years and two additional Sabbath years, making the profit sharing, so to speak, as 16 percent. However, in addition, there was an annual tithe of 10 percent, so the 84 harvest years yielded nine-tenths of the total harvest, or 75.6 percent to the farmer and, so to speak, 24.4 percent to God. (There were additional tithes that have been the subject of some 2,000 years of scholarly debate that we will not consider further here).
16. Although this last claim is really a circular argument, because the 25 Percent Rule is applied to profitability values.
17. An exception occurs when there are losses from previous years being carried forward, a frequent situation with startup or early-stage companies. Although even in these cases companies prefer not to consume the tax credit any faster than necessary. There can be circumstances where such companies are positioning themselves for other investors and actually want to increase their taxable profitability because it can dramatically increase the value of the company for sale. However, as a seller, it is advisable not to base the royalty on a number which can be computed in different ways for different purposes.
18. And not, as some have recently suggested, Earnings before Irregularities and Tampering.
19. This calculation assumes that the license is an all-equity company with no debt so there are no interest payments (or other excluded costs or adjustments) to account for in working an after-tax to EBIT calculation. And, yes, 7.54 was selected to make the royalty come out to 3.14.
20. Typical corporate income tax rates, which is a topic of current controversy, are in the low mid-30 to 40 percent range.
21. As noted before, to apply the 25 Percent Rule correctly, the interest expense and other non-operating or inappropriately allocated costs should be added to such pre-tax figures to produce the predicted EBIT value. Throughout this section, this adjustment will be ignored to simplify the analysis for illustration purposes.

22. The procedure followed in this example is using expert judgment to determine an appropriate benchmark population. Another approach is to include all the data available, the money losers and extraordinarily profitable cases, and deal with population as a whole. The issue boils down to this: Is the use of expert judgement improving the data set or simply biasing it? When there is reason to believe that expert judgements leads to valid insight into profitability, then there is every reason to do so. When uncertain of the situation, it may be better to be cautious and use all the available data. The decision is comparable to that faced by every interpreter of experimental data: When do I discard outliers?

23. "Scientific Management at Merck: An Interview with CFO Judy Lewent," by Nancy A. Nichols, *Harvard Business Review*, January–February 1994, p. 89.

24. Robert Morris Associates, *Annual Statement Studies*, Philadelphia PA.

25. Troy, Leo, *Almanac of Business and Industrial Financial Ratios*, 31st Annual Edition, 2000.

26. IRS Corporate Financial Ratios, Schonfeld & Associates, Inc. 15th Edition, January 2001.

27. The income tax rate for companies varies in a complex way during the history of a project because of how early losses can be carried forward, and various other tax treatment issues, which are beyond the scope of this book.

28. Depending upon the stage of development of the technology, and the scope and cost of further development required, such upfront license fee could be dwarfed by the investment that will be required just to get the technology into the marketplace. In such circumstances, the licensor may also seek evidence in addition to, or in some cases in lieu of, such upfront licensing fee.

29. When the licensee is a large company, a technology license could be one of many commercial opportunities that they then elect to pursue. Even with genuine commercial development intentions, companies change their priorities and what was once core to its strategy can now become peripheral, or their capital investment budget can be reduced by adverse business outcomes and cause them to drop certain projects that they had previously intended to commercialize. And, there are other cases, where such licensees simply plan on having a certain degree of project mortality, sometimes referred to as R&D Darwinianism (survival of the fittest) and so it can be that abandoning a license is a planned possible outcome right from the start. In still other cases, licensees have no serious intention of commercializing the technology themselves and are seeking only to make it unavailable to competitors and the marketplace for the lowest possible cost.

30. It could be argued that the presence of Licensee B will, at some point, become known to Customer 1 and lead Customer 1 to seek competitive bids from Licensees A and B for its purchase of license subject matter and thus drive down margins. Such a situation is possible but may never occur for any number of reasons (Licensee B does not wish to serve Customer 1, Licensee B does not have the manufacturing capacity to supply 1 in addition to its other sales, etc.).

31. It can be argued that the licensor is, to some extent, already providing working capital to the licensee by virtue of the delay in royalty payment, from the licensee's receipt of revenue, based on quarterly, semi-annual, or annual royalty payment schedule.

32. Goldscheider, Robert; Jarosz, John; and Mulhern, Carla; "Use of the 25 Percent Rule in Valuing IP," *les Nouvelles* (January 2003). This very recent paper is the most empirically-based example known of discerning evidence of the 25% Rule.

CHAPTER 7

Method Four: Discounted Cash Flow Method to Determine Valuation

INTRODUCTION TO DISCOUNTED CASH FLOW METHODOLOGY

Our fourth valuation method is commonly known as the Discounted Cash Flow (or just DCF) Method. It is much more mathematically based than our previous methods. However, it is founded on a very simple idea: in the business world, something is worth what it can generate in cash over its life. Suppose you were offered, say, a ten-year license to operate some sort of zero operating cost, zero investment cost street corner stand that would produce in cash $1,000 at the end of each year, just like clockwork. What would such a license be worth, or in negotiating terms, what should be the most one should be willing to pay for such a license? This is related to the more common question of what is the value of an equity investment in one share of common stock that pays out annually all its earnings as shareholder dividends, and each such share is projected to receive such a $1,000 dividend at the end of each year; the difference from our street corner license is that there is the presumption that the company issuing the stock will operate as a going concern in perpetuity, not just a fixed 10 years. The difference in the two examples amounts to the value of the infinity of years of dividends beyond the tenth year.

The use of the DCF Method for valuing a license right is closely related to its use in valuing companies and their stock. Both of these questions can be answered by the DCF method of this chapter because it enables one to create a present calculation of all the future cash flows from earnings (net of all expenses), which is commonly termed the Net Present Value (NPV). It is the "weight" of these expected future cash flows that derive from the investment that determines the most one should be willing to pay for such investment. This is the underlying idea of the public stock (equity) market and the wide-spread use, or citation, of the price-earnings (or, P-E) ratio: the current price one is willing to pay is somehow scaled in terms of the current earnings of the enterprise because there is some presumed relationship between its current and future earnings. Historically, such a P-E ratio has been about 15[1], meaning that buyers are willing to pay 15 times the current year's earnings, both numbers expressed on a per share basis. So, if the enterprise has 1 million shares outstanding, and the current earnings of the enterprise is $1 billion, then the earnings per share is just our example of $1,000. According to a valuation based on a P-E ratio of 15, a buyer would be willing to pay $15,000 for each such share. As the stock market has recently evidenced, people may be willing to pay much more than 15 times earnings when it believes that (1) earnings will grow substantially in the future, or (2) there will be someone willing to pay me more for my share in the future for whatever reason. This split in the rationality of P-E multiple derives from our uncertainty of and faith in the future, and by the froth caused by people who bid, and pay, for reasons and on bases that God only knows. There is a well-known quote attributed to Benjamin Graham, a historical giant in the field of stock valuation, that goes: "in the short run, the stock market is a voting machine, but in the long run it is a weighing machine." In Method 6, we will consider the voting machine, which corresponds to valuation by auction, but here, we will consider the weighing machine, which values opportunities by the weight of earnings that they are expected to be able to produce.

THE DCF METHOD IN THE CONTEXT OF RECENT STOCK MARKET TURBULENCE

As the twentieth century closed on 12/31/00 (not 12/31/99), there were dramatic declines in the stock market especially for so-called "technology stocks."

Because, in theory, such stock valuations were and are made based on a DCF analysis (assuming that investors are buying the right to receive a distribution of future earnings or the right to sell such right to others who are themselves buying this right), it is reasonable to ask whether the recent market tumult reflects a fundamental flaw in the DCF Method.

To illustrate the issue, let us consider such a DCF analysis performed by one analyst during the twilight of market innocence and the year 2000. Published on December 18, 2000 in *Red Herring*, one primary source of technology company information, was an analysis of fuel cell company stocks;[2] I have selected this example, instead of the multitude of "dot bomb" or telecom stories which were and are plagued by other kinds of issues, so as to have an illustration that just focuses on certain keys of a DCF analysis. Here in this article is the analysis of a Lehman Brothers analyst (Maureen Murphy) of Fuel Cell Energy (FCE), a company then (reportedly) "the leading developer of . . . stationary [fuel] cells . . . which is poised to be the first to commercialize them [stationary fuel cells] in 2001."[3] At the time of the article, FCE's stock had increased 791 percent to $73.50 in the *year* ending October 2000, which is quite a nice gain for one year in comparison, say, to T-Bills at 5 percent, particularly since the company was not expected to be profitable until 2006. However, the

Lehman analyst expressed the following view of the future: when FCE does become profitable in 2006 when its revenues (not earnings) were forecast to be $1 billion, its market value then would be five times such revenues (not earnings), making the 2006 market value of the company $5 billion. Then the Lehman analyst discounted such future value using a discount rate (which we shall designate later as "k" or "RAHR," for risk adjusted hurdle rate) of 17.5 percent to determine the October 2001 value (1 year hence) of FCE and then divided by the outstanding shares, concluded such "1 year target price" of FCE is $124, or a projected increase of 69 percent (124/73.3) over the then present share price. So, one could have chosen to buy a T-Bill and receive a guaranteed increase of 5 percent, or buy shares in FCE at higher risk (reflected by the discount rate of 17.5, together with the other assumptions) for the prospect of a one-year 69 percent return.

Another example from the same article was the Merrill Lynch view (analyst Christine Farkas) of another fuel cell company, Ballard Power Systems. Although Ballard was then continuing to report losses, Merrill Lynch projected Ballard's earnings to be $24.22 a share in the year 2013 (13 *years* hence). Then using a 25 multiple on those earnings (namely a P/E multiple of 25) to project Ballard's market value in 2013, and using a 15 percent discount rate to bring such value back to the present, Merrill Lynch projected a Ballard stock price in October 2001 (1 year hence) of $150 a share, an increase of 44 percent above its 2000 share price.[4] So, if the 17.5 percent discount (risk) rate associated with the projected 69 percent return of FCE was too risky, one could presumably opt for the 15 percent rate associated with the projected 44 rate of return and instead have bought Ballard.

A third example from this same article is an analysis by First Albany (analyst William Fogel) of Impco Technologies, another company then heavily involved in the fuel cell market. First Albany projected Impco's 2006 earnings of $2.86 a share and a P/E multiple on such 2006 earnings of 45. First Albany then discounted such projected future value using a discount rate of 20 percent to project a one year Impco target price increase of 100 percent.

These are interesting examples for several reasons. These company valuations were more akin to technology valuations because of the early stage of fuel cell technology and market development. They also show the choices that are made on discount rate (15, 17.5, and 20 percent) based on a belief about the risk of the underlying assumptions being realized. Finally, they also show that use of DCF analysis requires one to make predictions about the future, often a humbling experience. If the assumptions are not realized, because of some technology or market or other failure or difficulty, then the projected value will not be realized. The DCF Method is not "wrong" because its prediction did not come true. The Method is tied to assumptions about tomorrow, and such tomorrows are never knowable things. The keys to DCF's reasonable use is reasonable assumptions and a discount rate appropriately risk adjusted to account for the uncertainties and risks associated with such assumptions. In these above examples, there is a reason why projected one-year rates of return are so high (44, 69, and 100 percent): the attendant risk is high. You want risk-free? Try 10-year U.S. Treasury notes and you get 5 percent; it's as close to risk-free as is humanly available, or so it seems. You want the potential of greater return? You take risk. DCF is a method, together with a selection criteria for an appropriate risk adjusted hurdle (discount) rates as a tool with such method, that enables us to be as wise as we possibly can in properly aligning present value with projected future value and the risk associated with it being realized.

This does not mean that any math correct calculation is equally valid. Consider the following example from a *Business Week* story also from the year 2000.[5] In this article are the calculations of the CEO of MicroStrategy, Inc., Michael J. Saylor, justifying a $30 billion valuation for his company. Here is what he is reported to have said: (1) In 2010, U.S. consumer spending will be $11 trillion annually. (2) Wireless e-commerce will be the means by which 33 percent of such $11 trillion spending occurs. (3) MicroStrategy Inc., via its website strategy.com, will be the means by which 25 percent of such 33 percent of such $11 trillion annual spending (in 2010) will occur. (4) MicroStrategy will be paid a 1.1 percent sales commission on all such sales. (Now, a brief intermission for some math: the above four assumptions yield 2010 MicroStrategy revenues of $10 billion). (5) The market will value MicroStrategy in 2010 at a multiple of three times annual sales (3 times $10 billion = $30 billion, QED). Therefore, MicroStrategy should be worth $30 billion, though it is not clear why the market should put such value on MicroStrategy in 2000, 10 years before this is even supposed to come true. Selecting a risk adjusted discount rate appropriate to this set of five assumptions would be a challenge.

One more example also from the year 2000 published in *The Industry Standard*, itself now bankrupt.[6] The article summarizes the assessment of the CEO of InfoSpace, Naveen Jain, of why InfoSpace is on its way to a $1 trillion market cap. InfoSpace's business model was to garner a "tax" on all e-commerce transactions that it enabled; according to Jain: "We have 2,500 paying partners. Every time you go to NBCi looking for a plumber [I wonder how many plumbers have been so hired?] we get paid. Every time you go to Go Network [since shut down] looking for a phone number, we get paid. We are probably the only partner to both Disney and Playboy at the same time." At the time of these remarks, InfoSpace was not profitable, but was trading at 659 times trailing annual *revenues*.

A last concluding example comes from a 2002 *Business Week* interview with Scott McNealy, the CEO of Sun Microsystems looking back at the market's valuation of Sun in this same year 2000.[7] He was asked: "Sun's stock hit a high of $64. Did you think what tech stocks were doing two years ago was too good to be true?" Mr. McNealy, in an amazingly candid answer, replied: ". . . . two years ago [2000] we [Sun] were selling at 10 times revenues when we were at $64. At 10 times revenues, to give you a 10-year payback, I have to pay you 100% of revenues for 10 straight years in dividends. That assumes I can get that by my shareholders. That assumes I have zero cost of goods sold, which is very hard for a computer company. That assumes zero expenses, which is really hard with 39,000 employees. That assumes I pay no taxes, which is very hard. And that assumes you pay no taxes on your dividends, which is kind of illegal. And that assumes with zero R&D for the next 10 years, I can maintain the current revenue run rate. Now, having done that, would any of you like to buy my stock at $64? Do you realize how ridiculous those basic assumptions are? You don't need any footnotes. What were you thinking?"

The DCF Method, and the associated RAHR tool, is only as good as the thinking that goes with it.

This chapter has two objectives: (1) to aid in the development of financial tools and perspectives that can be used in support of all valuation approaches, and (2) to apply such tools to the fourth valuation approach, "Discounted Cash Flow" (see Exhibit 7.1).

Underlying all of the discussion in this chapter is the issue of computing the value of money that becomes available at various times and with varying degrees of certainty. Considering one's own personal finances, when transferring control of $1,000 to an institution for five years one must consider the relative value of the $1,000 today and what will be returned, or paid back, five years hence. As a result of inflation, which appears to be a permanent fixture, it would not be reasonable to expect to get back the same $1,000 investment in five years, because by then $1,000 will be less valuable than it is today, even though the face value of the currency is unchanged. Therefore, an invester must seek a return that is large enough to cover this diminished value caused by inflation.[8]

In addition to covering the cost of inflation, there are a variety of investment options. Suppose a person could pay down a home mortgage with an interest rate on the unpaid balance of 7 percent. With such an option, one would ordinarily conclude that this hypothetical

EXHIBIT 7.1   METHOD 4: DISCOUNTED CASH FLOW (NPV)

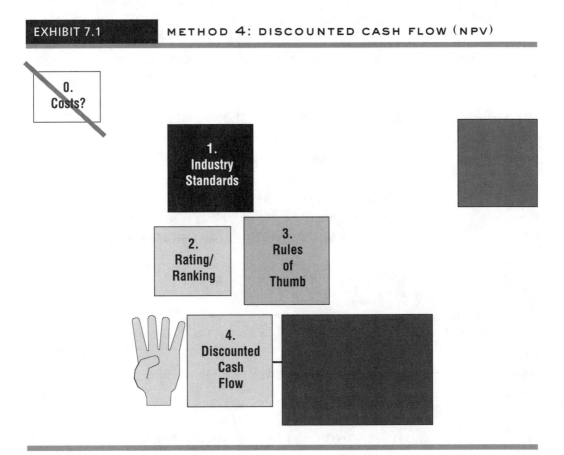

Source: ©2003 Razgaitis, richard@razgaitis.com.

five-year investment should return at least 7 percent compounded; the basis of this perspective is simply that one has an alternative investment yielding such return.

In addition to inflation and returns on alternative investments available, one must consider the risk that either the increase above $1,000 might not occur, or that some or all of the $1,000 itself might be lost.

This kind of assessment is what buyers go through when valuing an investment opportunity in commercializing a technology. In this chapter some very simple but powerful equations will be developed that will aid such assessments. They will be used in conjunction with discounting future cash flows for valuation purposes and in combination with the 25 Percent Rule discussed in Chapter 6.

BASIC FINANCIAL CONCEPTS

The key concept required to use the Discounted Cash Flow Method is the means of converting future cash payments into their present equivalent, taking into account the time such payments would be made and the risk associated with their being paid. A very simple derivation provides useful insight.

If one lends an entity "A" dollars (such as the $1,000 example), and expects a "k" rate of return (such 7 percent), then after one year, one expects to receive the following:

Money received a year from now = $A + k \times A$, where A is the amount given at the beginning of such year, and k the annualized rate of expected return. Using the $1,000 and 7 percent example:

Money one year from now = $1,000 + 0.07 \times \$1,000 = \$1,000 + \$70 = \$1,070.$

Calculating the money due two years from now utilizes the following formula:

Money two years from now = Money one year from now
+ the additional benefit of another year
= $\$1070 + 0.07 \times \$1070 = \$1070 + \$74.49 = \$1144.90.$

Expressing this equation in more general terms, we have:

Money two years from now = $(A + k \times A) + (A + k \times A) \times k =$
$A \times (1 + k) + A \times (1 + k) \times k = A \times (1 + k) \times (1 + k) = A \times (1 + k)^2,$

where A is $1,000 and k is 7 percent (or 0.07 when used in equation form). So, using this formula,

Money two years from now =
$\$1,000 \times (1 + 0.07)^2 = \$1,000 \times 1.1449 = \$1144.90,$

which is the same value obtained by doing the calculation one year at a time.

Now, extending the formula to three years adds another factor of $(1 + k)$ or, in this example $(1 + 0.07)$, so the formula reads:

$$\text{Money three years from now} = A \times (1 + k)^3$$
$$= \$1000 \times (1.07)^3 = \$1000 \times 1.22504 = \$1225.04.$$

The generalized formula then can be expressed as follows:

$B = A \times (1 + k)^n$, where A is the money invested at the beginning of the analysis period, B is the money received after "n" years, and k is the expected annual rate of return (or return on investment, in any case always expressed as a decimal). In finance textbooks, "A" is usually presented as "PV" for "present value" (i.e., money now), and "B" as "FV" for "future value" (i.e., money returned after "n" years)[9].

As used in valuation, this same equation is re-expressed as follows:

$$A = B/(1 + k)^n\text{, which is obtained by solving for "A."}$$

When used in this fashion, "B" is the money at the end of year "n" and "A" is the present value of that money for the chosen value of "k." Normally the term used for "A" is "DCF" for Discounted Cash Flow, "B" is simply the value of the money in year "n," and "k" is the risk factor or, more formally, the "risk-adjusted hurdle rate." The reason these terms are used is as follows. The normal valuation situation is that the buyer agrees to pay to the seller a prescribed amount of money at a defined date. So, rather than calculating the future value of the present $1,000, one is calculating the present value of a future payment of $1,000, as follows:

$$A \text{ or } DCF = B/(1 + k)^n = \$1,000/(1 + 0.07)^5 = \$1,000/1.40255 = \$712.99.$$

Expressed in this way, the idea is simply that in today's dollars, the value of receiving $1,000 five years from now is $712.99 if the "k" value is 7 percent. The reason the $712.99 is called the "Discounted Cash Flow" is that one has reduced or discounted the value of the future $1,000 payment by virtue of the fact it will not be received for five years and the belief that there was a 7 percent loss of value in money each year either through inflation alone, or (more commonly) through a combination of inflation and opportunity cost, given alternatives for investing the money.

With this single simple equation, $DCF = B/(1 + k)^n$, and a computer spreadsheet software program such as Excel, one can perform some very complex financial models as will be shown in the next sections. However, before doing so an in-depth understanding of "k," more generally known as the Risk-Adjusted Hurdle Rate (RAHR) is needed.

CONSIDERATION OF THE RISK-ADJUSTED HURDLE RATE (K OR RAHR)

In the opening paragraphs of this chapter, "k" was considered from three points of view: (1) inflation, (2) alternative available rates of return, and (3) risk of return. In the following subsections further consideration of these points of view will be developed.

Inflation and "k"

Essentially with no exceptions, money in all countries of the world for the last 100 years has suffered from inflation and is expected to continue to do so indefinitely. Inflation simply means that it will take more dollars to buy in the future what less dollars could buy today. Presently in the United States, inflation is running in the range of 2 to 3 percent. What that means with the DCF equation is as follows (using the 3 percent value):

A or DCF = $B/(1.03)^n$, where B is the value of money to be received at the end of "n" years, and (A or) DCF is then the resulting equivalent value of such money in today's dollars. So, considering the example of $1,000 to be received five years hence we have:

$$DCF = \$1,000/1.03^5 = \$1,000/1.15927 = \$862.61.$$

To put this in words, providing inflation continues at 3 percent, which is by no means certain, then someone promising to pay $1,000 five years from now is really promising $862.61 in terms of value in today's dollars. (Note: we can perform the calculation the other way around and say that $1,000 today is equivalent to $1159.27 five years from now using exactly the same factor of 1.15927 obtained from calculating 1.03^5). Another term used to describe the $862.61 is "Present Value " or "Net Present Value" (or NPV) which means that today, the perceived value of $1000 five years from now is exactly $862.61. When considering a *single* future payment, DCF and NPV are exactly the same concept and equation. When dealing with multiple future payments, then the *sum* of *all* the DCF values is exactly the NPV of the opportunity; examples later in this chapter will make this clear.

A key idea with DCF and NPV is the following. If a company is considering conveying a right, such as a license, in return for a promised future payment, and the appropriate RAHR (i.e., k-value) is used, then it is assumed that the promise to pay "B" in year "n" or the present payment of the DCF are exactly equivalent. In the previous example, if it is perceived that the 3 percent value of k is appropriate, then there should be no preference between $1000 five years hence or $862.61 now. The test of this perception is a buyer offering the seller the choice of these two situations and being indifferent to the election made.

The DCF concept is crucial in licensing transactions. The buyer will experience the commercial benefit of the license over a period of years and must characterize that benefit in terms of a willingness to pay a lump sum on closing or and royalties or annual payments over time in order for the project to be worth doing. When a license is being granted for a single lump sum (so called "paid ups," a useful short-hand for "paid up licenses"), then the entire future benefit to the buyer is being consolidated into one single, "present day" number. However, even when there is no upfront license payment, the buyer typically performs a spreadsheet calculation of the prospective income including anticipated royalty payments. This will enable the buyer to determine whether the overall returns, net of royalties, will be sufficiently attractive to make the additional, needed development investments, given the perceived risk.

Alternative Available Rates of Return and "k"

The inflationary value of k, 3 percent, reflects no real gain (or loss) in value given the *assumption* that the inflation rate will remain constant over the period. Thus, $862.61 is actually identical to $1,000 five years hence, under the circumstances of 3 percent inflation. However in business circumstances, there are numerous investment opportunities that provide greater-than-inflation returns and such returns are used to calculate the value of money for various times and risks.

One standard value of k used is the interest rate on a Treasury Bill (commonly termed a "T-Bill"), which is a short-term debt instrument used by the U.S. Government to fund its deficit and debt. Historically, the rate of return on a T-Bill has been approximately 7 percent,[10] although in 2002 the rate was approximately 5 percent (on a 10-year note). This value is generally considered the risk-free rate of return that every owner of cash would expect. Put in other terms, if one had $1,000 that could be committed for five years, a risk-free investment would be a T-Bill at 7 percent (using the historic value) which would yield the following result:

$$B = \$1,000 \times (1.07)^5 = \$1402.55.$$

That is, an owner of $1,000 today would expect to receive no less than $1402.55 in five years. Of course nothing in life is risk free or guaranteed; however, a T-Bill is backed by the full faith of the U.S. Government so barring default of the United States, the T-Bill will be paid at the face value return rate (7 percent in this example). Of all investments available, T-Bills are considered to be the most secure (one would be tempted to say a "gold standard," however, the United States no longer bases the value of its currency on the value of gold). Another investment opportunity that may be considered equally secure to a T-Bill is the repayment of existing debt; assuming one is able to do so without penalties for early repayment and ignoring any tax benefit associated with debt payment, then the investment value of such payment is exactly the interest rate of the debt being paid off.

Staying with the T-Bill example, a payment of $1,000 promised five years in the future would be considered to have the present value as follows:

$$DCF = \$1,000/(1.07)^5 = \$712.99.$$

Remember that earlier, the present value (DCF) of $1,000 five years hence was deemed to be $862.61, for a k of 3 percent, and here, with a k of 7 percent it is deemed to be $712.99, or $149.62 less. Why would $1,000 five years from now be worth $149.62 less than the previous inflation-based calculation? The answer is because there exists a means of investing money risk-free at a k of 7 percent, so that it is possible to produce $1,000 in face value five years hence by the present investment of $712.99, not $862.61. In other words, the larger the investment opportunity that's available, expressed in terms of k, the smaller the amount of money required today to produce specified value in the future (such as the $1,000 in these examples).

Consider another investment opportunity. Corporations borrow money just like the U.S. Government and, like the government, they may issue bonds that pay interest. However, because the guarantee of payment is the promise of the issuing corporation secured only by corporate assets, investors correctly perceive a higher risk. This then requires corporations to pay a higher rate of return than a T-Bill in order to persuade investors to take that risk and lend the corporation money. The premium that corporations must pay in order to attract investment depends upon the financial soundness of the corporation. Historically, when T-Bills have yielded 7 percent, corporate bonds have yielded 12 to 18 percent, or a premium of 5 to 11 percentage points above the T-Bill rate. The lower rates are obtained by blue chip companies such as IBM and Coca Cola and the higher rates, sometimes called junk bonds, are paid by companies in high-risk situations and even sometimes in bankruptcy. In 2002, a period of low inflation and low perceived overall economic risk, corporations with strong credit ratings offered what is known as investment grade bond instruments in the sub-10 percent range. When one considers the total rate of return a corporation must pay back to its investors, it is necessary to account for the bond (or debt) capital and the stock (or equity) capital—equity investors rightly expect a higher rate of return because they own a less secure right of return than a bond-holder. Accordingly, the weighted average cost of capital is typically higher than 10 percent, depending upon overall rate of inflation, the perceived risk of the corporation's bonds, and the proportion of debt and equity funding the corporation's operations.

Consideration of all these factors is beyond the scope of this book. For purposes of illustration, a value of 15 percent will be used as this has been a reasonable figure during higher inflation periods. With this value, the present value of $1,000 five years hence is as follows:

$$DCF = 1,000/(1.15)^5 = \$1,000/2.0133 = \$497.18.$$

Compared to the DCF value of $712.99 obtained for a T-Bill rate of 7 percent, this calculation shows that from the point of view of an investor in debt used by corporations, the present value of $1,000 five years hence is $215.81 less (or $497.18).

Essentially, the value of $1,000 five years from now is, to an extent, in the eye of the beholder, who has available various other means of converting money today to money tomorrow. The higher the available alternative returns (k value), the lower any fixed future amount appears to be worth today. In mathematical terms, the DCF of a fixed, future sum declines with increasing k.

Although this seems to trouble people, the rationale behind it is very straightforward. If George is a business person who considers investments solely in T-Bills (at a k of 7 percent), then George will correlate money now with any future year by the factor $(1 + 0.07)^n$ whether George is borrowing or lending. This factor is simply the way of creating monetary equivalence between now and year "n" from the point of view of George, who does business buying and selling T-Bill investments at 7 percent returns. If Sally is a business person who considers investments solely in corporate bonds at a k of 15 percent, then Sally correlates money at different time periods with the factor $(1 + 0.15)^n$ simply because to Sally that is how future money "looks" today (and Sally will need the inner constitution to deal with increased risks she is taking to secure such higher return). Because licenses typically involve a business either on the selling or buying side (or both) a k value of 15 percent, plus or minus a few points, is typically the way money is viewed by the parties. Stated more accurately, corporate borrowings are commonly 5 to 11 points above T-Bills, so in the mid-1998 economy this means typical rates are in the 12 to 13 percent range although historic values were more like 15 percent.

Risk-Adjusted Hurdle Rates and Corporate Rates of Borrowing

The previous consideration of corporate rates of return which yielded DCF factors of $(1 + 0.15)^n$ is derived from what corporations have to pay investors for the use of their money. It must, therefore, represent the floor of the overall rate of return of a corporation if it is to be able to pay back all its lenders in the future. However, when an individual project is considered, the risk of that project is normally higher than the overall risk and return of the corporation (15 percent in this example).

Why is this the case? The answer turns out to be essentially the same reason that an individual stock is more risky than a mutual fund. The corporation borrowing money invests it in many different kinds of projects: energy efficiency to reduce utility bills, opening a new sales office overseas to increase sales, building another plant to increase production volumes (and consequently revenues) based upon anticipated higher demand, and R&D projects that will produce entire new products that will be sold at a profit. A large company could easily have thousands of investments of all types being made in any given year. Even though each of these investments might have been made with the expectation that they would succeed in returning an investment of 15 percent or more, it can be expected that some of these investments will turn out to perform more poorly than expected—in some cases returning 10 percent, in others perhaps 5 percent, in others 0 percent (i.e., zero net gain), and in still others the entire investment will be lost (i.e., a 100 percent loss). If money is lent to a corporation at the individual *project* level, then the risk of the investment is higher than if the money is lent to the *corporation* to be applied to all its projects, because in investment of diversified projects it is highly unlikely that all of them will turn out poorly. Another way to look at this is as follows: If one wants to make a consevative $1,000 investment in corporate bonds, one could invest $100 in each of 10 different companies all in different industries rather than invest all the money in just one company.

However, in a technology licensing situation, a corporation would logically conclude that the overall risk of creating a profitable business is higher than, say, the risk of investing in insulation to reduce its utility costs. Accordingly, corporations typically consider each investment as belonging to a risk category and require higher risk investments to exhibit higher rates of return. For the purposes of illustration, consider the case where a corporation has concluded that investments in R&D require a RAHR (k value) of 30 percent. Therefore we have:

$$DCF = \$1,000/(1.30)^5 = \$1,000/3.71293 = \$269.33.$$

In other words, for a k of 30 percent, an upfront investment of $269.33 must show a return of $1,000 in five years. Conversely, a return of $1,000 in five years based upon an investment in projects that can be counted on to have a RAHR of 30 percent should be thought to have a present value of only $269.33, because the risk of bad things happening over the next five years is relatively high in comparison to T-Bills or typical corporate bonds.

Summarizing Four Points of View of "k" (RAHR)

The values calculated in the preceding sections are summarized in Exhibit 7.2.

The interpretation of the values shown in the third column is as follows: $1,000 five years hence under the corresponding risk perspective (k-value) should be considered to be worth the shown amounts in today's dollars. For this reason, when expressed in this way, the k-value is known as the discount rate because it is used to discount future payments.

In the remainder of this chapter, extensive use will be made of this DCF calculation using the $(1 + k)^n$ factor. However, it is first important to consider risk issues in more detail.

FURTHER CONSIDERATIONS OF RISK

The present value of future payments, known as the DCF, is dependent on three factors: the timing, magnitude, and risk of such future payments. In the DCF equation, the timing shows up in "n," which is normally the number of years from the present for such future payment, the magnitude is value in the numerator (symbolized by "B" or "FV"), and the risk is embodied in "k."

Getting back to the *TR R A DE*™ acronym where, "*TR*" designated Technology Rights, and "*DE*" Deal Economics or Equity, now we are prepared to consider formally "R^k" as "Risk expressed in k." Critical to translating Technology Rights into Deal Economics is an understanding and judgment of the risk associated with converting the technology rights conveyed into a stream of profits from which royalties can be justified and paid.

In the eyes of the seller, especially in the eyes of the inventor-seller, the risk associated

EXHIBIT 7.2	THE EFFECT OF VARIOUS POINTS OF VIEW OF DISCOUNTED CASH FLOW

Point of View	k-value	DCF of $1,000 in 5 years
Inflation	3%	$862.61
T-Bill	7%	$712.99
Corporation	15%	$497.18
R&D Project	30%	$269.33

with obtaining a profit from such rights can appear to be very low. This can be attributed to two primary factors. First, the seller has an intimate understanding of all the difficulties that have been overcome in bringing the technology to its present state (and in many cases it has been a multi-year or even decade-long trail of tears interspersed with transitory joys). Secondly, it is human nature to underestimate the complexities that await the recipient of one's work product. This is particularly true in high technology contexts because the science embodied in the "TR" can be extraordinarily complicated while the seller's expectations of the buyer amounts to "all they have to do is make it and sell it." Although making and selling may not involve differential equations (although sometimes it does), even simple process steps involve risk

Buyers who are too optimistic in valuing technology quickly find themselves providing very low returns on investment and unable to attract capital to make subsequent investments. The purest example of such a situation is the venture capital industry. Venture capitalists, commonly known as VCs, raise money in "funds" from high net worth investors and from high-risk segments of large, traditional investment pools. Typically such "funds" are raised during a recruiting period. If a VC firm is raising "Fund I," then, as the joke goes, their track record is in front of them. Potential investors would examine the performance history of the individuals raising the money and the business model for its subsequent investment and reach a judgment on whether to take the risk. When a VC firm is raising "Fund IV," investors tend to look at the financial performances of "Fund I" and "Fund II" and some preliminary results from "Fund III." From such examples, investors make a judgment on what kind of return might be expected from this new fund and how such return compares with all the other VC firms also seeking investors. Although the volatility of returns in the VC industry is high, investors appear to expect a return of at least 20 percent from the portfolio of investments made by any given fund. In some recent cases, there are funds that have returned more than 40 percent and during the Internet/telecom/Y2K mania closing the twentieth century transition, returns of more than 100 percent occurred."[11]

In this context, when VCs look at startup deals, they will need to see projected returns on their investment well above 20 or 30 percent because (1) there are VC management costs which dilute the returns to their fund-investors, and (2) it will happen that not all their investments will pan out as planned. (There is a rule of thumb in the risk capital industry that says: "all surprises are negative." It's a pessimistic outlook, but people who have been managing such investments over many years attest to its general validity.) Accordingly, when a technology seller is negotiating a license with a VC buyer, the VC may required a RAHR of 50 percent or more in order to attract their investment. Using such values on the example of $1000 in five years results in the following expression:

$$DCF = 1000/1.5^5 = \$131.69$$

Compared to the DCF of inflation ($862.61) or of a T-Bill ($712.99) or even of a corporate bond ($497.18), this $131.69 seems like an extraordinary low valuation for the promise of $1,000 five years hence. However, what a VC is likely to claim is that, based upon (often painful) experience, using a RAHR threshold of 50 percent is needed to produce investment portfolio returns which, after VC costs, are adequate to induce investors to make such risky investments. There is another factor at work in such high-risk situations: there is almost zero probability that any investment of $131.69 will yield $1000 in five years. Unlike the T-Bill example, or even the corporate bond example, what will happen is unknowable to any human. The technology-based startup could easily fail completely consuming all the original investment (in this example, $131.69). There is some chance that it could be wildly successful producing a 40-times return (known in the art as a "40-bagger"); Microsoft, for example, was a 400-bagger from its initial public offering (IPO) date to mid-1998. The above calculation yielding a DCF of $131.69 is a 7.6-bagger in five years (1000/131.69 = 7.594). Risk capital investors expect that a reasonable number of their startup investments will be 10-baggers and more. Given that some investments will be totally lost, some must be 10 or more baggers in order to yield, on average, an attractive return.

RAHR is not a static value for a given opportunity. As the subject technology is advanced one normally expects to learn more, get closer to commercialization, and reduce the total risk, although in some cases the more one learns the worse it looks. As additional investments are made and risks reduced, the value of the technology should increase, all other factors being equal, because of both stage of development considerations (discussed in Chapter 6) and a reduction in appropriate RAHR. Empirical evidence and examples are not readily available in most cases because companies do not normally publish histories of all their projects, including commercially unsuccessful ones. One example where such data is available is the FDA approval process for new drugs. Shown in Exhibit 7.3 are data from a recent *Scientific American* article that studied the history of what happened to new drugs entering the approval process (by the filing of an IND, Investigation of New Drug) in 1976--78 (which early period is needed in order to be able to follow the history).

Shown are the data for the drugs successfully entering each subsequent gate: Phase 1, 2, and 3 clinical trials, New Drug Application (NDA) applied for and granted (enabling sale). As shown, only 20 percent of the drug candidates that began the process emerged with approval to be sold. If the licensor makes the investment and takes the risk of generating additional of such results, then the appropriate RAHR for a license valuation will decrease and, correspondingly, the value of the projected cash flows will increase.[12]

Exhibit 7.4 presents, in the author's experience, how various categories of investment/licensing opportunities are viewed by technology investors. These RAHR estimates are very approximate values based upon buyers' general perceptions of the required rate of return, or the associated risk, of commercializing the technology. These values are not hard and fast numbers, but reflect commonly-used values. This information can be useful in negotiations between buyers and sellers to share perceptions of risk and the associated RAHR. Such discussions can help parties understand why they look at the same opportunity and see different values and, in some cases, may aid by removing some of the uncertainty and lowering the RAHR, thereby increasing the perceived value to the buyer. This subject will be discussed in more detail in Chapter 11.

EXHIBIT 7.3   **PRODUCT DEVELOPMENT AS RESULTS-CREATION AND RISK-REDUCTION**

Source: *Scientific American*, April 2000, p. 74.

A 1987 case study on hurdle rates used by venture capitalists provides another persepective.[13] Looking at the opportunity to invest from startup to IPO, these authors suggest the following RAHR values at "seed stage" (raw idea, pre-business plan) > 80 percent, "startup" 50 to 70 percent, "first stage" (existing company but with limited or no customers) 40 to 60 percent, "second stage" (to fuel growth) 30 to 40 percent, "bridge" financing (to carry to an IPO) 20 to 35 percent. It should be remembered that these rates reflect the added risk of creating a startup company, which approximately corresponds to the situation for the bottom two entries of Exhibit 7.4.

The reader is cautioned that the phrase characterizing each risk category in Exhibit 7.4 is a simplification for purposes of illustration of what must be a case-specific analysis. There are many dimensions to risk; the characterization of Exhibit 7.4 is focused on just two: the technology risk and the target market segment. A buyer could ascribe a low k value to a potential opportunity because it perceives that the risk of *not* adopting the subject technology or enter-

EXHIBIT 7.4	APPROXIMATE VALUES OF RISK-ADJUSTED HURDLE RATE USED IN LICENSE NEGOTIATIONS

Characterization of Risk	Approximate RAHR (k value)
0. "Risk-free," such as building a duplicate plant to make more of a currently made and sold product in response to presently high demand.	Approximates the corporate rate of borrowing, which can be in the range of 10–18%
IA. Very low risk, such as incremental improvements with a well-understood technology into making a product presently made and sold in response to existing demand.	15–20%; discernibly above the corporation's goals for return on investment to its shareholders
IB. Low risk, such as making a product with new features using well-understood technology into a presently served and understood customer segment with evidence of demand for such features.	20–30%
II. Moderate risk, such as making a new product using well-understood technology to a customer segment presently served by other products made by the corporation and with evidence of demand for such a new product.	25–35%
III. High risk, such as making a new product using a not well-understood technology and marketing it to an existing segment or a well-understood technology to a new market segment.	30–40%
IV. Very high risk, such as making a new product with new technology to a new segment.	35–45%
V. Extremely high risk (sometimes known as "wildcatting," borrowing an expression from the oil exploration industry), such as creating a startup company to go into the business of making a product not presently sold or even known to exist using unproven technologies.	50–70% or even higher

ing the target market is significant relative to the long-term well-being of the company. In the other situations, the buyer may possess inside information from known customers on the high value already placed on potential products or have valuable insights as to how the technology can be scaled commercially.

A graphical portrayal of such RAHR values together with other benchmark rates is given in Exhibit 7.5.

EXHIBIT 7.5   RAHR VS. RISK: TYPES & VALUES

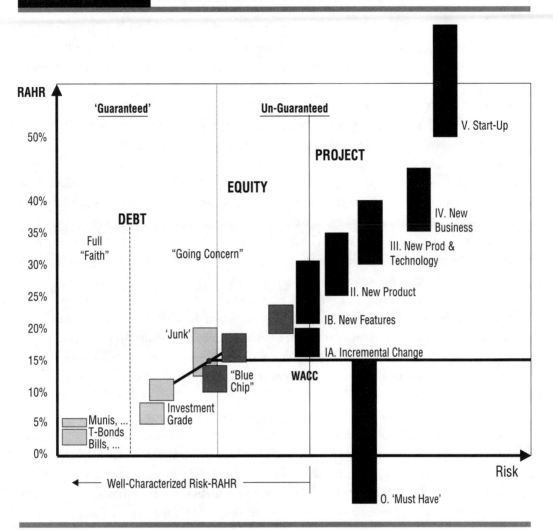

Source: ©2003 Razgaitis, richard@razgaitis.com.

This exhibit seeks to show how investors expect and receive higher rates of return for high-risk investments. The leftmost group are debt forms of investments (bonds). These are traditionally considered as guaranteed, but such guarantees are only as good as the guarantor. In the case of the governments, the full faith and power of the respective government or agency stands behind the repayment and the risk is generally considered to be very low. Next up the risk ladder are corporate bonds. As discussed previously, they are rated by various agencies into a dozen or more categories from very low risk to extremely high risk; for risks above some demarcation such bonds are considered junk (meaning not appropriate for investment grade purposes where the risk of loss of capital is supposed to be extremely low).

Overlapping somewhat the debt categories are the equity classes of investments (stocks). Such investments are viewed as riskier than bonds because returns are not guaranteed. However, the lowest-risk stocks are less risky than the highest-risk bonds, so these areas of the figure should overlap but have not been shown so to make the figure more readable. As the stock is perceived to be more risky, the expected rate of returns by investors goes up, as shown by the fuel cell valuation examples at the beginning of this chapter.

The next category is the project investments we have just been considering and summarized in Exhibit 7.4. Like the equity type investments, these are not guaranteed. They are generally considered to be more risky than equity investments because, for one reason, they are investments in a single project whereas equity investments in a typical company involve investment in multiple company projects. So one would expect less investment failure with a company investment than a single project. However, as with the overlap between debt and stocks, there can be instances where the risk of a particular project under consideration is less, even substantially less, than that in a company; again this overlap has not been shown in order to make the chart readable. The Roman numerals on each of the vertical bars corresponds to their designation in Exhibit 7.3.

The horizontal line designated WACC represents an important corporate finance concept which is the Weighted Average Cost of Capital. A company's WACC is the average cost of capital based upon their particular balance between debt and equity. In principle, it represents the floor of its expected rate of returns. So, companies not only seek high rate of return projects, they are highly motivated, on average, to exceed their WACC return on the portfolio of investments.

However, there are some projects that companies undertake which are shown by the O category of Must Have. For instance, suppose the government passes a law that requires companies that make a chemical, say benzene, to reduce ambient emissions of benzene. On a return on investment basis, this could be a purely negative number because there will be no return because the market for benzene may be no higher nor the margins any greater, but, nonetheless, the company must comply or get out of the business.[14] In such a circumstance, the company may look at a range of compliance solutions, all of which have projected returns below their WACC. Another, less obvious example are the effects of market forces. As discussed earlier, fuel cells are currently receiving revived commercial interest as non-polluting transportation engines and to provide portable electronic power for laptops and the like. A maker of conventional internal combustion engines could face a situation soon where on a return on investment prospect it would just as soon stick with improving its conventional engine but knows (or believes) that if it does not make some investments in fuel cell technology, regardless of the immediate prospective return (but mindful of the total investment and potential ultimate, total return), that it will be out of business like the proverbial buggy whip manufacturer.

Finally, Exhibit 7.5 shows that the domain of well-characterized RAHR values are the debt and equity investments. This is so because of their associated public markets establishing rates in a very real form auction. As one might imagine, there are web sites dedicated to provide rate information, such as *www.rate.net* which purports to have nearly 100,000 such rates ranging from commercial debt instruments (bonds), to home mortgage rates, to auto loan rates and credit card rates. And we should be reminded that even with such well-characterized values, the future does not always turn out the way we expected it.

A summary of the DCF values as a function of RAHR is portrayed in Exhibit 7.6. The present value of $1,000 five years hence is highly dependent on the perceived risk of the investment. Unless one understands how the buyer or seller perceives the risk it is not possible to appreciate how they would create a DCF.

Expressing the same concepts in terms of future returns for a given present investment, we use the following form of the DCF equation:

$$B = A \times (1 + k)^n,$$

where A is the present investment (at time equal to zero), and B is the future value; when this equation was solved for "A" previously, "A" was replaced by the more commonly known term: DCF.

By expressing the equation as a ratio of B/A, we obtain a very useful form because it is independent of any particular dollar (or currency) value:

$$B/A = (1 + k)^n.$$

When the values substituted for k and n result in a value equal to or greater than 2, the result is sometimes referred to by the "bagger" term introduced above. So, for instance, a "5

EXHIBIT 7.6	DISCOUNTED CASH FLOW (DCF) OF A FUTURE PAYMENT OF $1,000 FIVE YEARS HENCE AS A FUNCTION OF THE RISK-ADJUSTED HURDLE RATE (K)

DCF of $1,000 Five Years Hence

bagger" (that is, a five times return) in five years is obtained for a k-value of 38 percent (i.e., 0.38), namely:

$$B/A = (1 + 0.38)^5 = 5.0$$

When used in this way, the k-value or RAHR can be thought of as that rate of return, given the risks of the specific valuation, required to attract investors to contribute "A" with the reasonable potential, but not guarantee, of obtaining "B" in "n" years. Risk capital investors, VCs and some corporate managers think in terms of "payback" (B/A ratio as used here) or, more colloquially, "baggers." Exhibit 7.7 shows several such "payback" or "bagger" curves.

Exhibit 7.7 shows an important interaction between "n" and "k." For short periods of time, such as three years, the impact of different values of "k" is small. If one is debating whether the appropriate "k" value for a particular investment is 20 percent or 30 percent, the impact on B/A is small: 1.73 for 20 percent, versus 2.20 for 30 percent, an increase of a little more than 25 percent. However, if one is doing this same comparison for a period of seven years, then the impact on B/A is large: 3.58 for 20 percent, versus 6.27 for 30 percent. The 30 percent value of "k" results in a 75 percent larger value of B/A than the 20 percent value of "k." What this means is simply this: when dealing with short investment

EXHIBIT 7.7	EFFECT OF K-VALUE AND TIME (N) ON THE RATIO (KNOWN AS "PAYBACK" OR "BAGGER") OF THE RETURN (B, THE FUTURE VALUE) TO THE INVESTMENT (A, THE PRESENT VALUE)

periods, the uncertainty in appropriate "k" is not highly significant in determining the value of an opportunity, but when the investment periods are longer, say seven years or more, then the value of "k" plays a critical role in the perception of value. This observation is what makes the prediction and assessment of returns associated with inherently long term projects, such as a new pharmaceutical, a challenge using a DCF method.

AN EXAMPLE CASH FLOW PROJECTION FROM A LICENSE

The previous sections of this chapter considered simple situations; the present value of one future payment, or the converse of one future payment derived from a single initial investment. One simple formula was used to make such present-to-future (or vice versa) dollar conversions requiring only two other factors: the time to the future payment (n, usually expressed in years) and the RAHR or k-value.

The bad news is that such single-payment calculations are not sufficient to treat most real-life license valuations. The good news is that with the one trusty equation $\{DCF = B/(1 + k)^n$ or $B/A = (1 + k)^n\}$ and spreadsheet software such as Microsoft Excel or Lotus 1-2-3, it is relatively simple to deal with as many future payments and upfront investments as necessary.

First, let us consider why multiple payment calculations are necessary. In a typical licensing transaction, the buyer performs (and the seller *should* perform) a calculation of the future economic benefit of obtaining the subject license agreement. The buyer does this by creating a prospective income statement, known as a *pro forma* because it is being projected into the future and is, by necessity, somewhere between a wild guess and (closer, hopefully to) a well-founded and reasonable estimate. The *pro forma* income statement provides a year-by-year cash stream to the buyer over the projected life of the technology being licensed. In order for the buyer to rationalize the present value of such future cash flows, it is necessary to use a RAHR. Further, to compute a royalty payment to the seller, such payment must be reflected as a year-by-year cost of business in the *pro forma*.

The way this is handled is to compute each year's revenues in that year's dollars, for example, the calculation for the year 2005 estimates the revenues for 2005 in 2005 dollars and all the costs in 2005 dollars so the net cash produced by the business also is expressed in 2005 dollars. Then, in a separate calculation, those 2005 net cash dollars are converted back to current dollars using the DCF equation with the appropriate k-value and "n." Finally, all the DCF values for each year are then added resulting in the total present value of the future benefit of commercializing the technology. As part of such calculation the investment costs in the early years need to be considered; any upfront or progress payments to the seller are also included as part of such costs. When all the projected cost outlays and revenues have been estimated and converted to present value (that is, all the DCF values positive and negative have been added), then the result is known as the "NPV" for Net Present Value. Incidentally, there are embedded NPV formulas in spreadsheet programs that can perform this calculation in one step, although this is not recommended because it is useful to see the year-by-year DCF values and, computationally, the use of computer spread sheets makes it easy to perform.

Shown in Exhibit 7.8 is a hypothetical example of cash flows that would be experienced by a buyer as a result of commercializing a licensed technology. This exhibit assumes that the buyer invests a total of $10 million by the end of the sixth year from the date of the license, and then receives a total of $136 million from the end of the seventh year through the end of the twentieth year, netting $126 million (136 less 10). The $10 million invested is assumed to be: $1 million in one lump sum at the end of Year 1, $1 million at the end of Year 2, $2 million at the end of Year 3, and so forth. Similarly, incoming net cash flow begins at the end of Year 7 in the amount of $1 million, then at the end of Year 8 an additional $4 million comes in, and so on.

Each year's cash flow can then be discounted by the value of "k" to determine the *present* value of such future payment. The first row of Exhibit 7.5 considers the simple case of k = 0%, for which the Discounted Cash Flow (DCF) is identical to the Gross Cash Flow (GCF). Such an example would correspond to a world of zero inflation where no alternative investment opportunities were available that could produce a greater than zero return, clearly an impractical example.

The second row of Exhibit 7.8 shows the effects of k = 7%. This assumes world money decreases in value by 7 percent per year, and no alternative investments greater than a 7 percent return exist. As discussed previously, 7 percent corresponds to the historic level of a risk-free return such as a T-Bill. From such a perspective, the *present* value of the $10 million in net cash flow projected for the seventeenth year is worth only $3.2 million. The $10 million in net cash flow projected for the ninth year is worth more, namely $5.4 million. The cash outflows projected at the end of years one through six are treated in exactly the same way, so, the $1 million spent at the end of Year 2 is only $900K in present dollars, and the like amount spent at the end of Year 6 is even less at $700K. The net effect of this perspective is that the buyer will enjoy the net benefit of $49 million in present dollars, taking all the projected DCF inflows and subtracting all the DCF outflows. This $49 million is known as the NPV, for the Net Present Value, which is simply obtained by adding all the DCFs.

The third and fourth rows of Exhibit 7.8 show the effect of higher values of k: 15 percent and 30 percent. Such values reduce the NPV of the opportunity from $49 million (for k = 7%) to $17.3 million (k = 15%) and to $1.6 million (k = 30%). Because the projected cash inflows occur far into the future, peak GCF does not occur until the end of the twelfth year, and the discounting effect of larger values of k is huge. From the buyer's perspective, the cash outflows occur early and are certain, whereas the inflows occur late and are not at all certain. Assuming this value of k is appropriate to the opportunity (i.e., 30%), then the seller is entitled to 100 percent of the $1.6 million. From the seller's perspective such a small figure does not seem fair given that the buyer should have $126 million in the bank after the project is completed. The buyer's response to the seller is likely to be, "You, instead receive all your return in the form of royalties paid on the inflow GCFs starting at the end of Year 8 and continuing through the end of Year 19."

EXHIBIT 7.8

DISCOUNTED CASH FLOWS AS A FUNCTION OF YEAR & κ

Year	k	1	2	3	4	5	6	7	8	9	10	11	12	13	14	15	16	17	18	19	20	Net
GCF	0%	−1	−1	−2	−3	−2	−1	1	5	10	13	14	15	15	15	14	13	10	8	3	0	126
DCF(k)	7%	−0.9	−0.9	−1.6	−2.3	−1.4	−0.7	0.6	2.9	5.4	6.6	6.7	6.7	6.2	5.8	5.1	4.4	3.2	2.4	0.8	0	49.0
DCF(k)	15%	−0.9	−0.8	−1.3	−1.7	−1.0	−0.4	0.4	1.6	2.8	3.2	3.0	2.8	2.4	2.1	1.7	1.4	0.9	0.6	0.2	0	17.3
DCF(k)	30%	−0.8	−0.6	−0.9	−1.1	−0.5	−0.2	0.2	0.6	0.9	0.9	0.8	0.6	0.5	0.4	0.3	0.2	0.1	0.1	0.0	0	1.568

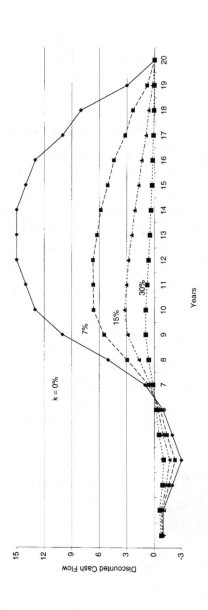

DISCOUNTED CASH FLOWS AS A FUNCTION OF YEAR & κ

201

Computing Royalties from a Rate of Return Perspective Using DCF

There are several perspectives possible on the splitting of the NPV resulting from the use of the DCF Method. The most straightforward perspective is that the buyer and seller reach a common understanding of the rewards, the timing of such rewards, and the overall risk of receiving the rewards as would occur if the parties agreed on a DCF table shown in Exhibit 7.8 with an appropriate k value. Continuing with this example, if it is assumed that the buyer contends and the seller agrees that the appropriate k value to be used to determine the buyer's justifiable return is 30 percent, then *all* of the $1.6 million NPV shown in Exhibit 7.8 (resulting from using k = 30 percent) belongs to the *seller*. This is built on the assumption that the buyer concluded that it is entitled to all the benefits of a Risk Adjusted Hurdle Rate of 30 percent. Exhibit 7.9 is based on the model given in Exhibit 7.8. Starting just below the row of "years," the first row is simply a repeat of the Gross Cash Flows (GCF) paid to the buyer by its customers for sale of products made by the licensed technology. The next row is a calculation of the GCF amounts to be paid by the buyer to the seller as a royalty. The way this royalty payment is calculated involves an iteration between the second, third, and fourth rows. The third row shows the GCF retained by the buyer after payment of the royalty to the seller. The fourth row shows the DCF of such net buyer's GCF using k = 30% as the hurdle rate, which in this instance can be thought of as the buyer's rate of return.

Because the underlying assumption of this example is that the buyer has proposed that it is entitled to a 30 percent return on investment and the seller has agreed, the fourth row discounts the net GCF of the third row. The iteration takes place by adjusting the royalty rate used in the second row so that the sum of the DCFs of the fourth row, i.e., the NPV to the buyer, is identically zero. Such iteration can be done by hand by substituting trial values of the royalty rate until the NPV becomes zero or, much more easily, by using the "Goal Seek" function of the spreadsheet usually available under the "Tools" menu option.

What this example shows is that for a royalty of 28 percent on the basis of the GCF received by the buyer, the net cash flow retained by the buyer produces a return on invest-

EXHIBIT 7.9 VALUE OF THE OPPORTUNITY SHOWN IN EXHIBIT 7.8 AS APPORTIONED BETWEEN BUYER AND SELLER (ASSUMING K = 30%)

Year		1	2	3	4	5	6	7	8	9
GCF		−1	−1	−2	−3	−2	−1	1	5	10
Royalty	28% (on basis of GCF)							0.28	1.39	2.78
Net GCF		−1	−1	−2	−3	−2	−1	0.72	3.61	7.22
DCF Buyer	30%	−0.8	−0.6	−0.9	−1.1	−0.5	−0.2	0.1	0.4	0.7
DCF Seller	30%							0.04	0.17	0.26

ment of 30 percent. The buyer will net (if the plan comes true) in GCF terms $88.16 million, $10 million in investment, offset by $98.16 million in cash inflows. Using k = 30% for all the gross outflows and inflows results in an NPV of $0, which means the seller obtained 30% return on investment (ROI). The seller will receive a total of $37.84 million in royalties paid out in Years 7 through 19 as shown. If the seller's perspective of the risk of such payments is also reflected by k = 30%, then the seller perceives the present value of these royalties as shown in the fifth row: namely $1.6 million, just as was determined previously. Put another way, if the buyer counter-proposes to the seller that instead of paying royalties yearly and a single, upfront payment is made, the seller should be entirely indifferent as to whether it receives the royalties shown over time or the $1.57 million upfront payment (providing the seller's perception of k is 30%).[15]

The royalty rate in this example is based upon the gross cash flows received by the buyer. Such cash flows result from taking the sales revenues and subtracting all the seller's costs in producing and selling the products. Royalties should normally be based upon sales not on cash flows; therefore in any agreement between the parties, there would need to be a separate calculation that would convert the royalty rate from 28 percent based on cash flows to an amount based on sales. Although this will be discussed later in this chapter, for illustration purposes let it be assumed that gross cash flows of this example were 20 percent of the sales: that is, 80 percent of the total sales dollars were consumed in expenses, taxes, and the like. This means that a royalty of 28 percent based upon cash flows that comprise 20 percent of sales revenues is exactly equivalent to a royalty of 5.6 percent based on such sales revenues (which is normally how royalties are expressed). A quick demonstration makes this clear:

$$Sales\ Revenues = 100$$
$$Cash\ Flow = 20\ (for\ the\ assumption\ that\ cash\ flow$$
$$is\ 20\%\ of\ sales\ revenues)$$
$$28\%\ royalty\ based\ on\ Cash\ Flow = 5.6\%$$
$$Alternatively,\ a\ 5.6\%\ royalty\ based\ on\ sales\ also = 5.6.$$

10	11	12	13	14	15	16	17	18	19	20	Sum
13	14	15	15	15	14	13	10	8	3	0	126
3.62	3.90	4.17	4.17	4.17	3.90	3.62	2.78	2.23	0.83	0	37.84
9.38	10.10	10.83	10.83	10.83	10.10	9.38	7.22	5.77	2.17	0	88.16
0.7	0.6	0.5	0.4	0.3	0.2	0.1	0.1	0.1	0.0	0.0	0.00
0.26	0.22	0.18	0.14	0.11	0.08	0.05	0.03	0.02	0.01	0.00	1.57

Incorporating Upfront and Royalty Payments in a DCF Model

Other variations of royalty payments can be similarly calculated. For example, suppose the parties agree that the seller should receive an upfront license fee of $100K. Now the costs to the buyer would increase by $100K at time zero (at the beginning of Year 1) and so the royalty payments would have to be reduced in order to provide the same 30 percent return on investment to the buyer. This case is shown in Exhibit 7.10.

In the first row (below the "Year" row) the column for "Year 0" (representing the date of execution of the agreement) a $100K expense to the buyer is shown in rows 2, 3, and 4, and a $100K revenue to the seller appears in row 5. The royalties paid by the buyer will need to be reduced in order to provide the same 30 percent ROI due to of the initial $100K payment. Performing the "Goal Seek" function results in a royalty of 26 percent corresponding to the cash flow basis, which is two points less than the 28 percent for the no-upfront payment case in Exhibit 7.9. As shown in row 5, the NPV of the seller is also unchanged in this example because both the seller and buyer are using the same "k" value of 30 percent to calculate DCFs.

Computing Royalties from a 25 Percent Rule Perspective

In Exhibits 7.9 and 7.10, it was assumed that the value of k = 30% provided a fair return to the buyer so that all the excess DCFs, i.e., the NPV, was the value attributable to the seller and that this value could then be provided in royalties only, in an upfront payment only, or in an infinite number of lump sum payments and royalties as long as NPV for the *buyer* was $0 with a k of 30 percent.

Another perspective on this approach is that the value of k = 30% (or whatever final value is deemed appropriate) be "neutral" to the buyer, and not reflective of an adequate rate of return. In other words, the buyer could argue that the 30 percent is simply that value of "k" for which the project is just worth doing, and if the buyer does not obtain the bene-

EXHIBIT 7.10	THE EFFECT OF A $100K UPFRONT LICENSE FEE ON EXAMPLE GIVEN IN EXHIBIT 7.9

Year	0	1	2	3	4	5	6	7	8	9
GCF	−0.1	−1	−1	−2	−3	−2	−1	1	5	10
Royalty	26% (on basis of GCF)							0.26	1.30	2.61
Net GCF	−0.1	−1	−1	−2	−3	−2	−1	0.74	3.70	7.39
DCF Buyer	−30%	−0.1	−0.8	−0.6	−0.9	−1.1	−0.5	−0.2	0.1	0.5
0.7										
DCF Seller	30%	0.1						0.04	0.16	0.25

fit of some or most of the excess NPV, then the buyer will not seek the license or undertake the project.

From this perspective the 30 percent is not an adequate rate of return but is the appropriate way of creating a neutral consideration of all future cash flows in the context of the overall perceived risks. From this situation, the logical follow-up issue is how the NPV above 30 percent, namely the $1.57 million in this example (Exhibits 7.8 through 7.10) should be divided between the parties. Here is where the Rule of Thumb Method can be combined with the DCF Method: the $1.57 million could be divided using a 25 percent split or any other split factor.[16] Using the 25 percent split, this would say that the seller's share of the $1.57 million NPV is $393K (25 percent) and the buyer's share is $1.18 million (75 percent). From this perspective, the royalty rates can be recalculated as shown in Exhibit 7.11. Using the "Goal Seek" function and setting the outcome sought to 1.18 results in a royalty of 5 percent on the basis of cash flows in addition to the $100K upfront payment.

To recap, there are two basic perspectives that can be employed in using the DCF Method to provide a valuation:

1. A "k" value that includes the effect of risk *and* justifiable returns (given the contributions of the buyer to achieving commercialization) so that the resulting NPV belongs to the seller either in the form of royalties only, upfront only, or a combination, or

2. A "k" value that provides only the appropriate present values of all the future benefits, given the risk of the project, so that the resulting NPV should then be *divided* between the buyer and seller in a way that reflects their comparative contributions.

The first perspective, sometimes referred to as an "allocated return" approach, can be grounded by analyzing what the buyer and comparable companies can expect to receive as a return for the deployment of the particular assets involved in the license. For instance, the buyer could deploy numerous kinds of assets such as cash, plant and equipment, design engineers, proprietary design tools and approaches, trademarks, patents and trade secrets, and so forth. For each asset so deployed, one could perform an analysis of the magnitude of

10	11	12	13	14	15	16	17	18	19	20	Sum
13	14	15	15	15	14	13	10	8	3	0	126
3.39	3.65	3.91	3.91	3.91	3.65	3.39	2.61	2.08	0.78	0	35.43
9.61	10.35	11.09	11.09	11.09	10.35	9.61	7.39	5.92	2.22	0	90.47
0.7	0.6	0.5	0.4	0.3	0.2	0.1	0.1	0.1	0.0	0.0	0.00
0.25	0.20	0.17	0.13	0.10	0.07	0.05	0.03	0.02	0.01	0.00	1.57

| EXHIBIT 7.11 | | USING THE 25 PERCENT RULE TO APPORTION THE NPV (K OF 30%) | | | | | | | | |

Year	0	1	2	3	4	5	6	7	8	9
GCF	−0.1	−1	−1	−2	−3	−2	−1	1	5	10
Royalty	5% (on basis of GCF)							0.05	0.26	0.51
Net GCF	−0.1	−1	−1	−2	−3	−2	−1	0.95	4.74	9.49
DCF Buyer	30%	−0.1	−0.8	−0.6	−0.9	−1.1	−0.5	−0.2	0.6	0.9
DCF Seller	30%	0.1						0.01	0.03	0.05

such asset and the appropriate market-based rate of return. The outcome of such analysis would be a weighted-average, market-based rate of return. Done in this way, the logic of the process would then say that all of the excess NPV should belong to the seller.

Thus, if one used such grounded methodologies for each of the two perspectives, one would expect the resulting value to be the same. That is, if one performed a reasonable "allocated return" analysis and found k = 30%, so that the NPV of $1.57 million belonged to the seller, and then separately did an analysis of the appropriate "risk adjusted" perspective, one would expect that the risk adjusted "k" value would be less than 30 percent. In this way, when the NPV was divided between the buyer and seller (using, for example, a 25 percent split) the seller would still be entitled to an NPV of $1.57 million. Exhibit 7.12 shows how this could develop. The top set of rows shows that for a 30 percent allocated return to the buyer, the seller receives 100 percent of the $1.57 million which results in a royalty of 26 percent (on the basis of the cash flows) plus an initial $100K license fee. In the bottom group of rows, the seller experiences exactly the same return: $1.57 million NPV with a k of 30 percent. However, in this case a RAHR of 20.4 percent provides an NPV which, when split 75:25 (buyer:seller), provides the aforementioned $1.57 million for the seller and $4.70 million for the buyer. Notice that for this latter case the royalty rate remains unchanged, so the payments made by the buyer to the seller do not change. Also unchanged is what the buyer receives and the buyer's perspective of risk (k = 30%). What has changed is that the "k" value that is used as a risk-adjusted hurdle rate has become 20.4 percent instead of 30 percent as in the top table.

From a negotiation perspective, the seller should be indifferent as to which of these perspectives is employed and can tell the buyer: "Either we discount all the GCF at 30 percent and I (the seller) keep *all* the NPV, *or* we discount the GCFs by 20.4 percent and we *split* the NPV 75:25 buyer:seller."

Although either interpretation and use of DCF can be employed, the normal method is the former: the k-value used includes the effect of the buyer's profit so 100 percent of the resulting NPV belongs to the seller.

10	11	12	13	14	15	16	17	18	19	20	Sum
13	14	15	15	15	14	13	10	8	3	0	126
0.66	0.72	0.77	0.77	0.77	0.72	0.66	0.51	0.41	0.15	0	6.95
12.34	13.28	14.23	14.23	14.23	13.28	12.34	9.49	7.59	2.85	0	111.95
0.9	0.7	0.6	0.5	0.4	0.3	0.2	0.1	0.1	0.0	0.0	1.18
0.05	0.04	0.03	0.03	0.02	0.01	0.01	0.01	0.00	0.00	0.00	0.39

ADDITIONAL CONSIDERATIONS FOR CALCULATING DCF

In all the previous examples, a single value for k (RAHR) was used to discount both the outflow GCFs and inflow GCFs. When one uses a risk-free value of k such as 7 percent, so that dollars tomorrow are made to look like dollars today, then it makes sense to use such k value on all the GCFs. However, what about the case when the parties agree that an appropriate k value is 20 or 30 percent?

For such cases, there is logic to structuring a model that discounts the outflow GCFs at the risk-free rate (such as 7 percent) and the inflow GCFs at the appropriate risk rate (here 20 or 30 percent). The rationale for this distinction is as follows: from the buyer's perspective, the outflow GCFs are much more certain than the inflow GCFs. This is because it is known that the prescribed outflow GCFs will be required to complete development of the technology, purchase manufacturing equipment, gear up for production, prepare marketing materials, train the sales force, conduct an advertising launch campaign, and so forth. However, the inflow GCFs will depend on the willingness of customers to buy the product, which is considered to be less knowable and subject to far less control than making expenditures. For this reason, outflow GCFs logically could be discounted by a k value appropriate to inflation, and the inflow GCFs discounted by a k value appropriate to the overall risk of project success. So, in this example, the outflow GCFs could be discounted at k = 7% and the inflow GCFs at k = 20% or 30% or whatever the appropriate number.

In some cases, the outflow GCFs are not even discounted by this lesser amount (7 percent). This is a result of considering how the outflow estimates are made. Consider a simple case where the only investment required is in people and the seller computes such cost as follows: in Year 1, 10 people will be needed at $100K/person in salary, benefits, and supplies, for a total of $1 million. If Year 2 requires these same 10 people, then it could be expected that, because of inflation each person would cost the seller $107K. Thus, the estimate of $1 million spent in Year 2 has *already* discounted the cost of the 10 people required. Consequently, to discount or not to discount the outflow GCFs depends upon how such estimates were made.

EXHIBIT 7.12		SAME NET OUTCOME OF TWO PERSPECTIVES OF K-VALUE								

Year	0	1	2	3	4	5	6	7	8	9
Allocated Return Perspective: 30% Return on Investment to the Buyer										
GCF		−0.1	−1	−1	−2	−3	−2	−1	1	5	10
Royalty	26% (on basis of GCF)							0.26	1.30	2.61
Net GCF		−0.1	−1	−1	−2	−3	−2	−1	0.74	3.70	7.39
DCF Buyer	30%	−0.1	−0.8	−0.6	−0.9	−1.1	−0.5	−0.2	0.1	0.5	0.7
DCF Seller	30%	0.1							0.04	0.16	0.25
Risk-Adjusted Perspective: 25% Rule Split of NPV between Buyer and Seller										
GCF		−0.1	−1	−1	−2	−3	−2	−1	1	5	10
Royalty	26.0% (on basis of GCF)							0.26	1.30	2.60
Net GCF		−0.1	−1	−1	−2	−3	−2	−1	0.74	3.70	7.40
DCF Buyer	20.4%	−0.1	−0.8	−0.7	−1.1	−1.4	−0.8	−0.3	0.2	0.8	1.4
DCF Seller	30.0%	0.1							0.04	0.16	0.25

Despite the logic of this two-valued "k" approach, it leads to unusable results when applied to long-term projects such as shown in Exhibit 7.8. The resulting problem is shown in Exhibit 7.13. Discounting all the Exhibit 7.8 outflow GCFs at 7 percent causes the NPV of all such outflows to be −$7.8 million, with the minus designating that it is an outflow. The gross total outflow was actually $10 million over six years, but discounting all the inflow GCFs at 30 percent causes the NPV of all such inflows to be only $5.6 million, even though the total GCF was $136 million. The reason this effect is so dramatic is the same one as discussed with respect to Exhibit 7.7: When the duration is long, the impact of large "k" values is huge. If one then combines the NPV of the outflows (−$7.8 million) and the NPV of the inflows ($5.6 million), the result is −$2.2 million and therefore not worth doing from the buyer's perspective.

Fortunately, in many cases the outflow GCFs are made over a sufficiently short period of time, such as two or three years, so that the DCF values obtained are reasonably unaffected by the choice of "k." The development of a new pharmaceutical from the license of an initially tested compound would be an example of a very long investment period. In this case, consideration of a different "k" to discount outflow GCFs would be appropriate.

When dealing with long return periods such as in Exhibits 7.8 through 7.11, there are other valuation approaches based on real options. These will be briefly addressed in Chapter 8. In most analysis of short-term investments, the parties do not attempt to include the

10	11	12	13	14	15	16	17	18	19	20	Sum
13	14	15	15	15	14	13	10	8	3	0	126
3.39	3.65	3.91	3.91	3.91	3.65	3.39	2.61	2.08	0.78	0	35.43
9.61	10.35	11.09	11.09	11.09	10.35	9.61	7.39	5.92	2.22	0	90.47
0.7	0.6	0.5	0.4	0.3	0.2	0.1	0.1	0.1	0.0	0.0	0.00
0.25	0.20	0.17	0.13	0.10	0.07	0.05	0.03	0.02	0.01	0.00	1.57
13	14	15	15	15	14	13	10	8	3	0	126
3.38	3.64	3.90	3.90	3.90	3.64	3.38	2.60	2.08	0.78	0	35.36
9.62	10.36	11.10	11.10	11.10	10.36	9.62	7.40	5.92	2.22	0	90.54
1.5	1.3	1.2	1.0	0.8	0.6	0.5	0.3	0.2	0.1	0.0	4.70
0.25	0.20	0.17	0.13	0.10	0.07	0.05	0.03	0.02	0.01	0.00	1.57
											1.57
											0.00

complication of different inflow and outflow k-values. The simplification is justified partly because the k value applied to the inflow is sufficient to account for this effect, and since this estimating process is sufficiently tenuous such attempts at precision are not justified.

USE OF THE MID-YEAR CONVENTION

There is one additional refinement to be considered. As developed earlier in this chapter, the equation $A = B/(1 + k)^n$, where A is the DCF (present value) of any given future gross cash flow and B assumes that the amount "B" occurs all at once at the end of period "n." Normally, payments are made more or less uniformly throughout a year, not just all at once at the end of the year. Accordingly, the outflow GCFs of Year 1 occur monthly during the year, not all at once at the end of the year. Likewise, the inflow GCFs for, say Year 10, occur throughout the year, not all at once at the end of the year. The way this phenomenon is usually handled is by means of the so-called "mid-year" convention. How this works is as follows: all the outflows (or inflows) of a year are assumed to have occurred throughout the year; for purposes of computing a DCF one can consider them to have occurred half-way through the year. Thus, the time period of the outflow GCFs for the first year occurred actually at mid-year, so that n = 0.5 for Year 1. Likewise for Year 2, all the outflows occurred at n = 1.5, and so on. Thus, the DCF equation becomes:

| EXHIBIT 7.13 | | EFFECT OF DISCOUNTING CASH OUTFLOWS AT A LOWER K THAN INFLOWS | | | | | | | | | |

Year	k	1	2	3	4	5	6	7	8	9
GCF	0%	−1	−1	−2	−3	−2	−1	1	5	10
Outflow DCF	7%	−0.9	−0.9	−1.6	−2.3	−1.4	−0.7			
Inflow DCF	30%							0.2	0.6	0.9

$$A = B/(1 + k)^{(2n-1)/2}, \text{ so for } n = 1 \text{ for Year 1,}$$
the exponent equals 0.5, for Year 2 (n = 2),
the exponent equals 1.5, for Year 3 it equals 2.5, and so on.

To be even more precise, which is rarely warranted, one could make monthly estimates of outflow and inflow GCFs and discount by a monthly "k." Normally the mid-year convention is as precise as needed, given all the other uncertainties associated with making such estimates.

INCOME STATEMENTS AND CASH-FLOW STATEMENTS

Creating an income statement is a fundamental requirement for performing the DCF valuation method discussed in this chapter. There is some bad news and some good news. The bad news is that done properly, creating an income statement is a daunting task, as it involves numerous assumptions involving future sales, the cost of raw materials and labor, the cost of the manufacturing plant, distribution costs, sales and marketing costs, efficiency of manufacture (yield ratios), administrative costs, product development and "R&D" costs, taxes (federal, state, and local), and any and every cost associated with producing the revenue.

The good news? The good news is that for purposes of valuing technology for a license negotiation, there are so many inherent uncertainties involved that it is often possible with some skill and experience to create a useful business model without resorting to a highly detailed calculation of individual costs.

In the previous examples, the gross cash flows were simply assumed. In order to perform a valuation, it is necessary to make estimates of cash flows. How does one obtain the future cash flows year by year?

Generally this is performed in two steps. Step 1 is to perform an "income statement" projection; step 2 is to use the "net income" obtained at the bottom of the income statement (the origin of the term "the bottom line"), and adjust it in a "cash flow" statement. To review, an income statement is derived as follows:

- Revenues (sometimes termed Sales or, in Europe, Turnover)
- Less "Cost of Goods Sold" (known as COGS)

10	11	12	13	14	15	16	17	18	19	20	Net
13	14	15	15	15	14	13	10	8	3	0	126
											−7.822
0.9	0.8	0.6	0.5	0.4	0.3	0.2	0.1	0.1	0.0	0	5.6
											−2.2

- Equals Gross Margin
- Less all appropriate overheads (known as "SG&A," for Sales, General, and Administrative, including relevant R&D)
- Equals "Earnings before Interest and Taxes" (known as EBIT)
- Less interest expense and provision for taxes
- Equals "Earnings after Tax" (known as EAT)

A cash flow statement can be obtained from the income statement as follows:

- Start with "Earnings after Tax" off the bottom line of the income statement
- Add back all depreciation expenses which were embedded in COGS and SG&A or other
- Less the increase in working capital or other investments required, and not included in SG&A of the income statement, to sustain the growth of the business
- Equals Gross Cash Flow (GCF)

EXHIBIT 7.14

DILBERT reprinted by permission of United Feature Syndicate, Inc.

The income statement is not directly useful for performing DCF or NPV analysis. This is because the calculation of the income statement handles investments in ways that do not reflect cash generated or consumed in the year being considered. For example, assume there is a need to build a physical plant in the first year of the license to be able to manufacture licensed products starting in year 2 and extending until Year 10 when the plant will be obsolete. On the income statement such an investment would be spread out over the ten years of useful life according to a depreciation model. One such depreciation model is "the straight line" wherein the initial investment is simply divided by the number of years of useful life and that amount is deducted each year from the revenues as though it were a current year cost. In order to convert an income statement to a cash flow statement, one would need to "add back" the amount of such year-by-year depreciation because the depreciation is not a current year cash expense. Further, one would also need to account for the cash amount of the investment in the year or years it occurred as a current year expense.

Returning to the example of Eli Lilly introduced in Chapter 6, Exhibit 7.15 shows how their cash flow statement is calculated from their income statement, using data contained in their public filings.

This example is somewhat unusual in that it shows a decrease in working capital (WC) requirements, when normally growing companies exhibit an increase in WC. Also, it should be noted that all such cash flow calculations should be made for licensing purposes with costs and adjustments that are appropriate to the subject opportunity being valued so that other, extraneous financial effects do not influence the analysis.

Consult a finance textbook[17,18,19] for background on these terms and concepts and Smith and Parr's book for examples of cash flow statements.[20]

Depending on the significance of the opportunity, there are several levels at which such a cash flow analysis can be conducted. It turns out that there are reasonable benchmark values for COGS, SG&A, and provisions for taxes that can be obtained and expressed as percentages of Revenues. For example, Robert Morris Associates publishes a summary organized by SIC codes of such ratios for companies of various sizes and over various periods.[21] A typical page from this type of source is shown as Exhibit 7.16. It should be noted that these data tend to have been compiled for smaller companies seeking loans because this is how such data is collected. For that reason, in many cases the values shown tend to under-predict profitability.

Other sources of such information include Bloomberg, Ibbotson Associates, *The Almanac of Business and Industrial Financial Ratios*, and Schonfeld & Associates, cited in Chapter 6.

In more important cases, a higher level of effort is justified. Consult annual or quarterly reports of public companies that reflect, as closely as possible, the subject license opportunity and from these reports calculate such ratios, as were discussed in Chapter 6. For instance, a company such as Tektronix may be selected to act as a general proxy for a high-tech device manufacturer. Using their reported results for year-ending May 31, 1997, reveals the following ratios:

EXHIBIT 7.15	ELI LILLY CASH FLOW CALCULATION

Year Ended December 31, 2000	Op. Income Statement	Cash Flow Statement
Net sales..................................	$10,862.2	**Increases to Cash Flow**
		• Dep/Amor **435.8**
Cost of sales.................................	2,055.7	**Incr or Decr to Cash Flow**
Research and development......................	2,018.5	• WC **+777.7** (normally
Marketing and administrative..................	3,228.3	a negative, for a
Interest expense.............................	182.3	growing business)
Other income--net............................	(481.3)	• Other (change in
		deferred taxes, gains
	7,003.5	on sales, asset
		impairment, etc.)
Income from continuing operations before		**(539.8)**
income taxes and extraordinary item........	3,858.7	
Income taxes (Note 11)........................	800.9	
		Net Operating Cash Flow
Income from continuing operations before		
extraordinary item..........................	3,057.8	**3,731.5**

Source: ©2003 Razgaitis, richard@razgaitis.com.

- COGS = 57%
- SG&A = 25% + 10% for R&D = 35%
- Provision for Tax = 32% (more typical numbers are closer to 40%)

By analyzing multiple companies over multiple time periods, one can make reasonable approximations of such ratios. By further analyzing how companies prepare their cash flow statements, also part of the public record, it is possible to make some ballpark estimates for the key adjustments to the income statement: depreciation (which is not a current year expense) and increases in investment required (for working capital or other purposes).

With even more effort, one could make estimates from first principles of what it will cost to manufacture the licensed technology. To do so would require domain expertise in manufacturing for the subject area, and in marketing, sales, and general administration. Where the opportunity warrants such increased investment in analysis, such expertise can be found within one's own organization or, more likely, by employing outside consultants.

A final source of such information is the buyer. Because they are in the business of commercialization, buyers normally have the resources, experience, and the need to develop such detailed projections. Although it is not reasonable to expect the buyer to provide the seller complete access to their records and projections (particularly if the seller is

EXHIBIT 7.16   MANUFACTURERS-ELECTRONIC COMPUTERS SIC# 3571

	Comparative Historical Data			Current Data Sorted By Sales					
					48(4/1–9/30/91)		51(10/1/91–3/31/92)		
Type of Statement	6/30/89–3/31/90	4/1/90–3/31/91	4/1/91–3/31/92	0–1MM	1–3MM	3–5MM	5–10MM	10–25MM	25MM & over
	ALL	ALL	ALL						
Unqualified	66	43	43	1	2	1	4	10	25
Reviewed	7	13	18		9	2	3	1	3
Compiled	12	9	16	1	7	2	2		4
Tax Returns			4	2	1	1			
Other	23	13	18		2	3	5	7	5
Number of Statements	108	78	99	4	21	9	14	18	33
ASSETS	%	%	%	%	%	%	%	%	%
Cash & Equivalents	10.4	12.3	10.4		8.0		7.3	8.7	16.0
Trade Receivables - (net)	31.4	31.5	33.9		38.0		32.9	31.9	31.1
Inventory	25.6	25.1	27.4		27.3		29.2	34.4	19.1
All Other Current	3.3	3.1	3.1		3.8		4.4	1.6	3.9
Total Current	70.7	71.9	74.8		77.0		73.8	76.6	70.0
Fixed Assets (net)	19.2	17.7	14.5		11.9		16.8	15.7	17.0
Intangibles (net)	2.6	4.0	4.5		5.0		4.2	2.8	5.5
All Other Non-Current	7.5	6.3	6.2		6.1		5.2	4.9	7.4
Total	100.0	100.0	100.0		100.0		100.0	100.0	100.0
LIABILITIES									
Notes Payable-Short Term	10.6	8.7	10.9		17.6		9.2	10.0	7.8
Cur. Mat.-L/T/D	2.4	2.7	3.1		1.9		3.1	5.0	1.8
Trade Payables	15.7	15.8	16.8		15.4		21.2	19.2	14.8
Income Taxes Payable	1.2	1.2	.8		.8		2.1	.5	.7
All Other Current	11.7	12.0	12.2		10.6		11.4	12.3	14.0

Total Current	41.6	40.4	43.8	46.3	47.0	47.0
						39.1

	C1	C2	C3	C4	C5	C6	C7
Total Current	41.6	40.4	43.8	46.3	47.0	47.0	39.1
Long Term Debt	8.5	11.7	9.0	10.6	8.1	7.8	7.5
Deferred Taxes	.8	1.5	.4	.3	.2	.3	.8
All Other Non-Current	4.2	4.2	5.1	2.9	2.5	8.9	5.0
Net Worth	45.0	42.3	41.7	39.9	42.2	36.0	47.6
Total Liabilities & Net Worth	100.0	100.0	100.0	100.0	100.0	100.0	100.0
INCOME DATA							
Net Sales	100.0	100.0	100.0	100.0	100.0	100.0	100.0
Gross Profit	40.7	39.5	42.8	48.5	32.0	35.5	44.1
Operating Expenses	38.3	36.5	39.5	44.9	28.4	31.9	41.3
Operating Profit	2.4	2.9	3.3	3.5	3.5	3.6	2.8
All Other Expenses (net)	1.3	.8	1.5	2.6	1.3	.4	1.6
Profit Before Taxes	1.2	2.1	1.7	1.0	2.2	3.2	1.3
RATIOS							
Current	3.0	2.7	2.5	2.3	1.9	2.3	3.1
	1.8	1.8	1.7	1.6	1.5	1.6	1.9
	1.3	1.2	1.4	1.3	1.3	1.2	1.3
Quick	1.8	1.8	1.7	1.6	1.3	1.4	2.0
	1.0	1.2	1.0	1.1	.9	.9	1.2
	.7	.8	.7	.6	.5	.5	.8
Sales/Receivables	49 7.4	41 9.0	42 8.6	9.0	34 10.6	37 9.8	51 7.2
	64 5.7	54 6.7	56 6.5	5.7	45 8.1	47 7.8	78 4.7
	87 4.2	76 4.8	79 4.6	4.2	59 6.2	72 5.1	104 3.5

(Continued)

EXHIBIT 7.16 *(Continued)*

	Comparative Historical Data			Current Data Sorted By Sales					
Type of Statement	6/30/89–3/31/90 ALL	4/1/90–3/31/91 ALL	4/1/91–3/31/92 ALL	0–1MM	1–3MM	3–5MM	5–10MM	10–25MM	25MM & over
				48(4/1–9/30/91)			51(10/1/91–3/31/92)		
Unqualified	66	43	43	1	2	1	4	10	25
Reviewed	7	13	18		9	2	3	1	3
Compiled	12	9	16		7	1	2	1	5
Tax Returns			4	1	1	1	1		
Other	23	13	18	2	2	4	4	6	
Number of Statements	108	78	99	4	21	9	14	18	33
Cost of Sales/Inventory	54 6.8	36 10.1	45 8.2		22 16.3		30 12.1	40 9.2	41 8.8
	99 3.7	69 5.3	83 4.4		76 4.8		58 6.3	91 4.0	79 4.6
	148 2.5	107 3.4	114 3.2		122 3.0		79 4.6	140 2.6	114 3.2
Cost of Sales/Payable	33 11.2	23 15.6	28 13.0		14 26.7		28 12.9	29 12.6	38 9.7
	42 8.6	42 8.7	41 8.9		40 9.2		36 10.1	41 9.0	55 6.6
	69 5.3	63 5.8	69 5.3		85 4.3		41 9.0	51 7.2	87 4.2
Sales/Working Capital	3.0	3.6	4.1		5.3		5.6	4.9	2.8
	5.2	6.0	7.1		9.6		10.7	7.4	4.4
	14.7	16.5	15.1		15.9		22.4	19.4	10.8
EBIT/Interest	9.8	10.4	8.2		2.7		8.2	25.3	15.2
	(95) 3.7	(87) 2.2	(65) 2.0		(19) 1.5		(10) 2.4	(17) 2.7	(29) 2.0
	.5	.8	-.2		-.2		-6.5	1.0	-1.6
Net Profit + Depr., Dep., Amort./Cur. Mat. L/T/D	12.6	11.1	13.0						23.6
	(54) 6.2	(38) 3.6	3.3						(13) 5.5
	.7	1.3	.9						.6

	(1)	(2)	(3)	(4)	(5)	(6)	(7)	(8)	(9)
Fixed/Worth	.2 .4 .8	.2 .4 1.0	.2 .3 .7		.2 .3 .6	.2 .3 .6	.2 .4 .7	.2 .3 .9	.2 .3 .7
Debt/Worth	.6 1.1 2.8	.7 1.5 4.0	.6 1.5 4.7		.6 2.5 7.4	1.0 1.8 2.7	1.0 1.8 2.7	.6 1.3 9.5	.6 .8 3.8
% Profit Before Taxes/Tangible Net Worth	30.8 17.0 (102) 3.7	40.6 20.6 (90) 6.4	(70)		43.9 7.1 (19) -4.1		38.9 14.1 (15) -22.2	57.0 17.5 (29) 3.1	33.0 19.0 -4.4
% Profit Before Taxes.Total Assets	13.5 6.0 -4.4	13.4 7.7 1.1			8.5 1.5 -3.3		21.3 6.9 -7.3	20.7 6.8 -1.9	15.4 5.0 -4.4
Sales/Net Fixed Assets	23.2 13.3 5.1	25.0 12.9 6.2			54.3 33.6 9.6		38.3 16.0 8.5	33.0 23.5 7.0	15.7 8.0 5.2
Sales/Total Assets	2.4 1.7 1.2	2.6 2.0 1.3			3.1 2.4 1.9		4.8 2.0 1.3	3.1 2.2 1.6	1.9 1.5 1.1
% Depr., Dep., Amort/Sales	1.3 3.1 (89) 4.6	(53) .9 2.6 (68) 4.0			.9 1.6 (18) 2.9		.7 1.7 (11) 4.1	.8 2.0 (11) 2.6	1.8 3.8 6.6
% Officers', Directors', Owners' Comp/Sales	2.2 5.6 (20) 9.9								
Net Sales ($)	5167155M	3910447M	5701101M	2431M	41328M	35234M	103986M	260758M	5257364M
Total Assets ($)	4115028M	2639217M	3885095M	988M	28715M	15838M	49770M	123962M	3665822M

M = $thousand MM = $million

Source: ©1992 by Robert Morris Associates. All rights reserved. No part of this table may be reproduced or utilized in any form or by any means, electronic or mechanical, including photocopying, recording or by any information storage and retrieval system without permission in writing from Robert Morris Associates.

negotiating with multiple prospective buyers), it can be in both party's interests to share reasonable projections for the purpose of conducting win-win negotiations.

Once such ratios are determined, then by making an estimate of the total revenues year by year, an estimate of the year-by-year GCF can be obtained. Exhibit 7.17 shows how this can be done. Shown is a model for developing the revenues over time. Normally one has some idea about the selling price range of the prospective product and the size of the market, although each of these variables alone could be the subject of a detailed analysis. Once the revenue line has been calculated, then the ratios developed previously lead one to the Gross Cash Flow (GCF). It is from the GCF that the discounting techniques discussed in this chapter can be applied. Exhibit 7.17 will be the basis for a demonstration of the Monte Carlo Method in the next chapter.

USING DCF TO DETERMINE
THE VALUE OF FIXED PAYMENTS

One of the powerful features of the Discounted Cash Flow Method is that it can be used with any other valuation method or context to move money forward or back in time. For instance, if, using the "Industry Standard Method" of Chapter 4, the parties agree on a royalty of 5 percent but for some reason want to defer or move up some or all of certain royalties, the above DCF equations can be used to convert such moneys into equivalent value but at different times.

In some agreements, the seller definitely prefers to receive substantial early, fixed payments in lieu of some of its downstream royalties. These DCF equations can be used to restructure equitable financial agreements into equivalent forms with different payment times and amounts.

OTHER ISSUES TO BE CONSIDERED
WITH THE DCF METHOD

One assumption inherent in the examples selected is the zero terminal value. Such a situation is common, though not universal. It arises, for example, when the license is a bare patent license (no trade secrets). The patents all expire on a known date. Another case is when the product life will be short and there will be no existing residual benefit in a succeeding product generation. Another reason terminal value may be ignored is that the k-value used is sufficiently large so that the DCF value of even a significant GCF figure at the end of the forecast period is so low that it is unaccounted for given all the project uncertainties. However, it is always reasonable to ask: Is there a terminal value that should be considered?

Another assumption inherent in the examples considered is an assessment of potential peripheral benefit to the buyer. This effect may be accounted for by the use of an appropriate royalty base. Returning to the laser example, if the licensed subject matter is the lasing element only, the buyer will likely gain the benefit of selling entire laser components as a

EXHIBIT 7.17 — EXAMPLE CALCULATION OF GROSS CASH FLOWS (GCF) BASED ON TEKTRONIX RATIOS

	A	B	C	D	E	F	G	H
1	Year		1	2	3	4	5	6
2	Number of Units Sold (1)		100	200	300	350	400	400
3	Average Selling Price (1)		$10,000	$10,000	$9,500	$9,000	$8,0000	$8,000
4	Revenues		$1,000,000	$2,000,000	$2,850,000	$3,150,000	$3,200,000	$3,200,000
5								
6	COGS (2)	57%	$570,000	$1,140,000	$1,624,500	$1,795,500	$1,824,000	$1,824,000
7	SG&A and R&D (2)	35%	$350,000	$700,000	$997,500	$1,102,500	$1,120,000	$1,120,000
8	EBIT	8%	$80,000	$160,000	$228,000	$252,000	$256,000	$256,000
9	Provision for Taxes (2)	32%	$25,600	$51,200	$72,960	$80,640	$81,920	$81,920
10	EAT		$54,400	$108,800	$155,040	$171,360	$174,080	$174,080
11								
12	Depreciation (3)	5%	$28,500	$57,000	$81,225	$89,775	$91,200	$91,200
13	Increase in Investment (4)	10%	$100,000	$85,000	$30,000	$5,000	$-	$-
14	GCF		$(17,100)	$80,800	$206,265	$256,135	$265,280	$265,280
15								

Notes

(1) Values which would be developed from market assessment (illustrated here)

(2) Ratios in Col. B are Tektronix annual report May 31, 1997

(3) Assumed to be 5% of current year COGS

(4) Assumed increase in working capital based on 10% of increase in year over year sales

result of having such new element. By using the selling price of the entire component, and appropriately adjusting the royalty, the seller can be fairly compensated. But what about the situation where the buyer will now be able to sell additional components not directly tied to the laser but bought from the buyer by the same customers? Accounting for such peripheral sales is normally much more uncertain than the products made directly by the licensed technology. As in the case of the terminal value issue, in many instances this effect is deemed too distant or minor to be included. However, it is always a reasonable question to ask: What is the total benefit of the licensed technology?

CONCLUSION

The DCF method requires delving into the origins of expected profit from the use of the licensed technology. If this is done primarily by reliance on ratios, such as EBIT as a percentage of revenues projected by year, then the DCF resembles the Rule of Thumb Method. However, even in this situation, the DCF can provide additional information to enable moving payments in time such as reduced royalties to create a larger upfront license fee. The DCF method can also provide insight into the sensitivity of the value to perceived risk (k).

If the DCF method is implemented by a detailed analysis of each component of the income and cash flow methods, then it can provide significantly more insight than the Rule of Thumb Method if there is a reasonable basis for making such analysis.

For the valuation of significant opportunities, the DCF Method is often used in addition to other methods to increase one's insight into value and confidence in the calculated result.

Summarized below are the equations developed and used in this chapter.

- A or DCF = $B/(1 + k)^n$, where A or DCF is the present value of a future gross cash flow B, or, A = $B/(1 + k)^{(2n-1)/2}$, using the midyear convention.
- B/A = $(1 + k)^n$, where such B/A ratio is known as payback or baggers
- B/A = $(1 + k)^{(2n-1)/2}$, using the mid-year convention
- NPV = the sum of all the DCFs (noting outflows offset inflows)

SOURCES OF INFORMATION TO DEVELOP BUSINESS PROJECTIONS

Although details on how to develop pro forma financials are beyond the scope of this book, provided in Appendices A and B are lists of numerous available business resources. I am in debt to Michael Odza formerly of *Technology Access Reports* and my colleague Dan McGavock of InteCap, Inc. for permission to include these references. Additional useful links are available at the author's website: www.razgaitis.com.

NOTES

1. The S&P 500 stock index has traded at an average price-to-earnings multiple of 15.7 over the past 42 years, and as of July 2002 is trading at 20 times projected 2002 earnings.
2. "Sector Watch: Fuel Cells Fire Up Alternative Energy Stocks," by Beverly Goodman, *Red Herring*, December 18, 2000, p.234.
3. Ibid.
4. Ibid.
5. "Wireless Plaything," by Timothy J. Mullaney, *Business Week E.Biz*, July 24, 2000, p. EB21.
6. "InfoSpace Evangelist," by Cory Johnson, *The Industry Standard*, March 20, 2000, p. 79.
7. "A Talk with Scott McNealy," by Editor-in-Chief Stephen B. Shepard, *Business Week*, April 1, 2002, p. 66.
8. Throughout the book we have generally ignored tax issues that may affect a party's decision-making or valuation because such issues are beyond the scope of this book and are situation specific.
9. The value of "k" has to be based on the same time period as "n" in order for these equations to work. In all the examples provided, "n" was expressed in years; so, the value of "k" was given in *annualized* (yearly) values. One could use monthly periods, but in such an instance the "k' value would be interest expressed per month; for example, the future value (B) of a present sum (A) could be:

$$B/A = (1 + k)^n.$$

For k = 12% on an annualized basis and a period of five years, one obtains

$$B/A = (1 + 0.12)^5 = 1.76$$

Equivalently, one could consider this same example as consisting of 60 monthly periods, such that n = 60. However, in such a case, "k" must be expressed as the monthly interest rate. Here, the equivalent monthly value of "k" is 0.9489 percent or 0.009489, so that

$$B/A = (1 + 0.009489)^{60} = 1.76$$

10. The average yield on a 10-year Treasury note has been 7.25% for the 42-year period 1960–2002.
11. And in keeping with such high rates of return are high risks for VC's, their investors, and the management, employees, vendors, and customers of their invested companies. The average VC returns has been 41 percent in 1995, declining year after year to 18 percent in 1998, then surging to 160 percent in 1999, returning to 23 percent in 2000, and becoming negative (-20 percent) in 2001, and expected to be negative in 2002.
12. They will also increase because presumably the time-to-market has shortened.
13. "A Method for Valuing High-Risk, Long-Term Investments: The Venture Capital Method", Harvard Business School Case Study, 9-288-006, published 1987, Rev. 6/89, Harvard Business School, Cambridge, MA.
14. Of course the scope of the analysis could be expanded to include a financial analysis of *losing* the incumbent business, and on such basis conclude that that investment in the project has a high rate of return.
15. The seller's appropriate k-value is normally different, and lower than the buyers. The buyer is using the k-value to scale risk and reward of a future investment. The seller is moving money expected to be paid in the future to the present. The discussion of such k-values and how they relate to the weighted average corporate cost of capital is outside the scope of this book.
16. It should be noted that this is not the same use of 25% as the 25% Rule of Chapter 6. The 25% Rule applies to the split of EBIT.
17. McKinsey & Company, Inc., Tom Copeland, Tim Koller, and Jack Murin, *Valuation: Measuring and Managing the Value of Companies* 3rd ed., New York: John Wiley & Sons, Inc., 2002.
18. Luenberger, David G., *Investment Science*, New York: Oxford University Press, 1998.
19. Brealey, Richard A. and Stewart C. Myers, *Principles of Corporate Finance*, New York: McGraw-Hill, 2000.
20. Smith, Gordon V., and Parr, Russell, L., *Intellectual Property, Licensing and Joint Venture Profit Strategies*, 2nd Ed., New York: John Wiley & Sons, 1998.
21. Robert Morris Associates, *Annual Statement Studies*, 1992, Philadelphia PA.

CHAPTER 8

Method Five: Advanced Valuation Methods: Monte Carlo and Real Options

INTRODUCTION

Chapter 7 presented a mathematical structure for performing valuation using projected, or pro forma, income and cash flow statements, together with equations and methodology to assess the present value of future sums based upon timing and risk. This Discounted Cash Flow Method is the most mathematical valuation approach considered thus far and can be used in most valuation situations.

However, in recent years, more sophisticated methods of valuation have been developed. In this chapter, two such advanced methods will be considered: Monte Carlo (or Probabilistic) Method and Real Option Methods (see Exhibit 8.1).

Both techniques are based upon the Discounted Cash Flow Method. They are similar approaches in that both are based on cash flow models derived from specific assumptions about revenues and costs. However, they do differ. With Monte Carlo techniques, one is not constrained to make single-value predictions of key variables such as revenues, costs, or even the technical risk of success; instead, estimates are made of ranges of outcomes with associated probabilities. Surprisingly, in many cases this turns out to be easier to do than making discrete value projections.

The second method considered in this chapter is real options. DCF plays an important role here as well. When dealing with long-lived projects, particularly when the expenses are significant and early, and the projected returns are far into the future, the use of a single Risk-Adjusted Hurdle Rates (RAHR, or k) tends to make all such projects look economically unattractive because of the heavy discounting that takes place by the factor $B/(1 + k)^n$

EXHIBIT 8.1   **METHOD 5: ADVANCED METHODS**

Source: ©2003 Razgaitis, richard@razgaitis.com.

when "n" is large. Option pricing methods evaluate investments and returns in an incremental way that better handles such circumstances.

MONTE CARLO METHOD

Monte Carlo, more generally known as probabilistic, techniques have a long history, primarily in engineering applications. Within the past 25 years, they have been increasingly
applied to business modeling in support of decision-making. These methods are very powerful ways to solve equations and situations so complex that a closed form solution is not
possible.[1] With the advent of powerful and inexpensive personal computers, such sophisticated tools are now widely available although not yet widely used. However, in most MBA
programs, the Monte Carlo method is taught, used, and required. Such method will be increasingly used in license valuation contexts.

There are two personal computer products available that work with PC-compatibles and
with Macintosh operating systems:

- Crystal Ball® by Decisioneering, Inc. (*www.decisioneering.com*)

- @Risk by Palisade Corporation (*www.palisade.com*)

They each work with and require a spreadsheet program such as Excel or Lotus 1-2-3. Different MBA programs have standardized one or the other of these products; they each have a prestigious list of university adoptions. Although both products are suitable for use in license valuation contexts, the examples provided in this chapter have been obtained using Crystal Ball.

To illustrate the Monte Carlo method we will use the previous cash flow projection example considered in Chapter 7 as Exhibit 7.17, repeated here as Exhibit 8.2. In this context, we will assume that Exhibit 8.2 is the projected situation agreed to by both seller and buyer for the purpose of valuing a technology license. Exhibit 8.2 contains an additional Discounted Cash Flow (DCF) calculation, based upon an assumed Risk-Adjusted Hurdle Rate of 25 percent, enabling the calculation of a Net Present Value (NPV) of $452,827 as shown.

This model says that based on the single valued assumptions of the model and the assumed RAHR of 25 percent, both the buyer and seller would conclude that the licensing opportunity was "worth" approximately $453K. As discussed in Chapter 7, the perspective on the RAHR selected (25 percent) determines whether the buyer would be willing to pay as much as $453K. In our consideration of the Monte Carlo Method, we will make certain probabilistic assumptions of the factors in this model to obtain a richer understanding of the NPV value of this hypothetical license.

How the Monte Carlo Method Works

The basic idea behind the Monte Carlo Method is that instead of prescribing a *value* for a cell in a spreadsheet model of a valuation, one prescribes an *expression* for the cell based upon some mathematical model of reality. When the calculation scheme gets to the point where it must ascribe a value to that cell, the Monte Carlo software program conducts a computation using the mathematical model specified to deduce the one specific number that is then used to compute the final result. What makes this approach probabilistic is that the mathematical expressions used to provide the one specific number are structured to provide a prescribed randomness (also known as a *distribution*). This seems peculiar and nonproductive, but it turns out to be very useful.

Two immediate questions arise: what is a prescribed randomness (or distribution), and why would the selection of a parameter having such randomness lead to a useful result?

Prescribed Randomness (Distribution) Expressions

With regard to the first question, the issue of prescribed randomness, it is useful to revisit the idea of predicting the future. Although it is universally accepted that no one knows the future, there are many aspects of life for which we do know the future in practical everyday terms. The sun will rise tomorrow, pretty much in the east. If it is spring, summer will follow. Even in human affairs, much of life is predictable. The stock market will rise, not every day, not every stock, but overall. The New York Yankees will win the World Series again before the Chicago Cubs will.

EXHIBIT 8.2 OBTAINING DCF AND NPV WITH REVENUE PROJECTION THROUGH RATIOS

	A	B	C	D	E	F	G	H
1	Year		1	2	3	4	5	6
2	Number of Units Sold		100	200	300	350	400	400
3	Average Selling Price		$10,000	$10,000	$9,500	$9,000	$8,0000	$8,000
4	Revenues		$1,000,000	$2,000,000	$2,850,000	$3,150,000	$3,200,000	$3,200,000
5								
6	COGS	57%	$570,000	$1,140,000	$1,624,500	$1,795,500	$1,824,000	$1,824,000
7	SG&A and R&D	35%	$350,000	$700,000	$997,500	$1,102,500	$1,120,000	$1,120,000
8	EBIT	22%	$80,000	$160,000	$228,000	$252,000	$256,000	$256,000
9	Provision for Taxes	32%	$25,600	$51,200	$72,960	$80,640	$81,920	$81,920
10	EAT		$54,400	$108,800	$155,040	$171,360	$174,080	$174,080
11								
12	Depreciation	5%	$28,500	$57,000	$81,225	$89,775	$91,200	$91,200
13	Increase in Investment	10%	$100,000	$85,000	$30,000	$5,000	–	–
14	GCF		$(17,100)	$80,800	$206,265	$256,135	$265,280	$265,280
15								
16	RAHR [=k]	25%						
17	DCF(k)		$(15,295)	$57,816	$118,073	$117,296	$97,187	$77,750
18	NPV(k)		$452,827					

There are basically three ways that one can have what philosophers sometimes term a "justified true belief" (JTB)[2] about the future: (1) a scientific law, (2) an established historical trend, or (3) a rational argument. Predicting the sun's rising and the change of seasons is an example of scientific law; there are known and knowable facts concerning the motion of the earth with respect to its own axis (rotation) and with respect to the sun (revolution), and of the tilt of the earth, and of the energy emission rate of the sun that enable predicting the "rising" of the sun, for example. In fact everyone's certainty is sufficiently high about such matters that the word "prediction" would emit a laugh: Imagine a local evening news forecast that proclaims "tonight it will be dark, but tomorrow it will be light again."

The second example of a JTB about the future, reliance on an established trend, is similar to the use of a scientific law. Scientific laws, after all, are simply codified experience. It comes as something of a shock to some college students that there is no "proof" of Newton's Laws of Motion or of the First Law of Thermodynamics. After careful study by many people in many different contexts, no exception to these dogmas has ever been observed and so a critical mass of people have declared them "law" and everyone pretty much agrees to stop wondering about them. Reliance on an established trend to predict the future is simply an uncodified way of asserting that what happened before will happen again. Prior to man's understanding of celestial mechanics, the existence and date of the shortest and longest days of the year (in the Northern Hemisphere, December 21 and June 21, respectively) was widely known. It appears certain that Stonehenge, for example, was constructed in such a way that at sunrise on the Summer Solstice the sun would project its light through a special keyway in the stones on that day and only that day. Other cultures many thousands of years ago similarly understood these dates and all of them did so (apparently) with either an inadequate understanding of celestial mechanics or a completely false one. What they were able to do was to capture an observation that occurs once a year, year after year, and communicate it down through a sufficient number of generations such that it was accepted as a law of life. The rising stock market, or the existence of inflation, is this same type of prediction by extrapolation. There exist approximately 100 years of stock market history encompassing two world wars, numerous presidential administrations and policies, countless numbers of new products being introduced and old ones being abandoned, and, yet there has been a surprisingly uniform rise in value of about 10 percent per year. Underneath such rise, there are "fundamentals" that can be used to explain why stocks as a whole are more valuable now than they were before, and why stocks on an individual basis are more, or in some cases less, valuable than in the past. So, does anyone "know" that the stock market will be higher by 10 percent one year hence? In the philosophical sense of JTB, the answer is "no." In the business sense of PDM (Prudent Decision Making), the answer is "yes." In a business context, certainty is an unaffordable luxury. If there is historical data, then it is frequently prudent to predict the future and act on such predictions as though the future were known.

The third way of knowing the future is rational argument. As shown in Exhibit 8.3, Dilbert and his boss are able to use rational argument to make bold predictions: Dilbert predicts that his project will never be completed with the boss's "help," and both Dilbert and his boss surmise what life will be like when the sun stops shining.

EXHIBIT 8.3

DILBERT reprinted by permission of United Feature Syndicate, Inc.

When an investment decision is to be made regarding whether or not to develop a new product, business decision-makers frequently have only rational argument as the basis for PDM. Although there may be both historical data for similar products or previous new product introductions and market assessments based upon surveys and trials, in almost all circumstances the commitment is made by the credibility of an argument. Thus, in the previous edition of this book it was predicted, pro forma, that the Yankees would (again) win the World Series of Baseball. This was based on a rational argument that *because* the Yankees won in 1998, and *because* off-season trades and acquisitions had made the team stronger than any other team, they *should* win again in 1999. Of course this was by no means certain, which is one reason why they play the game, but if the 1999 Yankees were an investment opportunity, PDM would have been to expect their winning (and they did).

When business forecasts are made, the future values selected for cells in a spreadsheet model are some combination of extrapolations of data or experience and a rational argument as to how circumstances should turn out. With traditional, non-Monte Carlo methods, each "best guess" is but one value from a range of reasonably possible choices. Monte Carlo tools enable the replacement of the single-valued best guess with a *prescribed randomness* that characterizes not only what is believed to be the most likely outcome but also includes treatment of reasonably probable but less likely outcomes. Normally the solution sought is the Net Present Value (NPV) of the total value of the project. Each time the software program performs a complete NPV calculation, it will determine a somewhat different value for NPV because at least some of the cells have the prescribed randomness expression rather than a single value.

Let us consider three classic examples of prescribed randomness: uniform, triangular, and Gaussian (also known as "normal").

Uniform Distribution   A uniform distribution, or "uniform" prescribed randomness, can be used in estimating the effect of the Cost of Goods Sold (COGS, as defined in Chapter

7). In Exhibit 7.18, we used a value of 57 percent based upon data from Tektronics for the year ending May 31, 1997. In modeling a prospective licensing transaction, we will typically use data wherever possible and deal with the uncertainty in the following way: Although we may believe that 57 percent is toward the middle of the most likely range, it may be equally likely that the COGS could be anywhere from 55 to 59 percent. Alternatively, we are sufficiently confident that the value of COGS will not be less than 55 percent that we are prepared to predict that there is zero percent probability for values less than 55 percent, and similarly, zero percent probability for values greater than 59 percent. However, any value between 55 and 59 percent is equally probable. Exhibit 8.4 illustrates how such a distribution is portrayed; it is derived from Crystal Ball 4.0 Pro for a PC.

Such a uniform distribution acts to put the maximum amount of uncertainty possible within the prescribed upper and lower bounds (here 55 and 59 percent) because we are saying that any value within such bounds is equally probable; on the other hand, this type of distribution has the most certainty possible with respect to values outside the upper and lower bounds because it ascribes zero probability to such values. Clearly, if we had set the upper and lower bounds at 56.99 and 57.01 percent, we would have for all practical purposes reduced the prediction to the single value of 57 percent at 100 percent certainty.

EXHIBIT 8.4   **UNIFORM DISTRIBUTION FOR COST OF GOODS SOLD**

Source: © 1988–2002 Decisioneering, Inc. Reprinted with permission.

Uniform distributions work best for those situations where the certainty is bifurcated: it is highly probable that the values will be within a prescribed range but highly uncertain as to exactly where within such a range.

Triangular Distribution (Prescribed Randomness)   A variation of Uniform Distribution is the triangular distribution. Triangular distribution is similar to the uniform type in that both types assume zero probability of values below the specified lower bound and above the upper bound. They differ in that the triangular distribution selects a most likely value and constructs a triangle of probability that varies linearly from the maximum probability at the most likely value to zero at the upper and lower bounds. Using a concrete example, consider again Exhibit 8.2. We will use triangular distribution to predict values for the average selling price in any given year, as shown in Row 3 of this exhibit.

The existing model portrays a 5 percent decline in selling price after the second year as a result of price erosion. Looking at the first year only, let us assume that as a result of market studies we are confident that the selling price can be at least $9,000 per unit, but not more than $11,000 per unit, to achieve the 100 units sold projected in Year 1. A triangular distribution would then look as shown in Exhibit 8.5.

Thus, this distribution assumes that the likelihood of the selling price differing from $10,000 declines linearly with price differential from $10,000 until, at plus or minus $1,000, the probability is zero. In comparison to the previously considered uniform distribution, the triangle distribution is appropriate when one has reason to believe that a most-likely value does exist, and that the probability of other values declines with separation from such a most-likely value. Because it is reasonable to hold a "most likely" outcome belief, the triangular distribution is appropriate for many circumstances.

The Normal, or Bell, Distribution   Another commonly used distribution is known by several names: Gaussian, normal, or bell distribution (or bell curve). This distribution, hereafter "bell" or "normal," is similar to the triangular in that the probability peaks at the "most likely" value and declines with distance from the most-likely value. However, unlike the triangle distribution, the bell distribution shows a probability which declines to zero asymptotically, not abruptly, at end points. Further, the probability decline is not a straight line but rather a curve that is described by a complex mathematical formula.

There is another important difference between the triangular and bell distribution: the bell distribution is observed experimentally in many different physical circumstances. If one were to measure the height of a large number of people and then calculated the average height, one would find that most people's height is close to the average. The number of people with heights far from the mean decreases rapidly as one moves away from the mean. For example, if the mean was determined to be 5 feet 6 inches, then one would find many people who stand between 5 feet 4 inches and 5 feet 6 inches, fewer between 5 feet 2 and 5 feet 4, still fewer between 5 feet and 5 feet 2, and still fewer between 4 feet 10 and 5 feet.

EXHIBIT 8.5   TRIANGULAR DISTRIBUTION FOR THE SELLING PRICE IN YEAR I

Source: © 1988–2002 Decisioneering, Inc. Reprinted with permission.

The distribution of such heights would closely follow a mathematical expression that pre-scribes the bell curve. The use of such a bell distribution is particularly suited when there exists a natural mean around which there is some randomness and the randomness is equally likely to be higher or lower than the mean. Even for situations where there is no "natural" mean, such a distribution can be used to express a belief that the mean or ex-pected value is highly likely to occur. Essentially, any value is possible, but the probability of values far from the mean is much lower than values closer to the mean.

Considering again the example of Exhibit 8.2, let us assume that the number of units sold each year can be characterized by such a normal or bell distribution as shown in Exhibit 8.6.

The relative slenderness of the distribution is determined by a mathematical quantity known as the standard deviation. One standard deviation, plus and minus, encompasses ap-proximately 68 percent of the total probability of occurrence. That is, in the example shown in Exhibit 8.6, the selection of a standard deviation value of 10 means that the distribution provides that 68 percent of the values selected for the units sold in Year 1 are between 90 and 110 units (plus and minus 10 around the most-likely value of 100). Three standard de-viations, in this example plus or minus 30, encompasses 98 percent of all occurrences.

EXHIBIT 8.6	EXAMPLE OF BELL DISTRIBUTION FOR UNITS SOLD

Source: © 1988–2002 Decisioneering, Inc. Reprinted with permission.

Custom Distribution

The Crystal Ball software provides more than a dozen different types of distributions that can be readily modeled and used. In technology valuation contexts, there is usually no basis for identifying a particular distribution from scientific principles because the valuation is driven by business variables. Exceptions can occur. For instance, if the licensed subject matter were a pharmaceutical that was still undergoing trials, then there could be valid reason and basis on which to select a distribution that accurately represents the rate of patient cures and to use such distributions to model FDA approval, market applications, and size.

In addition to such standard distributions, the Crystal Ball software has the built-in capability of easily creating a custom distribution that allows for the creation of any combination of probabilities at any arbitrary set of values. An example of the use of such distribution is shown in Exhibit 8.7.

This exhibit shows how the probable values of the sum of SG&A (Sales, General and Administrative) plus R&D (Research and Development) can be easily modeled. The original example, shown in Exhibit 8.2, used a value of 35 percent for the single, best assumption. Exhibit 8.7 shows how one can select probabilities at three discrete values: 50

EXHIBIT 8.7   EXAMPLE OF CUSTOM DISTRIBUTION TO MODEL SG&A + R&D

Source: © 1988–2002 Decisioneering, Inc. Reprinted with permission.

percent probability at 35 percent SG&A + R&D, 30 percent at 34 percent, and 20 percent at 36 percent. Crystal Ball allows one to easily specify any number of pairs and then normalize the entire result so that the integrated probability is 100 percent. This allows one to construct distributions based upon historical experience (data) obtained from previous licensing situations, or other new product development projects.

How Distributions Are Used in Monte Carlo Calculations

The ability to use prescribed randomness is what makes the Monte Carlo Method powerful. It works in the following way. Consider a desire to calculate the predicted value of Net Present Value (NPV) for a new business development opportunity. The various factors that will drive the value are all estimated by using discrete values and distributions as discussed in this chapter. The way Monte Carlo works is that the software performs the calculation for NPV over and over again to create a distribution of outcomes of NPV that can be analyzed and interpreted. Each time the program calculates an NPV, called one "iteration," the result can be thought of as one lifetime of running the business through its entire life cycle.

Each new iteration is exactly as though someone else in a parallel universe is able to run the business also through its entire life cycle. Typically one performs 1000 to 5000 such parallel universe calculations of NPV and then all the outcomes are reported and analyzed. By examining the statistics of all the NPV outcomes one can obtain a deeper understanding of the business prospects than from a one-time-through NPV calculation as was done in Chapter 7.

Just as distributions are used for certain of the inputs, the outputs of a Monte Carlo approach are likewise a distribution, rather than a single value. How to interpret such distributions will be discussed later.

Example Valuation Monte Carlo Calculation

Exhibit 8.8 repeats Exhibit 8.2 except the cells affected by the Monte Carlo method in Crystal Ball are highlighted: darker shading are the assumption cells, the ones for which some distribution has been selected, and lighter shading is the forecast cell, the value being predicted by the method.

As shown the shaded cells in Rows 2 and 3, Columns C through H, and in Column B, Rows 6 and 7, are the cells for which the previously described distributions have been provided. The "units sold" in Row 2 is modeled by the normal (or bell) distribution. The "average selling price" in Row 3 is modeled by the triangular distribution. The COGS is modeled by the uniform distribution, and the SG&A plus R&D by the custom distribution. All the other cells are assumed to maintain their single-value as was the case in Exhibit 8.2.

To use the method, the software is set to "run" the iterations. For the first iteration, or "parallel universe," when Crystal Ball needs a value from any of the probabilistic cells (units sold, selling price, COGS, or SG&A plus R&D) it uses the distribution recipe for the respective cell to determine a value that will be used for the remainder of the calculation to determine the first NPV. For the second "parallel universe" the process repeats but a different value will be selected for all the probabilistic cells (those containing distribution expressions rather than single values). Over the course of many iterations, usually 1000 or more, a sufficient number of selections are made from each of the probabilistic cells that, over the entire set of assumptions, a reasonable approximation of values will correspond to the assumed distribution.

The results from this Monte Carlo calculation can be presented in many ways. Exhibit 8.9 is a frequency chart that shows the number of trials occurring in each of the shown "slices" of NPV values over 1000 iterations.

In Exhibit 8.2, we found that a single-value DCF model produced a single-valued NPV of $452,827. From a visual inspection of Exhibit 8.9, such a value falls in the middle of the results here and appears to be the most probable value. However, what the distribution of NPV values shows is that there are plausible situations where the NPV was in the range of $350,000 to $550,000. Crystal Ball allows us to easily determine the relative probabilities for any specified value of NPV. So in this example, by moving the cursor or by entering the prescribed range, Crystal Ball provides the following information:

EXHIBIT 8.8 MONTE CARLO METHOD APPLIED TO EXHIBIT 8.2

	A	B	C	D	E	F	G	H
1	Year		1	2	3	4	5	6
2	Number of Units Sold		100	200	300	350	400	400
3	Average Selling Price		$10,000	$10,000	$9,500	$9,000	$8,0000	$8,000
4	Revenues		$1,000,000	$2,000,000	$2,850,000	$3,150,000	$3,200,000	$3,200,000
5								
6	COGS	57%	$570,000	$1,140,000	$1,624,500	$1,795,500	$1,824,000	$1,824,000
7	SG&A and R&D	35%	$350,000	$700,000	$997,500	$1,102,500	$1,120,000	$1,120,000
8	EBIT	22%	$80,000	$160,000	$228,000	$252,000	$256,000	$256,000
9	Provision for Taxes	32%	$25,600	$51,200	$72,960	$80,640	$81,920	$81,920
10	EAT		$54,400	$108,800	$155,040	$171,360	$174,080	$174,080
11								
12	Depreciation	5%	$28,500	$57,000	$81,225	$89,775	$91,200	$91,200
13	Increase in Investment	10%	$100,000	$85,000	$30,000	$5,000	—	—
14	GCF		$(17,100)	$80,800	$206,265	$256,135	$265,280	$265,280
15								
16	RAHR [=k]	25%						
17	DCF(k)		$(15,295)	$57,816	$118,073	$117,296	$97,187	$77,750
18	NPV(k)		$452,827					

Source: © 1988–2002 Decisioneering, Inc. Reprinted with permission.

EXHIBIT 8.9	MONTE CARLO RESULTS FOR THE EXAMPLE IN EXHIBIT 8.8

Source: © 1988–2002 Decisioneering, Inc. Reprinted with permission.

- Minimum NPV = $282K
- Twentieth Percentile NPV (i.e., 80 percent of the NPV results were higher) = $394K
- Mean NPV = $458K
- Eightieth Percentile NPV (i.e., 20 percent of the NPV results were higher) = $518K
- Maximum NPV = $662K

Thus, for the middle 60 percent of the cases, the NPV was bounded by $394 and $518K (i.e., between the twentieth and eightieth percentiles).

There is substantial additional information available from such data. A sample report is provided in Appendix 8A.

If one repeats the calculations for a new set of 1000 iterations, it is not a surprise that the numbers are different, but yet they yield the same general result. Exhibit 8.10 shows the results of such a second group of 1000 iterations. Looking at the frequency chart one can see that the overall shape is similar to the one shown in Exhibit 8.9 although there are individual differences. Exhibit 8.11 shows a cumulative distribution chart; such a chart makes it easy to isolate the NPV values corresponding to any degree of probability one chooses. For example, from this chart it appears that there is approximately a 90 percent (1 − 0.1) probability that the NPV will be greater than $360K.

| EXHIBIT 8.10 | NPV RESULTS DURING A SECOND GROUP OF 1000 ITERATIONS—FREQUENCY CHART |

Source: © 1988–2002 Decisioneering, Inc. Reprinted with permission.

Adjusting the Model Based Upon Critical Assumptions

Before making an interpretation of the NPV distributions, it is important to consider how the Monte Carlo Method can be used to highlight the important uncertainties. Although many different factors are unknown in every projection, the significance of these uncertainties is not equal. In every model there are usually one or two variables whose uncertainty determine substantially all the uncertainty in NPV. Identifying such critical variables can be very useful because reducing the uncertainty in these quantities greatly improves the quality of the prediction.

Shown in Exhibit 8.12 is a sensitivity chart produced by Crystal Ball for the 1000 iterations shown in Exhibit 8.10 and 8.11. What is shown in Exhibit 8.12 is that the two most important sources of uncertainty in NPV are first, the uncertainty in COGS, and second, the uncertainty in SG&A plus R&D. This may be surprising given the natural inclination to place high importance on the assumptions behind the revenue line, namely the assumed number of units sold and the average selling price. However, the COGS and SG&A plus R&D numbers have a direct and important bearing on operating margin and, therefore, cash flow. For the assumptions made here, these effects are actually much more significant than the revenue model.

| EXHIBIT 8.11 | NPV RESULTS DURING A SECOND GROUP OF 1000 ITERATIONS—CUMULATIVE CHART |

Source: © 1988–2002 Decisioneering, Inc. Reprinted with permission.

In a license valuation situation, one would then direct attention to the values assumed for COGS and SG&A plus R&D and, if additional precision in NPV is needed, make additional investments to develop more precise estimates of these numbers to the extent possible. In some cases, it may be practical to conduct additional proof of principle experiments to demonstrate, for example, that the cost of manufacture (COGS) is either lower than previously assumed (good for the seller's position) or known to a higher degree of certainty (better for both party's negotiations).

Interpretation and Valuation of NPV Distributions

As discussed in Chapter 7, there are two general perspectives on dividing NPV between seller and buyer: (1) the seller deserves 100 percent of the NPV because the RAHR (k-value) has the justified return built in for the buyer, or (2) the NPV should be split between the seller and buyer because the RAHR produces an NPV that only minimally accounts for the risk, making the buyer "whole" so that all the excess value (NPV using such k-value) is the true benefit of the opportunity. The normal perspective is the first perspective.

Often, buyers use k-values that provide the required internal return given the riskiness of

EXHIBIT 8.12	SENSITIVITY CHART FOR THE 1000 ITERATIONS IN EXHIBITS 8.10 AND 8.11

Source: © 1988–2002 Decisioneering, Inc. Reprinted with permission.

the project. For such a situation, all excess NPV justifiably belongs to the seller. Buyers will still want to have as much of the excess NPV as possible because business is all about paying $5 for $10, when possible.

Assuming such a perspective, how might a seller use the results of the Crystal Ball forecasts to support a negotiation position? With the buyer's assumed "right" to 100 percent of the NPV, what NPV does one choose? Clearly, if the seller settles on the maximum observed NPV ($662K) then there is less than one chance in a 1000 that the buyer will meet its targeted RAHR. At the other extreme, using the minimum observed NPV ($282K), there is less than one chance in a 1000 that the buyer won't achieve its RAHR and, on average, it will obtain a substantial additional return (in addition to its RAHR) of $176K ($458K less $282K) and could receive (one time in a 1000) as much as $380K ($662K less $282K) of additional value.

There is no simple way to decide such matters. If a single one-time payment is the remuneration approach favored by the parties, then it is a matter of dividing the uncertainty. If the parties "split it down the middle" then the result in this case is not much different than would have been obtained by using a straight DCF method without the Monte Carlo structure.[3] The argument for or against the seller receiving more than half of the

NPV hinges on this: Where is it more likely to find surprises? If the surprises are more likely to be found in new markets and applications (more than considered in the model) and/or in cost efficiencies of manufacture and/or synergies with other products or processes controlled by the buyer, then the seller should get more than the 50 percentile NPV. On the other hand, if the surprises are more likely to occur when bringing the technology to commercial fruition or as a result of new and superior products and technologies unexpectedly introduced by the competition, then the seller should get less than 50 percentile NPV.

The results of a Monte Carlo analysis can provide the basis for other payment structures that can more fairly reward the parties based on the uncertainty. One example would be that the buyer pays the seller 33 percent on closing with a second 33 percent payable based upon well-defined outcomes of the key assumptions (such as the COGS value in the previous example). Thus, the deal might be that the buyer pays $420K on closing, approximately the thirty-third percentile, and the difference between the sixty-seventh percentile (approximately $485K) and the $420K (i.e., $65K) would be payable in, say, three years if the COGS (carefully defined) did not exceed 57 percent.

Another approach for using Monte Carlo analysis is to use a RAHR that corresponds to the perceived or known standard value used as a baseline by the buyer, for example, 20 percent. By performing the Monte Carlo with all future cash flows projections discounted by such amount, the resulting NPV projections show the percentages when such 20 percent RAHR will be exceeded (corresponding to the area of positive NPV), and missed (negative NPV). Then one can determine an appropriate NPV based upon a reasonable standard of success that a willing buyer should be prepared to experience considering the opportunity. For most situations, a company's use of a baseline RAHR (such as the 20 percent example here) is that most projects, but certainly not all, will satisfy this standard. Additionally, in this example, a value of 20 percentile has been used for the Monte Carlo determined value, meaning that 80 percent of the time the NPV will be positive; this particular combination would be an example of a 20:20 "rule:" a 20 percent RAHR with a 20 percentile NPV value.

If this same buying company's WACC is 15 percent, then the above standard suggests that 80 percent of its projects will return in excess of 20 percent of investment, and 20 percent less. For a portfolio of opportunities, such company should succeed in exceeding its WACC, depending on the specific levels achieved in each such project undertaken.

There is no right single answer to the appropriate percentile selection. When companies consider their baseline earning projections on which public reliance will be made, the expectation standard is typically very high, perhaps in the range of 90 to 95 percent. The strong suggestion is that if the number is not made, and there is not a very good "story," it could cost you your job. However, at the project level, such a standard would result in only very low risk, and corresponding modest return potential pursuits. Enlightened companies seeking high returns will correspondingly seek selected projects, in a portfolio of opportunities, that have high risk providing they correspond to high potential returns. So, if the positive NPV zone of the Monte Carlo forecast shows large and noteworthy values, reasonable buyers could justifiably pursue the opportunity even at value points corresponding to probabilities of less than 50 percentile.

For highly risky undertakings, some form of real options becomes an attractive alternative.

Other Issues Relating to the Monte Carlo Method

There are many theoretical issues that can be argued about the use of normal or bell distributions for a selling price. There is no mathematical or scientific basis justifying such use. (Statistical purists have probably already discarded this book by now anyway.) However, the distribution closely clusters values around the expected value and, given all the other uncertainties, seems to offer reasonably useful results.

Likewise, one can argue about the interrelationship between price and volume distributions, namely that one should account for higher pricing causing lower volumes and vice versa, rather than permitting both of these variables to act independently and be represented by different distributions to boot.[4] Again the answer is that, given all the uncertainties one deals with in technology licensing, such arguments should not cause immobilization. The physicist Denis Diderot (1713–1784), editor of the classic French *Encyclopédie,* told the story of the man walking in the absolute darkness with a poor torch-lamp who encountered another man who said "it is very dark here, turn out the light!" Diderot, a champion of science and the Enlightenment, said of the second man: he must have been a theologian. The joke, weak as it may be, applies here: a poor light in the midst of great darkness is better than no light at all.

An expanded discussion of the use of Monte Carlo in a negotiating context, is available in *Dealmaking Using Monte Carlo and Real Options Analysis* (Razgaitis, Hoboken, NJ: John Wiley & Sons, Inc., 2003), and other resources at *www.razgaitis.com.*

RISK-ADJUSTED NPV METHOD

The rest of this chapter will consider three additional advanced[5] valuation methods: Risk Adjusted NPV, Probability Trees, and Real Option. These methods have arisen to treat longer term/higher risk valuation which may not be well handled by other approaches. The Risk Adjusted NPV Method builds on the DCF Method of Chapter 7.

Regarding DCF calculations (Chapter 7), when one value of RAHR (k) is used for long term projects, the equations compute very little value in later years because of the compounding effect of the value of k. For projects that end, by IPO or strategic acquisition, in five years or less, this compounding effect can be serious but not catastrophic. For pharmaceutical projects, where the first revenues may not occur for seven or even 10 years after a technology license, using high values of RAHR make it virtually impossible to justify any investment. Yet, everyone recognizes that with the technical, regulatory, and market hurdles, new drugs are high risk projects. What to do?

One approach is to de-aggregate the RAHR into its respective components: a component that represents the time value of money, a component for the opportunity cost value of money, a component for the technical risk, another for the regulatory risk, and so on. By this means, one can use lower values of RAHR as various hurdles are successfully passed and that particular risk is eliminated.

In a paper, Ashley Stevens has extensively described the use of such a stage-gating process on RAHR.[6] He also notes that Research Corporation Technologies applies a similar approach in deciding whether to invest in a university discovery. In this paper he contrasts such adjusted NPV, designated by raNPV (for risk adjusted NPV) with valuation models done by Larry Smith of Hambrecht & Quist[7] and Mary Tanner of Lehman Brothers.[8]

The examples he presents shows that such raNPV provides a higher estimated valuation of the opportunity, more in line with common sense. The reader is referred to the paper for the details of his approach and results.

THE USE OF PROBABILITY TREES FOR VALUATION

One very appealing method, both visually and conceptually appealing, is the use of probability trees for valuation. This method is best explained from an example. Consider the example in Exhibit 8.13.

Valuation using decision trees is best viewed from right to left, from the end to the beginning. Shown in Exhibit 8.13, in the five boxes on the right-hand side, are five perceived scenarios or outcomes going from highest to lowest in value as one goes from the top to the bottom. Three of them are associated with commercial success, and two of them with failure. For purposes of this illustration, we will assume that all the monetary values associated with this figure are on an appropriated discounted basis, such as a company's WACC or at a project hurdle rate.

For the three commercially successful outcomes we can conceive of a baseline or most likely result, shown by the $70 million outcome, but we can also readily visualize an even better possibility and one worse. The method works with any number of such scenarios, but a common approach is to use three: high, medium (base), and low. Failure also needs to be considered. Sometimes one uses only one failure condition, but here are shown two: a nice, quick death due to obvious failure, and a slow painful one (that is often the most costly).

For each of these five scenarios, one would calculate the value of the outcome using the DCF Method of Chapter 7. It is important that in developing such scenarios that the underlying assumptions are self-consistent. In other words, if one assumes a high scenario situation, all the underlying assumptions should be logically related with this envisioned situation.

The essence of the probability tree valuation method is projecting the weighted probabilities of each of the hypothesized scenarios coming to pass. For the commercially successful three, it is common to heavily weight the mid or baseline scenario as by definition it is perceived to be the most likely one; in this example it is assumed to occur 70 percent of the time. Then by some similar means one assesses the probability of the high and low scenarios occurring; shown here are 20 percent and 10 percent, respectively. The probability tree

EXHIBIT 8.13   PROBABILITY TREE VALUATION EXAMPLE

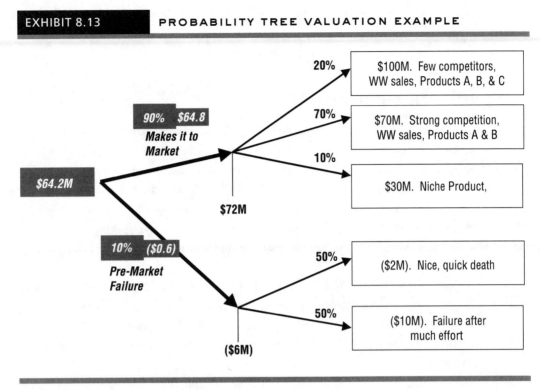

Source: ©2003 Razgaitis, richard@razgaitis.com.

method then simply determines the value of node to the left of these three commercially successful outcomes as the weighted average of the respective probabilities multiplied by their value, namely: $0.2 \times 100 + 0.7 \times 70 \times 0.1 \times 30 = \$64.8$ million.

A similar analysis is done for the two failure scenarios (here taken to be equally likely) yielding a weighted loss of $0.6 million.

Finally, the method requires the specification of the relative probability of success versus failure. Here it is taken as 90:10 (90 percent probability that one of the three successful scenarios will result). The value, then, of the opportunity is simply determined by: $0.9 \times \$64.8 + 0.1 \times (-\$0.6) = \$64.2$ million.

The appeal of this method is compelling and obvious. The problem is that of determining the appropriate probabilities of each of the five scenarios. How would one know that the breakdown is 20 percent, 70 percent, and 10 percent for the three successes, and that 90 percent of the time one of the successes will occur? One way would be to have a very large portfolio of very similar projects for which there is an established track record. This affords the power of history with the law of large numbers. However, for technology opportunities, there is normally an inherent uniqueness about each one and it is difficult to correlate success probabilities to historic numbers, even in such circumstances where such numbers were known. Yet, people with lots of experience, the equivalent of a Dr. DeBakey from a lifetime of performing heart surgeries, can often render just such judgment.

Another approach would be to combine this method with Monte Carlo. Using Monte Carlo, one can make estimates of the probability of different scenarios by doing aggregations among the (say) 1000 outcomes calculated.

REAL OPTION METHODS

As discussed here and in Chapter 7, long-lived projects are not analyzed well by the use of single values of "k" to compute DCFs and NPV. When "n" (the number of years) is large, the discounting effect causes very small DCFs in the later years, even for projects with very significant cash flows. For example, DCF = $B/(1.3)^{10}$, for k = 30% and 10 years results in DCF = B/13.8. So even if the buyer has a cash flow of $100 million in the tenth year, the perceived value is only 100/13.8 or $7.25 million. For projects involving long development times, new pharmaceuticals would be a noteworthy but not unique example; this circumstance arises all the time.

Another problem with the DCF approach is that it assumes that all the investment money will be spent, regardless of intermediate outcomes. What actually happens is that a technology commercializer can terminate a project early if it looks like the risks are going to be higher than anticipated (or the profit less), thereby saving some or much of the investment that would have been committed and lost.

Real option techniques that can deal with such complexities have been developed. The preponderance of such work has been in creating investment hedges primarily for European and American call options, which requires extensive data to be able to characterize various traits of the investment, such as volatility. In some respects this creates the same distinction made in Chapter 1 between sales of businesses and licensing of technologies: businesses have track records. Similarly, real option methods have been developed and applied to investments, such as stocks, that have extensive track records. Although such highly mathematical methods are now widely used in analyzing investment vehicles, their use in technology licensing is restricted to more simplified approaches as will be discussed next.

STRATEGY AS A PORTFOLIO OF REAL OPTIONS

Timothy Luehrman has published a series of papers in the *Harvard Business Review* on decision-making strategy from the perspective of taking and exercising options. In his October 1998 paper, he defines an option space determined by two variables: one based upon NPV modified to incorporate the time value of the ability to defer investment, and the other a measurement of volatility illustrating how much circumstances can change prior to the commitment of a decision.[9]

The underlying goal is to recognize that having an option to an NPV in high-volatility situations is an opportunity to spend a little and learn a little, deferring decisions of major investments until there is much higher certainty. In this sense, the concept is similar to the raNPV approach.

Professor Luehrman also describes the use of a modified NPV—APV, or adjusted present value—in modeling the present value of future returns.[10] In another article, he shows how such options relate to the Black-Scholes Model.[11]

A useful, concrete example is provided in a related paper by Dixit and Pindyck.[12] The description here is adapted from their example and applied to a licensing context. For simplicity we will focus attention on the option aspects; no time-value of money calculations will be made. The situation is this. A buyer is given an opportunity to acquire a license for an initial payment of $5 million after which the buyer will have to expend $10 million in additional R&D. After careful analysis, the buyer has concluded that the ultimate additional cost to commercialize the technology (after the $5 million plus $10 million) will be (1) $40 million, (2) $80 million, or (3) $120 million, based upon certain assumptions. At the moment, all three outcomes are believed to be equally probable. The payoff from a successful implementation is predicted to be either (A) $50 million or (B) $130 million. Should the buyer license the technology?

Identifying the two payoffs as A and B, and the three costs as C1, C2, and C3, there are six equally likely possibilities. AC1, AC2, AC3, BC1, BC2, and BC3. The payoffs are as follows:

$$AC1 = \$50 - \$40 = +\$10 \text{ million}$$
$$AC2 = \$50 - \$80 = -\$30 \text{ million}$$
$$AC3 = \$50 - \$120 = -\$70 \text{ million}$$
$$BC1 = \$130 - \$40 = +\$90 \text{ million}$$
$$BC2 = \$130 - \$80 = +\$50 \text{ million}$$
$$BC3 = \$130 - \$120 = +\$10 \text{ million.}$$

However, in all cases, there is a $15 million investment required just to determine which outcome is expected to occur, so including this cost there are only two outcomes that are net positive, BC1 and BC2.

If one takes a decision tree approach and weighs the outcomes according to their relative probabilities, then one finds the following:

$$\text{Value of the opportunity} = 1/6(10 - 30 - 70 + 90 + 50 + 10) - 15 = -\$5 \text{ million}$$

where the $15 million is always subtracted from the net payoff because in all cases, under these assumptions, it requires a $5 million license fee and $10 million of initial R&D to determine which of the six outcomes occurs. From such an NPV perspective, even if the seller cuts the license fee to zero, the opportunity does not yield a positive value to the buyer.

However, through real options, these authors illustrate that such NPV approaches portray a faulty thought process because by the $15 million investment, the buyer acquires an *option* to determine which of the three costs and two payoffs will occur. Once that is known, one does not incur the poor outcomes because if that is the perceived outcome, then one does not exercise the second option. To illustrate, if the outcome of the R&D is AC3 (payoff of $50 million and cost to commercialize of $120 million), no rational buyer will proceed any further because the buyer will lose an additional $70 million to the sunk cost of $15 million.

If the outcome is BC2 (payoff of $130 million and cost of $80 million), the buyer would then proceed with the project and net $50 million less the $15 million for the option, yielding $35 million net profit for having taken and implemented the option. Finally, if the outcome is C3, at a cost of $40 million, then the buyer should go forward in either payoff A or B (because the $15 million is an already sunk cost), yielding a net profit either –$5 million or +$75 million.

The six possible net profit outcomes are shown in Exhibit 8.14. At the left of each cell is the net of payoff (A or B) less costs (C1, C2, or C3). At the right of each cell is the net profit including the $15 million cost of obtaining the option.

The two unshaded cells show outcomes which are clearly positive even accounting for the $15 million option cost.

The two lightly shaded cells show a profit of $10 million by exercising the option, but when the option cost is considered show a net of –$5 million.

The two dark shaded cells show outcomes which would cause the buyer to terminate the project, incurring a net loss of the option cost ($15 million).

Since it was assumed that each of these six outcomes was equally probable, an option valuation shows the following:

$$\text{Value of the option} = 1/6(-5 - 15 - 15 + 75 + 35 - 5)$$
$$= 1/6(70)$$
$$= \$11.7 \text{ million}$$

Therefore, by viewing this opportunity from an option pricing perspective, it is worth a positive $11.7 million to the buyer instead of the negative result found by NPV analysis. The difference is a result of the actions taken for the two darker cells in Exhibit 8.14. In the NPV case, it is assumed that the buyer would commercialize these two possibilities just as is done in the other four cells and lose even more money than the sunk $15 mil-

| EXHIBIT 8.14 | NET PROFIT TABLE FOR THE REAL OPTION EXAMPLE |

		Commercializing Cost		
		C1 $40 million	C2 $80 million	C3 $120 million
Pay off	A $50 million	$10 / –$5	–$30 / –$15	–$70 / –$15
	B $130 million	$90 / $75	$50 / $35	$10 / –$5

lion in option cost. Whereas in the option perspective it is recognized that the buyer will not ever lose more than $15 million net for any outcome.

The six options are graphically shown in Exhibit 8.15.

As shown, after the "more facts period" afforded by the internal R&D investment of $10 million, there are then six options: two of them reflect a further net loss, so are not exercised, two of them represent a recovery of some of the previous investment, and so are exercised, and two of them are dreams come true and are delightedly exercised. The weighted average of these outcomes is to bring a positive $26.7 million to the holder of the option, which must be offset by the $15 million paid to have such option, leaving a value of the option of $11.7 million as calculated above.

EXHIBIT 8.15	DCF VERSUS REAL OPTION THINKING

Source: ©2003 Razgaitis. richard@razgaitis.com.

This result can also be shown using a probability tree structure as shown in Exhibit 8.16. (The respective percentages have not been shown because in this example they are all equal.)

Therefore, the license fee could actually be up to $11.7 million *higher* and still be net positive for the buyer.

One particular expression of real options has become quite famous because of its association with the pricing of financial (stock) options: the Black-Scholes Method, named after its co-discovers Francis Black (now deceased) and Myron Scholes. It has the appeal of being a closed form equation, namely: if one can determine the specific values of the inputs required, then a cell in a spreadsheet can directly compute the value of the option. This equation and approach has been widely used in financial options because, among other reasons, there is a wealth of data available from which the calculation of the needed inputs to the Black-Scholes equation can be made. Financial options also reasonably approximate the underlying assumptions required for the Black-Scholes method to be valid; these assumptions are:

| EXHIBIT 8.16 | WHEN AN OPTION EXISTS, A PROBABILITY TREE BECOMES A "DECISION TREE" |

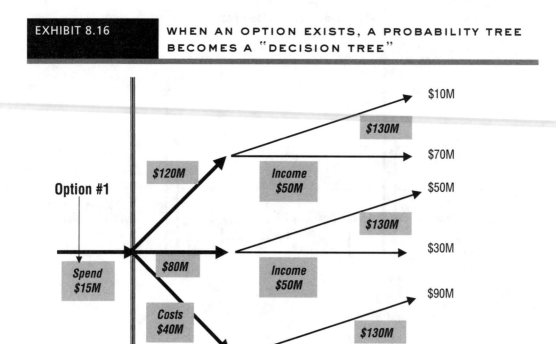

(Total Value to Buyer, Net of R&D Cost: = $26.7–10 = $16.7)

Source: ©2003 Razgaitis. richard@razgaitis.com.

- One uncertainty (volatility)
- Volatility knowable (generally by public trade data) at time of pricing the call value
- One time period
- Constant volatility during such time period
- Volatility characterizable by a continuous-time stochastic process arising from log-normal diffusion (LND). Such LND requires no below-zero values, and an infinitely long tail representing low probability but extraordinary value potential, and causes volatility to increase with the square root of time.
- The "Law of One Price" holds (two assets that have the same future value must have the same current value), or "no arbitrage" condition (known as dynamic tracking)
- European Call conditions (option is exercisable only on the expiration date, not before).
- No dividends (or ongoing costs), known as "asset leakage," occur (or if they occur, Black-Scholes must be modified by the Merton extension).
- "Continuous time finance," meaning that prices change continuous, one infinitesimal increments, without jumps.

Even for financial options, people have developed their own corrections to Black-Scholes to detail with these and other effects of the real world. For technology valuations, the luxury of data is simply not available, nor do most of these assumptions hold true, and other manifestations of real options is more appropriate, a subject beyond the scope of this book.

In the previously cited interview with the CFO of Merck,[13] the importance of Monte Carlo and real options to pharmaceutical investing is apparent. With huge, long-term investment decisions required to achieve "blockbuster" drugs (and earnings), sophisticated methods for characterizing, and value, risk versus reward are needed. Numerous additional companies in recent years have announced their use of real options for decision making. Some of these companies include P&W, HP, Anadarko, Cadence, Exxon, Texaco, TVA, Apple, Mobil, Airbus, and ICI.[14]

Dealmaking Using Monte Carlo and Real Options Analysis (Razgaitis, Hoboken, NJ: John Wiley & Sons, Inc., 2003), provides an expanded discussion of the use of Real Options including the use of now commercially available software for performing such calculation.

CONCLUSION

Real option is the subject of active research. Monte Carlo techniques are being more widely applied. The challenge is in applying such insights to the technology valuation problem at hand and dealing with the scarcity of data available to be able to exploit these tools.

However, as shown in the Monte Carlo example, it is now quite easy to develop much deeper insights into risk and reward using software available for the PC and the Mac. Some study of the software manuals is required, but experience will be gained mostly through use. The software vendors offer helpful courses and seminars. Also, insights can be gained with some simple math by viewing technology investments as options.

Valuation tools will continue to be an area for active development in order to assist businesspeople trying to make important valuation decisions in conditions of high uncertainty.

NOTES

1. "Closed form solution" means that all the variables involved in the problem can be arranged in equations such that the value being solved for can be determined by simply substituting for all the variables. A simple form of such a solution is $z = ax + by$, where z is the thing sought, x and y are variables for which one has values (known or assumed) and a and b are known constants. For any x and y, one can always determine z in "closed form." Complex problems cannot be reduced to such simple forms.
2. Justified True Belief (JTB) deals with beliefs that are not only *true* (lots of people believe things that are false) but also *justifiable* (it is possible to hold a belief that is true but for false or unjustifiable reasons).
3. In general, the assumption cells are not uniformly centered about the most likely value as was shown here. For instance, one could build in a probability of total project failure (such as due to FDA non-approval). In such more general cases, the median NPC valve will be skewed lower (or higher) than the corresponding simple DCF Method calculation.
4. The Crystal Ball software provides a very easy means to correlate, either positively or negatively, any pair of assumption cells. A further refinement of this example could include the use of a negative correlation between selling price and units sold.
5. The use of the term "advanced" is meant to designate methods that involve more complex mathematical calculations than the DCF Method and which are not as widely used.
6. Ashley J. Stevens, "Risk-Adjusted Net Present Value—A New Approach to Valuing Early Stage Technologies," *Journal of Biotechnology in Healthcare*, Vol. 2, No. 4, January, 1996.
7. Larry D. Smith, "Valuation of Life Sciences Companies—An Empirical and Scientific Approach," *Hambrecht & Quist Monograph*, January 4, 1994.
8. Mary Tanner, "Financing Biotechnology Companies," presentation at Association of Biotechnology Companies, NYC, September 1991.
9. Timothy A. Luehrman, "Strategy as a Portfolio of Real Options," *Harvard Business Review*, Sept.-Oct. 1998, p. 89 ff.
10. Timothy A. Luehrman, "Using APV: A Better Tool for Valuing Operations," *Harvard Business Review*, May-June 1997, p. 145 ff.
11. Timothy A. Leuhrman, "Investment Opportunities as Real Options: Getting Started on the Numbers," *Harvard Business Review*, July-Aug. 1998, reprint 98404.
12. Avinash K. Dixit and Robert S. Pindyck, "The Options Approach to Capital Investment," *Harvard Business Review*," May-June 1995, p. 105 ff.
13. "Scientific Management at Merck: An Interview with CFO Judy Lewent," by Nancy A. Nichols, *Harvard Business Review*, January–February 1994, p.89.
14. Copeland, Tom; and Anitkarov, Vladimir; *Real Options*, Texere, New York, 2001.

Crystal Ball Report

Crystal Ball Report
Simulation started on 3/10/99 at 17:18:06
Simulation stopped on 3/10/99 at 17:21:34

Sensitivity Chart

Target Forecast: NPV

COGS	-.75	
SG&A + R&D	-.40	
Units Sold Year 1	.22	
Units Sold Year 5	.19	
Units Sold Year 2	.16	
Units Sold Year 6	-.13	
Units Sold Year 3	.13	
Selling Price Year 1	.09	
Units Sold Year 4	.08	
Selling Price Year 6	-.07	
Selling Price Year 4	.07	
Selling Price Year 3	.05	
Selling Price Year 5	.04	
Selling Price Year 2	.03	

Measured by Rank Correlation

Forecast: NPV   **Cell: C18**

Summary:
Display Range is from $250,000 to $650,000.
Entire Range is from $282,179 to $661,632.
After 1,000 Trials, the standard Error of the Mean is $2,257.

Statistics:	Value
Trials	1000
Mean	$457,773
Median	$458,247
Mode	—
Standard Deviation	$71,362
Variance	$5,092,594,733
Skewness	0.14
Kurtosis	2.58
Coeff. of Variability	0.16
Range Minimum	$282,179
Range Maximum	$661,632
Range Width	$379,452
Mean Std. Error	$2,256.68

Percentiles:

Percentile	Value
0%	$282,179
10%	$366,192
20%	$393,817
30%	$414,635
40%	$438,070
50%	$458,247
60%	$477,084
70%	$493,614
80%	$517,890
90%	$555,341
100%	$661,632

End of Forecast

Assumptions

Assumption: Selling Price Year 1

Cell: C3

Triangular distribution with parameters:
Minimum	$9,000
Likeliest	$10,000
Maximum	$11,000

Selected range is from $9,000 to $11,000.
Mean value in simulation was $10,002.

Assumption: Selling Price Year 2

Cell: D3

Triangular distribution with parameters:
Minimum	$9,000
Likeliest	$10,000
Maximum	$11,000

Selected range is from $9,000 to $11,000.
Mean value in simulation was $9,990.

Assumption: Selling Price Year 3

Cell: E3

Triangular distribution with parameters:
Minimum	$8,550
Likeliest	$9,500
Maximum	$10,450

Selected range is from $8,550 to $10,450.
Mean value in simulation was $9,496.

Assumption: Selling Price Year 4

Cell: F3

Triangular distribution with parameters:
Minimum	$8,100
Likeliest	$9,000
Maximum	$9,900

Selected range is from $8,100 to $9,900.
Mean value in simulation was $8,982.

Assumption: Selling Price Year 5   Cell: G3

Triangular distribution with parameters:
    Minimum $7,200
    Likeliest $8,000
    Maximum $8,800

Selected range is from $7,200 to $8,800.
Mean value in simulation was $8,006.

Assumption: Selling Price Year 6   Cell: H3

Triangular distribution with parameters:
    Minimum $7,200
    Likeliest $8,000
    Maximum $8,800

Selected range is from $7,200 to $8,800.
Mean value in simulation was $8,007.

Assumption: Units Sold Year 1   Cell: C2

Normal distribution with parameters:
    Mean   100.00
    Standard Deviation   10.00

Selected range is from −Infinity to +Infinity.
Mean value in simulation was 100.07.

Assumption: Units Sold Year 2   Cell: D2

Normal distribution with parameters:
    Mean   200.00
    Standard Deviation   20.00

Selected range is from −Infinity to +Infinity.
Mean value in simulation was 199.82.

Assumption: Units Sold Year 3   **Cell: E2**

Normal distribution with parameters:
    Mean   300.00
    Standard Deviation   30.00

Selected range is from −Infinity to +Infinity.
Mean value in simulation was 301.56.

Assumption: Units Sold Year 4   **Cell: F2**

Normal distribution with parameters:
    Mean   350.00
    Standard Deviation   35.00

Selected range is from −Infinity to +Infinity.
Mean value in simulation was 348.79.

Assumption: Units Sold Year 5   **Cell: G2**

Normal distribution with parameters:
    Mean   400.00
    Standard Deviation   40.00

Selected range is from −Infinity to +Infinity.
Mean value in simulation was 400.98.

Assumption: Units Sold Year 6   **Cell: H2**

Normal distribution with parameters:
    Mean   400.00
    Standard Deviation   40.00

Selected range is from −Infinity to +Infinity.
Mean value in simulation was 399.06.

Assumption: COGS   **Cell: B6**

Uniform distribution with parameters:
    Minimum   55%
    Maximum   59%

Mean value in simulation was 57%.

Assumption: SG&A + R&D   **Cell: B7**

Custom distribution with parameters:		*Relative Prob.*
Single point	34%	0.300000
Single point	35%	0.500000
Single point	36%	0.200000
Total Relative Probability		1.000000

Mean value in simulation was 35%.

End of Assumptions

Source: Crystall Ball 4.0g, Decisioneering, Inc., Denver, CO. © 1988–2002 Decisioneering, Inc. Reprinted with permission.

CHAPTER 9

Method Six: Auctions

INTRODUCTION

While the Monte Carlo Method and the various option pricing techniques discussed in this book are fairly recent, this chapter deals with the oldest form of valuation known: obtaining bids under an auction format.

Since antiquity, auctions have been used as a simple, powerful means of determining the value of goods offered for sale. Auctioning is similar to the Industry Standards Method of Chapter 4 in that both methods are based on direct market determinations. However, the Industry Standards Method used market information for *previous* transactions *similar* to the one in question; the Auction Method uses existing and pending offers for precisely the technology being valued. (See Exhibit 9.1.)

In a certain sense, one can interpret typical negotiations as being "auctions." Even in mundane contexts such as bananas in a grocery store, the offering price is based upon the seller's perception of the price buyers are willing to pay, given the benefits and the alternatives. There really is nothing inherent in a banana that says it should sell for $X a pound. If for some reason buyers begin to want more bananas than are available, the sellers (all the sellers in the value chain) sense the demand and use it as a signal to deliver more bananas and to charge a higher price. Because bananas are perishable commodity items, the supply will eventually increase to the point where the abundance of bananas will cause sellers to reduce the price in order to clear out stock and a new market equilibrium price and demand will be established.

In offering technology for license, sellers typically call on multiple potential buyers to determine interest. The response from such inquiries can influence a seller's pricing decisions, even though no formal offer or bid has been made. Even if there are only discussions with one prospective buyer, imagine what a seller would think if that buyer said

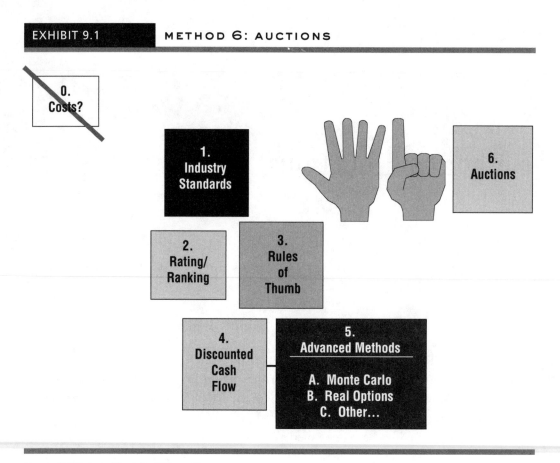

EXHIBIT 9.1   METHOD 6: AUCTIONS

Source: ©2003 Razgaitis, richard@razgaitis.com.

something like, "This is the best opportunity I've ever seen," "We absolutely have to have this technology," and "Hey, look, money is no object here, how much do you want?" Would not such words, or equivalent body language, be interpreted by the seller as bidding language even without formal bids? This is why, in the author's experience, the seller instead hears: "It looks very risky," "It's going to take a lot of money to get this to the market and then I'm not sure anyone is going to buy it," and "Maybe, just maybe, if we can get it for no upfront license fee and for a very reasonable royalty, I might be able to persuade my boss to take a chance on this."

The Auction Method is a way for a seller to structure a series of parallel, very short-term discussions with multiple prospective buyers and reduce all positioning statements into a simple monetary bid in a winner-take-all framework.

WHEN AUCTIONS ARE FEASIBLE

Before going into the operational issues of the Auction Method, it needs to be noted that the use of the method presumes a certain bargaining power on the part of the seller. Normally, if such power does not exist, then auctioning does not work. Also, from the perspective of the buyer, it is hard to envision circumstances where the use of auctions as a valuation method should be encouraged.[1]

In all five previous methods, there is no inherent limitation on the seller in making use of the described tools and techniques. There is always the challenge of gathering data, developing models, and applying good judgment, but there is nothing about these previous methods that requires a particular circumstance for the methods to be applied by either the buyer or the seller. Also in all the previous methods, there is nothing inherently disadvantageous to either the buyer or seller in the method itself. In the case of auctions, the buyer is at a disadvantage, and it requires some special circumstances in order to induce prospective buyers to "play."

Buyers always hope to be in a position to buy below the market value. It is important to recognize that if a seller and buyer each independently value a particular opportunity and, miraculously, both conclude that it is worth $10 million on an NPV basis net of an identically-assumed royalty, that it is the nature of buyers to try to pay something much less than $10 million. It has been said that business is about paying $5 for things worth $10; that is certainly the buyer's perspective. So, from a "win-win" negotiating standpoint, one might expect this situation to result in a quick settlement on the $10 million NPV. More often, what seems to happen is that the buyer will work very hard to see if the opportunity can be acquired for less than $10 million. The last thing that a buyer wants is a competitive bid situation with other buyers because such a situation would, in this hypothetical example, inevitably lead to a bid of $10 million, thus extinguishing the buyer's hope of paying $5 for a $10 item (Lest buyers feel abandoned, a counter-measure buyers can use to avoid auctions will be briefly discussed in the last section of this chapter.)

The other special circumstance of an auction is that it presumes (1) an inherently strong bargaining position on the seller's part and (2) that the technology in question can be apprehended relatively quickly by prospective buyers.[2] Considering first the issue of bargaining power, buyers will resist being herded into an auction. The primary reason buyers will go along with this method is that the licensing opportunity is so compelling that passing it up is even worse than bidding. Unless the seller can attract at least two or three bidders, the auction method is unlikely to produce a desirable result, although a sole buyer who is unaware of the non-existence of significant (or any) competition could be induced to making a full-NPV bid. Three or more bidders are optimal because it is common to have "low-ball bidders" at auctions—buyers who have not conducted a serious valuation but who bid a number so low that they are confident they can make money regardless of what it is they are buying (which by the way, is not reliably true of technology opportunities). In some cases, low-ball bidders even construct their offer in such a way as to tie up the technology for little or no money for the purpose of conducting their due diligence in a non-competitive environment. (This approach will be included in the buyer's alternatives to auctions section.)

A variant of low-ball bids is "fire sale" bids. The term refers to the insurance industry's practice of offering for quick sale goods that have been damaged in a fire. The insured had already been paid the full value for the damaged goods; a fire sale was a way for the insurance company to recoup something on its loss. The fire sale also carried the notion that what was not sold immediately was literally trashed, so any offer above zero was considered a potential winning bid.[3] Sellers should, of course, do everything they can to avoid the fire sale perception, signaling buyers that the auction is a disposal situation. Savvy buyers, as part of their due diligence, investigate the selling circumstances for exactly this reason. In the previously-cited Arthur Miller play, *The Price*, the used furniture buyer does not quote a price until he is able to determine the circumstances of the sale, wherein he learns: (1) neither heir can or will take the furniture, (2) there are no other bidders or takers, (3) the lease is about to run out on the apartment in which the furniture is being stored, and (4) the buyer's family is in a "get it over with" frame of mind. Did this affect his price? Not for nothing did an 89-year old man spend the entire first act pumping the seller for information. (Did Arthur Miller want us to think about our self-limiting natural inclinations, causing us to sell ourselves cheaply?) (Ah, back to work. . . .)

If an auction fails, due to a lack of bids or only low-ball bids, then the seller is at a bargaining disadvantage in seeking out subsequent buyers (assuming such buyers knew of the auction) because they would know that there was little or no interest by other buyers. Therefore, one of the seller's big risks in auctioning is that it can fail, which then can make it difficult to sell at all. At the very least, the seller might have to propose terms even less attractive than would have otherwise occurred sans auction.

The second assumption behind conducting an auction is that a buyer can reasonably apprehend the opportunity without a significant level of due diligence. To use estate auctions as a colloquial example, typical formats provide a catalog description of all the items offered for sale and an inspection period during which all bidders can examine the merchandise. When the goods being auctioned are seen and valued in a few minutes' time, then it is possible to get a large number of bidders to make the small investment in their time for the prospect of making and winning a bid. Even if a buyer's perception is that the odds of winning a bid are low, the investment required to ascertain the potential value is also low. In the case of technology, such low due diligence cost situations are rare if not non-existent. All the risk issues discussed in Chapters 2 and 7 normally need to be evaluated through a serious investment of time and, sometimes, testing (laboratory, manufacturing, and/or market). In such circumstances, buyers tell sellers that they simply will not exert such due diligence without some reasonable chance of being able to acquire the license if the opportunity checks out and the terms are affordable. Serious buyers will often express such a position by counter-offering an option agreement (discussed in Chapter 11), together with a cash payment to maintain an exclusive right to bid for a prescribed period. To some extent, sellers can help reduce the buyer's investment requirement by creating extensive data packages and even disclosure "rooms" where prospective buyers can study comprehensively prepared background information. It is in the seller's interest to make the due diligence burdens as low as possible in order to induce as many bidders as possible.

From time to time a particular auction-related selling concept is tried, that of having a technology fair. At such fairs, all technology sellers are in individual booths hawking their wares to prospective invitee-buyers, a technology flea market, so to speak. There are many problems with this concept. The principal underlying hypothesis is that it is possible, while standing in front of display tables with patents and prototypes, for a buyer to conduct sufficient due diligence to make a purchase decision and engage in negotiation. Such a process works well for baseball cards, collectible dolls, and shishkabob, but not for technology.

In summary, the more complex the opportunity, the more the seller must do to make it easier for buyers to conduct due diligence, and despite such efforts, the less likely it is that enough prospective buyers will take advantage of the opportunity. Likewise, the less compelling the opportunity, the more infeasible it becomes that a group of buyers will follow a seller's schedule in reviewing the opportunity and offering bids.

ROCKEFELLER "FAT GENE," AND OTHER EXAMPLES

One recent example of an auction that turned out very well for the seller has to do with a "fat gene" discovered by Rockefeller Institute.[4] Investigators at Rockefeller discovered a gene that appears to control obesity in mice and filed a patent application. The invention was described as "the hottest property to come out of biotech in years,"[5] a characterization not surprising given the ever-popular subject of weight loss. A startup company, Millennium, sought to obtain rights to the patent. Rockefeller, reasonably concerned about obtaining fair value by an arm's length negotiation, invited the interest of more than a dozen pharmaceutical firms including Amgen, Eli Lilly, BMS, and others. The interest turned out to be very high, and Rockefeller found itself being pursued with ever-increasing terms. Rockefeller conducted a series of discussions with interested parties in what emerged as a bidding process in January and February of 1995. Then on February 28, 1995, Rockefeller announced that Amgen agreed to pay a $20 million "signing fee" for a license; royalties (to be determined) were estimated at an additional $70 to $80 million. According to the Rockefeller Vice President for Academic Affairs, "Amgen purchased a scientific concept."[6]

This example has received a lot of press and may have created unrealistic expectations in some sellers. Clearly the Rockefeller auction was a case where the two necessary factors for a successful auction were present: strong bargaining power on the part of the seller, and relative ease in conducting due diligence by potential buyers. As further evidence of the bargaining power, in 1998 Pfizer was reported to have paid Phytopharm PLC up to $32 million for exclusive rights to an experimental drug to treat obesity based upon extracts of plants native to South America.[7] Clearly, market demand for drugs to control obesity creates intense interest in identifying promising technologies.

Although the price obtained by Rockefeller may be unusual, the use of an auction process for technology is not uncommon. The following are briefly summarized examples of auctions used to value and sell technology. They are based upon a recent paper by Bob Bramson which was written using publicly available information:[8]

- Exponential Technologies offered semiconductor patents alleged to cover Intel's Merced architecture. Rights were acquired by S3 for a price in the range of $10 to $12 million. Apple Computer has sued Exponential Technologies over the proceeds of the sale.

- Wang offered 200 patents organized in 34 technology groups. Certain groups sold during a so-called "quiet period." Additional groups sold through the auction process.

- AR Accessories Group, Inc. sold its patents at a bankruptcy auction.

- Carl W. Cooke had a patent on a child-resistant closure for pharmaceuticals. Its bankruptcy plan appraised the value of the patent at $375 million. An auction was conducted supervised by the Internal Revenue Service, but no bids were received.

- Cray Computer Corporation had patents on various technologies relating to supercomputing manufacturing packaging and processes. These patents and related intellectual property were acquired by Dasu L.L.C. for $100,000.

- IL Med had patents relating to surgical laser scanners. Under an auction format these patents were acquired by Laser Industries.

- Lamplighter Industries had patents relating to electroluminescent light technologies. The patents were offered at a bankruptcy auction and were acquired by CEL Technologies.

- Orca Technology had patents relating to disc drives which it had bought three years previously from Priam for $500,000 as part of a technology package. At a bankruptcy auction, Orca received $3.65 million by a Samsung winning bid.

- BioPolymers, Inc. had patents on medical adhesives which also were sold off also via a bankruptcy auction.

- Thinking Machines Corporation's massively parallel process patents were on track to be offered at auction. It is unclear whether such an auction took place. Likewise, VideOcart Inc.'s patent of shopping cart video display terminals was planned to be auctioned but the results are unknown.

- See additional auction examples in Chapter 4, News Sources of License Agreement Information.

These examples and others show not only the feasibility of using auctions but also act as another category of "Industry Standard" data to assist both buyers and sellers in performing technology valuations.

TYPES OF AUCTIONS

At the heart of the Auction Method is establishing an unambiguous process that prospective buyers can rely upon as being fair. Integrity in the process is essential as prospective buyers must believe that the highest qualifying bid will in fact be the successful bid. From the standpoint of a buyer, the nightmare scenario is that the seller has a hidden understanding with one of the buyers enabling the favored buyer to make a final bid after learning of all the other bids. Not only is such behavior unfair, but it also runs against the seller's own interests because it saves the favored buyer from having to make an aggressive bid by enabling that company to make only a matching or a slightly higher bid (known in the industry as a winning "McBid").

A simple form of an auction is to establish a time and place for written, binding bids to be submitted and the arrangements and time period whereby due diligence can occur. The seller should do everything possible to maintain the confidentiality of the number and identity of the bidders, although on many occasions the bidders all learn who the other parties are. Nevertheless, in some cases the prospective buyer views its interest as highly sensitive information, and the seller needs to take all reasonable steps to protect it as such.

Some "buyers" are really just doing competitive intelligence by participating in the process. Such buyers know or believe that someone will acquire the technology and put it into the marketplace, and they want to understand what the competitive effect is likely to be. Although such parties do not directly harm the auction process, they do take time and resources away from assisting serious prospects. Sellers have the right to exclude parties who they believe are not serious buyers. Strong non-disclosure agreements can act to dissuade some "tire kickers" because of the fear of later legal exposure if they independently develop features or products that appear to be derived from what they learned in the due diligence process.

The process normally involves written offers rather than calling out numbers as in estate auctions, although oral bidding processes have been used. The seller should create a standard form for such bids to assure that bidders respond with answers to all terms relevant to the seller. Otherwise, it can be impossible to know what exactly a buyer has bid.[9]

The seller then reviews the bids, which may take some time because each bid could be structured in such different ways that it requires "moving money around in time" using the Discounted Cash Flow Method. Of course, as part of such money movement, a risk factor must be selected which could vary from bidder to bidder depending upon the assets they can deploy in support of commercialization. The Rating/Ranking Method can be useful in comparing the various bids and bidders. The Industry Standard Method can help the seller compare all the offers received with those received by others in other auctions. Finally, the seller can use the Monte Carlo Method to create multiple return scenarios with various bidders or with various options under each bid.

The seller is not precluded from proposing modifications in the winning bid. Of course, the buyer is not obligated to accept such variations. However, it is possible that some changes advantageous to both parties could be found, (or at least changes that are advantageous to one and neutral to the other).

It is important upon selection of the winning bid that the consummation of the sale take place quickly as the losing bidders are likely to lose interest and go on to other projects. If for some reason the winner bidder does not complete the transaction, the seller wants to be able to conclude a deal with the next best bid. This hurdle can be cleared by having a complete agreement already drafted, one that outlines many of the key terms and requires all bidders to accept such terms for their bid to be qualified and considered for award. The U.S. Government has conducted such auctions for various contracts and in some cases even requires all bidders to sign the contract with their bid. The Government then executes only the winning contract. (It takes a *lot* of bargaining power to be able to do this.) In most licensing situations, the bids are sufficiently different in structure and the transaction complex enough that such pre-signed licenses are not feasible.

Sellers can further protect themselves by requiring that a non-refundable license fee or partial licensing fee accompany a bid. If the seller accepts the bid and the buyer has a change in heart, the licensing fee is forfeited. Such a fee is sometimes known as a "break up" fee, although that term is also used for the exit price paid by the party that terminates the deal after it has been executed. The rationale of this lost fee in an auction context is that the seller has been harmed by the buyer's refusal or inability to consummate its successful bid.

Open bidding auctions such as those commonly used for paintings, antiques, and cars work best when there are many items to be sold and many bidders to be managed. For technology deals, such an approach is generally not feasible.

However, other variants of auctions could be useful. One such variant is the "short list" auction. The initial bidders are pared down to (usually) just two or three parties who make "the short list." Then more detailed negotiations (and possibly further due diligence) are held, and a last, "best and final" bid is made by the two or three parties. This approach is particularly useful if an ongoing relationship between the seller and buyer will be needed; the negotiating period will permit each party to discern what working with the other party will be like. Such discussions can also be helpful to a seller who is attempting to determine the likelihood of actually receiving future payments or royalties based upon a buyer's successful commercialization.

Appendix 9A, courtesy of Dale Hogue, provides a sample letter used to conduct an actual patent auction.

AD HOC AUCTIONS

What about the approach of the seller using an ad hoc, namely: a seller describes the opportunity to a prospective buyer and then asks for an offer to initiate negotiations? This approach has obvious appeal to the seller as the easiest of all approaches, just ask and see what happens. However, any buyer who senses that the seller does not know its value will be sorely tempted to make a very low offer such that regardless of how the present uncertainties work out, or some upward adjustments in price as a result of ad hoc bargaining, the buyer will still be very happy with the result. So ad hoc are often simply easy, low-cost ways for sellers to receive very low offers. If a seller is in a "just get rid of it" mode this may be a justifiable approach. This could also make sense if the seller is in a unusual, long-term relationship with a remarkably fair-minded buyer who, in such circumstances, will make a fair offer as though they were being dragged through an auction. And it is possible that the reason the seller has such a long-term relationship is that the particular buyer has been getting opportunities for 10 cents on a dollar for years.

Any structured marketing and negotiating process has elements of an auction because there are offers, counter-offers, and adjustments in bids. However, in these circumstances both the seller and the buyer normally have some foundation for belief in the value of the opportunity and they are not relying for such foundational information to come in response to a question "what'll you give me for it?"

APPROACHES BUYERS CAN USE IN LIEU OF AN AUCTION

As discussed above, buyers generally find auctions to be to their disadvantage and, consequently, they seek ways of avoiding such situations. There are several techniques that buyers can use to prevent auctions.

The reason sellers seek auctions is to maximize the price and to have followed a process that can be argued to have done so. Buyers, then, can meet the desires of a seller by (1) offering a "preemptive," attractive bid, and (2) providing information that will persuade the seller that their offer is in fact fair and attractive. Further, the buyer can (when legitimate) create a reasonable sense of urgency. Focusing on concluding the negotiations as soon as possible will speed the subsequent commercialization of the technology.

At the beginning of this chapter there is the hypothetical example where the seller and buyers both have the same perception of value, that is, an NPV of $10 million. A buyer can use a business model to justify a bid of $10 million. Being greedy or attempting to get $10 for $1 may result only in getting forced into an auction process and a lost opportunity. This will certainly increase transaction cost and time spent. Instead, a buyer can sometimes induce a seller to accept somewhat less than the full $10 million for a quick deal. In the end, if the buyer believes that such NPV was calculated using an appropriate risk-adjusted hurdle rate (k), then the buyer should be prepared to pay the full $10 million.

CONCLUSION

In one sense, the Auction Method is the easiest valuation method because the seller does not have to calculate or develop a valuation model. However, it involves significant work of a different sort: the seller has to create and manage a valuation process that attracts a sufficient number of prospective buyers. Also, it is a good idea for the seller, and of course the buyer, to perform a valution using the other methods described in this book. Otherwise, without such insight, it is not often obvious if the auction has produced a reasonoable result, particularly with few or modest bidders. Overall, it may not be simpler, or easier, or even faster. The greatest value of auctions is that when they succeed they provide concrete evidence of market value by virtue of the fact that multiple buyers are each making offers in their own reasonable self-interest. For those circumstances where it makes sense, the Auction Method can be very useful, but overall it is not the norm. Its frequent use in bankruptcy settings and other emergency liquidations is testament not to the desirability of the method but rather to the need for a rapid resolution of the sale, much like our earlier reference to fire sales.

NOTES

1.   There is a least one case of buyer-encouraged auctions. If a prospective buyer believes that it has made a very high offer and, for reasons unique to the buyer, can afford to pay more for the technology than can other buyers, but the seller is still reluctant to sell because it believes that the technology is worth even more, then it could be in the buyer's best interest to encourage an auction, formal or informal, to dislodge the seller from its position.

2.   There is another context where auctions "work," a context that is a current growth market, and that is bankruptcy proceedings. When a trustee is harvesting what value he or she can from a failed company, then generally interested parties accept the proposition that an auction will take place and, depending on their interest, will or will not pursue it. There is normally limited or no ability to control or object to the behavior of the seller in such circumstances.

3.   In cases where there is a significant disposal (trashing) costs, even offers below zero, (i.e., the *seller* pays the buyer), can actually be advantageous to the seller. This situation is what buyers dream about in alpha-state sleep.

4.   The source of the information provided about the Rockefeller Institute auction is based upon *Business Week* articles, March 13, 1995, p. 46; March 20, 1995, p. 100; and August 7, 1995, p. 29.

5.   Ibid.

6.   Ibid.

7.   "Pfizer Gives Phytopharm a Boost; Pact Centers on Obesity Treatment," *Wall Street Journal*, August 25, 1998.

8.   Special thanks to Bob Bramson of Bramson and Pressman for the examples cited, as given in his paper, "Patent Auctions, An Alternative Method of Generating Value from Patents," presented at the 1998 Annual Meeting of the Licensing Executives Society in Miami, October 28, 1998.

9.   Some buyers create ambiguity on purpose. If a seller who does not fully understand such an ambiguous offer enters into negotiations with such a buyer, other buyers are likely to vanish and the seller could be left in a negotiating situation very different from what had been anticipated.

Bidder's Agreement

This agreement made between _____ (hereinafter Bidder) and Hogue Management, LLC (Hereinafter Auctioneer) is for the purpose of allowing Bidder to participate as a bidder in a live auction of U.S. Patent No. 5,664,115, Interactive Computer System to Match Buyers and Sellers of Real Estate, Businesses and other Property Using the Internet, now owned by Richard Fraser.

If the Bidder is the highest bidder, he agrees to pay his bid amount payable to the transfer agent, Antonelli, Terry, Stout & Kraus, LLP, 1300 North Seventeenth Street, Suite 1800, Arlington, Virginia 22209, by 5 PM EDT, Friday, May 15, 1999 at the above address. Payment may be by cashiers check or a wire transfer of good funds. Payment made after this time period may be accepted at the sole discretion of Richard Fraser. If there is not timely payment or acceptance by Richard Fraser of a late tender, Richard Fraser may reject the bid and resell the patent at the cost of Bidder and may recover any negative difference between the ultimate sale price of said patent and the Bidder's highest offer.

Bidder agrees that he will clearly communicate his bid to the auctioneer. Once the auctioneer acknowledges the bid it is final and may not be withdrawn.

Bidder agrees to abide by the laws of the Commonwealth of Virginia pertaining to the sale of intangible property sold by auction.

The Bidder may bid anonymously. If he wishes to do so he must identify his nominee to the auctioneer in writing by June 11, 1999, no later then 5 PM EDT, addressed to the auctioneer at the address of the Antonelli, Terry et al. law firm above identified.

Bidder will be assigned a number for bidding purposes and will receive a numbered bidding card. Bidder agrees to bid by this assigned number and is responsible for retaining possession of said card and all bids made using that number. Auctioneer will not disclose the identity of any bidder.

The auctioneer will cause to be delivered an assignment of all right, title and interest in said U.S. Patent 5,664,115 upon payment in good funds of the successful bid price to the transfer agent. The assignment will include all rights, past and present. Richard Fraser will warrant that there are no claims to title or licenses granted under said patent, or claims as to validity or enforceability of said patent. No other warranties or representations will be made nor indemnifications given.

Accepted by: Accepted by:

_____   _____
Signature   Signature

_____   _____
Title   Principal Manager

_____   _____
Company Name and Address   Hogue Management, LLC
Tele. No.

_____   _____
Date   Date

Source: Dale Hogue, Hogue Management, LLC, Hilton Head, SC, dchoguesr@aol.com.

CHAPTER 10

Equity Considerations

One hundred million
Could not keep us in business.
Jeez do we look dumb.[1]

Since publication of the previous edition of this book, the venture capital (VC) funding of new startups (NEWCOs) and the attendant returns from initial public offerings (IPOs) has dramatically declined from historically high levels. This decrease is principally due to what appears to have been an overreaction to the business opportunities associated with the Internet, computer networks, and deregulation of the telecom industry. These opportunities and their attendant components of optical fiber, photonic components, high-speed circuit switches and packet routers and related systems, and software that makes it all work, led to an explosion of investment interest by private capitalists, high risk capitalists, strategic acquirers (such as Cisco), investment bankers, and the IPO public. This led to the creation of enormous wealth in some situations, a financial black hole in others, and both (wealth, followed by a black hole) in still others.

The numbers are staggering. According to Vinod Khosla, a general partner with famous Silicon Valley venture capital (VC) firm of Kleiner Perkins Caufield & Beyers, in a talk given at an annual VC meeting in San Francisco in mid-June 2002, here are the VC statistics for the period 1995 through 2000:[2]

- 14,463 companies received VC funding.
- 978 went public (less than 7 percent)
- 1,529 were acquired (less than 11 percent; for a total with the IPOs of only 17 percent)
- 1,180 have by this date gone out of business
- 10,776 are somewhere out there (no doubt on the phone looking for money)

Yet, just the *month* previous to Khosla's talk (May 2002), VCs invested at total of $790 million into 59 rounds of technology companies, including $171 million into 14 rounds for "internet services."[3] And, according to "VC Buzz," an internet daily deal information source, U.S. Internet-related deals during the first six months of 2002 have attracted approximately $12 billion in investment. So, the equity investment industry still exists and NEWCO opportunities are still being created based on technology. Health care and biotech (sometimes collectively referred to as "life science"), including emerging areas such as genomics, proteomics, drug delivery, nanotechnology, and microfluidics, remains strong. During the past two years VCs invested a record $13 billion.[4] A summary of the change in the VC industry ("v-cindustry") is shown in Exhibit 10.1.

The public markets of technology companies have risen and fallen in similarly spectacular fashion. At their recent peak in March 2000, the "DICE" (digital information, communication, and electronics, including telecom and software/IT, but not life sciences, pharmaceuticals, health care, or biotech) public companies comprised some 44 percent of the total $17 trillion of market cap of all U.S. companies. As of this writing, the total market cap has dropped to approximately $10 trillion and as a percentage the DICE companies have plunged in value even faster to comprise just approximately 17 percent of that diminished total. Yet, during this period some dramatic transformations in our communication and IT structure has taken place. Between 1996 and 2001, internet traffic increased by a factor of 3,000.[5] There are now 440 million email accounts in the U.S. and 890 million worldwide (unfortunately many of them are receiving daily offers of lower rates on their credit card balances and various nefarious services and products).

Microsoft is in many ways the posterchild of the technology industry and new economy. To give perspective on what has happened consider this statistic: taking one recent day, December 4, 2001, Microsoft's market capitalization was $355 billion. This value was substantially more than the $288 billion for *all 25* companies comprising four S&P indices of steel ($8 billion), automobiles ($58 billion), chemicals and plastics ($109 billion), and aerospace and defense ($113 billion). That is, Microsoft itself had a greater market capitalization than Ford, GM, DuPont, Dow, Boeing, US Steel, Eastman, Lockheed Martin, and 17 other of the largest companies in the U.S. *combined*.[6]

EXHIBIT 10.1	INTERNET "V-CINDUSTRY": THEN & NOW	
	Q1 2000	**Q1 2002**
"Internet VC" Firms	916	202 (−78%)
"Internet VC" Investments	1009	292 (−72%)
$ Invested	$15.7 billion	$1.3 b (−92%)
	Q4 1999	
IPOs (all)	159	16 (−90%)

Source: Data adapted from "Down from the Peaks," New York Times Magazine (June 9, 2002): 34.

Returning again to Vinod Khosla, in just the first eight months of 1999 he saw the following transactions for companies that he was instrumental in providing founding investments:[7]

- Cerent, which was acquired by Cisco Systems for $6.9 billion (Kleiner Perkins $8 million, 30% stake was thus valued at $2 billion).

- Juniper Networks which went public (Kleiner Perkins stake was another $2 billion based on an even smaller investment)

- Excite Inc. which was acquired by At Home Corp. for $6.7 billion.

INTRODUCTION

As discussed in Chapter 2, there are many possible forms of payment (or consideration) of interest to buyers and sellers in licensing negotiations. In this chapter we will consider the special circumstances where the buyer offers equity (stock) in an entity already created or to be created in order to commercialize the subject technology. Although stock can be considered as partial or full compensation for a license by performing a fair market valuation (FMV) of the stock, and as such, could be treated by any and all of the previous valuation methods, frequently there are special aspects of such a transaction that warrant treatment in a separate chapter.

INHERENT ADVANTAGES OF PERFORMANCE-BASED PAYMENTS

First, it is useful to distinguish among cash payments, royalties, and equity as forms of compensation in a license. Cash is the simplest rumuneration. Once the amount has been settled upon as a result of valuation, pricing, and negotiation, the cost to the buyer and the benefit to the seller is fixed, certain, and immediate.[8] If the licensed technology turns out to be more successful than the parties envisioned, then this fortuitous outcome benefits the buyer and the buyer only; likewise, if there is an unfortunate outcome, the direct financial consequences are felt by the buyer and the buyer only. In other words, "A deal is a deal." Once the parties have agreed on the worth of a technology, it is contrary to the nature of a cash license agreement for future events to cause the parties to change the valuation. It is precisely this certainty of valuation that makes it challenging to use only cash as the basis of a technology license. Sellers must make projections on the potential range of outcomes, high to zero, and settle on one number for which they are willing to part with the technology and live with that decision. Similarly, buyers need to reduce all the uncertainties to one number, and that number has to be equal to or higher than the seller's number or no deal will be possible.

In a sense, all cash license agreements can lead to a feeling by either the buyer or the seller that, in retrospect, the deal was unfair. This is because the NPV of what actually transpires will almost certainly be higher or lower than the license price. If, for example, it comes out higher, then the seller must face the fact that the deal is fair even though it did not receive the full value of the opportunity because it did not participate in the risk but instead opted for a certain sum. If the outcome is lower than originally agreed to, then the buyer has to remember that this is the price of agreeing to a fixed-cash license fee. The buyer took the risk of commerce and this particular time the outcome was unexpectedly low. A summary of these perspectives is shown in Exhibit 10.2.

Because of the difficulty in determining one single number as an equitable valuation, and the subsequent dissatisfaction that one or the other parties can be expected to feel, it is common for the parties to instead structure the valuation so that both the buyer and the seller share some of the risk and some of the reward associated with uncertain outcomes. Royalties are a very useful and simple means of doing this, which is in fact why they exist as an option—the marketplace created the royalty concept because of the need for dealing with vast future uncertainties. This "tying together" of like interests, (unlike the example shown in Exhibit 10.2) is one key advantage of a royalty structure. A second advantage is that it does not require the specification of one absolute dollar amount as the equitable consideration for a license; so in this sense, it is easier to reach agreements between sellers and buyers, and it is easier for both the seller and the buyer to feel that what they are to receive is fair. This latter virtue is important because, in most cases, there are multiple individuals at both companies who must approve the deal in order for it to take place. A licensing negotiator can sometimes face more difficulty trying to negotiate a consensus in his or her own organization than with the other side. Royalties and equity make this easier than lump sum payments.

RATIONALE FOR EQUITY AS A PERFORMANCE-BASED PAYMENT

However (and there is always a "however") royalties do not completely mirror the profitability or cash flow that will result from putting a technology into commerce. Royalties, as

EXHIBIT 10.2	PERSPECTIVES OF THE PARTIES TO FUTURE OUTCOMES WITH CASH LICENSES	
	Seller's Perspective	Buyer's Perspective
NPV of the Outcome is Greater than Cash Payment for the License	I elected not to risk my payment and, so, did not deserve the unexpected upside.	By my risk-taking (and perhaps commercial skill), I have managed to do better than planned.
NPV of the Outcome is Less than Cash Payment for the License	At the time, I received what both parties believed it was worth; I did not have the right to any upside surprise and, so, I do not participate in a downside surprise either.	I took the risk that in the end I would receive more value than originally estimated, but with that risk was the chance that I would not do as well as I'd planned.

the term is normally used, apply to a base of sales, the so-called "top line" of an income statement. Profitability, or cash flow, occurs at the "bottom line." In between are a lot of costs (and a lot of accounting). The buyer will feel success or failure, relative or absolute, by what happens principally at the bottom line.[9] Accordingly, it is possible that the seller could be quite happy with a royalty cash inflow based upon some percentage of sales, while the buyer is quite unhappy because after all the costs, including the royalty payment, the net on the bottom line is small, zero, or even negative. Because royalties are tied to sales, which occur only if there are customers, they are a step toward risk sharing between the seller and buyer, but a royalty structure does not equally balance the risks and interests between the parties. This is a similar reasoning that leads boards and senior management to use stock options as a behavior motivating and rewarding tool, particularly for startups.

From time to time, various buyers have proposed a modified royalty structure where the royalty base is in the bottom line, EBIT, or EAT (see Chapter 7), instead of being sales-based, arguing that such a net income basis is a truer reflection of the value of the license. However, because all the costs between the top line and the net income of the bottom line are largely controlled by the buyer, there are only rare and special cases where the parties agree to basing the royalty on any value below the top line and doing so is perilous to the seller as recent public accounting mischief has made all too clear.

There are various other lines below the top line (sales) and above the bottom line (EBIT or EAT) on which the royalty could be based. Gross Margin, defined as the sales less the cost of goods sold (the so-called direct costs), is one such possibility. In general, because of the auditing complexities in computing the royalty base anywhere below the top line, it is still rare that parties agree to such a provision.

There are certain other issues that arise with royalty agreements. Consider the following situation. The seller licenses patents and trade secrets (know how) to the buyer and, in so doing, launches the buyer in a new business. As the technology is developed and optimized, the buyer creates and then sells products that look generally like the licensed subject matter, but such products are outside the claims of the licensed patents and the scope of the licensed trade secrets. As a result, the buyer argues that it owes the seller nothing. The seller, in looking carefully at the terms of the license agreement, concludes that although the buyer is technically correct, an unjust outcome has occurred because despite having put the buyer in business, the seller will not receive any future compensation. The buyer's response is "a deal is a deal" and I have no obligation to pay for what I am not using (i.e., I am not benefiting from the scope of the licensed patent claims or trade secret information). Equity-based agreements can help prevent this situation.

With equity agreements, the seller receives a share in the company that receives the licensed technology. If the above scenario unfolds, it would not limit the seller's future prospects because it owns stock *in the company*, not a royalty right in specific kinds of *sales*. In this sense, the consideration received by the seller is somewhat like ownership of a mutual fund comprised of anything and everything the buyer can or will create in terms of value. Even if the buyer abandons the licensed technology and instead opens a hamburger stand, as long as the corporate entity remains, the seller will retain its equity share in a burgers and fries enterprise.

Equity deals can also create a downside outcome for the seller. Consider a buyer that has two products, one based on the licensed subject matter and one developed independently. In this scenario, the licensed subject matter is wildly successful in both a top line and bottom line sense. However, the second product turns out to be a disaster and causes the loss of all the profits of the firm. Had the seller a royalty-only interest, it would have received payment possibly unaffected by the misfortune occurring elsewhere in the buyer's company, providing the buyer continued to make sales of the licensed technology. But with an equity interest, the "mutual fund" right the seller acquired could result in the destruction of all value of the company. Other concerns of sellers, which are outside the scope of this book, have to do with liability. Exhibit 10.3 summarizes the principal distinctions between a traditional royalty interest and an equity interest.

THE EXTREME UPSIDE POTENTIAL OF EQUITY-BASED AGREEMENTS

There is one additional, and extremely important, factor that explains the keen and increasing interest in equity-based agreements: the upside potential to the seller. Consider the following situation. In Case A, there is a straight royalty agreement of 5 percent of sales and

EXHIBIT 10.3	CONTRASTING THE BENEFITS AND LIMITATIONS OF ROYALTY AND EQUITY-BASED LICENSE AGREEMENTS	
	Royalty Agreements	**Equity Agreements**
1. Base of payment	Sales of licensed subject matter	Value of the buyer-entity
2. Upside Potential	Increased sales of licensed subject matter	Increased value of the company
3. Downside Potential	Decreased or no sales of licensed subject matter	Failure of the company
4. Payments Made to Seller	Quarterly or annually on sales	Conversion (sale) of stock
5. Payment Stream to Seller	Each quarter for the life of the agreement (could extend to 10 years or more)	No payments until an equity conversion (realization) is possible and exercised
6. Importance of Patents and other forms of IP	Crucial to the seller receiving payments under the terms of the license	Relevant to the general competitive position of the buyer, but irrelevant to the rights of the seller

such sales are $100 million per year for 10 years. Ignoring DCF considerations for simplicity, the math for the seller looks like this:

$$\text{Annual Royalty} = 5\% \times \$100 \text{ Million} = \$5 \text{ Million} \times 10 \text{ years} = \$50 \text{ Million}.$$

In Case B, assuming somehow there is a parallel universe where the exact same technology is put into practice under an equity-based agreement where, instead of a 5 percent royalty, the seller received 10 percent of the pre-public stock, the math for the seller could look like this:

$$\text{Annual Royalty} = \$0. \text{Value of the company, as determined by the}$$
market at an initial public offering (IPO) turns out to be 10 times the
company's revenues (which are solely from the licensed technology),
then the value of the seller's stock $= \$100 \text{ million} \times 10 \times 10\%$
$= \$100 \text{ million}$ (ignoring, for the moment, dilution),
at the date of the IPO which is in (say) three years hence.

So for Case A, the seller received a total of $50 million in equal $5 million payments over 10 years, whereas in Case B, the seller received $100 million in one payment three years after the license was signed. Most sellers would prefer Case B to Case A; if the perceived risks were the same, no rational seller would prefer Case A. The key driver for value in Case B is the market's perception of company value scaled on the company's sales at the time of the IPO. In this example, 10 times sales was used; had the valuation been two times sales, then the seller would have received:

$$\$100 \text{ million} \times 2 \times 10 \text{ percent} = \$20 \text{ million}.$$

For most sellers, this would look less attractive than the Case A outcome.

The general recipe for comparison is as follows:

$$\text{Case A/Case B} = \text{Royalty} \times \text{Sales/Share} \times M \times \text{Sales} = \text{Royalty/Share}$$
$\times M$, where royalty is the royalty rate as a percentage of sales,
share is the percentage of the company owned by the seller
at the time of IPO, and M is the market's valuation of
the company as a multiple of sales at the time of the IPO.

Historically, companies were valued at approximately one to three times sales. Using two times sales, the formula becomes:

$$\text{Case A/Case B} = \text{Royalty}/2 \times \text{Share}.$$

This equation shows that without consideration of risk or the time value of money (and the attendant timing of an IPO), Case A would be preferred by the seller if the royalty percentage was more than twice the share ownership at the time of IPO. If the share ownership is greater than half the royalty (again expressed as a percentage), then Case B would be more attractive to the seller. Using 5 percent royalty as an example, and again neglecting the issues of risk and time value of money and taxes, the seller should prefer an equity deal

(Case B) for any circumstance where the share interest exceeds 2.5 percent at the time of an IPO, and should prefer a royalty deal (Case A) when the shares offered were less (or projected to become less) than 2.5 percent at the time of an IPO. All these values are derived from the assumption that the market value is twice the annual revenues.

If the market valuation (M) is 10 times revenues, which occurred not infrequently during the late 1990s, then the crossover value for preferring equity over royalty is one-tenth the royalty rate, namely, the seller is better off in an equity model, rather than a royalty payment, when the shares offered make up greater than 0.5 percent of the company at the time of an IPO. Exhibit 10.4 shows how this works for various values of M.

The historical basis for valuations in the range of one to three times revenues is this: If a company produces after-tax profits (EAT) of 10 percent of revenues, then $100 of annual sales creates a stream of profits of $10 per year. What would an owner pay for a stream of payments of $10 per year? Using the Discounted Cash Flow equation (Chapter 7), the present value of each $10 payment is equal to $10/(1 + k)^n$ where k is the risk-adjusted hurdle rate and n is the year in which such payment occurs. What is the sum of an infinite stream of such payments made year by year? It turns out that the equation is very simple: Present Value of an infinite stream of annual payments = B/k, where B is the magnitude of such annual payments. So for a k-value of 7 percent (0.07), $PV = 14.3 \star B$. In other words, an investor believing that the future benefit of owning an asset will be "B" dollars per year, and perceiving the overall risk and time value of money as being 7 percent, would be willing to pay up to 14.3 times the value of B. Further, if the buyer believed that "B" would increase with time, perhaps as a result of expanding markets, then a value higher than 14.3 would be warranted. What this represents is the the price/earnings ratio (P/E ratio): the earnings are "B," and the buyer is willing to pay 14.3 (or more)

| EXHIBIT 10.4 | THE RELATIONSHIP BETWEEN ROYALTY RATE AND MARKET VALUATION MULTIPLE THAT MAKES AN EQUITY REALIZATION MORE ATTRACTIVE TO A SELLER |

Royalty rate for a royalty-based agreement (the Case A alternative)	Market Valuation Multiple, M (Value at IPO/Annual Revenues)	Share ownership that would create a more attractive return to a seller than a royalty interest
5%	2	2.5%
5%	10	0.5%
5%	20	0.25%
1%	2	0.5%
1%	10	0.1%
1%	20	0.05%

to own such future earnings. Historically, common stock has traded (been sold) at P/E ratios of 15 and more recently about 20 for perceived higher growth stocks.

Putting this together, the value of a company expressed as a percentage of its annual sales would be as follows:

Value of a company = (P/E)×(B/Sales)×Sales. For a P/E of 20, and
B/Sales (i.e., earnings after tax, or EAT) of 10 percent, the resulting
valuation is two times sales. The general result is shown in Exhibit 10.5.

The values shown in Exhibit 10.5 presume constant sales and profitability. Because the IPO market has recently valued many start-ups at very high multiples of revenues—the so called "dot com" effect—sellers have become increasingly interested in participating in equity realizations. When multiples on revenues at an IPO reach 10 or more, then even very small ownership percentages can create tremendous valuations.

SHARE STRUCTURES AND VALUE

When a company is publicly traded, such as on the NASDAQ exchange, the share price is known daily, even hourly, with great precision. The reason for such precision is that there is a continuous auction underway with numerous buyers and sellers, and imbalances in supply

EXHIBIT 10.5   **VALUATION AS A MULTIPLE OF SALES FOR VARIOUS VALUES OF P/E RATIO AND PROJECTED PROFITABILITY (EAT)**

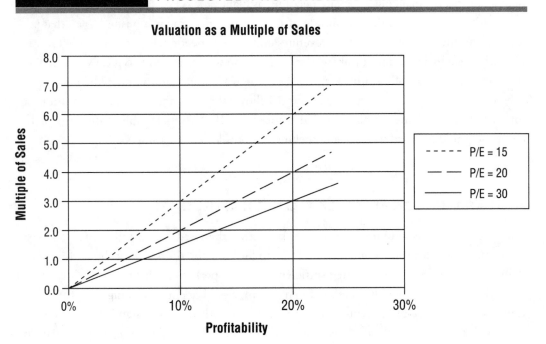

and demand cause the price of a share to go up and down. Such market determination is not present in a technology license to a start-up, because there is no public market.[10]

There are two licensing situations to be considered here: (1) the buying company pre-exists the license negotiation with previous investment and valuation, and (2) the buyer exists as individuals who will start a company, raise funds and hire additional management to commercialize the licensed technology. In the former case, there is some basis of valuation for the existing company because previous investors had to have determined how much each share was worth in order to rationalize their investment. In the latter case, the initial valuation of the company will be determined at the time of the license. We will deal with the latter case first because it's a more common situation.

The easiest way to perform a valuation is to assume a number of shares outstanding. For convenience we shall use 10 million shares, a commonly used number in technology start-ups. What is needed to create a company to commercialize a licensed technology is equity investors, parties who may not have any day-to-day management involvement but who in-vest money in the start-up with the expectation that at some future time (1) there will be a way to get their money out of the company (a liquidity event), and (2) there is a reasonable prospect that a return on the investment will occur that is commensurate with the risk. Eq-uity investment is critical because start-up companies often find it impossible to obtain debt investment (loans), because the start-up will require money to complete the technol-ogy, hire all the employees, perform market development, and manufacture and sell prod-ucts, all before there are substantial or even any revenues, and because lenders want security for such loans: Creating a business of unknown value is not what such lenders consider ideal collateral. Usually the finance model assumes only equity investment until the com-pany's profitability can support its operations and growth needs for capital; at such time, debt as a form of financing normally becomes available.

In order to determine the magnitude of such equity investment, a business plan that pro-jects all the investments and future revenues and costs is needed. Equity investors typically like to release their funding in phases, known as "rounds." A round is typically defined as a time period of 12 to 24 months, at the end of which additional funding will be needed in a subsequent round. A common business model shows the need for three or four rounds be-fore a start-up becomes publicly traded through an IPO (Initial Public Offering) or be-comes acquired by another company seeking a foothold in the business.

A START-UP CAPITALIZATION EXAMPLE

For simplicity, let us assume the business plan shows the need for $5 million for one year, then $10 million for the second year, and $20 million for the third year, at the end of which the start-up will have demonstrated sufficient sales and perhaps profits to enable it to attract an underwriter and a public market. Such a plan would ask its founding investors, those capitalizing the start-up in Round 1, for $5 million with the understanding that the plan calls for additional capital infusions totaling $30 million before the company can stand on its own. Now the question becomes, how much of the company at founding does $5 million buy? Put another way, what is the price per share of the 10 million initial shares?

Apportioning the Value to Start-Up Contributors

Generally this question is answered by looking at three primary contributions to the start-up: technology, management, and money, but not necessarily in that order. For simplicity, let us consider a case where the management is not a source of any money, so their stake in the company is determined solely by their commitment to the fortunes of the company. Further, for simplicity, let us also assume that the management is not the source of the technology. In such cases, investors tend to provide 10 to 20 percent or more of the founding stock as the management share, awarded (and vested) over time, based upon meeting certain milestones. In this example, we shall assume 20 percent, or 2 million shares are so allocated. Now, of the remaining 8 million shares, how shall they be divided between the money (investors) and the technology (the seller)?

This is a negotiation between the seller (the technology owner) and the buyer (the start-up investors) just like the ones considered previously in this book. What is different here is that these investors will develop a model for the future valuation of the company based on various scenarios, with a built-in expectation for a rate of return (k-value) from which a calculation can be made of how much of the company they should have (in their mind) given the risk they are taking. Likewise, sellers can perform the same business model assessment to determine a future cash value that can then be brought back to the present time using the DCF method (with a k-value appropriate to the risk). The seller then compares such DCF (or NPV) value to that obtainable from other licensing approaches, such as a royalty-bearing license, to an existing company using any of the methods and tools of the preceding chapters, and decides upon the minimum number of shares that would make this equity deal attractive. If the expectations of the seller and buyer overlap, then a deal will be possible. If they do not and cannot be made to overlap by further discussion and negotiation, then no grounds for an agreement will be reached on an equity model.[11]

The Use of "Step-Ups" to Characterize Round by Round Valuations

The challenge both the seller and buyer (investors) face is that the business model is based not only on a product that does not yet exist but also on a company that does not exist with customers who also do not yet exist. Accordingly, the uncertainty in the financial model tends to be very high. One tool commonly used to develop a valuation is the use of "step-ups." Let us suppose that in this example, the seller and the buyer agree to split the remaining 8 million shares 50:50 so that the founding capital structure is as follows: 2 million shares for management (albeit earned over time), 4 million for the technology (the sellers), and 4 million for the money (the investor-buyers). Thus, $5 million invested purchases 4 million shares. This ratio fixes the initial share price at $1.25/share ($5 million divided by 4 million shares). Thus, the management allowance of 2 million shares has an initial paper value of $2.5 million, and the technology has a value of $5 million, although because there is no market for the company's stock, none of the stock is sellable (there are also legal and contractual reasons why such shares cannot be sold, but these are outside the scope of this book).

A year hence, an additional $10 million will need to be raised. To do so, the company will issue and price additional stock, which leads to the infamous "dilution" problem for the seller and for management. Here's how the dilution problem is usually stated. If the future stock is priced at $1.25/share, then to raise $10 million, it will be necessary to issue 8 million new shares, creating a total pool of 18 million shares. Now management's 2 million shares, which had been 20 percent of the company, have become 11 percent of the company, and the seller of the founding technology has seen its 40 percent initial share become "diluted" to 22 percent because it still owns 4 million of the now 18 million shares. However, the value of the company has gone up as a result of the second round of funding. There are now 18 million shares with a value of $1.25/share or total value, known as the market capitalization (or market cap), of $22.5 million. When the management and technology sellers multiply their respective company shares against the $22.5 million they discover that their dollar value has not changed since the founding round, but their "say so" in company operations at the board level has been reduced by the addition of other seats for the new investors.[12]

This example of a second round of funding being priced the same as the founding round is known as "flat round" or a "step-up of 1.0." A step-up is defined as the ratio of the share price of the later round to the preceding round. Step-ups greater than 1.0 mean that the stock has become more valuable from one round to the next, and step-ups less than 1.0 mean that it has become less valuable.

Founding investors expect that the value of the shares at the time of the second round will be higher than at the founding round because the overall risk of the project should be less, and the time to liquidity should most certainly be less than faced by the founding investors. However, if there are significant problems in developing the technology or the market or building the management of the company, Round 2 investors could well conclude, based upon their projections of future rewards, that the risk is as high and the time to liquidity is as long as the first round investors perceived it to be. In business terms, either nothing was accomplished during the first year, or founding investors paid too much for the technology, or the market attractiveness has deteriorated.

Founding investors normally expect a very nice step-up to occur in the course of a year because the product should be defined and perhaps even prototyped, prospective customers should have been identified, and all the key management posts filled. Continuing with this example, let us assume that the results of the first year warrant a step-up of 2.0; that is, it is possible to find Round 2 investors who are willing to pay $2.50/share, or twice what founding investors paid. In this case, the number of new shares required to raise the needed $10 million is 4 million shares. Thus, there would now be 14 million shares, all valued at $2.50/share. The new "market" price is based on what cash investors at the one-year juncture are willing to pay, making the total value of the company (the market cap) equal to $35 million. The technology seller's ownership of the company has declined from 40 percent to 29 percent (4 million shares divided by the new total of 14 million shares) but its valuation has *increased* from $5 million (4 million shares at $1.25/share) to $10 million (4 million shares at $2.50/share). Likewise the management allowance has been "diluted" but become more valuable.

Let us assume that during the second year significant progress is made in that a product has been completed and demonstrated and customers have placed orders necessitating another $20 million for Round 3 in order to complete manufacturing and begin running the factory. As a result, let us assume that a step-up of 4.0 is attainable, making the price $10/share. Thus, only 2 million new shares must be printed (making a total of 16 million shares) for the Round 3 investors who are putting in $20 million, making the total value of the company $160 million. Accordingly, the seller of the technology has been diluted to 25 percent of the company (4 million shares divided by 16 million shares, the new total) but the value of each share is now $10/share (4 times the $2.50/share at Round 2) so that the total value of such shares is now $40 million.

Summary of All Capitalizations and Returns through IPO in an Example

Finally, let us assume that the company goes public at the end of the third year for $25/share, or a step-up of 2.5 over Round 3, which raises $100 million. This would require issuing 4 million additional shares, bringing the total to 20 million shares. The seller would now own 20 percent of the company, which is exactly half of the starting ownership percentage, but with a publicly traded (and liquid) value of $100 million! How is it that the seller can be diluted by a factor of two and yet the value is increased by a factor of 20? The answer is that the share price has been stepped up three times by factors of 2, 4, and 2.5. Multiplying these three factors together yields exactly 20, which is why the seller's value has gone up by this factor.

The step-up example is further illustrated in Exhibit 10.6. Following the row and column headings, we see in Row 3 the investment raised in each of the four rounds, including the IPO as the fourth and final round. A total equity capitalization of $135 million is shown. The seven shaded cells contain the key assumptions on which this example hinges: the initial share distribution among the investors, the technology sellers, and management; the initial share price of $1.25 which determines how much of the company the investors receive for their $5 million, and the three succeeding step-ups at Rounds 2, 3, and 4. With these assumptions, all the other values of this exhibit can be calculated. Focusing on Column C, the ownership percentages are determined by calculating the ratio of the shares owned by the total of 10 million shares outstanding (an arbitrary number). The post-round market capitalization of the company is determined by multiplying the share price ($1.25) by the number of total shares (10 million).

In Column D, the second round requires $10 million in new investment. The assumed step-up of 2.0 determines that the share price for the new money is $2.50 (2 times the $1.25 at the end of Round 1). Thus the investors providing the $10 million will receive 4

EXHIBIT 10.6 SAMPLE START-UP COMPANY VALUATION AS A FUNCTION OF STEP-UPS

	A	B	C	D	E	F	G
1		Year	1/1/00	1/1/01	1/1/02	1/1/03	
2		Round	Founding	2	3	IPO	
3		Round Investment	$5,000,000	$10,000,000	$20,000,000	$100,000,000	
4							
5		Post Round Shares	10,000,000	14,000,000	16,000,000	20,000,000	
6		Step-up in Share Value	—	2.0	4.0	2.5	
7		Post-Round Value: $/Share	$ 1.25	$ 2.50	$ 10.00	$ 25.00	
8		Post-Round Market Cap	$12,500,000	$35,000,000	$160,000,000	500,000,000	
9							
10		*Founding Investor's Shares*	**4,000,000**	4,000,000	4,000,000	4,000,000	
11		Ownership	40%	29%	25%	20%	
12		Valuation	$5,000,000	$10,000,000	$ 40,000,000	$100,000,000	
13							
14		*Technology Seller's Shares*	**4,000,000**	4,000,000	4,000,000	4,000,000	
15		Ownership	40%	29%	25%	20%	
16		Valuation	$5,000,000	$10,000,000	$ 40,000,000	$100,000,000	
17							

Management Shares	**2,000,000**	2,000,000	2,000,000	2,000,000
Ownership	20%	14%	13%	10%
Valuation	$2,500,000	$5,000,000	$ 20,000,000	$50,000,000
Round 2 Investors' Shares		4,000,000	4,000,000	4,000,000
Ownership		29%	25%	20%
Valuation		$10,000,000	$ 40,000,000	$100,000,000
Round 3 Investors' Shares			2,000,000	2,000,000
Ownership			13%	10%
Valuation			$ 20,000,000	$ 50,000,000
IPO Round Investors' Shares				4,000,000
Ownership				20%
Valuation				$100,000,000

million shares ($10 million divided by $2.50/share), creating a total of 14 million outstanding shares. The number of shares owned by the founding parties (shown within the lightly shaded outline) does not change. However what does change is the value of such shares: $2.50 instead of $1.25. Accordingly, the paper valuation of the founding investors, the technology sellers, and management has doubled to the values shown in Cells D12, D16, and D20. Their respective ownership as a percentage has declined as shown.

In Column E, the Round 3 investors provide $20 million. At the assumed step-up of 4.0, the share price corresponding to such new money is now $10, so only 2 million new shares need to be issued, raising the total to 16 million shares outstanding. The rest of the calculations follows what was done for Column D.

Finally, in Column F, it is assumed that the IPO investors will pay $25/share, the so-called IPO price.[13] At this juncture, with these assumptions, the value of the company is $500 million, and the shares belonging to the technology seller are worth $100 million. At this time, and subject to lockout restrictions (a specified period as an IPO where insiders cannot sell their shares), the seller can convert such shares to cash.

Now, in order to perform the initial valuation of share price, which determines how many shares the investors providing $5 million receive and how many shares are left for the technology sellers, this model has to be analyzed to provide a basis for all the aforementioned assumptions.

The first and most important assumption is the underlying business plan, which is not shown. At founding, the company had to create a "pro forma," a projection (based upon certain assumptions and models) of its future sales and profitability. In Exhibit 10.5, we considered how valuation depends upon profitability and P/E ratio. In order to obtain the IPO valuation of $500 million, for a sales multiple of 5, sales of $100 million annually would need to have been demonstrated, at the end of the third year. If the sales multiple were 10 times, then the sales needed would be $50 million to support the $500 million IPO valuation. Remarkably, there are examples of companies with lesser annualized sales supporting a more than $1 billion market cap at the initial public offering.

The determination of such multiples are figured, generally speaking, using the Industry Standards Method. Fortunately, because of the public nature of IPOs, there exist in any given year more than 100 examples of market valuations. By analyzing such recently-public companies (sales, growth, profitability, industry trends, etc.), investors and technology sellers can develop a range of expectations for future value based upon assumed performance. Likewise, there is a surprising amount of data available to determine step-ups. Although the companies receiving pre-IPO funding are not public, and thereby are not obligated to disclose their funding sources and valuation, normally such information is obtainable through a little digging. Sophisticated and experienced venture capitalists are much better able than technology sellers to create such models and estimates because of their experience and contacts in the industry.

Another tool for checking the overall sanity of the step-up assumptions is to use the DCF method of Chapter 7. Working backwards from the IPO, the question can be asked, what would lead the Round 3 investors to pay $10/share? And, again, would a Round 2 investor see \$2.50/share as reasonable? Finally, would the founding round investor accept \$1.25/share? Exhibit 10.7 analyzes all the investments from Exhibit 10.6 to determine what the corresponding "k" value is to each round's investors.

Looking at Row 14 of Exhibit 10.7, we see the k-value, or return on investment (ROI), on a round to round basis. What this means is: If after raising Round 2 funding as shown for 1/1/2001, and perceiving a paper value of the 4 million shares as \$10 million, what would the founding investor have experienced as a ROI? Referring back to the DCF equation where $B/A = (1 + k)^n$, or solving for $k = (B/A)^{1/n} - 1$, and substituting $B/A = 2$ and $n = 1$, results in $k = 1.0$ or 100 percent. Likewise, considering the effect of Round 3 funding and valuation, the ROI from the time of the second round is 300 percent; and the year-over-year return to the IPO round is 150 percent. Overall, from the founding of the company until the IPO event, the founding investor perceives an ROI of 171 percent, which corresponds to a 20 "bagger" (multiple) in just three years. Would a 171 percent ROI make a founding investor happy? Yes and no. If it were guaranteed, and the value of other comparable guaranteed returns was 7 percent, then of course the answer is "yes." But because it is not guaranteed, such an investor would review all the assumptions in the business plan and determine how speculative or realistic they are. If they were reasonable, then the answer should still be "yes," but investors would not be shy about trying to get an even better deal, especially if there are even better opportunities available to them elsewhere. In the late 1990s, the overall range of ROI for the more successful venture capital investors has been over 40 percent, a number obtained by a mixture of outcomes, some at 171 percent and some total losses.[14]

Looking at Exhibit 10.7 for the Round 2 investors, their 216 percent overall return is even higher than the founding investors', because their capital was tied up for only two years. Finally, the Round 3 investor experiences a 150 percent return.

In order to refine the assumptions, one would need to look carefully into the business plan and ascertain what risks will occur at what point in time and with how much money invested. The plan should be that the ROI of the founding investors should be higher than any of the later investors because joining the party at start-up entailed the highest risk. Statistically speaking some start-ups will never have a Round 2 and will fail out of the starting gate, losing all the founding capital, which is why investors who join only in the later rounds should normally receive a lower rate of return.

By adjusting the ROI projected for each round's investors in the context of the expected risk at that point, this model can be refined to provide a more rational prediction. Then, by comparing the return to the founding investor, compared to their alternatives, and to the technology seller, compared to their alternatives, the relative balance between their initial contributions can be analyzed. If the technology is genuinely the substance of the start-up company, then it is not unusual for the technology seller to receive founding shares equal to the investment, or even higher. On the other hand, if the investment yet required to commercialize is large and progress is likely to be slow, then founding investors will not fund a deal that allocates so much of the stock to the technology. To do so would not leave room for later investors to infuse additional needed money at attractive rates of return.

EXHIBIT 10.7   RETURN ON INVESTMENT TO THE VARIOUS ROUND FUNDERS OF EXHIBIT 10.6

A	B	C	D	E	F	G
1	Year	1/1/00	1/1/01	1/1/02	1/1/03	
3	Round	Founding	2	3	IPO	
4	Round Investment	$5,000,000	$10,000,000	$20,000,000	$100,000,000	
7	Step-up in Share Value	—	2.0	4.0	2.5	
8	Post-Round Value: $/Share	$ 1.25	$ 2.50	$ 10.00	$ 25.00	
9	Post-Round Market Cap	$12,500,000	$35,000,000	$160,000,000	500,000,000	
10						
11	*Founding Investor's Shares*	4,000,000	4,000,000	4,000,000	4,000,000	
13	Valuation	$5,000,000	$10,000,000	$ 40,000,000	$100,000,000	
14	Round-to-Found ROI (k)	—	100%	300%	150%	
15	Cumulative	—	100%	183%	171%	
23						
24	*Round 2 Investors' Shares*		4,000,000	4,000,000	4,000,000	
26	Valuation		$10,000,000	$ 40,000,000	$100,000,000	
27	Round-to-Round ROI (k)		—	300%	150%	
28	Cumulative		—	300%	216%	
29						
30	*Round 3 Investors' Shares*			2,000,000	2,000,000	
32	Valuation			$ 20,000,000	$50,000,000	
33	Round-to-Round ROI (k)			—	150%	

DILUTION ISSUES

Earlier we considered the effect of dilution, and we now need to return to the subject to consider what happens when things go more poorly than expected. If the step-ups are greater than 1.0, then the value of founding shares increase with each round. As shown in Exhibit 10.6, even as the percentage of the company owned goes down, the value of shares held goes up. That is the magic of step-ups.

For flat rounds, where the step-ups are exactly 1.0, the technology seller's ownership is diluted as a percentage, but the value of the shares held are unchanged. This is because there are more shares issued but the value of the shares remains what it was in the preceding round, and the start-up company has more money infused to support its operations and further development.

If a technology seller wanted a deal where its ownership percentage is unchanged even with the infusion of later investors, the founding investor would receive very poor returns on its investment because the dilution that occurs would come out of the founding investors' shares. Unless the percentage awarded to the technology seller was extremely low, then no investor is likely to want to fund the start-up company.

There is one other means that a technology seller, or founding investor, can use to avoid dilution: continue to invest in the company in all later rounds to maintain a larger share of ownership. Such a provision is common in start-up deals. The difficulty that arises is that technology sellers are not always in a position to make such investments, whereas founding investors exist for the purpose of making such investments. Ordinarily, founding investors are also second and third round investors. Perhaps they maintain their share, perhaps they are diluted a little as other investors are admitted to the club, but technology sellers, who have the right to match investments, often may not have the means or will. Another valid reason why technology sellers choose not to invest in subsequent rounds is to maintain a balanced portfolio. Because of risk, VCs are diligent about holding stakes in many different companies for each fund that they raise. A particular technology seller does not normally operate in this way and so may have only one or a few equity stakes by virtue of its R&D. To additionally invest scarce discretionary cash in later rounds of one of the opportunities puts them increasingly in a "eggs all in one basket" situation.

Assuming that such funding is secured through legitimate means using fair market value negotiations at each of the subsequent rounds, then technology sellers are not innately harmed by their inability to maintain their share. However, if the start-up is a success they will regret not having found the funds somehow and somewhere.

There is another phenomenon, however, that should be of great concern to a technology seller. In all the previous examples, the step-ups have been 1.0 or greater. What happens if progress during the year has been poor, or the market looks more distant, or competitors have emerged that were unexpected or stronger than expected? It is entirely possible for legitimate business reasons that the value in a later round is less than at the founding round. If this happens, then a true dilution will occur to a holder of previous round stock who does not invest to maintain his or her share: not only will the share of the company as a percentage decline but the aggregate value of their share holdings will also decline.

In such a situation, frustration arises when the adverse round is a result of management blunders over which the seller had no control. It should be recognized that technology sellers are not normally going to have a controlling interest or right to manage the company. In many cases, the reason for a start-up in the first place was that the technology seller wanted to put the technology in someone else's hands to develop and commercialize it. Otherwise, there would be no licensing situation. In essence, even though the technology seller may have one or more board seats and may express its opinion on various strategic matters, it is an opinion only. Decisions at the board level are made by the board majority. As a result of some bad decisions, the technology seller may, in retrospect, perceive that its dilution in value is unfair. However, the other owners also have incentive to increase the value of the shares (because they own shares too), so usually the board's decisions can be expected to have been made in good faith. An effective defense in such circumstances is for the technology seller to invest in subsequent "down rounds."[15]

There is, unfortunately, another kind of down round known in the industry as a "cram down" round. One technique that founding investors can use to unjustly dilute technology sellers (and management) is to lead a second round of funding at a valuation substantially below the founding round valuation. For Exhibit 10.6, say that instead of the second round being priced at $2.50/share, a step-up of 2.0, it was priced at 25 cents a share, step-"up" of 0.20. After the infusion of second round capital, primarily from the founding investors perpetrating this plan, the original allocation of stock among the founders has been significantly altered to the detriment of those founders who are not able to make the second round cash investment.

There are numerous such issues present in equity deals, more so than in licensing situations. Although there are various protective techniques that can be negotiated by technology sellers, they are outside the scope of this book. The general lesson here is to know with whom you are dealing. The same holds true for the management. This segment will receive a significant share of the founding stock, and the success or failure of the company will depend in large part on their skill, their industry, and their ethics. So, "Who am I dealing with?"—ever present in any licensing negotiation—is an even more significant question in an equity transaction.

INDUSTRY STANDARD AND RATING/RANKING METHODS APPLIED TO EQUITY VALUATION

For equity investments there is a unique window into valuation available. When a company intends to go public, it must file a document with the SEC known officially as an S-1 but commonly as a "Red Herring" (for reasons lost to antiquity). This document is typically over 100 pages in length and loaded with information on the company, its market, its current and historic financial performance. Further, once the company becomes publicly traded there is a simple means of establishing its valuation.

When performing valuations of NEWCOs, parties commonly look to such public documents as S-1s for comparables. Also, in the VC industry, there are many term sheets that are preferred and floated about that become part of individual consciousnesses. Further, there are so many NEWCO investments, even at their diminished scale today, that the law of large numbers makes it possible to find comparable agreements. The challenge is making the appropriate comparison given the different investment situations.

One of the most famous companies to go public, and in many ways the precursor and enabler of the internet revolution, was Netscape. The company was formed on April 4, 1994, just nine years ago. It went public via an IPO just 16 months later on August 8, 1995 priced at $28 a share creating a market capitalization of just over $1 billion, having cumulative losses of nearly $13 million and never having shown one quarter of profitabililty. By November 1995, Netscape was selling for over $100 a share and worth more than $4 billion, though still not profitable. Its share price at that time was 325 times (!) its *projected* 1996 earnings. The financial statements filed by Netscape in its S-1 together with several other relevant pages are provided at the following link: *www.razgaitis.com/Consulting/Valuation_and_Pricing_of_Technology_Book--Resources/*.

In a widely reported story, in 1997 Microsoft introduced their bundled competing product, Explorer, and succeeded in crushing Netscape. In November 1998, Netscape announced that it was being acquired by AOL and the acquisition was consummated on March 26, 1999, for a value of $10 billion at closing. So in just under five years as an independent company Netscape went from a raw idea to product to a public company to the highest of high flyers in the internet market place to being in the center of the Microsoft bullseye to disappearance as a stand-alone company but at a very substantial valuation and ultimately to being grounds of a legal finding against Microsoft for antitrust misbehavior. There are not many companies who have that kind of excitement in 100 years, let alone five. But the creators of Netscape (James Clark, Mark Andreessen, James Barksdale, the VC firm of Kleiner Perkins, and others), suggested dramatically new possibilities:

- It was possible, and even desirable, to go public in less than a year and a half,
- It was possible to be highly valued without having shown a profit, but by having a great story and widespread name and product use and recognition,
- The new recipe for success was "get big fast,"
- It need not require very much investment (about $30 million) to make a valuable company (about $1 billion), but timing is everything,
- The internet was the hottest hot thing in memory and money.

THE BARGAINING POWER OF START-UP CASH INVESTORS

In the current environment, there are numerous VC-founded companies needing additional capital to survive but not able to attract strategic investors (in many cases because potential acquirers are themselves experiencing financial straits) and not able to penetrate a much more skeptical IPO market. Some of these financial problems are due to poor business decisions in managing the NEWCO, compounded by a dramatic change in the market environment.

As just a few years ago there were numerous examples of extraordinarily high valuations of raw or primitive business ideas, so now the tables have been turned and prospective funders have been able to extract severe concessions in exchange for cash infusions. Two manifestations of such severe terms are extreme dilution and liquidation preference.

Extreme dilution basically wipes out or nearly wipes out all the investment value of the prior round investors (unless such investors participate in the new round). Then, by a separate means, such as the granting of stock options, they will provide new management incentives (because in large part the previous ones have been wiped out).

Liquidation preference is the provision that such later stage investors will receive a prescribed multiple such as 5 or 8 or 10 or even more on their investment upon a liquidation event *before* any other investor or management gets anything.[16–17] So if the company's value does not exceed say 5 times such later stage investment, all the realization will go to such later stage investors.

These buyer positions reflect the special, present value of cash with such equity situations.

EQUITY WHEN LICENSING TO AN EXISTING, PRE-PUBLIC COMPANY

The governing assumption in the previous discussion is that the start-up company is being created at the time of the license for the purpose of commercializing the licensed technology. At the beginning of this chapter, licensing to a public company was briefly discussed. What remains is to consider the intermediate situation: licensing to an already existing, pre-public company in exchange for stock.

If, in this circumstance, the start-up company is effectively restarting its operations (perhaps abandoning its previous technology for the subject license), then this reverts to the case considered in Exhibits 10.6 and 10.7. The founding valuation needs to be considered by all the parties as though it were a fresh start. The fact that significant sums were expended in a fruitless endeavor should not penalize the technology seller. Sunk costs are irrelevant. The re-started up company can argue that it has now established a management team and some market awareness that deserves recognition. That may be so. On the other hand, it is possible that the management team assembled is not particularly suited to the new direction of the company, or that the management has demonstrated only a lack of business acumen in its previous efforts. In any case, the seller should consider all these arguments just as though it were a true start-up, and value each party's contributions independently.

Another possibility is that a pre-public company seeks the seller's license to create a second product or to enhance its first product. Instead of paying a cash license fee or royalties, the buyer instead may propose issuance of stock. In this circumstance, the seller should consider that it is, in effect, a second or third round "funder" by infusing the company with technology and rights. The approach that should be used follows the structure of Exhibits 10.6 and 10.7. The seller should assess all the valuations that have gone into the company to date, the business plan and the actuals at the negotiation date, and determine what is the highest stock price, or fewest number of shares, it needs to get a fair return at the time of an IPO or strategic acquisition.

Such analysis is difficult for the seller because it necessarily involves performing due diligence on a company, its management and technology, and its business plan, without the advantage of having been part of the company's formation. Further, the seller may not have sufficient knowledge about the existing technology in the pre-public company to enable a fair assessment of its worth. The seller in these circumstances is really playing the role of a later-round venture capitalist without the experience and tools that come with doing this for a living. For these reasons, this form of valuation is more difficult than either getting stock in a true start-up or stock in a public company. In the former case, the founding technology is the seller's, and should be known; in the latter case, the value of the shares is determined by a public market and so it is known. This intermediate situation may have both little-known technology and hard-to-know share price.

The uncertainties might possibly be narrowed by performing due diligence, perhaps with support from an outside consultant. If the uncertainty remains large, then this can be reflected by a high "k" value in a DCF calculation. If the buyer's offer can meet the seller's requirements through an appropriately high discount rate, the seller then needs to decide whether it wants to take a high-risk opportunity. Such decisions are always best made when alternatives exist.

CONCLUSION

Equity as partial or sole recompense for the seller's technology is becoming an increasingly common and important event. There are certain innate advantages to equity participation that suggest its use when the opportunity is sufficiently valuable to warrant the attendant increase in deal costs because of the complexity of such arrangements.

Despite the many stories of startup company failures, and the purported demise of the VC industry, the level of investments remains very significant. According to analysts examining third quarter 2002 VC data, the anticipated VC committed investments for 2002 will be approximately $22 billion, which is approximately what it was in 1998, and a very significant total. There has been a shift to later stage funding primarily to expand existing NEWCOs so that they sell a product. During the height of the VC boom in the first quarter of 2000, approximately 44 percent of venture capital went to startups and 56 percent to existing NEWCOs. For the third quarter of 2002, approximately 75 percent of venture capital went to existing companies. Yet, the VC industry has about $90 billion in already raised but yet uncommitted capital.[18]

In start-up situations, the nature of the technology, money, and management are so different that it is a challenge to put them all on the same scale. There is a widespread perspective by technology sellers that, as a rule, they do not fare well in the monetization of their contribution. The thought is nicely captured in the Dilbert cartoon shown in Exhibit 10.8; note the enthusiastic tongue of the inventor, sardonically portrayed in panel 2.

Management's perspective is that in many start-up situations they make the difference in achieving commercial success (though the reciprocal is not true of failures!). There are numerous examples of start-up companies creating value by evolving away from the founding technology to reach more attractive market opportunites. Finally, there is the argument on behalf of the people investing the money. It is a special kind of high-risk adventure. Unlike other investments, there is a serious probability that every dime will be lost without any return—nada, zip, nothing. Also, overseeing the company as a board member is another kind of adventure and investment. People investing such risk capital are normally bringing much more than money to the venture, or at least so they say.

It should be noted that all six valuation methods discussed in this book can be applied to determine equity valuations, just as they can be used to determine a royalty or any other form of compensation. However, the non-liquidity of stock and the complexity of ownership bring with them a whole array of other business issues; those most-directly related to valuation were considered in this chapter.

A summary of the advantages and disadvantages of equity as the primary Wheelbarrow compensation is shown in Exhibit 10.9.

In Chapter 11 we will consider other issues of structuring licensing agreements and payments.

EXHIBIT 10.8

DILBERT reprinted by permission of United Feature Syndicate, Inc.

EXHIBIT 10.9	THE LURE OF EQUITY: ADVANTAGES AND DISADVANTAGES

Advantages	Disadvantages
• Closer identification with the results (for the company and for inventors) • Creates feeling of excitement/ownership; helps attract and retain the best talent • No inventing around patents/know-how and, so, supplanting our reward • Although royalty has an upside, because it is based on *sales*, equity has a greater upside potential because it is based on *value* • Create "solution" value (rather than "technology" value) • Creates highly-focused implementation • Creates highly-motivated implementers • Rapid response to new/changing markets increases the likelihood of commercial success • Can be a convenient exit path for employees and facilities in a 'sell it and shut down' strategy.	• The risk of total failure is high because of the high mortality of startups (therefore need portfolio of opportunities to create balanced returns) • Royalty-based returns start earlier, with the first sales, and come in steadier streams • Upfront payments tend to be small or even nonexistent because of need to conserve cash • Startups do not normally fund substantial external R&D, so they are not a likely services "customer;" least compatible with billable services business • May require key employees to leave and join the startup • Cash investment in multiple rounds may be required to retard significant dilution, especially in 'cram down' rounds • Cash investment may be required to attract investment (initially and/or later rounds) • Need experienced startup business management (to succeed, and to maximize valuation by investors • Numerous and complex agreements/issues • Have to know who you are dealing with

Source: ©2003 Razgaitis, richard@razgaitis.com.

NOTES

1. An anonymous haiku submitted to a web site dedicated to failed dot com companies.
2. "Talk about Scary," in the "Digits" column of Ann Grimes, *Wall Street Journal*, June 20, 2002, p. B5.
3. "Cashflow, May 2002," *Red Herring*, July 2002, p. 96.
4. According to Thomson Financial/Venture Economics, as cited by Samuel D. Colella in "Health Care Remains in a League of Its Own," *Red Herring*, July 2002, p. 32.
5. Gilder, George and Swanson, Bret, "Unleash Broadband," Wall Street Journal opinion page story, July 8, 2002, p. A22.
6. This statistic does not address comparative enterprise value, which would be the sum of equity plus debt.
7. "The Quiet Man Who Put Sizzle in the Cisco Deal," by Scott Thrum, *Wall Street Journal*, August 27, 1999, p. B1.
8. It is possible for cash payments to have some indeterminancy and/or to be paid for a period of time. Such matters will be considered in Chapter 11.
9. There are some exceptions to this broad statement that are outside the scope of this book.

10. Of course, publicly-traded stock could be part or all of a payment for a license. However, in such a case, the stock represents its cash equivalent because the seller receiving stock from the buyer could immediately convert the stock into cash (at the current trading price) or, conversely, if the seller wanted stock in the company it could take a cash license payment from the buyer and covert such cash into stock. The scope of this chapter deals with a more complex situation: when the stock of the buyer is not publicly traded and thereby not available and, generally speaking, is not valued in a well-defined way.

11. Investors in start-up companies are often not interested in a royalty relationship. They realize that the company will be a cash burner for many years and want to structure the company to limit such cash outflows. Royalty is simply another cash outflow. Accordingly, investors will attempt to defer royalties until the company is profitable, or encourage reducing or eliminating the royalty in lieu of stock.

12. In many cases the "new" investors are the old investors putting in additional money.

13. Once the initial selling price is determined, the company receives such proceeds less expenses to the underwriters, and thereafter the ups and downs of the market even on the opening day does not generate any additional cash for the company. Of course, the company could elect later to print and sell additional stock.

14. Article in *NY Times* dated 10/21/01 citing Venture One, Thompson, National Venture Capital Association.

15. There are, in addition, various down round protections known as "ratchet" provisions. Such provisions act to revalue, in whole or in part, previous round investments. Ordinarily only the founding investor expects to be the beneficiary of such provisions. A thorough discussion of such matters is outside the scope of this book.

16. "VCs reconsider tough terms for entrepreneurs," by Vyfyan Tenorio, in the Deal.Com, January 28, 2002.

17. "VCs Turn the Screws," *Business Week*, May 27, 2002, p. 82.

18. "Venture Capital Financial Falls to 1998 Levels, Continuing Slide," *Wall Street Journal*, October 29, 2002, p. B.4.

CHAPTER 11

Structure of Licensing Payments

INTRODUCTION

In the preceding chapters we have discussed methods of valuation and expressed the results in terms of royalty rates, DCF or NPV, and equity shares. This chapter discusses many different forms and structures of payment that can be used individually or in combination to establish the total value contained within a license agreement.

Although there are an infinite number of ways that payments can be structured, especially when considering non-monetary forms, this chapter reviews the principal forms and attempts to provide a framework for connecting the six valuation methods considered in Chapters 4 through 9 and the equity case reviewed in Chapter 10. Chapter 10 also provided a brief review of the advantages and some of the issues surrounding cash-only licenses versus royalty licenses versus equity licenses. This information is a useful backdrop for this chapter.

LUMP SUM LICENSES

Lump sum licenses are known by a variety of terms: cash licenses, upfront licenses, paid-ups (as in paid-up licenses). What is meant by such an agreement is that the parties will agree on a fixed amount to be paid by the buyer to the seller.

The most straightforward means of determining such an amount is by use of the Discounted Cash Flow method of Chapter 7. Recall that this approach uses k values, known as risk-adjusted hurdle rate (RAHR) or discount rate, to convert each future royalty payment to a discounted present-cash equivalent. Adding all the DCF values for all the years of the agreement yields the Net Present Value (NPV) of the agreement. For a single, lump sum cash agreement paid at closing, the amount simply equals the NPV of all the cash flows.

The buyer usually performs a wire transfer to the seller's bank account on the day of the closing, immediately following the signing of the license agreement. In some cases, with trusted buyers, the license agreement stipulates that such payment be made within a short time, such as ten days.

In Chapter 10, some of the limitations of using this form of agreement were discussed. The primary difficulty arises because all future predictions of value have to be reduced to one single number. A related difficulty is that, years later, either the buyer or the seller is likely to believe that they were at a disadvantage because it is unlikely that the commercial outcome will be identical to the terms of the agreement.

However, there are some advantages to lump sum agreements. Buyers often have a preference, if affordable, to conclude the relationship with the seller and avoid the accounting issues associated with making annual, semi-annual, or quarterly royalty payments. Normally, license agreements provide for auditing rights on behalf of the seller. Although there are limitations on the frequency of audits, and the seller must give fair notice before an audit, audits are still a burden on both parties. Further, the results of an audit can lead to a dispute. Furthermore, the disclosure of sales information is very sensitive business information and even though the seller is normally under confidentiality provisions, buyers do not like having to make such detailed disclosures to anyone.

From the seller's point of view there are also some advantages to paid-up licenses. The most obvious advantage is that the seller gets its money; there is no uncertainty of payment. Also, the payment is made now, so the seller can use such funds to invest in its other businesses. The seller also avoids the cost of administering the license on its end. Although royalties should be "checks in the mail," there are administrative costs involved, that may include reminding buyers to remit payments. In some cases this requires more extensive (and expensive) actions such as auditing the payments received, collecting and reporting the numbers, and making forecasts to management as to expected future royalties.

In the case of field of use licenses to multiple buyers, problems between different buyers can arise that will require the seller's intervention. For example, Buyer A could be exclusive in Europe, and Buyer B exclusive in the U.S.; however, Buyer B discovers (or thinks it discovers) that sales from Buyer A are being imported and wants the seller to put a stop to it and even negotiate reparations. If these parties have a competitive history, finding an amicable solution can be harrowing.

Other issues can relate to the minimum royalties. Buyers are not shy about coming back to sellers and arguing for a reduction in the minimums previously negotiated. The seller can simply say "no," but if the buyer ends up terminating the license due to economic necessity, the seller may be left with a technology it cannot easily license a second time.

Buyers have also been known to argue (even years later) for a reduction in royalties, not just minimum royalties. New management at the buyer's company can seek to change the deal because some of the projections have not borne out or simply because they believe that previous representatives agreed to pay too much. Future arguments about licensing terms will be further discussed later in this chapter.

When licensed patents are retained in the name of the seller, there can be disputes over filing or maintaining the patent in a particular country, or dealing with oppositions (as in Europe, where such oppositions are permitted).

Infringement (real or apparent) can arise. Buyers logically do not want to compete with companies who are not paying royalties to the seller, even in the case of a nonexclusive license. Buyers are even more concerned when they have paid a premium to obtain an exclusive right and other manufacturers turn up in the marketplace. How these issues can be handled in a license agreement are outside the scope of this book, but the point here is that because of an ongoing relationship between the buyer and seller, such infringement concerns can lead to complex issues requiring further negotiation.

Issues may arise surrounding future inventions made by the seller. Even though a license agreement might clearly state that the seller is not obligated to provide such future improvements to the seller, or to offer other technologies it may invent that could be used for similar products, the buyer may believe it is entitled to such rights because it is paying royalties year-by-year and it views the relationship as an informal partnership. Likewise, a seller can feel restricted in its options, not because of a legal requirement, but because it does not want to alienate a company paying annual royalties into its coffers. Sellers may likewise develop expectations that it should be entitled to invention rights to developments made by the buyer in the same technology area as the license.

In general, because royalty-bearing licenses can last 10 years or more, it can be expected that the particular individuals participating in the negotiation will have gone on to other jobs during the life of the agreement. Then the interpretation of the agreement will fall to individuals who were not privy to the original negotiation and who may not feel the same commitment or enthusiasm for the deal as the originators did.

All these issues have to be weighed against the difficulty of reaching an agreement on a lump sum payment to determine whether this form of an agreement makes the most sense. One factor not mentioned above is a subjective human one. In some negotiations the two parties were or are adversaries and do not want to work with each other because of a lack of trust or other issues. This situation would favor a lump sum agreement so that the parties can bring the negotiating relationship to a quick close. At the other extreme are cases where the parties have a longstanding strategic relationship that is much broader than the specific license and it is in each party's interest to stay involved with the other; this view would favor some form of royalty or even equity relationship.

Assuming the parties have agreed on a lump sum, how should it be determined and structured? If the valuation has been done by agreeing on a royalty rate and base, the creation of a sales projection is needed. This is done using a DCF method to bring all future payments back to the time of the negotiation, as described in Chapter 7. If a 25 Percent Rule of Thumb has been used to split profitability, then a profitability projection also must be made and discounted to create an NPV. If a DCF approach has been used, then the number has already been obtained. Monte Carlo techniques as described in Chapter 8 can be used with any of these projections to develop a best estimate for the range of uncertainties.

One standard of payment that comes up regularly is a lump sum tied to the costs of the seller in getting the technology to its present stage. One could argue that a cost basis is yet a seventh method. As discussed in Chapter 3, there are rare circumstances where a cost basis would be a useful proxy for determining value. One way that it does come up is when the seller is closing down an R&D activity that created something of value but not something perceived to be significant in value. In such a situation the seller may be willing to settle for a quick deal to simply get back what it put into developing the technology. If the buyer perceives that all the R&D activities would have been similarly costed in its own operation, then the buyer could view such a payment as reasonable. However, it is possible that the seller has spent an enormous sum and created a small opportunity, or a small sum and created an enormous opportunity. In the former case the buyer will never agree to pay such costs, and in the latter case the seller would be foolish to sell the opportunity solely for its costs.

One very practical situation that arises in such lump agreements has to do with budget issues within the respective organizations. For large sums, buyers may not wish or be able to make such a payment all at once. In some cases, sellers may prefer to receive payment in several years, also for budgetary reasons. One way to handle this is to create two or more lump sum payments instead of just one at closing. In such cases it needs to be made clear that future payments are not conditional on future outcomes and simply represent a payment schedule. Subsequent payments should be escalated to reflect a k value appropriate to inflation and lost opportunity to the seller, because presumably the earlier payment could have been invested elsewhere. The formula for performing such escalations was developed in Chapter 7: $B = A \times (1 + k)^n$, where A is the payment which would have been made now but instead will be made "n" years later, and B is the magnitude of such future payment.

Normally such multiple lump sum payments are limited to two or three payments made over two or three years. If they stretch out longer than this, then the parties will normally prefer some form of a royalty payment.

PURE ROYALTY LICENSES

Royalties are a payment made by the buyer to the seller based upon sales made by the seller of the licensed technology. Sometimes they are called "earned royalties" or "running royalties" to distinguish them from minimum royalties or other forms of payment. They are usually expressed as a percentage of sales made by the buyer, but they can also be expressed in dollars per item, per pound, or per anything. When expressed in fixed dollar amounts, it is generally a good idea to provide some form of inflation factor so that 10 years later (particularly if inflation has been significant) the amount paid is still reflective of the value of the license. In certain technology areas buyers may require that a deflating factor be included because the selling price is expected to decline with time; computer chips are an example, but not the only example, of such a phenomenon. For these reasons it is usually a good idea to simply express the royalty as a percentage of selling price.

Pure royalty licenses are licenses for which there are no lump sum payments. The buyer pays the seller a royalty based on sales and pays only once sales begin. Such agreements are rare, because ordinarily the seller expects to receive some form of down payment and, possibly, progressive payments before such earned royalties begin. Later in this chapter the more common case, a combination of upfront and running royalties, will be considered.

The advantages of royalties were discussed in Chapter 10. To review, they provide an opportunity for the seller to receive more than the parties would have or could have expected because the outcome of the license has been greater than expected. Likewise, they can be an advantage to the buyer if the market turns out to be much smaller than expected. With royalty structure, it is more likely that both parties will feel that they got a fair deal years later. However, there are the complexity issues of a long term relationship which were discussed earlier. The more uncertain the future, especially with large upside uncertainties, the more likely it is that a royalty form of payment will work best.

If the Industry Standard Method has been used, then a royalty is normally the direct result. If a 25 Percent Rule approach has been used, then a calculation must be made to infer what royalty rate will produce the agreed profit split. This can be done using the same spreadsheet income statement projections presented for the Discounted Cash Flow Method. Using DCF, the royalty rate should be adjusted by iteration, or using the "solve" spreadsheet function so as to create an NPV value of zero (or any arbitrary value). Again, the Monte Carlo Method can be used in combination with other methods to examine the sensitivity of various factors, such as growth in sales and costs of goods sold, upon profitability as a function of various royalty rates.

Often overlooked is the importance of the royalty base. What is important to both the buyer and the seller is the magnitude of the check, not the royalty percentage itself. The magnitude of the check is determined by the royalty rate multiplied by the royalty base. Although it may appear that the royalty base is obvious, it should be recognized that the license agreement will last ten years or more, and the way products get built and sold is likely to change dramatically during that term. The license agreement must carefully define both the licensed subject matter and which sales values are subject to the agreed upon royalty. If different products with different margins or with different mixes of licensed and unlicensed subject matter are envisioned, then some means of determining a fair split must be devised.

One example of such a situation is as follows. The buyer presently envisions making product A, which is covered by the definition of licensed subject matter, and then selling it to a customer who incorporates A into product B. However, in the future, the buyer decides to go into the business of making product B. Now, how shall the royalty base be calculated? If the buyer is still selling A, then that price can be used as an inferred selling price (known as a transfer price) to the part of its operations that makes product B and a royalty paid on both sales made externally and internally. If the buyer no longer sells A, then there needs to be some other means of determining a royalty base. Various methods have been used in such situations. One approach is to use a market-based price for A based upon sales made by third parties. Another is to calculate a selling price by some formula such as multiplying cost of goods sold by some factor. Yet another way is to create a recipe that determines the value-percentage of B that contains A. The use of different, lower royalty rates on sales of B is yet another way. All of these approaches can be made to work, although there are complexities involved that are beyond the scope of this book.

To the extent possible, the parties should consider all the possible manifestations of the licensed technology so that an agreement can be reached on all matters at the time of the license. If not so done, or if unforeseen circumstances arise, then the parties will have to conduct a future negotiation to determine the appropriate base.

As discussed in Chapter 10, basing the royalty on numbers below the sales line on an income statement creates other problems. Costs on a product income statement can be quite arbitrary, based upon allocations determined within the company among its various divisions and product lines. Such accounting could be adjusted to the disadvantage of a seller.

LICENSE (DOWN PAYMENT) FEES AND PROGRESS PAYMENT FEES

When creating a royalty form agreement, the seller typically expects a down payment on the license. This is particularly true when the license involves some form of exclusivity because the seller is then precluded from selling to others.

The framework for this thinking is similar to leasing a car or buying a house: There is a payment schedule in both cases which parallels a royalty, but there is also a down payment. One of the purposes of the down payment is to ensure that the buyer fulfills the commitment by risking the forfeit of the down payment. In licenses, particularly ones involving exclusivity, the seller wants to be assured that the buyer is not just "tying up" the technology without a serious intent to commercialize it.

How much should the down payment be? From the buyer's point of view, in many cases the view is that it should be as small as possible. The buyer makes the case that it will have to make significant investments in commercializing the technology, so it "cannot afford" to pay a license fee. This argument is strongly made by small start-up companies that are strapped for cash. On the other hand, the seller can say to the buyer: "Where were you when the page was blank?"[1] The seller logically believes that it has been investing in the technology for a long time and is entitled to payback in recognition for getting it to this state. Further, the seller can point out to the buyer that if the buyer's own R&D organization had created the technology, it would have already spent a significant sum before it could begin its design for manufacturing process.

One common basis for determining a down payment is to perform an NPV analysis and take some percentage as the down payment. A number in the range of 5 to 10 percent is common, but there is no hard and fast rule. Another approach is to take one year's royalties (at maturity) as a down payment; that is, if the royalty climbs from initial sales starting in year three to near maturity in, say, year seven and is then paying $1 million per year in royalties, parties have been known to use such a figure as the basis for the down payment. Yet another technique is to use some cost basis for the down payment; one example would be for the seller to recover their project costs in the down payment, assuming that the total value of the deal significantly exceeds such project costs. A key factor in determining a down payment is the importance of instant cash to the seller. In cases where the seller is meeting or exceeding the current year's budget, there actually may be a desire to defer upfront payments to a second or third year, or to have those payments made solely as royalties; in other cases where there is pressure to meet current year goals, a seller can be highly motivated, even too motivated, to take as large a portion of future gains in a present payment as possible.

If one assumes the formal DCF model for determining royalties, then a down payment is really a pre-payment on royalties due. In the DCF model, the royalty should be iterated to provide the total NPV owed to the seller. Then, for any given down payment, the royalty should be iterated so as to provide an NPV to the seller exactly equal to this down payment. Some money owed in yearly payments is being moved to form such down payments.

When determining a royalty rate using an Industry Standards Method, sometimes the parties agree to an arbitrary upfront payment that is not scaled on a DCF model because one has not been created yet. For instance, the seller and the buyer could agree that the subject license closely follows a certain comparable agreement that had a 5 percent royalty and, in addition, $100K as an upfront payment. Again, subject to negotiations between a willing buyer and a willing seller, the parties could agree to such terms without formally considering the $100K as a royalty pre-payment.

Another variation that occurs is that the buyer wants such a down payment to offset royalties. Following the example in the preceding paragraph, the buyer could insist that it pay no royalties until it receives "back" (gets full credit for) the $100K it paid as a down payment. From a seller's perspective, it is usually not a good idea not to receive any royalties once such a structure is agreed upon. Therefore, it may agree to credit some (or all) of the down payment but at a credit rate such that the buyer can credit up to half the royalties due (as an example). This approach at least enables the seller to receive diminished royalties, beginning with the initial sales.

Another form of down payment is known as progress payment or a license maintenance fee. When the delay from the time of the license until initial sales are made is long, sellers often expect to receive some additional lump sum payments after the down payment but before the initial royalty. The rationale is similar to that invoked for the down payment: it assures continued commitment by the buyer, and it provides some cash flow to the earliest investor (the seller). From the buyer's perspective these payments are additional prepayments against the royalties and, as such they resemble a lump sum agreement with a kicker (discussed later). Again, whatever is reasonable to both parties is subject to negotiation. Using the DCF model makes it straightforward to establish lump sum payments to the seller in any given year and then iterate on the royalty such that the NPV of the opportunity is unchanged. In principle, if this is done correctly and providing the sums are not large with respect to the total opportunity, both the buyer and seller should be indifferent to how money is moved around.

ROYALTY WITH FIXED SUM LICENSES

The most common form of royalty license involves one or more fixed sum payments, either down payments paid over multiple years, or down payments in conjunction with progressive payments.

As discussed in the last section, such fixed sum payments are normally viewed as prepayment of royalties. However, they need not be, especially if the amounts are small compared to the perceived opportunity.

The DCF Method is the primary tool for computing such licenses. As discussed, the royalty rate can be iterated to provide any pre-determined NPV, taking into account upfront and progress payment lump sums paid by the buyer. Normally, the k value used to perform DCF calculations on lump sums after the down payment is smaller than the k value used for the royalty rates, because the lump sum amounts are guaranteed by the contract.

A negotiation issue that arises is: What happens in the event of an early termination by the buyer? Such a situation presumes that the buyer is not going to make, use, or sell the licensed subject matter so no future royalty obligations exist. If all the lump sum payments have been made, then the remaining question is: Is there a termination fee? If all the lump sum payments have not been made, then there is the additional question: Are such payments still due upon termination? The answer to the latter question is usually yes and should be so worded in the contract. However, the matter is negotiable and the parties could agree that no further lump sums are due upon termination. Likewise, any termination fee is subject to negotiation, although because it deals with an event not expected to occur, it is not typically modeled as in a DCF approach.

ROYALTY KICKER LICENSES

One interesting variation on royalty agreements involves a bonus factor commonly known as a "kicker." The situation arises as follows. The parties agree on a reasonably certain financial projection of sales, costs, royalties, and profitability, say sales of $100 million per year at maturity and a royalty of 5 percent. However, the seller believes there are other markets that could be reached by the commercialized technology that are much larger and more profitable. The buyer counters that if such additional sales occur then there will be additional royalties at the rate of 5 percent. However, the seller argues that the 5 percent figure was agreed upon by considering certain fixed investment costs and other operating costs (overhead) that do not scale up linearly with volume. Put another way, if this is a $500 million per year sales opportunity, it will be much more profitable than the $100 million scenario, and the seller would be entitled to a higher royalty rate.

One way to handle such a circumstance is by means of a kicker that adds a payment to the seller after certain sales thresholds have been reached. Continuing with this example, the parties could agree that if the sales in any given year are more than $300 million, there will be an incremental royalty of 1 percent of sales over $300 million, and a second kicker of another 1 percent for sales over $500 million. The resulting payoff table would look like this:

Sales = \$100 million   Royalty = 5% = \$5 million
Sales = \$300 million   Royalty = \$5% = \$15 million
Sales = \$400 million   Royalty = 5%, + 1% of \$100 million = \$21 million
Sales = \$600 million   5%, + 1% of \$300 million + 1% of \$100 million = \$34 million

In the third case above, the kicker provided an incremental \$1 million over what would have otherwise been paid. In the fourth case, the kicker provided an additional \$4 million.

Such kickers could be applied to a series of lump sum payments. As another example, the parties could agree that the deal will be a license fee of \$6 million, paid in three equal \$2 million lump sums—one at closing, one at the first anniversary, and one at the second anniversary. In addition, a kicker of an additional \$2 million will be paid if sales in year five exceed \$200 million. This provides some of the advantages of a royalty structure but with less complexity.

As in our discussions on royalty bases, using as the trigger or scale of a kicker some value below the sales line on an income statement is perilous. Buyers, especially large buyers, have enormous discretion in creating bottom line numbers at the product, product line, or division level. Also, buyers are subject to reorganizations that could cause the application of bottom line provisions to be incomprehensible. Buyers should likewise be concerned about tying kickers to product profits because it opens up the possibility of a costly dispute and an interpretation beyond the limits of the original negotiation.

ROYALTY SCALING ON SALES

A common issue that arises when implementing royalties is the use of what is known as "wedding cake" rates. They work like this. If the parties agree to a 5 percent royalty, the buyer typically proposes that this rate should be scaled down with increasing sales as is commonly done in purchase agreements, perhaps proposing something like this: 5 percent for the first \$1 million in sales (i.e., resulting in a payment of \$50,000), and 3 percent for the next \$1 million in sales (an additional payment of \$30,000), and 1 percent for all sales beyond \$2 million (\$10,000 per each additional million in sales).

There are many problems with this approach. First the underlying premise of volume discounts is sharing the benefit caused by a larger orders by the buyer. If the buyer places an order for paper clips, it expects to pay less per clip for a box car full of them than it does for a single box full. Why? Because there is a built-in economy of manufacture and delivery for the paper clip vendor. Because of the buyer's large-volume purchase, a volume value opportunity is credited that can be apportioned between vendor and buyer. This is a widely recognized concept—even at the grocery store: 50 pound bags of dog food are priced less on a per pound basis than 5 pound bags.

But does this make sense in licensing? No. There are no manufacturing and delivery costs or economies of scale to be shared in technology licensing.

What about declining profitability with increased sales? This can be possible but, in the absence of data, the more likely case is *increasing* profitability with sales because the buyer is enjoying a volume value opportunity. It is the seller who should, on this basis, make the argument that the royalty rate should go up with increasing sales because of the increased value (profit) to the buyer.

Sometimes buyers propose a variant of the wedding cake structure on cumulative sales. Using the 5/3/1 royalty rate example given earlier, this might be expressed as follows: 5 percent on the first $50 million in cumulative sales under the license, 3 percent on the next $50 million, and 1 percent on everything over $100 million. This approach could be based on a rational examination of margins because it could happen that with time (expressible in terms of cumulative sales) that competitive pressures will erode margins and so should erode royalty rates.

The seller is cautioned to not casually adopt such structures without thinking through their potential implications, especially in the context of the total valuation determined beforehand. This is another example where the DCF Method can be very useful because all such wedding cake proposals can be evaluated and compared.

An extreme form of a wedding cake structure is a royalty cap, which works something like this. The seller says to the buyer, "After I've paid you royalties on $10 million in sales that year (or on $100 million in cumulative sales for that form of structure), all subsequent sales should be royalty free." This is the "enough is enough" argument and you, the seller, should not want more than the cap.

The seller's response to this should be to explore ways that both the buyer and seller can jointly contribute their profits to some charitable purpose, rather than just restricting such opportunity to the seller. The cap of the seller's profit should be similarly shared by the buyer. This usually puts an end to this line of negotiation.

Sellers can and do propose "inverse wedding cakes," royalty rates that increase with sales because, as argument goes, the margins increase with volume. Conceptually there can be a solid argument for such an approach, but this would normally require some fairly detailed modeling to convince both parties of its legitimacy.

Royalty Rate Step Downs

There are a variety of circumstances where it would make sense to the parties to provide in the license agreement reduced royalty rates, so-called "step downs," upon some licensee controlled event. One example would be the conversion of an exclusive license to nonexclusive. Normally, a license is negotiated to be exclusive or nonexclusive for its life. However, the parties could agree that after a fixed number of years, the license converts to nonexclusive, and at that point the royalty rate "steps down" to some lower, specified value. The parties could also agree that such conversion from exclusive to nonexclusive would be at the licensee's option, which, for the savings in royalty cost, they may or may not subsequently elect. Licensees are not likely to find it acceptable to have such conversion occur upon the licensor's election, but there could be instances where it would be in the parties' mutual interest, such as the instance by a large customer in the market for a second source.

Another trigger for such a step down would be the expiration of a certain patent or patents.

Reduced Royalty Sales

Although licensees are always seeking reduced royalty events, there are some reasonable circumstances where the parties could use such a provision. One such case is initial sales of the product, particularly if it is a very costly item for customers to purchase. It could be in both parties' interests to seed the market by having very low cost initial sales, and forgiving or deferring all or part of such early royalties is one way to do this. Licensors are advised to have some confidence that when they agree to such royalty reduction that the licensee is genuinely reducing its price on the sales, otherwise the licensor is effectively the sole subsidy of the reduction.

Another example is when sales could take place to leading opinion-makers, such as to doctors in a teaching hospital. The licensee may have a well-considered marketing plan of making its products available at very affordable, below market, terms because of the value of gaining opinion leaders experience with the product.

Convoyed Sales

A very contentious subject is that of licensee convoyed sales. An example of such sales is the following. Suppose the licensee is a computer printer and ink manufacturer with very limited market share in printers. Because its sales in printers is small, it is also difficult for it to have large sales of profitable inks or toner. A licensor provides them the technology and right to a new generation printer that should greatly increase their market share. The parties agree to a reasonable royalty on the sales of such printers, but then comes the matter of the inks and toner. The licensee objects to any royalty payment on such consumables under the reasonable argument that it is not licensing in such technology. However, the licensor makes the also reasonable "but for" argument, namely: without the new printer technology you would not be selling any (or as much) of such inks and toner.

In some cases the parties agree to a higher than otherwise justified royalty on the printer to account for this. In other situations, the parties might agree to a low royalty on such auxiliary (or convoyed) sales. In the latter case, the parties could compute such royalty base in a way to account for just the increase in ink and toner sales associated with the new printer technology.

ROYALTY BUYOUT AGREEMENTS

In some circumstances, the parties (especially the buyer) may seek to have a buyout provision. Such a provision is basically an option, exercisable by the buyer, to pay off the remaining financial obligations of the license by making a previously agreed upon lump sum payment.

The way it would normally work is that there is some formula for the buyout option that varies with time. If the buyout is exercised early in the license, then the lump sum payment is large because the foregone royalties were expected to be large due to the number of years remaining. The lump sum would decline with time as the number of years bought out declines. One way this can be done is to multiply the current year royalty by some ratio of the remaining number of years. For example, the parties might agree that the buyer can buy out the license by making a lump sum payment equal to the current year's royalties in dollars multiplied by half the remaining years of the license. In other words, the buyout takes place for 50 cents on the dollar, assuming the royalties were to stay flat for the remaining life of the agreement.

The financial basis is the Discounted Cash Flow Method. For each year of the license, the model calculates the NPV of all subsequent royalty payments using an appropriate k value. Based upon the perceived risk and estimated sales, a guideline can be developed.

Generally, such a provision is advantageous to the buyer, because the buyer has an option only it can exercise and that presumably, will only be exercised if it results in a better deal for the buyer. Sellers may find such risk acceptable if the formula used to calculate a prepayment provides a reasonable return. Care must be given to variabilities in royalties paid year by year. For example, it could happen that there would be a "down" year in royalties because of some problems with supplies, or a factory fire, or a one-year blip in the market; the seller would not want to enable the buyer to use a low royalty year as the basis of calculating a prepayment of the remaining royalties.

ROYALTIES ON RELATED PARTY TRANSACTIONS AND FAIR MARKET VALUE CONSIDERATIONS

A common situation is that of a licensee "selling" product to a related party, such as another division or even another company with common ownership. The reasonable concern from the licensor's perspective is that the sale price, really a transfer price, reflect fair market value as would have occurred if the parties had dealt at arm's length. There are several ways for dealing with this situation. Perhaps the simplest is to prescribe a minimum royalty amount in dollars per unit of sale, to assure that there is at least a reasonable floor on the royalty paid. Another more complex approach, but probably preferred overall, is to compute a fair market value (FMV) for the transaction based upon licensee sales to similar customers in similar circumstances where a price was established by an arms length transaction; obviously this can lead to some analytical complications and disputes.

Another issue that arises is when a licensee offers the subject technology/product as an add-on to an unlicensed product or service. In such situations it may be ambiguous from a purchase order or sales agreement exactly how much was paid for the licensed subject matter. Or, in other cases, the licensor may offer the licensed product for little or no cost to its customers conditioned on some other purchase. Again some approach of a minimum unit royalty or a royalty based on FMV could be used, although there are additional complications if the licensee makes no sales solely of the licensed subject matter as there would be no FMV data available. In such cases, the parties could develop a proxy for FMV such as some multiple like two or three of the manufactured cost (COGS), although that in turn can lead to accounting disputes as discussed earlier in this book.

AGREEMENTS TO NEGOTIATE ROYALTIES

Because technology licenses deal with so much uncertainty, parties have agreed to defer negotiations until the products and margins are better known. This can be done in a variety of ways. One is simply to agree to negotiate in good faith and, if negotiations are not successful, to submit the matter of royalty rates to some designated third party to act as an arbitrator. At this stage, both parties would submit their basis for their rates and the arbitrator would evaluate the arguments and set the rate.

This approach has been widely used, but the actual need for bringing in the arbitrator is rare because neither party wants to deal with the uncertainty of a third-party decision.

A variant of this approach is to provide a cap of the royalty *rate* with the rate to be negotiated subject to such cap. To be fair to the seller, at the same time there should be a floor, so the range is bookended.[2] When possible, the parties can also agree on principles or even a recipe for how the royalty rate will be determined within the prescribed range.

There are great advantages to deferring a royalty calculation to a time when commercial utility can be better predicted. Although this can appear advantageous to the seller because the buyer is advancing the technology without knowing the royalty rate that will ultimately be used, there are also advantages to the buyer. Later in the negotiations, the buyer will have a much better understanding of the value and use than the seller. Also, the buyer has the power of termination or selected use. Also, if the parties have an ongoing relationship and expect to do other deals, there should be a mutual confidence that both parties will act reasonably in the process.

AGREEMENTS TO RENEGOTIATE ROYALTIES

A variant of the deferred negotiation strategy is the renegotiation provision. This usually works as follows: The seller proposes that the rates agreed to will exist for a prescribed period, say five years, at which time the parties will renegotiate the license.

Buyers are understandably not keen on this idea because they fear that after all the investment in manufacturing, creating the market, and developing sales relationships, excessive claims will be made by the seller.

The seller can argue that the rate can also go down, benefiting the buyer, so the provision is not one-sided. The key issue hinges on what happens if the parties do not agree. If the seller can effectively terminate the license by demanding an increase in royalties from 7 percent to 70 percent, then the buyer will see this as one-sided because it does not have a comparable club to wield.

Two provisions can help equalize this situation. One is the use of a third party arbiter in the event negotiations break down. The other, and better, approach would be to "pre-agree" on the criteria by which any new royalty rate would be established. For example, suppose a polymer will be introduced that initially will go into the general industrial market at low margins and a low royalty (say 3 percent). However, there is a possibility that it could have medical device applications, but this will not be known for years. Although the parties could pre-agree on the royalty rate for such medical applications, there is good reason to agree to renegotiate the license in 5 years to take into account the markets being served and the margins enjoyed.

EQUITY LICENSES

In Chapter 10, equity licenses were considered in some detail. The subject is raised again here because equity can be used in combination with lump sum payments and royalties (and kickers, for that matter). For example, a license agreement with a start-up company could involve a nominal upfront lump sum payment, a low royalty, and some stock. The combined consideration would then reflect fair value for the transaction. In this case the seller receives a certain, immediate (though usually small) payment; the assurance of some payment based on sales, regardless of what happens to the stock; and finally, some share of the equity realization in the event the company has a big IPO gain. This could be attractive to the buyer because it minimizes the stock it must give up, yet it carries lower royalty payments than would otherwise be made, an important consideration when cash is tight. In some circumstances, buyers actually favor having the seller be a stock holder because they want the seller to be involved and supportive of the buyer's company. It can also add to the buyer's credibility to have the seller so involved.

Combining royalty and equity returns creates a lot of deal and management complexity. This must be balanced against the benefits of the multiple forms of compensation. Further complications (and creative solutions) are possible. There can be provisions to convert a royalty interest into additional stock, or vice versa. The primary concern of the seller would be that the buyer who controls the start-up might not decide to create a liquidity event such as an IPO. Under such circumstances, the seller would own a minority share of stock in a company that could remain small and private indefinitely. The seller would like to have some way to cash in on the value of the stock held; having a conversion right to increase the royalties would be one way of doing this.

MINIMUM ROYALTIES

Minimum royalties are fixed annual payments that the buyer pays the seller unless the earned royalties exceed the stated minimum. In other words, the buyer owes the seller the larger of the earned royalties or the minimum royalties.

Clearly buyers want to have low minimum royalties (or none), and they want payments to start far in the future. Sellers, on the other hand, want significant minimum royalties, approaching in magnitude the expected earned royalties according to a pro forma income statement. They want payments to begin at a time when such earned royalties are reasonably expected.

Like everything else in a license agreement, the minimums are negotiated through back and forth bargaining. If the pro forma has been conservative, i.e. assuming most circumstances do not turn out favorably, then the parties may agree that the royalties projected should be the minimum royalties. If the pro forma has been optimistic, then a fraction should be counted as minimum royalties. Parties seem to negotiate in the range of 25 to 75 percent of the most likely royalties, with sellers pressing for values of 50 percent or higher and buyers arguing for 25 percent.

One of the realities of licenses is that if the minimum royalties exceed the earned royalties for a number of years, the buyer can be expected to come back to the seller and ask (or demand) some relief. If the low return comes despite vigorous investment and development by the buyer, then the seller could be faced with a terminated license if it doesn't go along with a reasonable proposal. Also, a seller who gets back a technology years later as a result of a termination is often unable to license it to a third party because the market window may be gone, the key inventors may be gone, and the start-up investment to a third party simply may be too large to find an interested buyer. A third party would also (quite reasonably) question what it was that made the original licensee abandon the technology and its investment.

In the case of nonexclusive licenses, buyers often argue that minimum royalties should not exist because the seller can license the technology to as many buyers as it wishes. From the seller's perspective, each license, though nonexclusive, represents a commitment made and loss of opportunity to do something else. For example, a seller could end up with just two buyers, each with nonexclusive all-fields and all-territories licenses. If one of these buyers is not practicing the technology, and without a minimum has no incentive to terminate its license, then the seller cannot take advantage of creating an exclusive license with its other buyer; such a circumstance could arise because the non-practicing buyer simply wants to preserve its options to enter the market but doesn't really intend to do so. Accordingly, there is no innate reason not to have a minimum royalty even for nonexclusive licenses.

TERMINATION FEES

A license negotiation could result in an agreement with modest upfront and early payments by the licensee with the expectation that this would be more than compensated by substantial royalty and/or calendar/minimum payments in later years. If the licensee in such circumstance had the right to terminate its license at no cost at any time, there could create an economic disadvantage to the licensor that the parties did not envision at the time of negotiating the license. One way to protect against such result is to provide a termination fee to be paid by the licensee to the licensor in the event of its election to terminate prior to some specified date.

MARCH IN RIGHTS

It is common with exclusive licenses that the licensor have some right to "march in" and convert the license from exclusive to nonexclusive, reduce the allowed fields of use, reduce the allowed territories, and/or terminate the license entirely based on some standard of inadequate or non-performance by the licensee. Depending on the magnitude and timing of maintenance and minimum royalties and other periodic payments, the licensor may be harmed by a licensee's languid execution of its license rights. Some licensors, such as government agencies, require a march in provision to prevent the hypothetical situation of some oil company buying rights to the proverbial 200 mile per gallon carburetor solely to keep it off the market.

OTHER FORMS OF CONSIDERATION

In all the previous discussions, the form of compensation considered has been money, in the form of initial payments, royalties, minimums, kickers, and so forth. There are many other possible forms of compensation.

One example is a supply contract. A seller could license technology to a buyer and receive as compensation the right to purchase the buyer's licensed products at a discounted price (compared to fair market value) in lieu of any royalty or other payment. Alternatively, the deal could be structured so that the buyer pays a royalty to the seller for sales to third parties and must supply a certain minimum quantity of the product to the seller.

Another example is a purchase contract. In this case, the buyer is obligated to buy raw materials from the seller as part of the license agreement. (Note: In both of these examples there are some potentially significant legal issues that need to be carefully reviewed by counsel.)

Another common form of compensation in technology licenses is the payment for additional R&D by the seller. In many cases the reason a technology license arises is because there is an R&D capability within the seller that is not or can not be used directly for commercial purposes. In these and other cases, the seller can be highly motivated to receive funding to support the people and labs doing such work. This can also be important to a buyer because it can speed the commercialization process and/or lead to enhanced features in a second generation embodiment.

The following question arises; Should payment by the buyer for such R&D services come out of the NPV of the deal? Using the $10 million NPV example, suppose that the seller proposes an upfront cash payment of $500,000, the balance of the $9.5 million in royalties, and that the buyer commits to funding $1 million in additional R&D at the seller's lab. From the buyer's perspective, this now looks like an $11 million deal.

What happens here depends on the nature of the R&D and the rights flowing from such work. If the $1 million in R&D was to be precisely the work that the buyer was going to have to do anyway, and the buyer obtains, for no additional consideration, all rights to the fruit of such R&D, then it should not be considered as coming out of the $10 million (assuming that is the agreed upon figure) to which the seller is entitled. Taking the other extreme, if the R&D is not going to aid the buyer's commercialization, and the buyer receives no rights to the results, then the buyer will naturally take the position that the seller may spend its money however it likes but that it should come out of the $10 million (or elsewhere from the seller's budget), not as an additional buyer's payment.

The typical situation is somewhere between these two extremes. The proposed work is related but not exactly the same. The seller is willing to include an option to obtain rights to the new results but under terms to be negotiated when the time comes. In this case, the seller is really offering the buyer an option to a second grocery cart of technology rights as an add-on to the deal for the $10 million opportunity. The use of options will be discussed in the next section. However, the short answer here is that the parties should separately value the benefit of the option to the buyer and the funding to the seller to determine a valuation in addition to the $10 million. In order words, the seller is now offering more than the original deal (an option to additional rights), and the buyer is paying more (the R&D funding that will create such additional rights). This circumstance should be treated as a separate valuation, although there may be some economy of scale to consummate this additional agreement at the same time as the base agreement.

OPTION AGREEMENTS

An option is the right to make a future decision. Normally it presumes an exclusive right: If a buyer seeks an option on a license, it normally expects to receive the exclusive right to acquire such license. However, there are cases where the buyer is only seeking assurance that he can acquire a freedom to practice at some future point. In such cases an option to a non-exclusive license is sufficient.

Option agreements can be very useful in technology licensing because they allow a buyer a period of time to conduct due diligence, including possible test marketing. During this period the buyer has the assurance that the deal will not be sold out from under him (the phrase refers to the retailer who repossesses a bed while the occupant is still in it). For seller's options there is good news and bad news. The good news is that a serious buyer exists, and there has been some payment for the option. However, the bad news is that during the due diligence period the seller normally (for exclusive options) is prohibited from further marketing the opportunity (the so-call "no shop" provision) and other interested buyers must be turned away. Thus, it is possible that a more motivated buyer could offer more than the buyer holding the option but would have to be turned down. Finally, if the buyer-optionee elects not to exercise the option, other prospective buyers are likely to find out; this casts a pall over subsequent marketing efforts. Some options require a termination fee to compensate sellers for the pall effect. Although not common, some options provide for march in provisions similar to conditional offers in real estate: If a third party shows up with a bona fide offer, then the optionee has a shortened period of time to exercise the option or lose it.

Another issue to be considered in option agreements is what happens if the buyer says yes. If the buyer wants to know all the financial and other key terms prior to exercising the option, then essentially that means the entire agreement will have to be negotiated upfront, a costly exercise in both time and money. Without such agreement, what would a "yes" entitle a buyer? Generally the answer is, only a good faith effort to negotiate within a prescribed period.

The key elements of an option agreement are (1) the scope of the option (defining the TR, or technology rights), (2) the duration of the option, (3) restrictions and obligations on the seller, (4) rights of the buyer (access to information, consultation, etc.), (5) what happens if the buyer says "yes," and (6) payment(s) by the buyer to secure the option.

Like upfront fees, option fees can be considered to be down payments on the opportunity. Consider a case where the parties agree that the NPV of the opportunity is $10 million, subject to confirmation by due diligence. They might agree to the following approach: an option fee of $250,000 upfront and non-refundable (or creditable), an option termination fee of $250,000 in the event the option is not exercised, an upfront fee for the license of $500,000, and the balance of the value expressed in royalties. Normally the option fee does not subtract from the NPV of the deal because the buyer got more than the deal itself: It received the option to the deal, which has value of its own, and then the opportunity to acquire the deal.

Options can be very useful when two parties anticipate doing deals regularly. In that case, an almost form-like agreement can be negotiated once and used quickly many times. Such an approach also allows the option to have unspecified execution value, subject to negotiation, because parties expecting a long term relationship have confidence that both parties have a stake in being reasonable.

BALANCING SIMPLICITY WITH COMPREHENSIVENESS

Clearly, if any one license agreement attempted to incorporate all the various structural tools described in this chapter, in addition to others that can be conceived, the agreement would likely be so complicated as to defy comprehension, agreement, and management.

In Exhibit 11.1 the tension between simplicity and comprehensiveness is illustrated.

Simpler agreements are easier to negotiate in the sense that there are fewer issues to work on, they can be understood and communicated to all stakeholders more easily, and then, importantly, years later third parties responsible for their implementation can comprehend them. So, in general, simple agreements are good things.

However—and there is almost always a however—simple agreements normally do not take into account all the vagaries of the future which one or both parties may be concerned about because without such taking into account the agreement could become unfair. Many of the structural issues discussed in this chapter have arisen from this motive, making the agreement remain fair under some if/then situation. Also each party to a negotiation has things that are uniquely important to them, either in the box or in the wheelbarrow, for either or both the buyer and seller. Incorporating such priorities into the

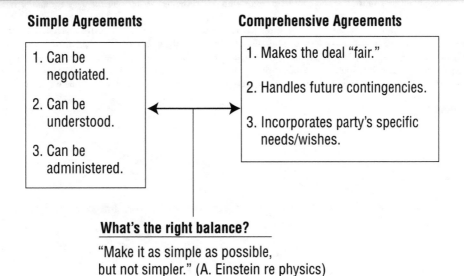

Source: ©2003 Razgaitis, richard@razgaitis.com.

agreement, even at the addition of complexity, can make the negotiation easier because a need has been accommodated, a concern about future fairness alleviated, or even a compensation for making some other concession as a means of reaching agreement closure (which is sometimes difficult to do without the use of such structure provisions).

So each negotiation and agreement represents some balance between KISS (keep it simple stupid) and providing for every possible issue and eventuality. Perhaps Albert Einstein said it best when he commented on ideal physics models: they should be made as simple as possible, but not simpler.

CONCLUSION

In this chapter we considered many of the ways that the economic value of a technology can be structured. The wonderful flexibility of technology licenses enables parties to customize the terms of payment to meet their respective goals. In many instances, the issues addressed in this chapter are a delight to work out because it becomes a mutual discovery process for how to meet the needs of all stakeholders.

In the final chapter we will deal with some of the negotiation principles that are part of converting valuations to prices.

NOTES

1. Reportedly said by Truman Capote to a film director who was changing the story line of the screenplay of a Capote book.
2. An example "bookend" structure would be as follows. At the time of the licenses the parties reach agreement on the most (reasonably) pessimistic and optimistic projections for the use of the technology, and these correspond to a royalty rate of 1% and 5% respectively. The agreement could then provide for a royalty rate to be negotiated at the time of commercial introduction that would be bound by these values. The parties could further provide a formula, or basis, by which future events or findings could be used to determine the neighborhood or even exact value in this range.

CHAPTER 12

Pricing, Negotiation Readiness, and Conclusion

If I see before me
The nervature of past life
In one image, I always think
That this has something to do
With truth. Our brains, after all,
Are always at work on some quivers
Of self-organization, however faint,
And it is from this that an order
Arises, in places beautiful
And comforting, though more cruel too,
Than the previous state of ignorance.[1]

INTRODUCTION

In this chapter we return to some of the "soft" issues originally introduced in Chapters 1 and 2, issues of risk perception and personalities. By means of the six valuation methods developed in Chapters 4 through 9, it is possible to make a judgment as to what a specific licensing opportunity is worth. Normally such an estimation contains inherent uncertainties due to computing a value based on future events. Through the use of a royalty or equity structure, and perhaps sweetened with kickers or renegotiation provisions, some of the effects of such uncertainty can be mitigated. Finally, through negotiation the seller and the buyer, can come to a price agreement or, in terms of the *TR R A DE*™ acronym, *DE (Deal Economics)*.

For a valuation to be realized, it is necessary that a negotiation take place between a willing buyer and willing seller in which, at the end, both parties agree on the same number with the associated terms. Because each party tends to look at matters in an egocentric way, even if the buyer and seller make use of the same method, it should be expected that their initial positions will not agree or overlap. One reason has to do with conservatism. Sellers know that they will never get more than they ask for, and that once an agreement is struck it will not normally be possible to reconstruct it for more money. Accordingly, the safe tack is to produce a valuation on the high side so that if a buyer accepts the proposed figure, the seller can be at ease with the outcome. However, the buyer is inclined to look at things pessimistically, at least initially, so that the odds of meeting or beating the market-value assumptions are very high. In most cases, the initial perspectives developed by the parties do not overlap, that is, the desired valuation by the seller is higher than that of the buyer.

For more in-depth information on negotiation as a discipline, see *Dealmaking Using Monte Carlo and Real Options Analysis* (Razgaitis, Hoboken: John Wiley & Sons, Inc., 2003). Following are some basic points that are essential to implementing the work of previous chapters. Addressing these basic points and wrapping up some of the soft side issues is the goal of this chapter.

REVIEW OF THE SIX VALUATION METHODS

The six valuation methods are displayed visually in Exhibit 12.1. Shown at the top are the two most commonly used methods: Industry Standards (Chapter 4), and Rules of Thumb, such as the 25 Percent Rule (Chapter 6). The Industry Standards Method requires the identification of an appropriate comparable agreement. In many cases, no single agreement exists that closely matches the subject valuation. Therefore, a common practice is to create a comparable scenario from existing agreements. This can be envisioned as an interpretation exercise that interpolates and extrapolates from existing data to predict how the market would have valued the subject opportunity had it been given a chance to do so.

There is a useful metaphor for this process. Airplanes reference their positions from fixed ground stations that emit a special signal. These signals, known as VORs, are coded in such a way that an onboard instrument can determine the heading, or direction, of the airplane moment-by-moment relative to the ground station. Originally, such VOR stations were used as byways whereby pilots would "hop" their way across the country flying from one VOR to the next until they got close enough to their destination that they could use visual observation or other forms of navigation. Then a very bright guy came up with a simple but powerful idea: Instead of flying from VOR station to VOR station, why not use the VOR signals and create virtual stations anywhere, ideally in direct lines toward the destination? This was the birth of what is now known as R-NAV. The process of using Industry Standards is a lot like R-NAV. If one can find a comparable agreement, or better yet, a family of them that happen to be located exactly where one wants to go, it's like having a VOR station conveniently located at one's destination (a rare event). It is more common

| EXHIBIT 12.1 | OVERVIEW OF SIX VALUATION TOOLS/METHODS |

Source: ©2003 Razgaitis, richard@razgaitis.com.

to find useful points of reference from previous agreements (similar to the scattered VOR stations). Analyzing the agreements through analysis such as Rating/Ranking, possibly coupled with Rules of Thumb and Discounted Cash Flow, one can create an R-NAV site directly where one needs to go. (The Rating/Ranking Method is particularly useful in this endeavor.)

The Rule of Thumb Method is commonly employed for three valuation purposes. First, it is a starting point for deriving a royalty rate, based upon an analysis of the benefit to the buyer, to create a price. Second, it is a sanity check on a number created in some other way. For instance, the seller's use of the Industry Standard Method coupled with Discounted Cash Flow can create a valuation that does not take into considerion what proportion of the expected financial benefit to the buyer is being allocated in royalties and equity. The Rule of Thumb Method can check the reasonableness of other methods. Finally, Rules of Thumb can be used as an early basis of agreement between a seller and buyer to frame subsequent detailed financial analysis. For instance, if the parties can agree at the earliest stage of due diligence and negotiation that they will apply the 25 Percent Rule with the value "25," then this process agreement can create confidence that a deal can ultimately be struck and a fair final number calculated. Conversely, if a prospective buyer discerns early in the process that the seller aspires to 50 percent or 75 percent of the profits, and such a high range is clearly incompatible with the nature of the opportunity, the buyer can focus on re-aligning the seller's perspective or else cut off further investment in due diligence.

The Discounted Cash Flow Method (Chapter 7) and other advanced methods such as Monte Carlo (Chapter 8), are based on creating pro forma spreadsheets of estimated in-come and cash flow statements. Such approaches are the most formal, and complex, meth-ods of valuation. They calculate a financial benefit that the buyer will accrue by virtue of the license. By applying Rules of Thumb to the projected profitability, a Net Present Value can be calculated, or a royalty such that the NPV is apportioned appropriately between seller and buyer.

In addition, these two methods serve other purposes. The DCF Method and its related equations enable money to be moved in time so that even if one performs a valuation solely based on the Industry Standard Method, it is possible to make rational judgments as to the appropriate upfront payments, or progress payments, or buyout value. Also, the DCF Method creates a way to think about and evaluate risk that is expressed in a concrete dollars and cents form.

Likewise, the Monte Carlo Method can be used to assess the effect of specific elements of risk or uncertainty and to understand its effect on the overall uncertainty of the project's profitability. Such analysis can suggest actions that sellers can take to reduce the business risk of a project and, thereby, attract more buyers and better terms. Also, such methods can help buyers construct agreements that provide conditional payments (such as kickers) to sellers based upon ultimate outcomes of highly variable risk factors.

Finally, the Auction Method (Chapter 6) is a way of creating an incontrovertible compa-rable, or as in the metaphor used earlier, creating a VOR site at the perfect location, by hav-ing the market bid for the specific opportunity. With perfect information, and multiple bidders, this process should yield a fair value to both the buyer and the seller.

THE "BEST" VALUATION METHOD

One of the foundational questions of philosophy is what is truth or its close corollary: what do I know and how do I know that I know it? This latter question falls within the disci-pline of epistemology, meaning a theory of knowledge.

Earlier, we considered the matter of uncertainty as an inherent element in future plan-ning. Here we want to briefly consider another aspect of uncertainty dealing with the val-uation and pricing methods and outcomes.

Epistemology is one of the core philosophical subjects that in the Western tradition dates back to at least the 400 B.C. Greek classics. Epistemology deals with the question of what can be known and how one can know it, but not with the specifics of what it is that one is trying to know. For us here, the epistemological question is this: What is knowable from the use of these valuation methods, and how do we know that we know?

In our scope of technology valuation, there are two, polar-opposite erroneous answers to the first of these questions: (1) nothing is knowable, or (2) epistemic certitude is possible. The first response has the effect of declaring valuation of technology as an utterly futile effort. This is the equivalent of you thinking of a number between one and a million and inviting me to predict the number. In this situation, nothing is knowable; regardless of my tools and endurance, I am not going to generate a better guess than the first number that enters my head. But is technology valuation really this epistemologically bleak? In general, the answer is no; the future may be dark, but it is not black.

What about the other extreme of contending that epistemic certitude is achievable? There is an old cartoon in which an elementary-school mathematics teacher asks a student: "Quickly, John, how much is 9 times 7?" To which the mathematically unaccomplished, but perhaps future senior management material, student replies, "High 50s, low 60s, somewhere in there." In many, if not most, mathematical settings we demand epistemic certitude. What about technology valuation? One of the virtues of having six methods is the opportunity for comparing results by multiple approaches. Each of the methods reviewed has its strengths and weaknesses. By using more than one approach, one frequently gains insight into a valuation that does not occur by the use of one method. Even though these multiple methods are likely to lead to multiple answers, they are also likely to lead to a deeper understanding of the key factors driving the value and how the process can be refined to develop a wiser answer.

So, in technology valuation, the epistemological aspiration is neither futility nor certitude, but coherence—where multiple methods produce a value or value range that makes sense from such multiple perspectives.

Having six methods, and even more when one counts sub-methods within these six (such as Monte Carlo and Real Options), which one is best? This is akin to the joke that when I had only one watch I always knew what time it was, but now that I have two watches, I never know.

As discussed back in Chapter 4, just taking the average of multiple views can be misleading. So does one choose one method as "supreme?" My answer to such questions is that the answer lies in a search for coherence. For any given valuation situation, there are varying degrees of information available and circumstances by which the license or transaction is to be done. Although it is generally a good idea to look at a valuation from the perspective of multiple methods, one generally gains an understanding when performing such valuation that the available data, or deal-making environment, just creates greater confidence in the values obtained by such preferred method. So, for instance, we might value an opportunity by a combination of Industry Standards, Rules of Thumb, and Discounted Cash Flow, perhaps with each one using some aspect of Rating/Ranking, and result in three different value models. But in performing this calculation, we come to believe that the availability of very relevant comparable agreements causes us to have a higher confidence in the Industry Standards Method. In such case, we could be well served to consider what was it that caused our valuation by Rules of Thumb and Discounted Cash Flow to deviate from what we believe is a most reasonable estimate.

This kind of thinking and subsequent method analysis of methods used is what is meant by a search for coherence. There is no one method that is the gold standard of valuation for any and all circumstances. Coherence is a process of seeking to apply practical wisdom to the array of results produced by each individual method used.

What About Cost?

Reinforcing a key point made in Chapter 3 about cost, it must be remembered that costs are, with special exceptions, irrelevant.

It is easily conceivable that a seller has already made enormous investments in getting the technology to its present state, and these costs would not have to be laid out by the buyer. One reason this must arise is simply poor project and investment management on the part of the seller. Another reason is that the seller's timing was poor; the cost of creating a new technology is heavily dependent on when one starts. In starting too late, one misses the window. If one starts too early and is the so-called pioneer, one has to invent everything and endure a long gestation period before the market is ready. Numerous other reasons can exist. The seller may have locked into a needlessly complex and expensive way of creating the technology because of the mindset of the inventors or corporate policy.

On the other hand, a low cost project might "get lucky" in that it creates something of significant value quickly and for a very modest investment. This is normally not a fortuitous accident: key capabilities that already exist were previously paid for at the seller's labs.

In both of these extremes, the cost basis of the project will have no bearing on a valuation. In the former case, no rational buyer will pay more than an opportunity is worth, looking only forward in time; the buyer perceives itself as striking a deal to benefit itself, not to undo the misfortunes of the seller. In the latter case of the "fortuitous" project, no rational seller will sell it for less than it is presently worth just because its costs were low. Sellers recognize that, just as in each life a little rain must fall, so does a little extra sunshine from time to time. Realizing fair value for sunny days helps compensate for the rainy times.

Yet there are certain circumstances where a cost analysis is worth performing. Often within the seller's organization there are stakeholders who approve or influence the approval of a deal. These stakeholders may be cognizant of the project's costs and they will want to know why the seller is receiving less than it spent and why it is getting a smaller ROI than expected. There can be circumstances where in-process R&D has been booked as a balance sheet asset; upon disposition, there could be an adverse balance sheet effect. Such circumstances would indicate the need for a cost-analysis.

Performing the cost analysis will help stakeholders in the selling company to come to one mind on the valuation. Such a process may require reconciliation with earlier (and not-to-be-realized) ROI expectations. Even if R&D expenses do not show up on the seller's official balance sheet, they can show up in key people's bonuses and so affect behavior. As will be discussed further, license negotiations include negotiations within one's own organization. For the seller, such negotiations involve reconciliation of already sunk project costs with proposed selling prices or terms offered by the buyer.

Another reason to analyze cost is to determine how a buyer might value an opportunity. What are the buyer's alternatives to a negotiated agreement with the seller? One simple alternative for the buyer is to do nothing, which is equivalent to investing its funds in buying down its debt or buying back its stock. Another option is to invest in a completely different project unrelated to the one offered by the seller. A third option, and a crucial issue with regard perceiving the value of the seller's technology, is to create the same or similar business opportunity as might result from a deal with the seller but to do so independently of the seller. This can be done by following a different technology path, or by following the same path but working around the seller's patents and/or independently recreating the seller's trade secrets.

The seller's project costs could be a useful starting point for estimating what it might cost a buyer to recreate the technology. If it will cost the buyer X to recreate the seller's technology, then the buyer will not pay much more than X unless there is a significant time-to-market advantage in doing so. Other reasons to consider technology licensing would be if there is significant risk that the buyer's re-creation might not work, or there is significant risk that the scope of the seller's patent claims might not be avoided, or the buyer wants to maintain good will between the parties because of broader business objectives, or for some other reason.

Accordingly, it is good practice to answer two cost questions: (1) What did it cost the seller to this point? (2) What would it cost the buyer to recreate the seller's technology? However, it is rare that either of such figures will be the basis of a final agreement.

Deciding on an Appropriate Level of Analysis

Using any of the described methods, it is possible to engage in an endless analytical exercise, leading to paralysis by analysis. This quote from Ross Perot captures well the frustration that can exist with excessive analysis:

> I come from an environment where, if you see a snake, you kill it. At GM, if you see a snake, the first thing you do is go hire a consultant on snakes. Then you get a committee on snakes, and then you discuss it for a couple of years. The most likely course of action is—nothing. You figure the snake hasn't bitten anybody yet, so you just let him crawl around on the factory floor.[2]

An appropriate question to ask is: How much of my resources are justifiably spent on analysis? Or, put another way, what is an appropriate cap on transaction costs, of which valuation analysis and other preparedness activities are the initial component?

Let us consider a simple example. Suppose there is a technology that a seller expects could result in a royalty of probably more than $100,000 per year, but probably less than $1 million per year; this is colloquially termed a six-figure deal. Further, it is believed that such royalties might be paid over a period of five to ten years starting three to five years hence. Using such approximate numbers, a seller might estimate that it should be able to receive an upfront licensing fee of at least $100,000, so in current-year terms the deal should be worth at least that much money. Over the life of such a license, the NPV could be roughly estimated as, say, seven times the DCF of a $300,000 royalty payment (on the conservative side of midway between $100,000 and $999,999), occurring seven years hence (about mid-term of the royalty payment after four years of further development). Using "7" as the multiple on the DCF is a somewhat conservative estimate of the number of years that a royalty would be paid. Overall, the risk level of the royalty stream (as an example) may be estimated to be 30 percent. Thus, the NPV may be calculated as follows:

$$\text{NPV} = 7 \times \$300,000/(1 + 0.3)^7 = \$330,000.$$

Such an estimate of potential impact can be done quickly, especially with experience, and used to gauge priority and significance. It can be argued that the range in the assumed values is so vast that the calculated result is meaningless. It can also be argued that the entire process has become circular because the calculation assumes the value which is to be determined to decide whether or not it is worth the effort to determine the value. However, making judgments about the importance of things without genuinely knowing the importance of things is something we all do every day. When you get a telephone call soliciting the "opportunity of a lifetime" do you invest time in figuring it out or not?[3] Sometimes it is impossible to invest all the due diligence time needed. Early, best-guess judgments and selections must be made.

Following up on this example, if it is reasonable to assume, as a ballpark estimate, a current-year value of $100,000 (assumed to be conservative) and a lifetime NPV value of $330,000 (modestly conservative), what is the appropriate level of investment to make a deal? Like many things, there is no hard and fast rule. One way to look at this from the seller's perspective is, what is the opportunity worth without a license agreement? If it is zero, then if there is even a 50 percent chance of reaching an agreement with a buyer under the previous terms, it is worth spending up to 50 percent of those figures. For sellers that think appropriately in NPV terms, that would put a cap of $165,000 on the transaction costs; for sellers who think in terms of current-year expenses and revenues, the cap would be $50,000. More accurately, the seller should view investment in creating a deal like any other investment made and, so, should be reasonably justified on an ROI basis. This might place the operational caps at 80 percent of these figures ($40,000 and $134,000).

Of course the goal of any seller is to determine rational behavior to maximize benefit, not to compute the worst tolerable performance. A way of valuing the benefit of perfect information is needed. Let us consider what might be meant by perfect seller information in a licensing valuation context. A good working definition of that number would be the most that any one buyer would be willing to pay after completing due diligence and hearing the seller's persuasive argument and that the transaction took place in a reasonable amount of time with reasonable selling costs. In many cases, such perfect valuation information would cause three to five buyers to take a serious look at the opportunity. Three might make serious counter-offers, all within a three-month period, and all with terms and conditions generally acceptable to the seller.

How would such perfect information differ from, say, the example proposed earlier? Because in that example the probable annual royalties varied by a factor of ten ($100,000 to just under $1 million); this would correspond to a royalty rate variation of 0.2 to 2 percent or 0.5 to 5 percent, a huge range. For the seller to be reasonably safe in quoting a figure, it would have to select a number at or close to the top end of the range. Such a figure may be so high as to dissuade any bidder. Alternatively, considering the range of 0.5 to 5 percent, what should the seller do if an early prospective buyer offers 1.5 percent "firm and final?" Most sellers, under these circumstances would view the investment of several tens of thousands of dollars as a prudent investment.

Sellers often find themselves at an information disadvantage with respect to the buyer. By definition, the buyer is planning to put the technology into commerce, so it should know many of the key issues of manufacturing and sales and marketing. If the opportunity is really significant, the buyer is not likely to tell the seller that it is valuing the opportunity too modestly.

Therefore, it is good practice for the seller to perform some preliminary analysis of potential significance to make a general determination of the value at stake. This can be done semi-quantitatively as shown in the previous example, or even more qualitatively by creating and using "high," "medium," and "low" categories. Then a seller can adopt deal investment levels and methodologies appropriate to the categories. For example, for a "high" opportunity (say, a potential of seven figures or more, i.e. $10 million or more), an extensive valuation will be performed using multiple cross checking methods and using outside experts to provide additional resources and confirmation. For a "medium" category (a six-figure deal), the seller could use one method, perhaps with external support and validation.

For "low" categories (a five-figure deal), judgment could be based upon an afternoon of thinking and consulting the records of previous deals (including networking with colleagues and friends). Also, for each of these categories a budget for selling and transaction costs should be established. Clearly for a five-figure deal one could spend more than the value of the deal in internal staff costs, especially for legal costs. If a seller has numerous opportunities in the "low" category, then it would be wise to create a very standard valuation approach with form licenses that are not subject to negotiation or customization to avoid consuming value in transaction costs. Also, there are some situations in which the opportunity is literally not worth the cost of creating the agreement to transfer the rights.

VALUATION VERSUS PRICING

As discussed in Chapter 1, we have used the term "valuation" to mean the worth of an opportunity and "pricing" as a communicated offer. When buying from street merchants in some countries, especially areas frequented by tourists, a seller's initial price can easily be ten times the product's value. In such circumstances, the number of potential buyers is practically endless. Sellers in such circumstances have little to lose by quoting enormus prices because there is literally always another buyer around the corner (or perhaps on the next cruise ship).

Further, if the buyer is not responding favorably, the price can be dropped quickly often, without losing the transaction. Such backpedaling by a seller normally causes a buyer to distrust the seller's representations. In the case of street goods, this is generally not a significant loss because the trust was probably not high in the first place, but, more importantly, the buyer can conduct rapid due diligence without the "assistance" of an untrusted seller.

Consequently, it should be no surprise that street sellers the world over have learned to deploy strategies of high price multiples. How would such a strategy work in licensing a technology? Not well. First, the number of potential buyers is normally not large and certainly not endless. Therefore, it is generally not a good idea to risk losing any buyer's interest by quoting unreasonably high numbers.

In addition, technology licensing requires significant levels of due diligence by buyers. Buyers are not inclined to make such investments if they have reason to believe that the seller is just looking for naïve or desperate buyers. Further, trust is an important element in most licensing transactions. A buyer will tend to devalue an opportunity if it concludes that the seller is hiding or misrepresenting information. There are serious adverse results to being too aggressive in pricing.

So, although a seller can count on not being offered more than it asks, it does not serve its own interests to ask for much more than it is perceived to be worth. A very reasonable approach to finding the middle ground is for the seller to value an opportunity several times under varying levels of optimism, the so-called scenario analysis. A common approach is a low scenario, a high scenario, and a most likely scenario. The low and high scenarios are usually labeled according to the assumptions made about them. For example, the low scenario could be "niche market, U.S." and the high scenario "mass market, worldwide." For a seller to select a price valuation at the high end is reasonable, providing that there is some basis for making such an assumption. During the course of discussions with prospective buyers, the feasibility (or not) of the optimistic assumptions can be tested.

Obviously, buyers may disagree with seller's assumptions, particularly for the more optimistic scenarios. However, buyers generally will respect a reasoned approach. Further, if the seller's assumptions are communicated to a buyer, then the buyer can move forward by developing its own most likely scenario and present those findings to the seller. If the seller says, "I want 100" and the buyer says, "I'll give you 10," convergence will be difficult if not impossible. If instead the seller says, "You will be able to sell licensed products for three major applications in all the industrialized countries of Europe, Asia, and America, and so it is worth 100," then the buyer can reply, "If I believed I could, I would agree with your number, but here is where I can see applying it. . . ." And so on.

Although the pricing discussion has been primarily focused on a seller's position, pricing is also an activity performed by the buyer. "Low ball" offers by a buyer often poison the relationship with the seller and can, in particular, offend inventors whose technology is being sold. Even if the buyer later makes a more reasonable offer, offended inventors (and others) can sometimes sabotage negotiations. Although some buyers might relish the prospect of getting something for almost nothing, most sellers are not naïve and, furthermore, they have long memories.

MARKETING AND SELLING STRATEGIES: SELLER'S VIEW

Although "marketing" as a term seems to carry a more professional image, what a seller really is doing is "selling." Marketing has more to do with creating future products and services that the target segments will want. Selling is getting a buyer to take what exists on the shipping dock. Theodore Leavitt has put this succinctly: "Selling is getting rid of what you have; marketing is making sure you have what you can get rid of."

Selling as an activity focuses on the specific "product" in the sales bag and how it will benefit specific customers. This process leads a seller to consider how the intrinsic features of the technology translate to the benefit of the buyer and the buyer's customer. It is helpful to consider the buyer as a value-added reseller (VAR) as the term is used in the information technology industry. The key attribute of VAR-thinking is that the buyer is an intermediary to the ultimate customer and, as an intermediary, has to contribute to and benefit from the value delivered to such customer. It is generally a very good idea for the seller to be able to express in income statement terms (such as used in the DCF Method) how the buyer will make money with the technology. This is the basic concept behind the phrase, "Sell the benefits not the features."

Another key aspect of selling is market segmentation. Not all categories of buyers will view the same opportunity as equally valuable. An astute seller will focus on the category of buyers that is most likely to be interested in becoming a licensee and that will put the highest value on the opportunity because they can extract the greatest benefit. Next we will consider four distinct buyer segments.

One poor buyer category that is frequently but unwisely considered is the ultimate customer. To make this concrete, let us consider a technology for making a special-purpose laser. Sellers can often more easily identify potential customers of such lasers than potential licensees who would want to build and sell such lasers. The identity and enthusiasm of potential customers can be helpful in attracting licensees, but rarely will such customers find the opportunity so compelling that they will seek to become laser manufacturers.

A better buyer for this category is a company that presently uses similar technologies but for other markets and applications. Again using the laser example, let us suppose that the laser is particularly suited to medical applications, both diagnostic and treatment. If a prospective buyer exists that already makes lasers, but only for the *industrial* laser market, then it can be a significant stretch for that buyer to enter the medical market. This is because there are many aspects of the medical market that would be unknown to the company, such FDA approval processes, the buying needs and patterns of hospitals and doctor's offices, the economics of the industry, especially the important involvement of third party payers, and so forth. Also, having trade name value and company recognition definitely plays a role. Finally, one needs an experienced sales force to call on the ultimate customer. Thus, although it is a positive that the prospective buyer understands lasers, its lack of experience in the niche market is usually a significant barrier.

An even better buyer segment would be a company making high-tech devices for the medical industry. Even if it does not presently make lasers, it inherently possesses an in-depth understanding of the market environment and customer requirements, and it is the perspective that is generally more important and difficult to obtain. If needed, the buyer could have some or all of the laser manufacturing contracted out to one of its vendors. Obviously, the best buyer segment would be a company already making lasers for the medical industry because it would have both the technology and the market understanding, but finding such a buyer is not always possible.

Using such perspectives, a seller needs to develop a sales strategy. Because it will be necessary to induce a buyer to make a significant due diligence investment, it is helpful to be able to show the prospective buyer how and why the opportunity is beneficial. To do this intelligently requires some effort on the seller's part and limits the number of prospective buyers that could be cost-effectively analyzed. Usually a seller should consider more than just three or four buyers; depending upon the potential significance of the deal, a reasonable upper limit might be in the range of six to ten. If a seller were to choose six in the laser example, the distribution should favor the last two buyer segments. A reasonable distribution would be as follows: two or three companies that make lasers for the medical market, one or two companies that make other high-tech equipment for the medical industry, and possibly one company that is experienced in making and selling lasers for many markets, but not the medical market. This approach benefits the seller by providing different perspectives from different segments; however, most of the selling energy goes into the most-likely-to-succeed category.

Another selling question that arises is determining what size companies are most likely to be serious buyers. In other words, should a seller approach the existing market leader, a strong "number 2," or a market laggard? There are two generalizations that can be useful to answering this question. First, the size of the opportunity should be scaled to the prospective buyer. For instance, if the seller's expected price is going to be seven figures, it is generally not fruitful to consider buyers whose annual revenues are just seven figures. Big opportunities, particularly ones that will require large R&D and developmental investments, will need the resources and grand visions of big companies. Likewise, profitable but small opportunities seem to be more attractive to smaller prospective buyers; bigger companies are generally not interested in licensing opportunities that, even if successful, will be almost undetectable on their income statements.

The second generalization deals with the attitude of market leaders. It appears to be both a human and corporate trait that large size and success lead to hubris and the belief that one knows more than anyone else. Compounding this, market leaders normally have a vested interest in maintaining the status quo. Although there can certainly be exceptions, it is not surprising when market leaders turn down an opportunity, and later that decision proves to be a short-sighted judgment. At the other end of the market share spectrum, the smallest companies are often so limited in their resources that they are unable to effectively implement opportunities. Generally, the companies ranging number two through number four in terms of market size frequently are better targets than the market leader or the smallest players.

OPPORTUNITY PRIORITIZATION AND
DUE DILIGENCE: BUYER'S VIEW

The high cost of conducting due diligence, coupled with the high mortality of even the most promising projects, makes a strong argument for a strategic approach for a buyer. If every prospective opportunity has to be analyzed from first principles, then the cost of analysis will be high and the likelihood of failure will be equally high. On the other hand, if licensing opportunities can be investigated from a pre-established framework of company priorities and strongest assets, success becomes more likely.

By being proactive, a buyer can increase its odds for being the first in line to negotiate. By having a checklist of key functions, features, and benefits sought, together with an understanding of the customer needs it seeks to meet, the buyer is also better able to quickly recognize significant opportunities.

An ability to understand the value of a license early in the process enables the buyer to do a reality assessment. In some cases such an assessment may actually precede the seller's own valuation activities (which from a seller's perspective, is not a preferred method). By being early, the buyer can create momentum for a quick and early deal that can induce the seller to accept a lower price than it might have otherwise. This is particularly so in a royalty-based agreement where the buyer can make the case that in its hands the technology will be exploited more fully and immediately because of the strategic fit and the proactivity of the buyer.

NEGOTIATION READINESS

Prior to a negotiation, there are certain basic preparations that are part of "negotiation readiness." The first two are obvious but often are not carefully thought through: (1) what do I have to offer?, and (2) What do I want in return? As discussed in Chapter 2, there are many things that can be offered and sought. Even if one considers only money, it can come in many forms. It can be tied to company value (equity), to sales (royalty), to profitability (a kicker), to fields of use and territories granted. Money can be fixed payments or conditional, and weighted to occur early (or not).

The nature of the buyer's commitment is another important element of a deal. Often this shows up as the diligence requirement of the license. This means that if the buyer/licensee does not fulfill the specified requirement, the license can be terminated, or made nonexclusive, or some penalty payment is made, depending upon what is negotiated. This is an example of an important "want" of the seller and "offer" of the buyer.

Another kind of commitment is future assistance by the seller, either in the form of tech transfer, troubleshooting, and/or improvement inventions. The ability of the seller to provide such assistance may be critical to the buyer's decision to enter the license agreement at all, no matter what the price.

A good practice is for both the buyer and seller to create a simple table of "offer" and "want" elements around which to frame a deal. A common way to communicate such elements is in what is called a term sheet offer, which can be made by either the seller or buyer. Usually a term sheet is one to three pages in length and deals with the principal elements that are being offered and what is proposed in return. It normally defers dealing with the details of a license agreement until it appears that there is consent to the basic terms.

In addition to offers and wants, there are two other elements that should be thought through prior to negotiations. The first is often known as a decision tree. In any negotiation, it normally happens that the offers and wants of each party do not exactly mirror the other. This leads to the need for compromise. In order to compromise effectively, it is necessary to formulate a decision tree by which comparisons can be made of the economic significance of each concession made or sought. In complex cases, there could be multiple rounds of such considerations and therefore multiple decision trees. By preparing alternatives of various decision trees in advance of negotiations, the parties can more readily propose compromises that preserve the value sought while still accommodating certain needs of the other side.

The alternative analysis, sometimes called a "Plan B Analysis," should always be: What happens if there is no deal? What are our alternatives, and the likely value of such alternatives, if we cannot reach an agreement with this party? For sellers who negotiate with only one prospective buyer and who believe that there are no other alternatives possible, this process reveals the vulnerability of not having a tenable Plan B. Accordingly, sellers should always sell and negotiate with a legitimate Plan B, even if it is significantly less desirable than Plan A. Without a Plan B, the seller can be convinced to accept a very low valuation because "something is better than nothing," (if their Plan B is truly nothing). In many situations, buyers inherently have a Plan B. That Plan B can be to invest its money in some completely unrelated but profitable project. The interaction between valuation, pricing, the Box/Wheelbarrow (deal elements) and deal structures is shown in Exhibit 12.2.

Valuation occurs in the context of all the elements with a Box and a Wheelbarrow, in consideration of the deal structure as discussed in Chapter 11. Such valuation normally is expressed in the form of a summary document known as a term sheet or "the deal." Prior to commencing negotiating it is normally a good idea to have more than one way of looking at such deal and the associated valuation and pricing. In some cases this may mean considering a range of possible "adders" that could be included in the deal, such as additional fields of use, or additional patents or software. In some cases it could be a completely alternative Wheelbarrow, such as an all-equity transaction as a "plan B" to a convention license fee and royalty approach.

The point of Exhibit 12.2 is that these matters are interrelated. One cannot value and price each possible variation, because there are likely to be too many possibilities. But, likewise, it is generally a good idea to have more than just one way of looking at the transaction, particularly with multiple prospective third parties.

In licensing negotiation, as in many other areas of life, the old saying holds true: proper preparation prevents poor performance.

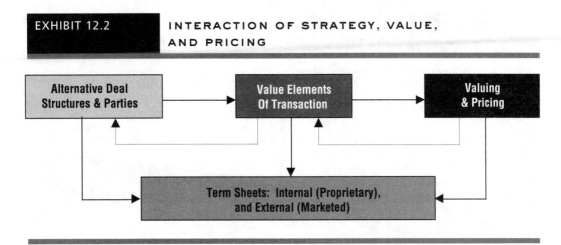

Source: ©2003 Razgaitis, richard@razgaitis.com.

BUYER-SELLER CONVERGENCE

At the beginning of this chapter it was noted that the seller's and buyer's positions commonly do not overlap when negotiations begin. If both parties have performed valuations based upon some rational methodology, and both have identified underlying assumptions, then there is hope that with an open exchange of information convergence can take place. It can be the buyer's valuation increasing to meet the seller's, or it can be the reverse. In other cases it might be movement by both parties, not just in the spirit of compromise, but due to a better understanding of the opportunities and risks.

Convergence is illustrated in Exhibit 12.3, which is based upon a similar figure in a book by Smith and Parr.[3] Early in this book, we introduced the acronym *TR R A DE*™, where *TR* stood for *Technology Rights*, *DE* for *Deal Economics* (or Equity), and *R* for the risk characterized by the risk-adjusted hurdle rate (k). The final element in the acronym is the *A*: *A* stands for the *Art* of the deal.

Once the buyer's and seller's valuations overlap, a deal should be possible. The art of the process is discovering ways that make the deal as valuable as possible to both parties and to do so quickly.

Dealmaking Using Monte Carlo and Real Options Analysis (Razgaitis, Hoboken, NJ: John Wiley & Sons, Inc., 2003), addresses these and other topics in considerably more detail.

CONCLUSION

Three other closing points remain. The first has to do with predicting the future. Technology, by definition, is unproven commercially. In some cases it carries with it bold promises of revolutionizing the way things are done. It is wise to have a little humility about such

EXHIBIT 12.3	ILLUSTRATION OF THE CONDITIONS FOR WHICH A NEGOTIATION OPPORTUNITY EXISTS

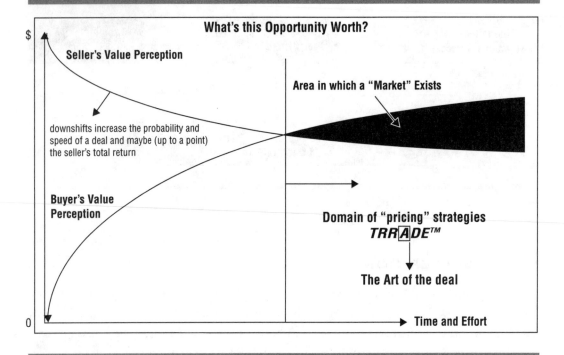

Source: Based on Figure 5.1 in Smith and Parr, *Valuation of Intellectual Property and Intangible Assets*, John Wiley & Sons, Inc., 1999.

bold forecasts. At the World's Fair of 1893, a group of 74 social commentators, an expert panel, was convened and asked to reach consensus on key features of the world in 100 years. Here were some of their predictions:

- Many people will live to be 150.

- Prisons will decline and divorce will be considered unnecessary.

- The Nicaraguan canal is as sure to be built as the tides are to ebb and flow and the seasons are to change.[5]

- The government will have grown more simple, as true greatness tends always toward simplicity.

On the other hand, ". . . . take a chance; Columbus did and he did OK." (Bobby Valentine, manager of the New York Mets, Oct. 17, 1999).

Secondly, it should be remembered that all of licensing is about creating value for end users. There is a Dilbert cartoon that has as its punchline: "Whoa! Are you saying we need *revenue* to make a profit?" (See Exhibit 12.4.) Nothing good happens unless the buyer can sell something.

EXHIBIT 12.4

DILBERT reprinted by permission of United Feature Syndicate, Inc.

Finally, you bought this big (not so) expensive book and were looking for a *number?* Based on having been asked this question many times, this author has developed an answer: 3.14. It's the best I can do without additional information.

NOTES

1. The opening lines of a poem by W.G. Sebald (1944-2001) entitled "Dark Night Sallies Forth," published in the *New Yorker* magazine, 6/17 & 24/2002, p. 126.
2. Ross Perot, "The GM System Is Like a Blanket of Fog," *Fortune*, 15, February 1988, pp. 48-49.
3. The author once received a collect long distance call from a man living in a homeless shelter in Florida who convincingly described the general outline of the "invention of the century." The deal was that he would offer negotiating rights in exchange for a Western Union transfer of $500, but that the deal had to be done now because the shelter lunch line was closing in two minutes. How does one decide such things?
4. Based on Fig. 5.1 in Smith & Parr, *Valuation of IP & Intangible Assets*, Wiley 1989 (p. 129).
5. This one is a personal favorite. The canal that got built just 15 years later under the leadership of President Theodore Roosevelt was the *Panama* Canal. The metaphor to express certainty is especially touching.

Technology Access Key Resource List

Here are important information sources and contacts for licensing professionals. This listing originated from a publication of Technology Access *and Michael Odza, who gave permission for its use here.*

American Association for the Advancement of Science
Open membership organization of 200,000 includes subscription to Science, runs large annual meeting in February with a growing tech transfer track, and maintains an excellent update on S & T legislative action.
ACCESS: 1200 New York Ave., NW Washington, D.C. 20005, 202/326-6400, fax 203/371-9526.

American Entrepreneurs for Economic Growth
Founded (and wholly funded) by the National Venture Capital Association in 1989, this no-fee group now numbers over 4,000 emerging growth companies. Surveys, legislative alerts, directory and annual meeting.
ACCESS: 1655 N. Fort Myer Dr., Ste. 850, Arlington, VA 22209, 703/524-3743, fax 703/524-3940.

American Intellectual Property Law Association
7500 attorneys covering patents, copyrights and trademarks. Three meetings per year.
ACCESS: 2001 Jefferson Davis Hwy., Suite. 203, Arlington, VA 22202, 703/415-0780, fax 703/415-0786.

Association for Technology Implementation
Official consortium of Europe's national (governmental) tech transfer agencies. Chair rotates to different countries.
ACCESS: Mr. Gag Kavlie, Norges Forskningsraad, Sognsveien 720801 Oslo 8, Norway, 9(47-2)237-685, fax (47-2)181-139.

Asssociation of Federal Technology Transfer Executives

New in 1992, open to all, focuses on the details of administration of technology transfer in federal agencies.

ACCESS: Reid Adler, Director, Office of Technology Transfer, National Institutes of Health, 6003 Executive Blvd., Bethesda, MD 20892, 301/496-0750, fax 301/402-0220.

Association of University Technology Managers

1,000+ university and medical center licensing officers (and company scouts). Membership and meetings open to all; fall business-oriented licensing course.

ACCESS: Bayfield Resources, (management company), 71 East Rd., Norwalk CT 06851, 203/852-7168, fax 203/838-5714.

Best-North America

Database of university research faculty profiles.

ACCESS: Ken Blaisdell, President, Best-North America, 1615 Thames St., Ste., 301, Baltimore, MD 21231, 301/563-2378, fax 301/563-5389.

BioScan

Leading database of close to 1,500 biotech company profiles and 6,000 executives; includes R&D and licensing agreements, new products, etc.

ACCESS: American Health Consultants, www.ahcpub.com/ahc_root_html/products/ newsletters/bsch.html

Center for Economic Conversion

Consults with communities and individual companies on positive actions to create economic benefits from base closings and cut-backs.

ACCESS: Michael Closson, 222 View St., Ste. C, Mtn. View, CA 94041-1344, 415/968-8798, fax 415/968-1126.

Commerce Business Daily

Notices of government contracts, RFPs, cooperative research opportunities.

ACCESS: Superintendent of Documents, Government Printing Office, Washington DC 20402, 202/512-1800.

Commercial Development Association

Merger of two chemical industry professional societies, with roots in marketing and commercial development, both sides dipping into technology licensing. Two annual meetings, foundation for training and scholarships in CD.

ACCESS: 1255 Twenty-third Street, NW, Washington, DC 20037-1174, 202/452-1620, fax 202/833-3636.

Community of Science

Commercial database collator, part-owned by Johns Hopkins University, with 46,000 U.S. and Canadian university research faculty profiles from some 125 U.S. and Canadian research institutions "Expertise", as well as funding opportunities, patents, Commerce Business Daily and the Federal Register, etc., searchable (for a fee), by entire organization domains.

ACCESS: Community of Science, 1629 Thames Street, Suite 200, Baltimore, MD 21231, 410/563-2378, fax 410/563-5389. www.cos.com

Corporate Technology Information Services (CorpTech)

Directory of 50,000 high technology companies public and private and 180,000 senior staff, including licensing contacts, in almost every conceivable format including paper, on-line, mailing labels, diskettes and in editions by state or region. Useful for targeted marketing of inventions by industry. Classifications are more up-to-date than old SIC codes.

ACCESS: 12 Alfred Street, Suite 200, Woburn, MA 01801-1915, 800/454-3647 (617/932-3939), fax 617/932-6335, www.corptech.com

Department of Commerce

The home of the Office of Technology Policy, "the only office in the federal government with the explicit mission of developing and advocating national policies that use technology to build America's economic strength."

ACCESS: Office of Technology Policy, Room 4418, 14th and Constitution Avenue, NW, Washington, DC 20230, 202/482-6102, fax 202/219-8667.

Disclosure, Inc.

Private service that maintains Securities and Exchange Commission filings by 11,000 companies on microfiche, including many documents detailing licensing and joint venture agreements.

ACCESS: 5161 River Rd., Bethedsda, MD 20816, 800/754-9690 (outside U.S., 44 171 278-8277).

Energy-Related Inventions Program/Innovative Concepts Program

Grant program "too small to cut" during Reagan-Bush years, has built enviable track record of successfully commercialized inventions, usually from independent inventors, by careful technical screening by NIST, and equally careful business training and supervision of grantees by ERIP staff.

ACCESS: Department of Energy, 1000 Independence Ave., CE521, 5E052, Washington, DC 20585, 202/586-1478, fax 202/586-8134.

European Association for the Transfer of Technologies, Innovation and Industrial Information (TII)

Private association of 300+ governmental private agencies and companies involved in various aspects of technology commercialization. Publishes cross-indexed directory.

ACCESS: TII asbl, 3 rue des Capuchins, L-1313, Luxembourg, (352)46.30.35, fax (352)46.21.85.

Federal Laboratory Consortium for Technology Transfer

Technology transfer officers for the 700+ federal laboratories, from every agency and department that performs research. Activities: a small demonstration grant program, a free newsletter, annual meetings, open to all. Fall meeting focuses on members' professional development; spring meeting includes displays of technologies available for license.

ACCESS: www.federallabs.org.

Federal Register
Proposed revised and enacted regulations, laws, including grant and procurement.
ACCESS: Superintendent of Documents, Government Printing Office, Washington DC 20402, 202/512-1800, fax 202/512-2250.

Find/SVP
Catalog of out-sourced product, market and technology reports.
ACCESS: 625 Ave. of the Americas, New York, NY 10011, 212/645-4500, fax 212/645-7681.

IBM Intellectual Property Network
The world leader in issued and new patents and patent licensing income had to create its own searchable database of all U.S. patents for internal purposes, then opened it to the public. It is slowly becoming a commercial venture, offering instant translation, document delivery, powerful patent analysis and graphing tools, both home-grown and by arrangement with outside vendors, and "pink dots," visible links from patents available for license to the owners' own websites.
ACCESS: www.patents.ibm.com

IC² Institute
Headed by George Kozmetzky, a founder of Teledyne Corp., then dean of the Graduate School of Business at UTA, and now widely heralded as the godfather of technology development in Austin and Texas, this research, publishing conference center focuses on Innovation, Creativity and Capital.
ACCESS: IC² Institute, 2815 San Gabriel, Austin, TX 78705, 512/475-8900 or 800/215-6782.

Industrial Research Institute
260 members, limited to for-profit companies conducting research in the U.S., across all industries; committees reach out to federal labs and universities. Company representatives are highest level managers of R&D. Publishes bimonthly journal *Research and Technology Management*, holds seminars and semi-annual meetings, conducts research on research.
ACCESS: Charles Larson, Executive Director, IRI, 1550 M St., NW, Washington, DC 20005, 202/872-6350.

Industry, Science and Technology Canada
Canada's government clearinghouse for information, online license opportunities and resources.
ACCESS: Ron Doherty, Market Intelligence & Technology Opportunity, ISTC, 235 Queen St., 1st Flr. E., Ottawa, Ontario K1A OH5, fax 613/954-5463.

Intellectual Property Owners Association
100 large with some small companies, universities, inventors and patent attorneys, advocating strong IP rights to government agencies. Publishes brief bulletins, awards inventor of the Year, and holds annual meeting.
ACCESS: 1255 23rd St., NW, Ste, 850, Washington, DC 20037, 202/466-2396, fax 202/833-3636.

Inventor-Assistance Program News
Free, limited circulation newsletter is the main information transfer mechanism of an Energy Department funded program to encourage inventor and inventor-assistance organizations. Short articles describe general business, entrepreneurship and technical information and assis-

tance resources for inventors and the organizations that assist them. Also publishes Inventor Assistance Source Directory.
ACCESS: Robin Conger, Program Manager, Inventor-Assistance Program, Pacific Northwest Laboratory, P.O. Box 999, K8-11, Richland, WA 99352, 509/372-4328, fax 509/372-4369.

Japan Information Access Project
Non-profit, non-partisan, membership organization dedicated to training U.S. public and private decision makers to access, evaluate, and use Japanese scientific, technical and business information. Study groups and conferences organized by industry sectors.
ACCESS: Mindy Kotler, Exec. Director, 2000 P Street, NW, Ste. 620, Washington, DC 20036, 202/822-6040, fax 202/822-6044.

Japan Patent Information Centre
"Information offer forms," (for patent applications), retroactive, on-line searches, patent abstracts, status inquiries, "watching service" and statistics. (Non-resident applicants must file through Japan-resident patent attorney or administrator.)
ACCESS: 1-5-16, Toranomon, Minato-ku, Tokyo 105, Japan, (03) 503-6181, fax (03) 501-3866.
ACCESS:Japan Institute of Invention and Innovation, 9-14, Toranomon 2-chome, Minato-ku, Tokyo 105, Japan, (03) 502-0511.

Knowledge Express
Online database package, with easy-to-use graphical, Al-enabled interface. Includes proprietary database of university inventions and data-bases of federal lab technologies, SBIR winners, federal research grants, etc.
ACCESS: 3000 Valley Forge Circle, Ste. 3800, King of Prussia, PA 19406, 800/529-5337.

Licensing Executives Society, U.S. & Canada
3000 corporate technology managers and scouts, inhouse and independent patent attorneys and consultants, increasing number of university and federal lab members. (Worldwide LES membership: close to 10,000.) Prospective members must be nominated by two members. Meetings, quarterly journal and annual spring intellectual property law-oriented licensing seminar, open to all.
ACCESS: 1800 Diagonal Road, Ste. 280, Alexandria, VA 22314-2840, 703/836-3106, fax 703/836-3107, e-mail: info@les.org

Licensing, Innovation and Technology Consultants' Association
Promotes exchange of experience and information among members. Publishes annual catalog of technologies and services offered and sought, and bimonthly newsletter, annual convention in Hanover.
ACCESS: Dr. Paolo Cattapan, c/o Teknomedia Intl., Viale Restelli 3, 1-20124 Milan, Italy, 2 66801272.

Modernization Forum
Alliance of non-profit technology extension service providers to small and medium manufacturers, sponsored by the National Institute of Standards and Technology and its five Manufacturing Technology Centers.
ACCESS: 20501 Ford Road, Dearborn, MI 48121, 313/271-2790, fax 313/271-2791.

MIT Enterprise Forum

30,000 members in 17 local chapters, open to all; chapters feature public critiques of selected entrepreneurs' business plans. National headquarters sponsors Venture Capital Network and meetings, including Entrepreneurial Tech Transfer.

ACCESS: MIT Enterprise Forum®, Inc., 28 Carlton St., Bldg. E32-336, Cambridge, MA 02139, 617/253-0015, fax 617/258-0532.

National Academy of Sciences

(Also: National Academy of Engineering, Institute of Medicine, National Research Council) Chartered by Congress but independent, non-profit, limited, honorific membership societies, which undertake studies of leading-edge developments and issues in science and technology. Advises government, holds conferences, publishes reports.

ACCESS: 2101 Constitution Ave., NW, Washington, DC 20418, 202/334-2138.

National Business Incubation Association

Maintains detailed statistics on incubators and their tenants; hosts practical annual meeting covering financing, best practices, economic development, international comparisons, and so on.

ACCESS: 20 E. Circle Drive, Ste. 190, Athens, OH 45701, 740/593-4331, fax 740/593-1996.

National Commission for Economic Conversion and Disarmament

Focuses on legislation and other national plans.

ACCESS: Dr. Greg Bischak, Executive Director, 1801 18th St., Ste. 9, Washington DC NW, 20009, 202/462-0091, fax 232-7087.

National Council for the Advancement of Research

Founded in 1945 with a slightly different title (but same acronym), this loose association of some 250 high-level people from across industry, government and academe, holds annual meetings.

ACCESS: c/o Lt. Gen. Austin W. Betts, US Army, Ret., NCAR Executive Secretary, Consultant to the President, Southwest Research Institute, P.O. Drawer 28510, San Antonio, TX, 78228-0510, 210/684-5111.

National Institutes of Health

The leading funder and creator of biomedical advances in the world, with funding growing faster. Lead licensor among federal research agencies, too.

ACCESS: Office of Technology Transfer, NIH, 6011 Executive Blvd., Suite 325, Rockville, MD 20852-3804, 301/496-7057, fax 301/402-0220, *www.nih.gov/of/ott*.

National Science Foundation

Independent federal agency, funds $3 billion in mostly basic research and education for non-medical, non-military science, mathematics and (more recently) engineering, via competitive grants to non-profit institutions and individual investigators, and SBIR grants.

ACCESS: 4201 Wilson Blvd., Arlington, VA 22230, 703/306-1234.

National Technical Information Service

Part of the Department of Commerce, collects and publishes most government technology resources, reports, databases, facility descriptions, and many inventions.

ACCESS: NTIS, 5285 Port Royal Rd., Springfield, VA 22161, 703/487-4600, fax 703/321-8547.

National Technological University

Consortium of major engineering schools delivers credit courses and non-credit short courses on specific technologies and the innovation process, via satellite.
ACCESS: Lionel Baldwin, President, NTU, 700 Centre Ave., Fort Collins, CO 80526, toll free800/582-9976, 970/495-6400, fax 970/484-0668.

National Technology Transfer Center

Mission: to assist all other federal tech transfer efforts by building outreach and training, and answering initial inquiries of companies seeking technical expertise or specific inventions from federal labs. Funded by NASA.
ACCESS: c/o Wheeling Jesuit University, 316 Washington Ave., Wheeling, WV 26003, 800/678-NTTC(6882), fax 304/243-4388.

National Venture Capital Association

Invitation-only (200 members), includes firms, corporate funds and individuals.
ACCESS: 1655 North Fort Myer Dr., Ste. 850, Arlington, VA 22209, 703/524-2549, fax 703/524-3940.

NERAC

Annual fee entitles companies to use non-profit center's technical and business problem-solving and tech transfer services, including access to its own technical team, automatic customized Tech Track® updates, Expert Match, fax document delivery, etc.
ACCESS: One Technology Dr., Tolland, CT 06084, 860/872-7000, *www.nerac.com*.

North Carolina Biotechnology Center

In addition to assisting state-based biotechnology industry and academia, the center prepares national databases and directories of faculty, research centers, resources and companies.
ACCESS: Biotechnology Information Program, P.O. Box 13547, 15 T. W. Alexander Drive, Research Triangle Park, NC 27709, 919/541-9366, fax 919/990-9544.

Office of Science and Technology Policy

Staff of Science Advisor to the President, home of future Critical Technologies Institute.
ACCESS: Dr. John H. Marburger, Director, OSTP, Executive Office of the President, Washington DC 20502, 202/456-7116.

Office of Technology Assessment

Analytical arm of Congress; produces and publishes thoughtful reports with options for action.
ACCESS: Director, OTA, U.S. Congress, Washington DC, 20510-8025, 202/224-9241.

Patent & Trademark Office

The world's largest and most compact collection of technological information. Essential for trend analysis and targeted searches. Accessible via commercial databases. CD-ROM, the central Public Search Room, and locally through 70+ Patent and Trademark Depository Libraries.
ACCESS: Room CM2-304, Washington DC 20231, General information, 703/308-HELP, Office of Information Product Develoment (electronic information only) 703/308-0322; PTDL Program: 703/308-3924.

Product Development & Management Association

Business and academic membership open to all; annual meeting, chapters, publishes *Journal of Product Innovation Management.*

ACCESS: 17000 Commerce Parkway, Ste. C, Mount Laurel, NJ 08054, 800/232-5241, fax 856/438-0525, *www.pdma.org.*

Regional Technology Transfer Centers

New in 1992, funded competitively by NASA (separately from NTTC) to assist businesses through fee for services programs: information retrieval, technical assessments, and technology and funding brokering.

ACCESS: Northeast: Westborough, MA, 508/8870-0042; Mid-Atlantic: Pittsburgh, PA, 412/648-7000; Southeast: Alahua, FL, 904/462-3913; Mid-Continent; College Station, TX 409/847-9217; Mid-West; Columbus, OH, 216/734-0094; Far-West; Los Angeles, 213/743-6132.

Science and Technology Council of the States

Designated representatives from every state and territory, supported by the Natl. Governors Assn.

ACCESS: Marianne Clark, NGA, 44 N. Capitol St. NW, Washington, DC 20001, 202/624-5300.

Small Business Administration

Loan programs, publications, central referral source for Small Business Innovation Research award programs (actual applications through each agency).

ACCESS: 409 Third St. SW, Washington, DC 20416, 800/U-ASK-SBA.

Small Business Innovation Research (SBIR)

Competitive, phased grants for proof of concept and prototyping set aside by each federal agency for businesses with fewer than 500 employees.

ACCESS: SBIR Programs, Office of Innovation Research & Technology, 1441 L St. NW, Mail Code 6470, Washington DC 20416, 202/653-7875.

Technology Access Report

Simply the best: concise, independent, highly *practical* monthly newsletter of analysis and opportunities in technology transfer, technology policy, defense conversion, economic development, and technology management. Includes comprehensive calendar of tech transfer events, technologies available for license, profiles of successful programs, and 400 to 500 contacts yearly, in every technology and industry. Editors in Washington, DC, Paris and San Francisco.

ACCESS: Technology Access, 8 Digital Drive, Ste. 250, Novato, CA 94949-5759, 800/733-1516; fax 415/883-6421.

Technology Exchange Ltd.

Annual forum for one-on-one appointments for buyers and sellers of technology; attendees receive book of 5-10,000 inventions prior to meeting.

ACCESS: Dr. David Lefever, Wrest Park, Silsoe, Bedfordshire, MK45 4HS UK, 44/1525-860333, fax 44/1525-860664.

Technology Targeting, Inc.

Database of 2000+ specific individuals in companies looking for inventions in technology areas they identified through detailed questionnaire.

ACCESS: Norman Brown, President, Technology Targeting, Inc., 2940 Warr Rd., Salt Lake City, UT 84109, 801/4887-9800, fax 801/486-0826.

Technology Transfer Conferences, Inc.

Bimonthly regional meetings present technologies from two dozen universities to audience of corporate scouts, with time for one-on-one sessions.

ACCESS: Lucy Malone, Executive Director, 325 Plus Park Blvd., Ste. 108, Nashville, TN 37217, 615/366-0680, fax 615/366-0695.

Technology Transfer Society

Individual open membership; publishes journal and newsletter; annual and chapter meetings.

ACCESS: 611 N. Capitol Ave., Indianapolis, IN 46204, 317/262-5022, fax 317/262-5044.

Technology Utilization Foundation

Affiliated with NASA and *NASA TechBriefs* publisher Associated Business Publications, presents Technology 2003 (1993) etc., annual showcase of federal lab and contractor technologies.

ACCESS: Bill Schnirring, President, 41 E. 42nd St., New York, NY 10017-5391, 212/490-3999, fax 212/986-7864.

Teknekron Corporation

Pioneer and exemplar of "open corporation" model for nurturing and spinning off technology ventures.

ACCESS: George Tuirin, Vice President, Technology, 1080 Marsh Rd., Menlo Park, CA 94025, 415/322-6390

Teltech, Inc.

Technology consulting service using a computerized search interface to draw from thousands of technology professionals who have agreed to provide the first hour for a pre-set fee.

ACCESS: Joseph Shuster, President, 2850 Metro Dr., Minneapolis, MN 55425-1566, 952/851-7500, fax 952/851-7744.

United States of America

ACCESS: President George W. Bush, The White House, 1600 Pennsylvania Ave., NW, Washington DC 20500, 202/456-1414 (voice mail 202/456-6213; to record comments on legislation: 202/456-6213), fax 202/456-2461. E-mail: president@whitehouse.gov. MCI-Mail: View White House BBS. Compuserve: Go Whitehouse. American Online: Bush.

ACCESS: Vice President Richard B. Cheney, 202/456-6213. E-mail: vicepresident@white house.gov.

ACCESS: U.S. Senate, Washington DC 20510, 202/224-3121.

ACCESS: U.S. House of Representatives, Washington DC 20515, 202/224-3121.

Wal-Mart Innovation Network

Quickly (since 1990) one of the largest company-sponsored programs for screening inventions for both technical merit and market potential. Uses network of 400-500 organizations as funnel. Recent pilot project used DOE's ERIP program to help screen and LES members to explore potential alternative commercialization route.

ACCESS: c/o The College of Business Administration at Southwest Missouri State University, 901 South National Ave., Springfield, MO 65804-0089.

World Intellectual Property Organization (WIPO)
Searchable database of published PCT applications.
ACCESS: http://pctgazette.wipo.int/eng/index.html

Source: © TECHNOLOGY ACCESS REPORT, newsletter for technology transfer and intellectual asset management professionals, NOVATO, CA, 800-733-1516, www.techaccess.com. Reprinted with permission from Michael Odza, editor and publisher of Technology Access Report and Digital Drive.

An Alphabetical Listing of Useful Resources

This resource material was originally compiled by Daniel M. McGavock of InteCap, who gave permission for its use here.

Almanac of Business & Industrial Financial Ratios

Balance sheet and income statement data along with key financial ratios, broken down by four-digit SIC code. Each SIC code breakdown shows data for current year and previous two years. Current data are further categorized down by sales ranges.

Publisher: Pearson Education
(201) 236–7000
(201) 909–6200
www.prenhall.com

American Statistics Index

Index of economic, demographic and statistical information. This resource is updated monthly and bound in annual volumes.

Publisher: Congressional Information Service
(301) 654–1550
www.cispubs.com

Bloomberg Financial Database

The Bloomberg Financial Database is extremely useful for finding significant amounts of information on public companies, broad industry news stories, stock prices, bond prices, and much more.

Provider: Bloomberg
(212) 318–2200
www.bloomberg.com

Bureau of Labor Statistics
This publication includes information on inflation indices, occupational earnings data, etc.

Publisher: United States Department of Labor
(202) 606-5886
www.bls.gov

Business Conditions Digest
This publication provides charts and statistical data for leading economic indicators. Information includes cyclical indicators, composite indicators and their components.

Publisher: U.S. Bureau of Economic Analysis
(202) 606-9900
www.bea.doc.gov

Census Bureau Database
The Census Bureau provides on-line access to its reports and studies. Some of the most useful information is found in the *Current Industrial Report* section. This on-line publication provides unit shipment and sales revenue data for specific products produced by domestic manufacturers. These products are categorized by SIC code.

Help-Line: (301) 457-1242
www.census.gov

Census of Manufacturers
This publication provides useful information on industry statistics and ratios. The publication is broken down by SIC code; however, in many cases the SIC code is extended to cover very detailed subjects.

Publisher: Available through the Superintendent of Documents
(202) 512-1800
www.access.gpo.gov/su_docs

Dialog
The Dialog on-line database has access to a significant number of industry or company publications, articles, journals that cover a wide variety of topics. This database may contain significant amounts of information helpful in understanding the marketplace in which a product or potential product may compete.

Publisher: Knight-Ridder Information
(800) 334-2564
www.dialog.com

Directory of Companies Required to File Reports with the Securities & Exchange Commission
This report lists, alphabetically and by industry group, all the firms required to file under the Securities Exchange Act of 1934.

Publisher: Superintendent of Documents
(202) 512-1800
www.access.gpo.gov/su_docs

Disclosure Services

The Washington office of this organization maintains copies of all the documents filed with the Securities and Exchange Commission ("SEC"). Useful information that can be obtained from Disclosure Services includes company financials and license agreements.

Publisher: Disclosure, Inc.
               (800) 777–3272
               www.disclosure.com

Dun & Bradstreet Reports

Dun & Bradstreet credit reports provide information on over 3 million companies. It is one of the best sources of information for private companies. These reports cover both U.S. and international companies.

Publisher: Dun & Bradstreet
               (800) 234–3867
               www.dnb.com

Dun & Bradstreet Industry Norms

This report summarizes key financial data for various industries. The report includes common-sized balance sheet and income statement information, as well as fourteen financial ratios. These financial ratios summarize the average profitability, efficiency, and solvency positions of companies participating in the industry.

Economic Indicators

This publication includes basic U.S. economic indicators such as GNP, spending, personal consumption, corporate profits, production activity and security market data. Information includes most recent six years.

Publisher: Council of Economic Advisors
               (202) 512–1800
               www.access.gpo.gov/su_docs

Economic Report of the President

Annual report to the U.S. Congress from the U.S. President (as prepared in consultation with the President's Council of Economic Advisors). Discusses projected economic policy of the administration, economic outlook and provides current economic statistical data.

Publisher: Superintendent of Documents
               (202) 512–1800
               www.access.gpo.gov/su_docs

Encyclopedia of Associations

This set covers most major national associations. It lists the address, phone number, number of members, publications, and functions of the association.

Publisher: Gale Research, Inc.
               (800) 877–4253
               www.galegroup.com

Encyclopedia of Business Information Sources

This publication provides a detailed listing of publications that cover certain industries. It lists the address, phone number, fax number and purpose of the publications it covers.

Publisher: Gale Research, Inc.
(800) 877-4253
www.galegroup.com

Federal Reserve Bulletin

This report is published by the Board of Governors of the Federal Reserve System. It contains a wide variety of financial, economic and business statistics primarily related to the formulation and implementation of monetary policy. The report is published monthly and is particularly useful in tracking interest rate and exchange rate movements.

Publisher: Publication Services
(202) 452-3244
www.bog.frb.fed.us

Handbook of Economic Statistics

Economic statistics for selected countries. Covers economic profile of the country, data on economic trends, energy, agriculture, minerals and metals, chemicals, manufactured goods and foreign trade.

Publisher: U.S. Department of Commerce
(703) 482-4883
www.doc.gov

Ibbotson Associates' Yearbooks

This book provides a history of capital market returns in the United States from 1926 to the present. This information is particularly useful in determinations of costs of capital.

Publisher: Ibbotson Associates
(312) 616-1620
www.ibbotson.com

Ibbotson Associates' Cost of Capital Quarterly

This book provides useful information such as profitability ratios, cost of equity, cost of debt, and cost of capital for many different industries. The publication is broken down by SIC code.

Publisher: Ibbotson Associates
(312) 616-1620
www.ibbotson.com

Info-Trak

This database contains information on thousands of articles from a comprehensive list of trade publications.

Location: Public Libraries

Instant Information

Listing of nearly 10,000 organizations, associations and government agencies. Includes the name, address, phone number and a brief description of each listing. Part one is an alphabetical listing by state (including Puerto Rico and Canada). Part two is an alphabetical listing by organization title. Part three is an alphabetical listing by subject.

Publisher: Pearson Education
(201) 909-6200
www.prenhall.com

Investment Analyst Reports

These reports, if available, are an excellent source of information pertaining to specific companies covered in the report as well as the industry in which the company competes. Significant information that may be obtained in an investment analyst report may include projected company market share, profitability, and competition.

Publisher: Call specific analyst or use Investext
(800) 662-7878
www.investext.com

Investext Database

The Investext Database is useful for finding both industry-wide and company-specific reports prepared by investment analysts. The search of this database can be structured by product, date, and company.

Provider: Investext
(800) 662-7878
www.investext.com

Licensing Economics Review (LER)

This publication covers many issues of interest to the licensing executive. The cover of each issue provides the reader with a synopsis of recent royalty transactions discussed in the issue as well as other highlights.

Publisher: AUS Consultants
(609) 234-1199
www.ausinc.com

Les Nouvelles

The *Les Nouvelles* is the journal of the Licensing Executives Society which discusses licensing issues. This resource is useful in identifying recent trends and issues as well as experts that follow licensing in various industries.

Publisher: Licensing Executive Society
(703) 836-3107
www.les.org

Licensing Law & Business Report

This publication contains significant information in many of their feature articles that discuss licensing and other IP transactions.

Publisher: West Group
(800) 328-4880
www.westgroup.com

Market Share Reporter

This report is an annual compilation of reported market share data on companies, products, brand names and services. It is an excellent resource for identifying major competitors and their relative strengths within certain markets.

Publisher: Gale Research, Inc.
(800) 877-4253
www.galegroup.com

Mergerstat Review

This is a statistical reference guide on all announced mergers and acquisitions in the past year. Also includes historical data on mergers, acquisitions, reorganizations, etc. for both U.S. and foreign-based companies.

Publisher: Houlihan Lokey Howard & Zukin
(800) 455-8871
www.mergerstat.com

Moody's Bank & Finance Manual

This manual provides five to seven years of balance sheet and income statement data, along with key financial ratios for companies in the insurance, finance, real estate and investment industries. Includes, for each company, a narrative of its business and a listing of all subsidiaries. Also includes analyses of the various firms' debt and equity structures.

Publisher: Moody's Investors Service, Inc.
(212) 553-1658
www.moodys.com

Moody's Industrial Manual

This manual provides five to seven years of balance sheet and income statement data, along with key financial ratios for companies listed on the NYSE, AMEX, and regional stock exchanges. Includes, for each company, a narrative of its business and a listing of all subsidiaries. Also includes analyses of the various firms' debt and equity structures.

Publisher: Moody's Investors Service, Inc.
(212) 553-1658
www.moodys.com

Moody's OTC Industrial Manual

This manual includes industrial companies listed on the over-the-counter stock market. Provides data such as historical background, mergers, subsidiaries, products, plants, officers and directors. Also includes financial information and analyses of the various firms' debt and equity structures.

Publisher: Moody's Investors Service, Inc.
(212) 553–1658
www.moodys.com

Moody's Public Utility Manual

This manual includes five to seven years of balance sheet and income statement data, along with key financial ratios for electric and gas utilities, gas transmission companies, and telephone and water companies. Includes, for each company, a narrative of its business and a listing of all subsidiaries. Also includes analyses of the various firms' debt and equity structures.

Publisher: Moody's Investors Service, Inc.
(202) 553–1658
www.moodys.com

Moody's Transportation Manual

This manual includes five to seven years of balance sheet and income statement data along with key financial ratios for railroads, airlines, shipping, bus and truck lines. Includes, for each company, a narrative of its business and a listing of all subsidiaries. Also includes analyses of the various firms' debt and equity structures.

Publisher: Moody's Investors Service, Inc.
(212) 553–1658
www.moodys.com

Robert Morris Associates Annual Statement Studies

These statement studies contain composite financial data on manufacturing, wholesaling, retailing, service, and contracting lines of business. The financial statements on each industry are shown in common size form and are accompanied by widely used financial ratios. The report is organized by SIC codes.

Publisher: Robert Morris Associates
(215) 446–4000
www.rmahq.org

Standard Industrial Classification Manual

The SIC code was developed for use in the classification of establishments by the type of activity in which they are engaged. The code consists of 20 major industry groups which cover the entire field of economic activity ranging from manufacturing to distribution and service. Each business establishment in the United States has been assigned an SIC code according to the nature of its business operations. As a result, these SIC codes are useful for collecting and tabulating economic data on business activity in the United States. Many of the information resources used in market research organize their materials and data according to these SIC codes.

Publisher: U.S. Office of Management and Budget
Superintendent of Documents
(202) 512–1800
www.access.gpo.gov/su_docs

Standard NYSE Stock Reports

Provides financial data such as sales, earnings, book value, dividends and stock trading range for individual companies. Also provides a narrative about the background of the company, recent events and the outlook for the future of the firm and its industry.

Publisher: Standard & Poor's Corporation
(877) 481–8724
www.standardpoor.com

Standard & Poor's Analyst's Handbook

This handbook provides statistical industry composite data, including sales, operating profits, dividends, earnings and depreciation. Data cover over 90 industries.

Publisher: Standard & Poor's Corporation
(877) 481–8724
www.standardpoor.com

Standard & Poor's Bond Guide

This guide covers over 6,100 domestic and Canadian corporate bonds as well as hundreds of convertible and international bonds. Includes corporate and government bond yields, comparative financial data for each corporate bond, S & P debt ratings, rating changes and more.

Publisher: Standard & Poor's Corporation
(877) 481–8724
www.standardpoor.com

Standard & Poor's Industry Surveys

These surveys provide basic financial data on 36 key industries. Each industry report includes a financial comparison of the leading companies in that industry.

Publisher: Standard & Poor's Corporation
(877) 481–8724
www.standardpoor.com

Standard & Poor's Register of Corporations, Directors, & Executives

Volume one: Alphabetical listing of over 37,000 companies with a description of each business, the address and telephone numbers, and corporate officers and directors. Volume two: Alphabetical listing of individuals serving as officers, directors, trustees or partners. Volume three: Indexed by SIC number.

Publisher: Standard & Poor's Corporation
(877) 481–8724
www.standardpoor.com

Standard & Poor's Statistical Service

This service covers current basic statistics for broad industry groups, including security price index record by industry group.

Publisher: Standard & Poor's Corporation
(877) 481-8724
www.standardpoor.com

Standard & Poor's Stock Guide

This guide covers stocks listed on all major U.S. stock exchanges. Provides information on institutional ownership, recent stock performance data, highs and lows for the past year and over a period of the past 20 years, balance sheet data, debt structure and earnings.

Publisher: Standard & Poor's Corporation
(877) 481-8724
www.standardpoor.com

Statistical Abstract of the United States

Summary of statistics covering social, political and economic organizations in the United States.

Publisher: U.S. Bureau of Census
Superintendent of Documents
(202) 512-1800
www.access.gpo.gov/su_docs

Survey of Current Business

This survey provides national income and product account data for past three years, real GNP trends and cycles, regional economic analysis, international economic indicator comparisons, and more.

Publisher: Superintendent of Documents
U.S. Government Printing Office
(202) 512-1800
www.access.gpo.gov/su_docs

TELTECH

This is an on-line database that provides information on how to contact experts for various industries.

Provider: TELTECH Technical Knowledge Service
(800) 367-8358
www.teltech.com

U.S. Industrial Outlook

This publication provides statistical and narrative analyses of recent trends and forecasts for over 200 industries. It includes analyses of industries' supply and demand, developments in domestic and foreign markets, employment trends and capital expenditure trends.

Publisher: U.S. Department of Commerce
Industry & Trade Information
(202) 512-1800
www.access.gpo.gov/su_docs

Value Line

This publication provides information that is useful for calculating a company's cost of capital. It summarizes individual company financial performance over the last decade by providing up to 15 years of simplified financial statement and ratio analysis data. The report specifically addresses the company's most recent results. Moreover, the report provides historical stock price performance and projections for the company.

Publisher: Value Line, Inc.
(800) 531-1425
www.valueline.com

Index